Dreams of Mars

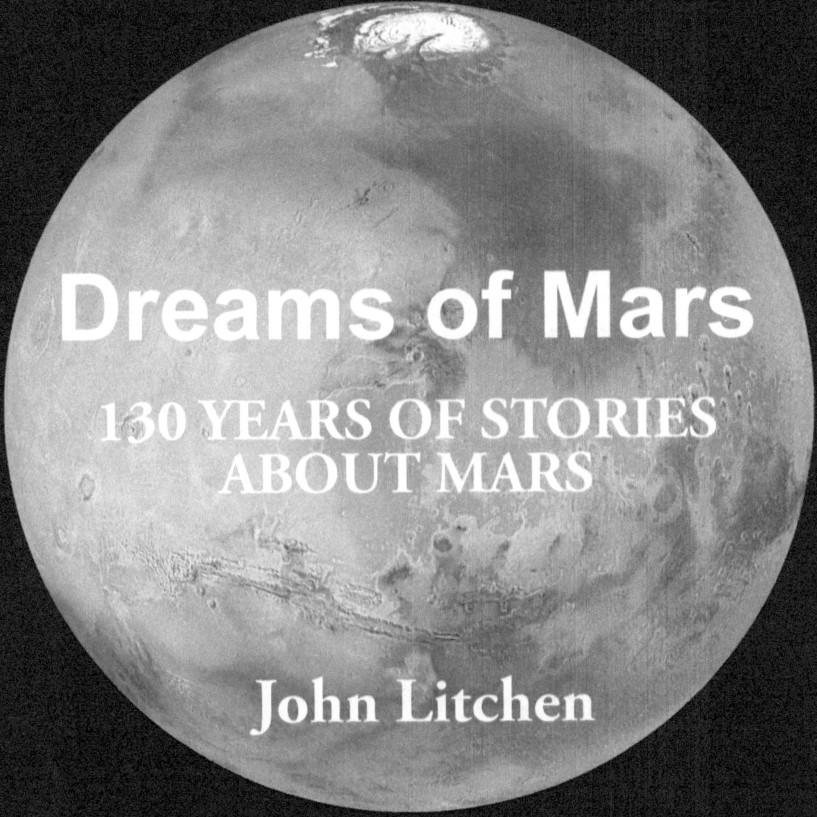

Dreams of Mars

130 YEARS OF STORIES ABOUT MARS

John Litchen

Yambu

Dreams of Mars
1st edition

ISBN: 978-0-9804104-9-5

NATIONAL LIBRARY OF AUSTRALIA

A catalogue record for this book is available from the National Library of Australia

Published by Yambu
PO Box 3503 Robina Town Centre QLD 4230
Contact: John Litchen:
jlitchen@bigpond.net.au

For **Bruce Gillespie**
who inadvertantly got me started on this,
and who was kind enough to publish a
shorter version in his beautiful magazines,
SFCommentary 93 and 95,
and for all of those readers who were kind
enough to comment on aspects of the work.
It was much appreciated and hopefully is
reflected in this longer version.

and for Dick (Ditmar) Jenssen
who supplied such beautiful covers
for both those issues.
His cover art 'Mars Attacks'
appears here with his kind permission.

All images of Mars in this book appear
Courtesy NASA/JPL/-Caltech.

Meridiani Planum North East of the site where Opportunity landed

Contents

page

Preface

Mars has fascinated people for thousands of years.

In the clear skies of ancient times its red colour was visible to the Greeks, the Babylonians and later the Romans who associated the colour with blood, and blood with warfare, and thus designated the Red Planet as the abode of the God of War.

The Babylonians called the planet **Nergal**, their god of war, the Greeks called the planet **Ares**, who was the son of Zeus and Hera, and their god of war. The Romans did the same, elevating **Mars** to a high status in their pantheon of Gods. Other cultures had different names, but in each the concept of what the Red Planet represented to them was the same as that of the Babylonians, Greeks and Romans.

Galileo was the first to observe Mars through the newly invented telescope. He saw an indistinct shape with little detail. As telescopes improved another astronomer, Giovanni Cassini, in 1666 saw ice caps on the planet.

In 1877 two moons were discovered orbiting Mars by astronomer Asaph Hall. He named them after the children of Ares, the Greek god of war: Phobos who personified fear and Deimos the creator of panic. It must be noted that this was a century and a half after the author Jonathon Swift had written in 1726 in his book ***Gulliver's Travels*** that Laputian astronomers had discovered that Mars had two moons and more or less accurately described their orbits and periodicity. How did he know? Was it just a lucky guess? At that time it was observed that Jupiter had four moons and of course Earth had one; was it not logical to suspect that Mars, being in between Earth and Jupiter would have two moons? Perhaps it was a common idea in the 1700's. People still speculate over how Swift decided Mars had two moons when they could not be seen with the naked eye or through the telescopes of that time...

A most important event relating to Mars was an announcement by the Italian astronomer Giovanni Schiaparelli which changed what people thought about Mars, altering their perception of the planet for the next hundred years. He observed Mars over a period of time from September 1877 and carefully drew maps showing darker areas linked together with faint lines. He exhibited his maps and drawings and announced that he had observed '**Canali**' on Mars. He also suggested that these canali naturally carried water from melting ice to other barren parts of the planet, since there was no rain on Mars.

He wasn't suggesting they were artificial or engineered structures, but the public took the idea of channelling water and mistranslated the word. In Italian canali means channels, but in English it was erroneously translated as canals and everyone immediately assumed that Mars was or had been inhabited. Why else would there be canals?

No other observers saw these lines in 1877 even though Mars was at its closest point to Earth. But once two other astronomers, Joseph Perrotin and Louis Thollon claimed to see 'the canals' in 1886, almost everyone who looked at Mars after that started to see them.

My fascination with Mars began when I was eleven years old in 1951. I discovered a science fiction magazine which included a short story that stood out from all the others. It was a story set on Mars. I can't remember the name of the story now, but what I clearly remember was I just had to read more stories like that.

Science fiction enthralled me with its gloriously positive images of a future Earth, about alien planets in different star systems that often sent shivers along my spine, and space operas with thrilling adventures that could take me out of everyday reality. They allowed my imagination to run wild. But the stories I especially loved were stories about Mars.

Turning thirteen in 1953 I discovered Arthur C Clarke's ***The Sands of Mars*** and enjoyed it immensely. This story more than any other reinforced my addiction to Science Fiction, and stories about Mars which has not diminished even now that I am in my late seventies.

Has any other place or locale fascinated people in general and writers of SF in particular more than Mars?

My approach to looking at books about Mars is not that of a scholar who studied them in a course on Science Fiction, but is that of a layman who enjoys reading and doesn't look for deeper meanings within the text— meanings that the authors probably never intended, but which in hindsight from a modern perspective, can be interpreted in many different ways. I don't care if a story is a disguised criticism of American or European Imperialism, of Communism, Fascism, or Capitalism. My concern is if it is enjoyable. Can I get lost in the story? Are the characters believable? Can I identify with a character and feel what they feel as events in the story unfold? Does the setting seem real without intruding on the events depicted? More importantly does the story transport me mentally to another world, in this case Mars? For me, reading is an enjoyable pastime, and if I don't enjoy a book, or can't get engaged with it, I will not persist. It gets put aside.

What follows then is an individual appreciation of Martian themed stories, and as such it reflects my opinions and biases on whether a story engaged me, thrilled me, left me feeling as if there should have been more to it or was simply something I couldn't read after the first couple of chapters.

This is not an anthology of Martian stories, nor is it a complete history of stories regarding Mars. The stories mentioned here are those that I have in my personal collection, some of which I bought as far back as 1953, and have been collecting since then, including recent reproductions and reprints of books published well before I was born. (1940).

Readers who have read the same books as those mentioned here will have different opinions, but for those who haven't read some of them, I hope this volume might encourage a search for those books and the subsequent pleasure involved in reading them.

My apologies to those who have read Mars books other than the stories mentioned in this volume: it wasn't possible even half a century ago when there was not the amount of books published like there is today to keep up with everything regarding Mars, or Science Fiction in general, especially in Australia where often books published in the US were not available because of US and UK copyrights; particularly American SF magazines along with other genre magazines. They were banned from being imported from 1938 through to the late 1950s for economic reasons rather than copyright reasons. The government wanted the publishing and printing jobs in Australia so some magazines were available as Australian reprints. The government also wanted the money spent on those books and magazines to stay in Australia rather than be transferred overseas, which is to America.

From the late 1950s as more books were published in each subsequent year, trying to keep up was soon beyond anyone's capacity. Today, with millions of books published and re-published as eBooks, as well as printed books and POD (print on demand) books, and limiting oneself to a specific genre like SF, or sub category like Martian themed books, it is impossible to be aware of everything that has been published, what is presently available, or what is about to be published, let alone being able read all of them. It is astounding that so many books featuring Mars in some way or another have been published, and continue to be published.

Looking at those that I have collected over the last 65 years, I am also surprised to find many I had forgotten about, which of course meant I had to re-read them. Not only that, I discovered others that I never knew existed back then, some of which were much better than I would have expected.

Reading again the earliest ones from my collection, as well as some extra early stories from the *'golden age'*, I found it was wonderfully nostalgic to rediscover those books that created within me a sense of wonder when I was a teenager. Some of them were astonishingly good.

Over the last century; it seems that every couple of decades, going to Mars was always 20 to 30 years ahead.

In the 1920s, 1930s and 1940s everyone optimistically expected we would go to the Moon and to Mars within 30 years. No one understood the complexity of the technology needed for such a journey, nor how little we knew about conditions in space, and how that could affect humans who left the protection of the Earth's atmosphere.

In the 1950s the dream of going to Mars within 30 years was strong enough to be almost a certain possibility.

But scientists tempered their enthusiasm as they began to realise the enormous problems which had to be solved before humans could even get into low orbit, let alone leave Earth altogether. But one highly enthusiastic scientist, Werner Von Braun, had dreams of fleets of ships being built in orbit and setting off for Mars in a grand flotilla.

Science fiction writers still expected going to Mars was only a few years ahead, and stories with a Martian setting proliferated from the 1940s to mid-1960s to such an extend it could almost be considered a 'golden age' for stories about Mars. They were either fantasies, often of the sword and sorcery type, attempts to depict events on Mars, or journeys to Mars in as realistic a manner as possible all the while still assuming Mars had a modicum of breathable atmosphere and some kind of native life. Mars was often the backdrop for interplanetary adventures and dark mysteries as well as romances, all of which abruptly ended in 1965.

A Moment in Time

July 1965 was the moment in time which divided the fanciful from the factual, when the Mariner-4 probe came within 10,000 kilometres of the surface of Mars and sent back the first photographic images of the planet's surface; images that shattered forever all previous concepts. It appeared that Mars was a dead world, cratered like the Moon. Mariners 6 and 7 in 1969 confirmed those initial findings.

Almost immediately incentives to write about going to Mars diminished and authors switched their speculations to other parts of the solar system or sent their protagonists off into interstellar space where any kind of star system could have whatever planets they imagined for their stories.

It wasn't until Mariner 9 went to Mars in 1971 and orbited the planet which was shrouded in a massive dust storm that perceptions of Mars changed once again. When the dust storm cleared in 1972 it sent back sensational photos enabling NASA scientists to create detailed maps of Mars, but what these photos showed was that Mars wasn't actually dead, like the Moon, but that although apparently barren of life, it did have a changing topography that was affected by weather and seasons; it was not geologically dead as they had thought after Mariner 4. And once again writers became interested in the new Mars.

Stories written before Mariner -4 sent back its low resolution images were fanciful or fantastic rather than factual. Whatever an author could imagine was fine because there was no one who could dispute it. There were few facts available and what had been observed through the primitive telescopes of the 19th century was extrapolated in many different ways depending on the inclination or imagination of the observer.

Subsequent missions to Mars with flybys and orbiters first, followed by rovers on the surface sending back thousands of astonishing high resolution images has shown Mars to be a much more interesting planet after all. Mars certainly isn't dead; it is very different, and still geologically active. There is recent evidence of water having caused features similar to what it does on

Earth, and frozen water has been confirmed beneath the surface. The possibility of finding some form of life has again emerged into the consciousness of the public as well as the SF writers who want to set stories on Mars.

After a dearth of Mars stories during the 1970s and early 80s, the 1990s came alive again with many new stories. Towards the end of the 1990s and as we entered the 21st century another golden age of stories about Mars began, this time focussed more on the real technicalities of how to get there and how to survive on the surface. This proliferation of stories has continued beyond 2000 to the present day and shows no sign of diminishing with the bulk of them accepting that a colony or a substantial group of people have managed to establish some kind of community on Mars and the stories now involve other aspects of human activities other than just exploring and surviving. They have become deeper and more complex as our understanding of Mars continues to increase.

In the first 30 to 50 years of 20th century thousands of stories were written about Mars. Very few fortunately have survived in the memories of people today. So what we have left that stand out are the longer works, the novels, novellas and novelettes. These were more carefully written because being longer more time and thought would have been taken to produce them, resulting in a more accurate depiction of Mars at the time the story was written.

Consequently this book falls into two parts: that which was thought of and expressed in stories and novels, as well as purportedly factual works created before July 1965, and stories and novels written after this date which included newly discovered facts about our neighbouring planet at the time the story was written. This continues to evolve as more information is transmitted from Mars and more stories are written.

To refer to all the novels, novellas and novelettes and short stories where Mars is prominent is an impossible task even for academic researchers — there are just too many of them — so I have limited myself to those novels, novellas and novelettes and a few anthologies of shorter works that are in my collection, including some recently obtained early books that I had not known about when I was younger, as well as a few eBooks along with some enthusiastically self published stories.

What really surprised me upon re-reading the early books, was that quite a few of them can hold their own against anything written today, being imbued with a sense of wonder that transcends time making them still as enjoyable today as they were half a century or more ago.

There are as many views of Mars as there are authors willing to express them, making the subject endlessly fascinating. Not every story will appeal to everyone, but amongst all those published across the last century readers will be sure to find many outstanding stories.

The much later post Mariner 4 stories improved from a factual point of view as we entered the twenty-first century with so much more known about Mars than before, but not always from a fictional point of view. While many writers are accurate in depicting details, some forget that stories are about people rather than the setting no matter how fascinating that might be. The best stories are always those that examine the characters: their motivation for what they do which effects their interaction with each other, and how they change and evolve, rather than the background setting of Mars. With characters of depth combined with a unique setting like Mars, great entertaining stories are inevitable.

Simple Categories

Looking through my collection of Mars books it seems most of those published during the 20th century fall into three simple categories: **fanciful**, **factual** and **transformative**.

But within those basic categories there are sub-categories, for example, the **factual**, where between a certain period many stories were about the first or nearly the first trip to Mars and what happened on arrival, the climax of the story being the arrival. At another period the stories involved a well established society on Mars and all the various activities that people living close together can get up to including murder, political corruption, and so on, which generally was a reflection of the US society of the time. Later stories became more or less adventures where small groups explore either willingly or unwillingly some aspect of Mars.

Those from the 2000s and on, the 21st century, sometimes fall into all three categories or a newly revived category altogether, often mixing genres, the most common being with detective or '*noir*' detective elements which combine quite well with SF elements. In fact mixing detective type stories with a Martian setting was also common in the 1950s. Although the detective elements were not as strong as they are in today's fiction, they managed to create a grungy noir feeling to the settings on Mars and Earth. This subgenre vanished after the photos came back from Mariner 4 and has only reappeared in some more modern stories.

SF and horror also go well together but this is more of a mixture in movies than it is in books; (see *Winds of Mars, Last Days on Mars,* and *Ghosts of Mars*) whereas books from the early part of the century usually fell into category one or two. But the categories are only a loose suggestion rather than being specific as many stories combine elements from all three groupings in various ways.

The first, Fanciful, contain stories that assume Mars was inhabited and there are remnants of ancient civilizations struggling to survive, or similarly dealing with situations that include the arrival of humans and their discovery of these ancient remnants, or straight out fantasies where exotic creatures live strange lives with all kinds of kingdoms and autocracies based vaguely on human models but set in a totally alien environment that was thought to exist. These fanciful and fantasy imaginings can mostly be blamed on Percival Lowell and his speculation about why there were canals on Mars. Edgar Rice Burroughs was the greatest exponent of this kind of story, but others also followed his lead, Michael Moorcock writing under the pseudonym of Edwin P Bradbury being one who started his career with fantasies about Mars. Leigh Bracket also wrote fantastic adventure stories set on Mars as well as other planets in the solar system that are still as exciting and entertaining today as they were 60 years ago. But even going back to ancient Greek times there was the expectation that life existed on all the heavenly bodies, and especially on Mars, and this expectation survived well into the twentieth century. Stories in this category are often thought of as 'romantic'.

The second, Factual, is where authors tried to include whatever scientific knowledge of Mars was current or believed to be true at the time of writing, and includes stories involving the trip to Mars and the difficulties this entails; stories about setting up and colonizing the planet and dealing with the harsh realities of Mars, which often included a situation where something disastrous happens and a small number of people struggle to survive until they can be rescued or must make an epic journey across the surface to a place where they can be safe. These are basically adventure stories.

An important aspect of these adventure stories is depiction of the surface of Mars along with the discovery is primitive life still surviving in the harsh Martian terrain. We want to find life there, so we can finally say we are not alone in the universe. Underlying this is the knowledge that once there must have been life of some sort on Mars because it had water and a thicker atmosphere billions of years ago. Almost every modern writer has their characters find bacteria deep underground, or primitive plant life partially protected in the valleys of massive chasms. Sometimes their characters find alien artefacts from an ancient Martian civilization, or something alien altogether that isn't from Mars, but this then is a crossover into elements of fantasy. Writers in the 1950s based their stories around the urban society they lived in with its fear of the cold war and extrapolated that into a Martian setting.

Also included in this second category is a smaller group of speculative stories that are basically non-fiction but slightly dramatized about how we would get to Mars and what we would or could do there. By adding characters and the situations they could get into, the technical details can be made more interesting for the non-technical reader. Modern television mini-series like ***The Race to Mar***s, and National Geographic's ***Mars,*** are beautifully dramatized documentaries.

Arthur C Clarke's book ***The Snows of Olympus — A Garden on Mars*** (1994) a coffee table book, falls into this category.

The third, Transformative, is where a major transformation is depicted. This is either modifying humans so they can actually exist unprotected on the surface of Mars (or any other planet) or alternatively by modifying Mars to create some resemblance to Earth, in other words terraforming Mars to make it more habitable for humans. It also includes stories in which the protagonists no longer feel they belong to Earth but have in effect become Martian, their transformation being internal and psychological rather than physical. An early example of modifying a human to be able to live on the surface is ***Crucifixus Etiam*** by Walter M Miller Jr. Much later examples are ***Man Plus*** by Frederick Pohl, and ***Climbing Olympus,*** by Kevin J Anderson.

There have always been crossovers within these categories which suggest they are amorphous. Most of the later crossovers are between categories two and three but the earlier ones are sometimes between category one and two rather than staying strictly in one or the other. If the protagonists in a story do find some kind of animal or alien being (presumably underground) it falls into the category of fantasy or fanciful imagination regardless of how the author tries to justify it. If there is some scientific basis for the speculation no matter how tenuous, then it remains acceptable until humans actually get to Mars and can prove otherwise, it may then fall into category two.

Another crossover is where something (*Martian bacteria, radiation or some other 'thing'*) inimical to humans affects them on Mars or is carried inadvertently onto their ship and as they return it either infects them or remains dormant until they arrive back on Earth where it will infect everyone when the ship lands. This is a variation of the alien invasion concept originating with H G Wells and his contemporaries, and is more popular in movies than it is in books. A recent example of this is a brilliantly scary film called ***Life***.

Another category has evolved in this new century — an evolution or de-evolution from both the **transformative** and **factual**, mostly involving an established colony on Mars having to survive after a major disaster on Earth has cut communications and supplies, leaving them to their own resources. This is usually a dystopian vision that ties in with the current worldwide general feeling of negativity towards the future, contrasted against the much earlier positive sense of wonder the early stories exhibited. This negativity is especially prevalent in fiction for young adults. Some of these stories are set many years into the future; while others take place not long after a colony begins to be self-sustaining, but still needs some assistance from Earth. Other stories have evolved from the noir detective mix of the early 1950s into a much more complex detective type story that takes place in large well established colonies. It seems old ideas never really die out but are simply recycled.

Whatever the category or sub-category, or crossover between them, it is best to enjoy the story for what it is, taking into consideration the time or the decade when it was written and what would have been known or thought to be known about Mars at that time. Every decade over the last century has some great stories, all of which deserve to be read.

Regardless of category, stories set on Mars are speculative.

No one knows what it feels like to walk on the surface, or to stand on a bluff and look towards the horizon. We have recent quite superb images sent back from the rovers on the surface which enhances our imagination, but until a human actually walks on the surface, any description or feelings attributed to being there can only be speculative.

Once we have landed on Mars, science fiction will become science fact and the stories from that moment on will certainly be different but no less interesting than what has been written before.

Today we have the knowledge and the technology to go to Mars, whereas back during the first half of the 20th Century we didn't. All we had were dreams.

The 1960s was a decade of great hope for space enthusiasts.

Astonishingly, we went to the Moon, but further human explorations were abandoned after Apollo 17, in favour of unmanned and robotic missions and going to Mars was postponed.

Some of the problems of travelling in space have been solved because of those trips to the Moon. We have also had people living and working in low earth orbit for decades; enabling many more problems associated with free-fall and lack of gravity and the long term effects of this on human bodies to be solved.

We know with certainty that we can go to Mars.

We have known this at least for the last 20 years.

The desire to go is there; all that is needed is the finance and commitment from Governments. Unfortunately governments and the majority of the people they serve always manage to find other areas where they think money could be better spent.

It seems however that privately owned companies such as SpaceX, Blue Horizons and others are leading the way to sending people to Mars... and it might happen much sooner than we think; perhaps as soon as 2020.

There is now a feeling of inevitability about going to Mars.

And the most exciting realization for me is that I will see someone journey to Mars in my lifetime.

It is no longer a dream.

Gale Crater

Part One

Before the Mariner 4 flyby

Chapter One

The Ascension of Mars

As the nineteenth century came to a close the idea firmly embedded in the public mind was that there were canals on Mars.

The astronomer Percival Lowell could hardly wait until Mars made its next closest approach to Earth, in October 1894, so that he too could see the canals that had been observed barely two decades earlier.

Percival Lowell was actually an amateur astronomer rather than a professional and was frowned upon by other professionals, but he couldn't be ignored because he was wealthy and this wealth had enabled him to build a magnificent observatory at a remote location he called *Mars Hill* which was better equipped than many of those used by other professional astronomers.

And sure enough he saw the canals in greater detail than ever before. It was his imagination rather than his professional competence which engendered dislike from other astronomers, but this imagination gave him great credence amongst the general population who devoured his books enthusiastically and believed every word he had written. He also backed his assertions with a plethora of photographs taken at his observatory which closely matched the earlier sketches and drawings he and other astronomers had made.

He published his first book about Mars in 1896, ***Mars***, and two more books followed in 1906 and 1908, ***Mars and Its Canals***, and ***Mars as the Abode of Life.*** He saw what he claimed were networks of canals that he believed carried water from the poles to the more arid and inhospitable equatorial regions of the planet. He truly believed these canals crisscrossed the planet and intersected at nodes he deemed to be oases and could only have been created by intelligent beings. He went to his grave in 1916 convinced he was right.

Percival Lowell believed and promoted the theory of planetary senescence to explain why Mars appeared to be a dying planet. In this theory planets closer to the sun would be younger and those further out older, thus Venus represented a planet still forming while Earth was in its middle age and Mars further out was old and dying: a ridiculous theory since basically all the planets would be about the same age regardless of how far out from the sun their orbits were. Yet this theory was widely accepted and Lowell postulated all kinds of struggles, with life on Mars desperately engineering their planet to enable them to survive. He wrote popular books on the subject and influenced many later SF writers who created limitless visions of a dying Mars and the struggle for survival of its inhabitants over millions of years. These books were devoured by the general public long before Science Fiction became ghettoized.

Authors like Edgar Rice Burroughs, Leigh Brackett, and Otis Adelbert Kline wrote many novels set on the kind of Mars imagined by Percival Lowell which became very popular and widely read. Burroughs' eleven Martian novels are still in print and still popular (spawning many modern imitators) today almost 100 years later, whereas the others are not widely remembered. Burroughs' earliest ones were published as books between 1917 and 1923. The later stories were published between 1931 and 1948. The final Mars novel, ***John Carter of Mars*** was published posthumously in 1964.

Burroughs died in 1950.

Lowell saw what he saw because he believed that was what he was going to see. The human mind will play tricks and subconsciously join disconnected spots together to make continuous lines, especially when the viewing is difficult with air that shimmers so nothing can be clearly seen for any length of time. Not only did he believe what he saw, a few other astronomers were also convinced that Mars was covered by a network of canals.

Some even saw canals on Venus and Mercury! — affirming that people will see what they believe they are going to see rather than what is actually there.

Other astronomers didn't believe it for one second, adamant that they had not seen anything like canals when they managed to get clear views.

Alfred Russell Wallace, a contemporary of Charles Darwin who came up independently with a similar theory of evolution based on his field studies in Indonesia, (*which actually forced Darwin to publish his* ***'On the Origin of Species'*** *before he was ready to do so*) didn't accept the idea of canals on Mars and publicly stated that, "not only is Mars not inhabited by intelligent beings, but it is uninhabitable."

He accepted that Lowell had seen lines across the surface, although Howell and his fellow believers were unable to capture photographic images to prove this.

What Wallace thought was that these were natural, a result of volcanic activity and 'planetary shrinkage'. He also suggested that because Mars was further from the sun than the Earth, it would be much colder and wouldn't have the pleasant earth-like climate people expected. He even suggested the daytime summer temperatures would still be well below the freezing point of water.

As arguments raged among astronomers and scientists, writers discovered a new source and location for weaving wonderful stories of planetary adventures; Mars and Venus, but especially Mars.

The populace at large was convinced that Mars had canals, and that for such canals to be seen from the Earth through telescopes they must have been very wide, at least 30 to fifty kilometres wide. They were also convinced that the planet still harboured ancient civilizations with skilled engineers — who or what else could have constructed such massive canals across the surface of the planet? Or alternatively there remained old ruins from extinct civilizations that were still inhabited with intelligent beings struggling desperately to survive. They believed the planet had once been far more advanced than Earth was at its present stage, but was now in its last desperate stages of dying.

It was these beliefs that enabled the populace to accept the terrifying proposition put forward by H G Wells in his story ***The War of the Worlds***.

A forgotten delight

Although several novels had been written about Mars in the late 19th century — Percy Greg's ***Across the Zodiac*** published in 1880 set wholly on a Mars which supported an advanced utopian human like civilization being one, another one describing a gentle utopia, ***Melbourne and Mars*** by John Fraser, was published in 1889 — most of these early attempts to depict life on Mars are long forgotten.

Melbourne and Mars (1889) by John (Joseph) Fraser

The author of this remarkable story worked as a Phrenologist and Physiognomist in Melbourne Australia in the 1880s and in collaboration with his wife, also a phrenologist, he wrote two other books: Husbands and how to select them, and How to read men as an open book. He also wrote a number of smaller chapbooks: Religion and Phrenology, Physiognomy made Easy, Hydropathy in the Household. There are several advertisements at the end of the book delineating J Fraser's services which include marriage advice and the use of photos to help match people who were considering marriage, all of which makes his book so much more remarkable since it was the only fiction he wrote.

Melbourne and Mars subtitled ***My Mysterious Life on two Planets*** is a memoir disguised as a novel, and is written as a first person narrative interspersed with diary summations. What is truly interesting about this story is that the first three chapters depict the narrator's life from being a boy in England who migrated with his mother to Melbourne Australia to join her husband who had been sent to this British Colony as punishment for a petty crime. This is the autobiographical memoir part. His descriptions of life in the Victorian Colony are evocative and harrowing, and even today more than 100 years later they still engender astonishment. They are contemporary and have the feel of being real whereas many modern attempts to set a story back in that time period ring false or seem artificial. This really was written and no doubt based entirely on the author's own life in Melbourne between 1850 and 1889. It seems it was the last thing he wrote because he is listed (*in The National Library Archives of Australia)* as having died in 1889, the same year this book was published.

The Martian part of the story begins in chapter four where because of his hard life he falls ill and is bedridden for some time. During his convalescence he begins having strange dreams. His first dream is of struggling in the dark with great forces pushing him from behind and on all sides until finally he emerges into a brilliant light where the air was so cold it made him pant and gasp until finally he could cry out for help. Gentle hands picked him up and cleaned him, comforted him until he fell asleep in his dream. He talks more about this and eventually concludes that he has been born somewhere else and is living the life of a happy healthy baby in a most comfortable and cheerful home.

He further notes that while he is living the life of a middle aged man in Melbourne he is also living the life of a young child somewhere else that is not remotely anything like Melbourne. He skips over some of his early life here and philosophises are all children rejuvenations with their old life forgotten? Is the soul always rising on a new life when setting on an old one? There are many other similar questions for which he has no answers. He talks about '*fissipation*' or the splitting of one life into two separate lives. He believes humans, especially the soul, are fissiparous because of his new experiences.

The next several chapters describe the world he experiences growing up in and it soon is obvious it is Mars. He includes some scientific facts that were known at the time; Mars is colder than Earth because it is further away from the sun, the day is slightly longer than an earth day, the year is almost twice as long, as are the seasons. In general the temperatures are much colder than those on Earth.

There is a sense of wonder as he describes how everything on Mars is powered by an abundant underground supply of electricity. The author believes that electricity is an all-powerful force generated by the sun, and that it is the force which keeps the planets spinning as well as moving around the sun creating the seasons. He goes at some length to explain how this marvellous power controls the functioning of the universe. Any electricity that the Martians extract from underground is instantly replenished by the sun so there is a never ending and abundant supply of power. The Martians even have 'electric fountains' where people can recharge their devices.

Other authors writing about Mars at the end of the nineteenth century also believed that electricity was the power of the future and that there would be an unending supply of it. Kurd Lassovitz's (***On Two Planets*** 1897) had Martians using solar power and they came to Earth to harvest it. Perhaps his thinking about the power source of the future was more advanced than his contemporaries. I don't think he explained how they converted the solar energy into usable power, but it certainly must have been the first mention in SF of harvesting solar power.

The society John Fraser describes is utopian. Everyone is happy. No one owns anything; they simply borrow it for as long as they need it. This includes their home, their flying vehicles, and all devices found in the homes and public places. When they no longer need it they return it to a depot for use by someone else. They only work five hours a day four days a week to earn credits against which they can borrow the necessities of living comfortably. The fifth day is a Sabbath and no work is done. He learns the history of how Martians were once warlike and fought each other over territory that was becoming ever increasingly barren, until finally an engineer discovered the power of electricity and how to use it to benefit the whole race. They transformed Mars from a dying, and drying planet into a much more benign world by draining swamps and channelling the water through canals to form two oceans, to reform the planet into a more hospitable environment. With no more wars the population increases until stability is reached.

(*Is this the first mention of planetary engineering in fiction...something later referred to as Terra-forming, only in this case would it be Mars-forming?*)

The narrative follows the life of the young child as he grows, goes to school, and has various adventures while learning about Mars, his home planet. The author uses the boy's experiences in school learning about Martian 'geography' as way of describing the planet and its history. As a young student he discovers a means of using electricity to heat the ground and increase fertility so more food can be grown. Because of this he becomes famous and no longer needs to work since his credit supply is endless. However he chooses to continue working so he can help his fellow Martians live a more comfortable life.

There is only one metropolis on Mars, a huge city 1000 miles long by 500 miles wide containing one fifth of the population. Population on the planet is 5000 million, all living happily together. Trains run underground because the land above is given over to agriculture. They can go as fast as 100 miles per hour, which must have seemed a phenomenal speed back in 1889.

We discover that there are three kinds of beings on Mars; *those who have lived on Earth and become fit for introduction to our higher life which to them is a kind of heaven and reward for virtuous living, those who while still living on Earth put out a new life and live here quite unconscious of the old life, and finally those who live on both planets and are conscious of both lives. Our protagonist is conscious in his Earth life of his life on Mars, but on Mars is entirely unaware of his life on Earth. Thus his soul can be on both planets no matter how far apart and can move back and forth without any loss of time.*

The author makes several comparisons between life on Earth (specifically in Melbourne in 1889) and life on Mars. His main observation being that on Earth humans make life for each other as miserable as possible whereas on Mars they strive to make life happier and better for all.

He meets an old man who also remembers being rejuvenated from an earlier Earth life and with the use of mesmerism he enables out protagonist to experience a half an hour of his life back in Melbourne. Here we have a description of a scene in the city that could very well be descriptive of the present day as it was of Melbourne in 1889. ...*What a roar of harsh sounds, grinding wheels, clanging bells, discordant and angry voices, and what faces —*

stern, hard, selfish, smile-less, sickly, pale, wrinkled, careworn, ugly as with sinful passion, and yet these are human faces and being human they are capable of happiness, though not one appears happy. He goes on to describe how he feels old at 60, heavy and tired as he walks from the Town hall in Collins Street and along Swanston Street towards the railway station at five o'clock, peak hour in the city. ...*and getting on a train, more clang and bang, more roar and shriek, more hurry and rush...*

Life on Mars seems so wonderful by comparison.

Most authors of the time believed that the lower the gravity the taller the beings would grow, and human-like beings on Mars would be giants compared to us. Gary P Serviss in his sequel to ***The War of the Worlds*** serialised in 1898 had his Martians as nine to twelve feet tall humanoids.

H G Wells in a later article published in 1908 described Martian plant life and drew conclusions based on the science of the time that humanoid Martians would be eight feet tall, have huge heads with bulging eyes and a long proboscis; quite a change from his original invasion story where his Martians with their superior intellect were completely unhuman and hideous, the first truly alien invaders. Other authors also postulated giant inhabitants...the smaller the celestial body, the larger the inhabitants were supposed to be.

Fraser was the complete opposite. He described his Martians as being no more than a metre in height. He believed the lesser gravity of Mars would mean people didn't need to grow as big because there was no need to struggle against heavy gravity as we do on Earth. If the planet had only one third the gravity of Earth and a thinner atmosphere there was no logical reason for giants to exist. Everything on Mars, Fraser believed, would be correspondingly smaller. Even his measurements of distance were smaller. One mile on Mars was two thirds of an Earth mile. A day was divided into 25 hours of fifty minutes each.

As the protagonist grows older he meets other people who also exist or existed on Earth and becomes a member of their club called *The Earthborn.* During his work on a major project to heat frozen areas for agricultural development he rescues a group of people whose air-car had an accident and one of these is a young woman who somehow seems familiar to him. A romance develops and finally after she rejects him several times he discovers that she is the rejuvenation of his wife of 40 years on Earth. His wife on Earth had died and by the end of the book he is an old man also not far from death. His new found love agrees to marry him again but only after he has died on Earth.

Here the story ends with a note from the editor saying that since Jacob (the name of the character whose diaries tell this story), has died there are no further notes or diaries which could tell of the wedding and his subsequent life on Mars.

Although the pace of the story is a little uneven being interspersed with descriptive summaries from the diaries of the Melbourne merchant, with dialogue between characters as well as action of the adventurous kind, it is a very interesting story. In 1889 it must have been an absolutely fascinating book to read.

Mars Attacks: *Art by Dick (Ditmar) Jenssen.*

Then along came H G Wells

H G Wells brought Mars to the forefront of people's imagination with his frightening novel ***The War of the Worlds*** published in 1897 as a serial in Pearson's magazine of London.

That same year Kurd Lassovitz's ***Auf Swei Planeten,*** (***On Two Planets***) published in German had equally great success in Europe. It had humanoid Martians invading Earth initially to harvest our sunlight for power, and for our water, after which it became more of an invasion story as the Martians decided to colonise the planet for our own good. It wasn't translated into English until 1961.

But it was Wells' serial that earlier captured the imagination of English speaking people with its horrifying alien Martians invading Earth to harvest humans for food.

His story has endured where most other contemporary 'Mars' novels vanished.

In January 1898 ***The War of the Worlds*** was licensed to appear in Hearst's *Cosmopolitan* Magazine. Since this was an expensive magazine, the Hearst newspapers also serialized a substantially rewritten version with American cities destroyed by the Martians rather than British ones. The various Hearst newspapers used alternative titles such as ***Fighters from Mars***, or ***The Terrible War of the Worlds as it Was Waged in or Near Boston in the Year 1900***... an awkward title to say the least. It ran until the end of February 1898 at which point the editors announced that a sequel to ***Fighters from Mars*** would begin immediately. This was ***The Conquest of Mars***, by Garrett P Serviss.

HG Wells upset previous ideas that life on Mars was benign.

He was the first to use the idea of an alien civilization struggling to survive on a dying planet deciding to invade the lush and beautiful planet Earth. At least he was the first to make this idea popular in the English speaking world.

The War of the Worlds stunned and terrified readers when it first appeared. What is also stunning is that more than a century later it is still being published and still thrills readers around the world.

Wells may not have been aware of Percival Lowell's ideas and his book Mars published a couple of years earlier in 1896, although I doubt this because in the third or fourth paragraph he mentions the Nebula Hypothesis of planetary formation and the belief that Mars being smaller, cooled quicker than Earth and therefore would have generated life earlier than Earth, ideas well propounded by Lowell and his associates both in lectures and books, but Wells, like everyone else, certainly knew about Schiaparelli's observations which had been widely publicised.

The decade before he published ***The War of the Worlds*** was full of speculation amongst scientists and the general public regarding life on Mars. The speculation was not if there could be life, but rather what kind of intelligent life existed on Mars and how it could have evolved?

In 1896, two years before publication of ***The War of the Worlds***, Wells had written an article discussing possible life on Mars and what the Martian climate may have been like for the ***London Saturday Review***, in which he referred to an earlier article published in Nature in 1894 about luminous flashes of light seen near Mars' poles when Mars was at its closest approach to Earth. Wells speculated that Martian evolution would be nothing like ours and that Martians would most certainly be very different in appearance from humans or any other earthly animals, unlike his contemporary novelists who depicted Martians as being humanoid if not actually human in appearance.

Wells also wrote a short story called ***The Crystal Egg*** (1897) wherein a London antique dealer came across a mysterious polished crystal egg that displayed images of another world, a verdant world with ethereal creatures which it was determined by the end of the story were inhabitants of Mars. Before anything more could be discovered the mysterious crystal egg (a device for communicating between planets) disappeared and that was the end of the story.

A year later when it came to ***The War of the Worlds***, Wells imbued his Martians with sinister and superior intellects that were technically far more advanced than humankind deciding to take over our world because theirs was no longer able to sustain them. There was nothing we could do to stop them.

After laying waste to vast areas of the English countryside and preparing to utterly destroy London, the Martian machines finally ground to a halt. The Martians, hideous and unstoppable — ***the first truly alien beings ever described in fiction, and the first invasion of Earth by aliens*** — had succumbed to the humble bacteria that caused the common cold, something humans had learned to resist or become immune to over untold generations. The Martians had never encountered this particular bacterium before and not having immunity to it they all died. After ***War of the Worlds*** Wells never returned to Mars and went on to other things. But he did leave a suggestion that the Martians would possibly try again and that we should be wary of a future invasion.

Incidentally he used the same plot device to resolve his later story ***First Men in the Moon*** where the Selenites all succumbed to the common cold carried by the inventor of the spaceship that took his characters to the Moon.

Wells had certainly been aware of this very thing happening in Africa and other places like the islands of the Pacific where contact with Europeans brought death and devastation to native populations through such common diseases as Measles, Mumps, Smallpox, and Syphilis to name a few. Those native populations had no immunity to the European diseases and dropped like flies. So too, thought Wells, would the Martians have no immunity to Earthly diseases because they had never come into contact with them. They also had no way of stopping colonization of their lands and the terrible consequences of that occupation. Most invasions of Earth stories inverted this idea and had humans suffering the same fate or worse as those inhabitants of countries colonized by European powers when aliens come to conquer Earth.

The Martian invaders dying from the moment they started breathing our atmosphere wasn't a *deux ex machina* cop out; it was a brilliant concept for the time and it showed Wells had thought carefully about how to resolve his enthralling story because he foreshadowed it in the very first paragraphs of the story when he clearly mentioned the mortality of the Martians.

The War of the Worlds started a renewed wave of stories about Earth being invaded by increasingly sinister aliens that still goes on today — more so in movies than in books since filmmakers generally prefer horrible and grotesque subject matter rather than the more realistic. It also engendered in people's subconscious the idea that any aliens coming to Earth came from Mars.

Every decade since there has been invasion stories, although they were not always about Martians. However, over the last decade or two there have been many unauthorised 'sequels' to Wells original book where the story is continued with a second invasion. But it was Wells who is generally credited as the first to establish the concept of the world being invaded from space.

Though ***The War of the Worlds*** is not a book about Mars, it is so imbued with popular images of what Mars and aliens from Mars in people's minds were like, it deserves to be here.

The War of the worlds was a seminal work that stunned the public with the idea — never truly considered before — that our world could be attacked by aliens inimical to us. Aliens who would treat us the way we treat insects like ants; aliens so superior that we had no defence against them; aliens who would harvest humans for food as we harvest sheep and cattle. The concept that humankind and all its civilized societies could be totally wiped out and reduced to rubble frightened everyone at the beginning of the 20th century. It still does, perhaps even more so today.

It must be remembered that when Wells published this story in 1898, the common mode of travel was via horseback or horse drawn vehicles; there were no aeroplanes and no motor cars although there were steam engines, limited railways and possibly steam motor road vehicles. The combustion engine had just been invented and motor cars as we know them were experimental and rarely seen, although the looming First World War a decade ahead spurned rapid development of all kinds of vehicles with combustion engines for land as well as air.

This one book spawned untold numbers of copies and variations on the same theme and authors today, more than a century later, are still using H G Wells' basic idea to create novels and films which always do well. It seems that our fascination with our own destruction is an endless source of contemplation and fear.

Wells clearly mentions the nebula theory of planetary evolution in the first chapter and his story referred to the beliefs of the time when people thought there were canals on Mars (although he never mentions canals) and that there was a dying civilization there, a civilization desperate to escape its fate, desperate to find a new world where it could thrive, and what better place than the third planet from the sun? — A world rich with life and abundant water, something desperately lacking on Mars. Percival Lowell and his enticing ideas of a benign Mars fired everyone's imagination. But Wells' Mars was frightening and sinister, although he never describes it in any detail he implies what it must be like through the actions of his hideous alien beings bent on the destruction of our own beautiful world.

The opening paragraph sets the mood and we know from that moment on nothing good is going to happen but we are compelled to keep reading.

Wells made it so real right from the beginning because he added true information reported about Mars, about flashes of light seen by astronomers that implied something strange was going on there. These reports were in leading newspapers of the time.

Wells also reminds us of ...*the ruthless and utter destruction our own spe-*

cies has wrought, not only upon the animals, such as the vanished bison and the dodo but upon its inferior races...and he goes on to mention the native Tasmanians being entirely swept out of existence in a war of extermination over 50 years, asking the question ...Are we such apostles of mercy as to complain if the Martians warred in the same spirit?

Who can forget the quotes taken from the beginning and the end of the first paragraph of the novel used in the filmed versions of the story as well as the radio play from 1938 that scared the wits out of Americans who actually believed they were being invaded by Martians, and panicked as they tried to evacuate major east coast cities. In the back of their minds was the fear that Germany would invade America, which it didn't, (this was the eve of the Second World War) but perhaps this subconscious fear was why they instantly accepted the Martian invasion.

...No one would have believed in the last years of the nineteenth century that this world was being watched keenly and closely by intelligences greater than man's and yet as mortal as his own; that as men busied themselves about their various concerns they were scrutinised and studied, perhaps almost as narrowly as a man with a microscope might scrutinise the transient creatures that swarm and multiply in a drop of water. ...across the gulf of space, minds that are to our minds as ours are to those of beasts that perish, intellects vast and cool, and unsympathetic, regarded this earth with envious eyes and slowly and surely drew their plans against us... (Part of H G Wells' opening paragraph to ***The War of the Worlds***)

Radio was something new and live broadcasts of news events were accepted as true. When Orson Welles broadcast his radio dramatization of the War of the Worlds — on Halloween night 1938, in a slot usually used for radio dramas — in the form of an interruption to what seemed to be a regular musical programme, with on-site news reports of events that were happening, listeners of the time couldn't distinguish the difference between *The Play* and a real news broadcast. Welles had one of his actors on the roof reporting about Martian tripod machines wading across the Hudson River while attacking the nearby buildings with its heat ray and in the background was the sound of heavy traffic from the streets of New York below which suggested that the city was being evacuated. It was very real to listeners of the broadcast and they panicked. They never bothered to look for themselves to see if there were tripod machines advancing on the city. En masse they tried to evacuate and absolute chaos ensued.

Even after it was known to have been a hoax, radio stations in South

America several years later emulated Orson Welles dramatization. On November 12, 1944 ***The War of the Worlds*** broadcast from a radio station in Santiago Chile caused widespread panic across the whole country with people fleeing into the streets or barricading themselves in their homes. In some provinces troops with artillery were mobilized to fight the Martians.

Four years later on February 12, 1949 in Ecuador, Radio Quito broadcast their version of ***The War of the Worlds*** but did it by interrupting a regular program with their fake invasion news reports. It too caused widespread panic. The capitol's citizens ran out into the streets in their night clothes believing they were either being attacked by Martians or invaded by neighbouring Peru.

When the radio station realised the panic it had caused, they broadcast an apology hoping it would calm people down. But this fired up the panicking citizens, giving them a purpose. They headed for the radio station, and with cans of petrol they set fire to the building. The employees of the radio station escaped through a back door. Unfortunately a number of rioters died during the attack and the police later arrested and jailed the radio station manager.

As late as 1986 when some radio stations in America announced they were going to play an updated version of the Play used by Orson Welles in his first broadcast, people still panicked and swamped authorities wanting to know what to do, and where to go to be safe.

There is just something about an invasion from space, but from Mars in particular, that terrifies people even when they have been told it isn't real.

In 1953 George Pal produced Byron Haskin's film version of ***The War of the Worlds*** starring Gene Barry inhis first movie appearance as Dr Clayton Forrester and set the story in Los Angeles and California, rather than England and London. He changed the appearance of the tripod machines described by H G Wells with floating triangular shaped ships that brought to mind images of manta rays (known as Devil Fish in some places). These floating machines destroyed everything in their path and were impervious. Even an atomic bomb, the most powerful weapon humans had in 1953 couldn't harm them.

America, in the middle of the Cold War, was primed to expect some kind of invasion. People flocked to see this film and were suitably terrified. The special effects won an Oscar that year, and although they look dated by today's standards the film still evokes a sense of innocence destroyed by an implacable invader. The very brief glimpse of a Martian flashing sideways past an open door in the wrecked house where Dr Clayton Forrester was hiding with his fiancée was absolutely scary. The only other glimpse of a Martian is at the end when the triangular space ships stop their destruction and slowly crash. A door in the base of a crashed ship opens and a three fingered hand that has suckers on its finger tips struggles to drag a dying Martian out of his machine but doesn't quite succeed. It dies before we can see the rest of it.

We never really get a good look at a complete Martian, which makes them and the threat they represent more horrifying. Often the monsters in other invasion films from that decade and the one after looked quite ridiculous which destroyed any possibility of believing they were real. But the brief glimpses of the Martians in this film succeeded in convincing viewers how horrible and real they were. The producers wisely left us with our imagination to fill in the details and this was far more effective than trying to show everything.

In the book, chapter eight goes into detail about how the bacteria of Earth have co-evolved with humans over millions of years; bacteria which did not exist on Mars and which immediately the Martians arrived began attacking them. Wells' character is almost sympathetic as he wonders what the Martians would have thought as they tried to explain the inexplicable… why they were dying and putrefying the moment they were exposed to Earth's atmosphere and water. There were no bacteria on Mars and the Martians would have been unable to explain why they were dying when whatever was attacking them was invisible.

In the 1953 film it is summed up with a succinct quote about Earth's smallest creatures, bacteria, being able to defeat the Martians while all of Man's weapons were of no use at all against them. I actually saw this film before reading the original book and I must admit I loved the film but didn't at that stage particularly care about the book.

The film, rightly or wrongly, is thought of with a degree of ambiguity. It is either a classic SF story, or a B grade horror film with SF elements. For me it is classic SF and always looks good.

Even though a much later film starring Tom Cruise (2005) was quite spectacular compared to the 1953 film, it didn't capture the essence of H G Wells' original idea which I feel the George Pal production, transplanted from England to California, did. The aliens in this later film have been here all along, lying dormant in their machines deep underground until something triggers their awakening after which they suddenly emerge with much noise and destruction, hell-bent on harvesting humans for food which they process in their giant tripod machines. This idea is much closer to other invasion novels of the 80s and 90s rather than HG Wells' original story. In the George Pal film production there was no mention at all of harvesting humans for food, an idea that may not have been popular in the 1950's. No doubt the producers of the new film thought this would be a more horrifying idea to emphasise and would appeal more to modern audiences. Who knows? There are many other films with monstrous alien machines or quasi-machines (*Transformers* and *Pacific Rim* spring to mind among other forgettable efforts) that makes them hard to distinguish from one another… just massive machines and mayhem mixed together with excessively loud sound effects.

As much as I enjoyed the newer film while watching it, it is eminently forgettable not long after.

Nobody forgot the original film if they saw it when it was released in 1953. There was something about it that stays in your memory, just like the original book which has never gone out of print and has editions in more languages than probably any other SF book.

There was a TV series that lasted 44 episodes in 1988 -89 — God knows why! It is dated by the hair styles and clothes of the women more than that of the men, but the premise established in the first episode is that the aliens from Mars didn't die but went into a coma or induced hibernation. They were stored (by whom?) in steel vats and hidden along with three of their flying machines in a secret American military base. Other locations around the world also had vats with dormant Martians hidden in secret locations.

In the first episode a small group of 'American' eco-terrorists wanting to broadcast a message on a captured satellite accidentally release them,. They attack remorselessly and take over the bodies of the terrorists turning them into super strong zombies. When shot they dissolve into a gooey mess. These Martians now have immunity to earth bacteria, and they want to continue their invasion.

Fortunately our intrepid scientist, his female micro-biologist sidekick, plus a few army Special Forces people who believe him, manage to plant bombs inside the three captured but dormant Martian war machines which the zombie-Martians reactivate. These machines look exactly like the ones from the 1953 movie. The machines blow up after using heat rays to blast out of the hangar where they had been stored. The episode concludes here with a brief shot of the remaining Martians hiding in an old abandoned underground bunker. They plan to re-activate the many Martians kept in containers stored all around the world.

As this series begins no one knows about the original invasion which was covered up in 1938 (referencing the panic induced by the Orson Welles radio Play) and the one that occurred in 1953, (the George Pal film), is also covered up, and the lead character, who was a boy then adopted by Dr Forrester after his parents were killed by Martians, is the only one who knows about them.

It beggars belief. How could an invasion which destroyed most major American cities (let alone other cities around the world) be covered up so no one knows about it 30 years later? People still talk about the devastation caused in both World Wars. They still talk about the damage done to San Francisco a hundred years after the massive earthquake that destroyed it. In a world where all the major cities were reduced to rubble by Martian war machines with millions supposedly killed as we saw in the clips shown from the 1953 film near the beginning of the first episode, (called ***The Resurrection***) how could that be covered up with no one remembering? How could the damage be repaired so the cities look as they always had without anyone knowing about it?

It was a silly series that eventually had to bring in other aliens attacking the earth as well as the original Martians to sustain it over 44 episodes. The characters simply weren't believable and the acting was so over the top it went beyond melodrama. But the very fact that it was such an awful show could be the reason it became successful enough to last two years.

There are some other telefilms that purport to be sequels or remakes of Wells' original story that went straight to video (early 2000s) and have seemingly vanished. I haven't seen them so can't comment other than to mention in passing that they exist.

One other interesting film which was made for TV was ***The Night That Panicked America***, about Orson Welles and the radio team that created the War of the Worlds broadcast. This telemovie won an Emmy Award for sound editing, and for many years was broadcast once a year on Halloween. It hasn't been seen much in recent years which is a pity because it is a good film.

Numerous sequels to Wells' novels are beginning to appear now that the original copyright has terminated. Some are officially sanctioned by the H G Wells Estate, such as ***The Time Ships*** by Stephen Baxter, an excellent lengthy sequel to the wonderful short novel *The Time Machine*, and ***The Massacre of Mankind***, (2017) an unnecessarily long sequel to ***The War***

of the Worlds also by Stephen Baxter. Baxter followed this with a novella called ***The Martian in the Wood*** a very creepy story published as an eBook.

There are many others that appear to be unsanctioned and of various qualities written by avid fans of the original novel, or of the Americanised version of it, who obviously want the story to continue; ***The War of the Worlds – Aftermath*** by Tony Wright (2010), ***The Great Martian War: Invasion*** and ***The Great Martian War: Breakthrough*** by Scott H Washburn (2015 – 2016), ***Counterattack*** (2017) and those three in one volume called ***America Aflame*** (2018), as well as ***Europe Ablaze*** are some of the many, but these alien invasion stories are not about going to Mars or being on Mars so they are not relevant here.

War of the Worlds Retaliation (2017) by Mark Gardner and John J Rust takes the battle back to Mars in 1924 using the technology gained from the remains of the Martian fighting machines abandoned on Earth after the invasion of 1898. It is a story big on action with massive space battles, and battles fought on the surface of Mars. It is seen from both the viewpoints of the humans invading Mars and from the desperate Martians trying to defend their planet from overwhelming human forces, a reversal of the basic concept of ***War of the Worlds***.

All the nations of the World united to develop the technology that would allow them to retaliate against the Martians so there is no 1st World War. This is as an alternate history story with the major characters being actual historical figures from the time between 1898 and 1924. I found it lacked the feeling of wonder that permeated the first sequel ***Edison's Conquest of Mars*** and was not as interesting. For me, this new retaliation had too much focus on the battles between opposing forces and very little on character development which ultimately made the story flat, whereas Serviss' story was certainly original being the first. It is a much more fascinating read than many of the modern sequels in my view.

The very first sequel to *The War of the Worlds*

Edison's Conquest of Mars appeared in February 1898 also as a serial, immediately after the serialization of ***The War of the Worlds*** had concluded in the American newspapers of the day. It was written by science journalist and astronomer Garrett P Serviss.

Although Wells' original serial shortly became published as a proper book, which is constantly reprinted, Garrett P Serviss' sequel vanished once the serial had concluded, and was not reprinted until a limited edition in

1947, years after the author's death in 1929. It is a pity because this sequel contains many technological concepts later adopted by almost every SF author, yet very little credit is given to this author who first came up with those ideas. People think of Wells and Verne as the progenitors of modern science fiction, but Serviss should also be added to that list.

A restored edition of ***Edison's Conquest of Mars*** with many original newspaper illustrations was reprinted in 2010, and this is definitely worth a closer look. It has an excellent cover design by Ron Miller, an author and illustrator with over 50 books to his credit. (Notably ***Spaceships: an illustrated history of the real and the imagined.*** 2016.)

Edison's Conquest of Mars begins shortly after the Martian invasion of Earth as humanity starts to rebuild the damage caused by the Martians and their war machines; more flashes are seen by Astronomers emanating from Mars. They fear a second invasion is underway.

The scientists of the day, led by American inventor Thomas Edison who has invented an electrical cigar shaped ship capable of travelling in space, propose a counter invasion. They will go to Mars and destroy the Martians, thus preventing them from ever attacking Earth again. All their resources are put towards building a fleet of space ships to be manned by scientists of all disciplines as well as fighting men. Edison has also invented a disintegrator, which he demonstrates to the world leaders. It is his answer to the Martian heat rays which caused so much devastation, What it does is break down and separate the atoms in whatever it is aimed at, so the target vanishes, broken into individual atoms and dispersed.

Apart from the disintergator, there are a number of firsts in this novel. Serviss has them fly to the moon for practice and preparation for the ongoing flight to Mars. Something NASA is considering as part of its attempt to go to Mars. They encounter an asteroid and his description of how they react to extremely low gravity as they explore the asteroid is spot on.

The disintegrator gun is used here for the first time, both as a small hand held weapon as well as a much larger weapon mounted within the space ships. How many stories have been produced since then (1898) where ray guns are used? Every space opera has ray guns and they continue to do so in more complex ways in modern stories. This is especially notable in TV series like ***Star Trek***, not to mention the ***Star Wars*** films.

On the way to Mars the fleet encounters an asteroid where Martians are mining for metals, and a space battle occurs between the fleet and the Martian ships. The humans prevail because of their superior disintegrator weapons. Space battles are now common in space opera stories but this was the first time such a battle was described.

His descriptions of space suits and how they look and work, and the way the crew enter and exit the ships through airlocks, and the methods used to move around in space between the ships had never been described so accurately before this story. It is exactly in principle, how it is done today in space. He even warns us that if someone gets too far away from the ship and runs out of propellant, there is no way back and they would drift forever. Who knew that way back in 1898, when no one considered going into space was even possible?

When the fleet arrives at Mars the story exhibits all the beliefs of what Mars was thought to be like in the nineteenth century: criss-crossed with canals, with massive urban complexes built around intersection points, with shallow seas, and industrial complexes where space projectiles were being built.

Wells' idea was based on the nebula theory proposed by Percival Lowell of a dying planet, but with a population desperate for water and other resources so its inhabitants attacked Earth for the riches they could obviously see.

Serviss' idea is that the Martians are a warlike race and enjoy conquering and enslaving the peoples of other planets and they have been to Earth before. He tosses in the idea that they built the pyramids and the monuments in ancient Egypt. Who before him ever suggested that aliens built the pyramids? He also had them destroy an early Himalayan civilization bringing the survivors back to Mars as captives which they enslaved. Only one of them has survived by the time the humans invade Mars, a beautiful young woman… *of course.*

Unlike Wells' tentacled and hideously alien Martians, Serviss' Martians are human looking except that they are more than twice as large as us. It was commonly thought that because Mars has a lower gravity, less than a third of what we have on Earth, that everything would be bigger and taller. His Martians are fourteen to sixteen feet tall and all their buildings etc. are similarly bigger to accommodate them.

In Serviss' version of Mars, it is not dying at all. There is plenty of water, oceans of it, kept at bay with locks and gates which allow sufficient to be fed into the canals in low lying areas for irrigation and other purposes. But his Martians are warlike, and the moment they see the Earth ships hovering in the atmosphere they attack with their heat rays destroying a number of ships.

The human fleet retaliates with devastating effects using their large mounted disintegrator guns. The Martians throw up a smoke cloud enveloping the planet so nothing can be seen from space. The human fleet travels to the other side of the planet where one of the ships goes down beneath the cloud to infiltrate their defences.

This is where they discover a beautiful human captive with whom they eventually communicate. She gives them the clues that they need to destroy the Martians, and this is done in spectacular fashion by opening the gates that hold back the oceans of Mars. They beat the Martians by flooding the whole planet which destroys their cities and their industrial capacity to build space ships and anything else, in the process killing millions of Martians. This is as exciting as it is spectacular.

This latter part of the novel is fantasy based on what people thought Mars was like, whereas the first part was much more scientific, extrapolating engineering and astronomical concepts into practical ideas.

For all its good points there are a couple of anomalies that jar, that remind the reader that no matter how futuristic or modern some of the story is, it was written more than 100 years ago. There are references to the pure Aryan Race, which is not how we think today especially after what happened during the 2nd World War.

However, it is an enjoyable story, and in many ways, surprisingly modern.

Or is it that modern stories use so much of what he first extrapolated 100 years ago which makes Garrett P Serviss seem so modern today?

H G Wells as a character

1966 was the centenary of the birth of H G Wells, and as a tribute Brian Aldiss wrote a delightful novella ***The Saliva Tree*** in which Wells appears as one of the main protagonists. Since that year other authors have written stories in which H G Wells appears as a secondary character or as a main character.

Two examples that spring to mind are Michael Moorcock's ***The Hollow Lands*** in which H G Wells gives some advice about Time Machines to Jherek Carnellian, a mysterious innocent from the ends of time (***Dancers at the End of Time*** series) — one of the funniest books Moorcock ever wrote with his perspective of the Victorian Age seen through his protagonist from the far future being absolutely riotous — and Christopher Priest's ***The Space Machine.***

Aldiss' ***The Saliva Tree*** opens with two English gentlemen walking along a country road when they see a huge meteor passing slowly overhead. It disappears over a hilltop where they presume it has crashed. The head to the site to find whatever it was has landed in a farmer's pond and cannot be seen. The farmer is known to the young gentleman who has amorous intentions towards the farmer's daughter, so he has no problems in gaining access to the farm.

Not long after, mysterious mist envelopes the whole farm where it lingers until the sun is strong enough to dissipate it. This mysterious event prompts our young man to write to his esteemed friend H G Wells whom he knows loves a good mystery. Meanwhile odd things begin to occur on the farm. There is the feeling that something strange is wandering about. It leaves footprints but can't be seen. There is an intense feeling of being watched. Again the young gentleman writes to his friend and invites him to come and look at what is happening.

Spring arrives and for some strange reason everything on the farm grows to enormous size. Pigs and Cows give birth to many more offspring than expected, and the farmer is happy. He considers what is happening as good luck. Other farms are struggling and hardly produce anything at all. While the farmer loads a wagon with piglets to take to market the young man sees a series of footprints approaching, then suddenly the wagon sags as if something heavy has jumped on it. The piglets go crazy and one manages to jump off breaking a leg in the process. While he watches the piglets one by one suffer disinflation as if everything has been sucked out of them leaving nothing but the skin behind. The young man is horrified. The farmer is dumbfounded and insists they must have had some mysterious disease. The farmer takes the injured piglet into his pregnant wife and she cooks it for dinner, but no one can eat it because it tastes horrible, as if it had been poisoned.

Later back in town the young man does some research and finds some snakes inject a poison that digests the victim from inside and all the snake has to do is suck the liquefied inside out. He believes something like that is coming up out of the lake and doing the same to the farm animals. Things turn from bad to worse and in terrible agony the farmer's wife gives birth to 9 babies. The young man now thinks that whatever is in the meteor in the lake has somehow fertilized the farm and is harvesting the creatures for food. She goes crazy and strangles the babies because she believes she can see a weird creature eating the animals for food and suspects the babies could be next.

The young man now believes the alien creature in the lake treats everything, people included, as a source of food. They set up a trap to capture it by spreading flour about so they will see the footprints appearing when it comes towards them. When this happens they throw bags of flour over it to reveal its shape. It is monstrous, almost two metre tall with writhing tentacles each with a mouth and teeth so it looks a bit like an octopus combined with a man of war jellyfish and all this mixed in with crablike legs and finned feet. They manage to stick pitchfork into it, and one of the farmer's assistants tries to strangle it but is thrown aside. It retreats and heads back into the pond. Later, in the barn it comes for the cows which are enormously bloated. The young man is trying to get the farmer's daughter to a safe place and they are caught in the barn. Trapped in there they manage to see the hideous creature through the dust raised by the panicking cows. The young man shoots it with the farmer's rifle stored in the barn and the monster retreats back to the pond.

Not long after there is a terrible noise and huge amounts of steam rise from the pond and slowly the meteorite rises up out of the pond and shoots up into the sky. The horrible visitor has gone. Did it come here for a holiday? Did it come to exploit the animal life for food? Will more of them come?

These are unanswered as the young man heads back into town with his fiancée and back at the hotel he finds his friend H G Wells has checked in. He rushes up to his friend's room to tell him all of the events that occurred. And that is the end of the story. Presumably H G Wells would relate this story in a much expanded form as ***The War of the Worlds.***

This is a beautifully crafted piece that captures the Victorian age perfectly. It is also both amusing and at the same time horrifying and creepy.

A magnificent tribute from Brian Aldiss!

In Christopher Priest's ***The Space Machine,*** the space machine is really a time machine in which our young hero and his lady love accidentally get themselves transported into the future. They also find themselves on Mars where they undertake some strange and wonderful adventures culminating their stay by starting a revolution. They help downtrodden slaves fight against their monstrous overlords, and when they find that these horrible creatures intend to invade Earth, they contrive to stow away in the first capsule to be catapulted towards Earth. They arrive as the spearhead of the Martian invasion.

No one believes them when they try to warn people, but the population soon finds out that all of Earth's (meaning England's) armies are no match for the Martian invasion.

Our two weary travellers decide to head back to where the inventor of the Time Machine lives who happens to be our heroine's guardian. On their way home they encounter another dishevelled gentleman. Yes, it is none other than H G Wells. They join forces to work their way down river, avoiding Martians and their destructive machines, and when they finally reach their destination, they find it abandoned.

H G Wells tells his new acquaintances that the inventor of the Time Machine was a friend of his and that he has already chronicled his adventures. HG and our hero proceed to build themselves a space time machine which they then use to attack and destroy the Martian war machines which by this time are stomping all over the countryside. There are too many of them and the task seems hopeless.

But just as they are about to give up hope, the Martians mysteriously begin to die. At the end of the book HG parts company with our young hero and his lady love. Each decides to write down their account of what happened. Of course HG will write ***The War of The Worlds***, and our hero, well he has already told his story — it is ***The Space Machine.***

The book is a delight… the story, the Victorian style of writing, in short everything about it is a joy to read.

In 1979 Arkady and Boris Strugatsky, Russia's best known writers of science fiction, published a novella called ***The Second Invasion from Mars.***

Having failed with their first invasion the Martians sent emissaries to Earth whose object was to buy their way into Earth's economy and thus gain acceptance. The setting is a small isolated country town and no one in this town has actually seen a Martian, although they certainly knew about the first failed attempt at conquest.

The story, in a style reminiscent of 19th century literature, is satirical and pokes fun at the changes by the Russian Government as it begins modernization but which in this story are attributed to the Martians. When the Martians do arrive they look exactly like humans so no one suspects they are not what they seem. One interesting detail concerns the establishment of a business which pays people to donate their blood and gastric juices. I don't recall any reasons given to convince the villagers other than they are to be paid, but the donations we can assume are used as food by the martians who in the origanl story by H G Wells harvested humans for their blood.

All the characters in the town have names from Greek mythology, which for me was confusing. Not many people would have seen this short sequel to War of the Worlds, since it was originally written in Russian and translated in 1979. Another novel written by the Strugatsky brothers was ***The Ugly Swans***, an invasion of Earth story that probably owes its basic theme to H G Wells, as do many other invasion of Earth stories.

SF translated from other languages into English did not seem that popular in the 1970s, and even today, so I have no doubt there are European Martian stories that have yet to be translated and seen by English readers. France for one had many authors who wrote stories that dealt with Mars, from the beginning of the 20th century to the present time, but few if any of these stories have been translated into English.

Many years later Kevin J Anderson also added to this selection of books with HG Wells as a featured character, really as a tribute, with two books: One using two novellas to form the basis of ***The Martian War***, which purports to be ***the true account of the war of the worlds***, featuring H G Wells prominently alongside many of the characters that Wells actually created in his own books, and the other, an anthology, ***War of the Worlds – Global Dispatches***, (1996 - 2013) which is much more than just a collection of stories.

Although this is an anthology, it reads like a novel. In fact it should be approached as if it is a novel, with each story seen as a separate chapter that illuminates what was happening while H G Wells as a character in some of the stories was reporting on and experiencing the events that led to his writing of ***The War of the Worlds.***

One of the stories that formed part of ***The Martian War*** also appears here in a different form titled ***Canals in the Sand,*** by Kevin J Anderson, and features Percival Lowell as a main character. Each story or chapter has the sense of the end of the Victorian Era, capturing the feelings and moods of the time, some of them quite humorously. Each presents the perception of the Martian invasion as it was experienced simultaneously in different places around the world by many different people, some of them to become famous later in life such as Winston Churchill, Teddy Roosevelt, Pablo Picasso, Albert Einstein, Tolstoy, Jules Verne, H P Lovecraft, Joseph Conrad and Jack London, among others each of whom presents the invasion from different perspectives which highlights H G Wells brilliant original work that was set entirely in England.

All of the stories in this volume, except for one were copyrighted in 1996, written as originals for this anthology. The only exception was Howard Waldrop's ***Night of the Cooters,*** copyrighted in 1987 and published the same year in *Omni*. It fits beautifully into this anthology and is used with permission of the author.

The authors of the stories in this volume are known for high quality, innovative and thought provoking work, (Robert Silverberg, Connie Willis, Walter Jon Williams, Mike Resnick, Gregory Benford and David Brin, to mention a few) which makes this book a superb complement for ***The War of the Worlds***. It makes H G Wells' original work appear to be much better, which is not something the many other later sequels managed to do.

Every story is good and worth reading, but for me a few stood out: ***Paris Conquers All***, by Gregory Benford and David Brin, with Jules Verne as a protagonist was an unexpected delight. ***After a lean Winter*** by Dave Wolverton, featuring Jack London was most unusual, definitely outstanding from my point of view. ***To See the World End,*** by M Shayne Bell with Joseph Conrad was another that impressed me. Also a delight was the appearance of Einstein in ***Determinism and the Martian War with Relativistic Corrections,*** by Doug Beason.

Don't bypass this book if you see it, it's worth every cent you pay for it.

The Martian War by Kevin J Anderson (2012)

Two novellas, ***A Scientific Romance*** (1998), and ***The Canals of Mars*** (1995) form the basis of this larger work, which Anderson has subtitled: *a thrilling eyewitness account of the recent alien invasion as reported by H G Wells.*

Not only has Anderson used real people, H G Wells himself along with his fiancé Jane, T H Huxley, Percival Lowell (the man who gave us the canals and dying civilizations on Mars), he also includes some familiar characters from Well's other novels, Dr Moreau, Hawley Griffin (the invisible man) and Professor Cavor (the inventor of cavorite that uses anti-gravity to power the sphere that goes to the moon), and mixed them together in such a way that we can almost believe how H G Wells came to write his famous stories — ***First Men in The Moon***, ***The Invisible Man***, ***The Crystal Egg***, ***The Shape of Things to Come***, ***The Island of Doctor Moreau***, and of course ***The War of The Worlds***.

Anderson gives us two parallel stories that are interlinked.

The first is with H G Wells and his romance with Jane, along with him being invited to participate in a forum where many different scientists are working on secret weapons to thwart a possible Prussian invasion of England. Among the scientists is Dr Cavor who while trying to invent an impenetrable shield against Prussian artillery comes up with anti-gravity, Hawley Griffin (almost a madman) who is experimenting with drugs to make things invisible, and many others all presided over by Professor T H Huxley, an eminent biologist/botanist and general man of the sciences.

The initial meeting is interrupted by Dr Moreau, who has been banned from attending these conferences in England because of his animal experiments on a mysterious tropical island. He tells them he has a remarkable tale regarding an invasion from Mars and actually has a specimen to show them. It's all documented in his notebooks which he gives to Huxley. The meeting breaks up in an uproar when the Martian specimen is revealed.

All sorts of things happen then, H G and his fiancé along with T H Huxley find themselves in the laboratory where professor Cavor has built his sphere when the mad Hawley Griffin comes in (he is a saboteur) and sets off an explosion. Somehow Wells anticipates what Hawley is about to do and thrusts Jane and Huxley into the sphere closing the hatch as he follows them in. The explosion set off by Hawley kills professor Cavor and blows the sphere up through the roof of the science lab, up through the atmosphere and out into space. They learn how to control the sphere as it rushes towards the Moon.

The second parallel story begins when Moreau's notebooks are revealed to H G Wells who begins to peruse them. Lowell has got Moreau to help him build an enormous triangular canal 10 miles long on each side in the desert of North Africa. They fill this with gasoline and bitumen and set it alight in order to send a signal to Mars which is rapidly approaching its closest distance to Earth.

Sure enough a mysterious cylinder flies past overhead leaving a fiery trail. It crashes in the desert not too far away and Lowell and Moreau rush to the site to find the crashed space ship cooling down. They open it and a hideous Martian appears. They knock it back down inside and climb in after it to find the ship full of desiccated insect like creatures and one other dead Martian. They capture the Martian who is trying to do something with a crystal egg and they bring it back to their camp.

Meanwhile, landing on the moon H G opens the hatch and discovers there is an atmosphere which appears when the sun comes out, and presumably disappears when the two week night commences. He and Huxley argue about who should step out first. H G wants it to be Huxley but Huxley insists H G should step out saying… "*It is but a small step.*" Wells stood firm.

"*No Professor. When history looks back on this it will be seen as a giant leap for mankind.*" (page 147, Titan Books 2012 edition)

There are many delightful moments like this as well as references to H G Wells' novels and stories.

While our explorers discover the selenites and their history we also discover what Lowell and Moreau are up to. They have taken their Martian to America where Lowell is building a huge telescope in Arizona at a place he calls *Mars Hill.* The Martian runs amok but not before we discover its true nature, how it feeds by sucking the life fluids out of a living being, and the fact that it is a scout for an invasion force preparing to attack Earth. Moreau eventually kills the Martian and it is this specimen he takes to England to show his colleagues.

At the same time as this unfolds H G, Jane, and Huxley set off for Mars and on arrival are captured and the sphere is locked away in a huge warehouse. H G and Jane are made into slaves and put to work alongside the Selenites which had previously been captured and taken to Mars to work at building the invasion fleet.

The Martians can't do much on their own and need mechanical assistance in getting around. These are the tripod walking machines among other things.

Jane who has been given a crystal from the Selenite Mastermind, the mother of all the Selenites, induces the slaves to revolt. They obey her because they recognize the crystal and because she is female. H G and Jane escape and rescue Huxley and an enthralling chase across the Martian surface follows with the Martians trying to stop the escapees.

They finally destroy or escape their pursuers and reach the polar ice cap where they first landed. They release vials of cholera (*which mysteriously they happened to have*) into the water system that channels water from the ice cap so that all Martians will be affected by this disease, thus wiping them out. The selenites remain untouched since they are insectivorous and not at all like the Martians.

Huxley decides to stay on Mars while H G and Jane return to Earth, landing in the courtyard of the same science foundation where they were before being blown out into space.

The story ends here with the implication that H G will go on and write his many famous books, both to entertain as well as to warn people of the possible dire consequence the future may hold.

This homage to H G Wells is a most enjoyable story, full of nostalgia and clever references to historical events to which we can all relate.

Chapter Two

The Golden Age begins

The idea suggested by Percival Lowell of a dying civilization struggling to survive ever worsening conditions by building a planetary system of canals to bring water from the poles was embraced by the public at large and used by many authors in stories set on Mars. They embraced the idea of canals and the oases that linked them together. They peopled the planet with fantastic animals and semi human beings as well as very human like beings using both primitive and advanced machines congruently to portray collapsing civilizations battling against creatures from earlier cultures that had degenerated into more primitive states.

There was no limit to what could be imagined and Edgar Rice Burroughs was one of the most exciting and imaginative of these writers who crafted stories set on Mars. He wasn't a great writer from a technical standpoint, but he could tell fabulous stories that had all the excitement of great romances and adventures with thrilling battles between weird things and humanlike people. There were six legged animals and six limbed intelligent beings that co-existed with others who might as well have been human. There was magic and mysticism interspersed with clunky Victorian science that made these books unputdownable for young readers like me who discovered them in their early teenage years. They were fantasy buttressed with a bit of science. They were full of wonder and excitement. What more could you want?

Burroughs, the epitome of an entertaining writer, was also the creator of *Carson of Venus* series in the 1930s in which the lead character crash lands his space ship on a super tropical world with massive oceans and has to survive against incredible odds. But before any of the Venusian stories Burroughs created his most memorable character, *Tarzan*, who appeared in many books and become a cinematic hero for generations. ***Tarzan of the Apes*** was the first Tarzan book published (1912) and most likely the first book he actually published, although he had many stories before that published in magazines. I read all the Tarzan books, saw all the Tarzan movies and devoured the Tarzan serials at my local movie theatre.

Burroughs alternated writing about Tarzan concurrently while he wrote about *Barsoom*, his word for Mars. The series of eleven books about Mars started with ***A Princess of Mars*** (originally serialized in a pulp magazine as '***Under the Moons of Mars***' in 1912). It didn't appear in book form until 1917.

Burroughs also challenged Sir Arthur Conan Doyle's ***Journey to the Centre of the Earth***, with his creation of *Pellucidar*, a world inside the Earth that had dinosaurs and monsters from the Age of Reptiles co-existing along with tribal humans who were his examples of the 'Noble Savage'. The first in this series was also published in 1914, ***At the Earth's Core***. It was followed in 1923 with ***Pellucidar*** and then with ***Tanar of Pellucidar*** (1928) and ***Back to the Stone Age*** in 1937.

One of his later books even linked Tarzan, a very modern day Noble Savage, with this new and primitive world in a book called ***Tarzan at the Earth's Core*** (1929) Perhaps his last Tarzan book was ***Tarzan and the Foreign Legion*** (1947). I don't remember reading that one but I did read the Pellucidar books. But it is his Mars books that have endured and are the books most often reprinted.

The first of his Mars books that I read was ***Thuvia, Maid of Mars.*** It was the 4th in his Barsoom series with John Carter, and was incredibly different from Arthur C Clarke's ***The Sands of Mars*** which I read the year before when I was thirteen.

I was fourteen when I discovered the Burroughs' Mars' books. I had already devoured several Tarzan books, and this and subsequent Mars books which I snatched up as soon as I saw them at my local newsagent/general store were absolutely amazing as far as I was concerned. I thought they were real, convinced because Burroughs explained how he came to have the manuscript given to him by his uncle, John Carter himself, putting him into the story along with us readers as well.

When these books were written the colonial era of Europeans in Africa was about to end (*although I knew nothing about that*) and writers searched for more unknown and exotic places to set their adventures. What place could be more exotic and exciting than Mars? It was still thought that there were canals there, and dying civilizations. Burroughs imagined this Mars in all its glory and convincingly set grand adventures there using his uncle as chief protagonist. Well, I assumed it was his uncle. I believed it was his uncle, and so I fell into these thrilling stories and couldn't put down whichever book I was reading until the last word was read.

If nothing else had already hooked me into science fiction, stories by Edgar Rice Burroughs would surely have done it. I dreamed about Mars, of being up there doing fantastic stuff. I eventually outgrew these books slowly realizing that Mars was probably more like what had been described in ***The Sands of Mars*** rather than in the *John Carter of Mars* series, and discovered other equally as exciting stories set in space, on other worlds, or in our own world's future history.

I was tempted to get new copies of Edgar Rice Burroughs's Mars books to read again, but after thinking about it, I decided that I didn't want to be disappointed if the books weren't as good as I remembered them. I prefer to remember the essence of them and how they affected me as a young reader in the early1950s. Since the memory of the details in these books is more than 60 years old and lost in the mists of time, all I have left is the vague fuzzy feeling of excitement that reading them generated, and that is something I would like to keep.

Burroughs was already dead when I discovered his books. He died in 1950.

He also wrote about Venus depicting it as a world of massive seas and jungle covered land much like the Amazon only hotter and wetter, and filled with extremely dangerous creatures like those that existed during the latter part of the Mesozoic Era, as well as zombie-like weird terrifying creatures.

It was common for early writers of fantastic fiction to think of Venus as being hotter because it was closer to the Sun and wetter because it was perpetually covered in clouds. Whereas Mars being further away from the Sun was considered to be more of a desert and colder, perhaps like the Gobi desert only like that over the whole planet.

Most writers assumed the atmosphere of Mars was thin like one would find at the top of a mountain range such as The Andes, and left it at that. The Martians had adapted to it over millennia while humans had to use some kind of mask to assist with breathing until they could accustom themselves to the thinner atmosphere. No one suggested it could be cold since naked or semi naked women and scantily clad warriors always abounded.

It was only Burroughs however who suggested the inhabitants used some kind of air producing machine to replenish the extremely thin atmosphere so life could continue. This early suggestion of 'terra-forming' brought his books into the realm of Science Fiction although basically they were exotic fantasies overlaid with Victorian Age scientific speculation.

Burroughs was a prolific writer and wrote across genres including westerns and murder mysteries as well as his fantastic tales of Mars and Venus. Even the Tarzan books which are the most realistic of his stories are fantasies, based vaguely on the idea of a human baby being brought up by wild animals, in this case an unknown species of Great Apes. Other contemporary authors used similar ideas with other animals, but the Tarzan stories have endured longer than most.

It was inevitable that Burroughs would have copycats. His Mars books were so popular many other writers decided to produce similar material in a similar style. Otis Adelbert Kline garnered a degree of success with his novels ***The Outlaws of Mars*** and ***The Swordsmen of Mars.***

It seems that every couple of decades Burroughs and his early copycats are rediscovered and new writers produce similar work, some more successfully than others. Some newer writers brazenly add Edgar Rice Burroughs' name to the title page. It's okay to be inspired by an earlier famous writer like Burroughs, but it's not good to copy him or his style of writing. It's definitely not good in my view to use his name to help sell their books.

One who didn't copy but was influenced by Burroughs was Leigh Brackett who wrote for the pulp magazines before switching to scriptwriting in Hollywood where she began her scriptwriting career as co-writer of ***The Big Sleep***, (1946) starring Humphrey Bogart. She wrote many Martian stories beginning in 1940 before branching out into other areas of SF in the 1960s and on. She is probably more famous now for being the scriptwriter for ***The Empire Strikes Back*** in the first ***Star Wars*** trilogy of films for which she won a posthumous Hugo award in 1981. She died in 1978.

John Carter of Mars is the Disney Studios massive film production of Edgar Rice Burroughs' famous book, ***A Princess of Mars.*** It cost well over 200 million dollars to produce and looks spectacular on screen. Since I didn't want to spoil the memories of those early books that fascinated me as a teenager, I decided to look at this film instead of re-reading those ancient classics.

There were many familiar faces in various roles, but I couldn't put names to any of them. One of the actors listed was Willem Dafoe whose face I do know but I couldn't see him anywhere so I assume he voiced or played the lead Martian *Thark*, the two legged four armed green creatures that John Carter becomes involved with from the moment he arrives on Mars.

I also don't know how close the film followed the original novel ***A Princess of Mars*** since I have no recollection of that book other than the fact that I read it when I was 13 or 14 in 1953 or 54 and thoroughly enjoyed it, as I did all Burroughs' books. One of the script writers listed was Michael Chabon which means there should be some good story in the film.

The film is epic and fantastically realized. It does create a world image which is absolute fantasy just as Burroughs books were fantasy with SF elements. The depiction of Mars seems quite convincing. There is a hint here that some eternal beings (who actually can be killed) who can change their appearance are in control of all nine planets and they continually foment war between the various races of each planet, especially Mars, and by implication Earth since they can travel there, presumably for their own pleasure. Any further suggestions of how this may work out is buried under the action that takes place and the simple plot of one warring tribe to marry into the other so they can control all of Barsoom (Mars).

Perhaps the plot was too simplistic for such a grand film. Perhaps the warrior tribes looked too much like roman legionnaires and didn't quite fit an idea of what Martians may look like. Perhaps the leading actor wasn't good enough or well-known enough to attract an audience, although I thought he was good. Perhaps the *Tharks* weren't very likeable in appearance looking like a cross between a praying mantis and a mountain goat… who knows?

It was released about the same time as Disney's release of the new Star Wars film which had plenty of publicity. I suspect that Disney Studios, having spent an enormous sum to buy *Lucas Film* and the *Star Wars* franchise, decided to put their entire advertising budget into promoting *Star Wars* to make sure they got a big audience to help them recover the cost of acquiring *Lucas Film* and its future movies and spin-offs.

With virtually no publicity ***John Carter of Mars*** was doomed before it was released. It failed to make a decent return at the box office. The film appeared and quickly disappeared, but over time it did recover its costs through DVD and BRD sales.

Whatever the reasons for the film not doing well at the box-office, it killed any chance of subsequent films of Burroughs Mars books. However, it still makes a wonderful addition to anyone's collection of films and books about Mars. For me it certainly was enjoyable, and much better than I had expected it would be.

The Maker of modern myths

Not long after discovering Burroughs I came across an English paperback with a beautiful cover depicting thousands of silvery space ships rising up into a deep blue sky, ***The Silver Locusts*** by Ray Bradbury. The real name of the book which was a collection of stories Bradbury had been publishing through the late 1940s was ***The Martian Chronicles*** (1950).

Although not a novel it can be read as if it were, with each story a chapter in the ongoing establishment of humankind on Mars. It bowled me over because it was so different from what Burroughs had created. Yet it was equally as unrealistic as any other earlier fantasy.

The Martian Chronicles endures because of Bradbuty's poetic use of language combined with a mythic nostalgia. It is continually being reprinted, whereas many other more realistic novels about Mars have disappeared which is something to regret because there were some fine works amongst them.

The Martian Chronicles (1949 -50) by Ray Bradbury.

The edition I have, replacing my early edition of ***The Silver Locusts*** which disappeared years ago, was published in 1973, and is a special edition with illustrations by Karel Thole. (*He also did covers for early Brian Aldiss paperbacks as well as many European SF books and magazines.*). This book doesn't have the story that I read as a youth where the protagonist sleeps at night in a Martian house and while sleeping microscopic tendrils emerge from the bed and penetrate his body all over slowly altering him so he turns into a Martian. It was a creepy story and it gave me bad dreams for a while. Bradbury must have written this after the original publication of ***The Martian Chronicles*** in 1950 but it was not added to this 1973 edition.

It appears that different editions don't always have the same stories. Some editions contain stories he later wrote, while removing some that were in the original. Bradbury has commented that ***The Martian Chronicles*** endures because it is not science fiction but is fantasy. He never considered himself as a writer of science fiction. The term ascribed to him, *The Poet of Science Fiction* was a marketing ploy from his publishers. It made his books easily identifiable to the general reader who may never read an SF story but would read Bradbury because he was different, more literary, more poetical.

Bradbury's Mars has always been about the myth of going to Mars and his ideas of what Mars was like could have been engendered by what he read as a boy from Edgar Rice Burroughs and his series of books set on Mars, and the older idea promulgated by Percival Lowell that Mars harboured a dying civilization and that the lines seen in telescopes were canals built to bring water from the poles to the arid tropical areas. Even H G Wells thought Mars harboured an ancient civilization, though his Martians were much more malevolent whereas Bradbury's were wise, benign, and sometimes even funny, (*see the 2nd story, **The Summer Night***) and certainly very human.

Bradbury wasn't concerned with the reality of Mars but with the myth of a lost civilization that had endured aeons of a dying planet, and the myth of country America. His recollections of small town America were more a fantasy than a reality, something he could have remembered as a child, but he projected that childlike fantasy into his present time (1940 to 1950) and what he imagined the near future would be. This non-existent past America projected into the near future gives the stories *the sense of wonder tinged with nostalgia* that permeates the book. It is also this same feeling that after more than half a century keeps most of these stories alive, fresh, and enjoyable.

Bradbury had the foresight to set his stories far enough ahead of his time, unlike many other authors. The first story ***Rocket Summer*** is set in1999 (originally published in 1947 in *Planet Stories*), while most of the other stories take place over the years 1999 to 2005. The final three stories are set in the year 2026. Oddly enough, the very last story, ***The Million Year Picnic***, set in 2026 was one of the earliest written, (1946).

Bradbury was a master story teller. His backgrounds were barely sketched in because what the characters did and said was more important. How they expressed their emotions and their feelings always took precedence over the setting. It is claimed his stories are like prose poems and many of them are studied in schools alongside other more famous American writers of literature. His language sings and is remembered long after the story has been read and put aside.

Bradbury's old Martian cities are built along these ancient canals. His only attempt at science is to claim the air is so thin it is hard for earth people to breathe and that it was not nourishing. He suggests it is like the high altitudes of villages in the Andes and that it will take time for humans to acclimatize. His descriptions of the Martian scenery are vague, and he focuses more on the problems the characters bring with them to Mars rather than what Mars could possibly be like.

Surely in 1950 people must have known that it was simply too cold to go about unprotected on Mars, that the air was far too thin to breathe regardless of how much acclimatization one cared to make, and that any outdoor activity would require protection as well as breathing gear.

I think what Bradbury expresses is what people in the 1920's and 30's would have believed Mars to be like, and so his visions of the future where just about anyone could build a rocket in their back yard, where rockets were as common as cars and busses and trucks and came in all sizes, and where every town had at least one rocket ready to lift off for Mars, are retro-futuristic, and decidedly quaint.

Can you imagine carrying enough lumber to rebuild exact replicas of small towns in country USA in thousands of rockets filling the sky like *silver locusts* in waves of voyages from Earth to Mars? They built these replicated 1920's American towns along the canals. He implies all the food and luxury items were brought in on rockets. There is no hint of anything being grown on Mars. One story though has a Johnny Appleseed character wandering across Mars planting seeds for trees, Oaks, Ashes, Elms, all the trees familiar to Americans. This one seems out of place because it is outright fantasy, compared to the other stories, with the trees sprouting into giants behind the character as he traverses the countryside.

When he wrote the Mars stories the only rockets Bradbury may have seen would have been German V2 rockets used in the 2nd World War against England. His vague descriptions suggest scaled up versions of these. He never thought about how enough of these could be made to make them as common as the family car, or the massive infrastructure that would be needed to accomplish this impossible feat.

His characters had no resemblance to Astronauts or Cosmonauts, nor even to Air Force pilots or any other person who may be able to fly a plane, they were ordinary people who suddenly decided they wanted to go to Mars and so going there was not much more than going outside and getting into the car to drive across the plains on a long journey, instead they got into a rocket and hopped off to Mars.

He hints at the reason why people wanted to go, suggesting a possible Atomic War looming on the horizon —a very real fear in the early fifties as the cold war was beginning to escalate— but when war finally breaks out everyone on Mars ups and leaves, taking themselves and their rockets back to Earth presumably to help fight this terrible Atomic War.

His vision of thousands of rockets falling into the sky like autumn leaves falling to earth covers the whole departure of most of the humans on Mars.

It is such a beautiful vision that any addition to it is superfluous. There are a few left stranded who for various reasons couldn't get back in time to take the rockets home.

When the original ship's captain from the third story arrives back after going out to Jupiter and Saturn he finds Earth destroyed and only a few people left to survive alone on Mars. This is the last story, ***The Million Year Picnic*** where he finds his wife and children and leaving a devastated Earth, returns to Mars. When the children ask to see real Martians he takes them to a nearby canal. "*There they are,*" he tells them. The real Martians, they see are reflected in the still waters of the canal.

Of all the stories in the book, most of them hold up well because Bradbury is a born storyteller.

In my view there is only one story that jars, that is racist and downbeat.I ***Way in The Middle of The Air*** just doesn't fit. In the 1950's it may have gone over as a powerful social comment, an indictment against southern White Supremacists, who no doubt still exist although more covertly today than in the fifties depicted by Bradbury. I didn't remember this story being in ***The Silver Locusts.*** Perhaps it *was* there and I found it so distasteful I erased it from my memory.There is no definitive edition of this book since various editions and reprints do not always contain the same stories.

The Martian Chronicles also appeared as a television mini-series (281 minutes long) in (1979) staring Rock Hudson, Gayle Hunnicutt, Bernie Casey, Roddy McDowell, Darren McGavin, Bernadette Peters, Maria Schell, Joyce Van Patten, and Fritz Weaver, with Screenplay by Richard Matheson.

It has been more than fifty years since I first read ***The Martian Chronicles*** in its English edition called ***The Silver Locusts***, and having come across a DVD of the 1979-80's mini-series, (which I remember seeing on TV, and at the time was quite impressed), I couldn't wait to have another look at it.

When it was made in 1979 Rock Hudson was a fading star, but his name still held some appeal and I suspect he was happy to have the work and be the lead. However his acting was wooden and emotionless. Back then to appear in a TV series was a real comedown for a film actor. They regarded TV disdainfully, and to all and sundry it indicated the end of a career; quite the opposite of the last decade or so, when many actors of TV series have crossed over into film and become massive stars. George Clooney springs to mind as a good example. Even the best and most famous actors are happy to do TV commercials and don't mind appearing in TV shows as well as Movies. A good TV series is often better than a movie as it can tell a story in great detail over an extended period and people will follow it and then buy the DVDs of the series so they can watch it again at their leisure.

With Richard Matheson authoring the script one would assume the series was going to be brilliant. Unfortunately, it wasn't. By the standards of 1979 or 1980 when ***The Martian Chronicles*** was shown on TV in Australia it was good. I didn't remember how cheap and tacky the animation of the space rockets appeared, and that was immediately off-putting when I started watching the DVD. The crude control centre I could accept as they were often like that in old films and they did reflect a degree of reality. But the rockets were absolutely silly with puffs of smoke spluttering out of the engines, and jerky animation, but fortunately these were brief moments. The stories' study of character and the underlying myths of Bradbury's Mars were more important.

Not all of the stories from the book are represented in this mini-series; the first story, ***YLLA***, the third and fourth are combined into one episode, ***The Third Expedition***, and ***The Moon be still as Night***, are there as separate episodes. The second story was used as a base for another episode but was completely changed. Other stories individually or combined are ***The Silent Towns, The long Years,*** and ***The Million Year Picnic***.

In ***The Silent Towns*** with the phone ringing in various buildings and one lone earthman chasing around to answer it but missing it, eventually deciding to call every number in the phone book, and finally he connects with the last woman on Mars.

Going off desperately to find her, he is staggered when he encounters a vain self-centred creature that wants her every whim catered for almost to the point of insanity. He finally jumps into his truck and leaves her there, preferring the solitude of the deserted mountains far away. In the book instead of a beautiful woman he encounters a hugely overweight slob who stuffs herself endlessly with chocolates and sweets. She is such a revolting creature he flees in despair in his gyrocopter. I suspect a morbidly overweight woman would have put off television viewers in 1979 so she was changed into something they could accept, a beautiful but vain woman. This was one of the stories I thought just didn't work as a TV episode.

But ***The Long Years*** with Rock Hudson returning from an expedition to Jupiter to find a lone man searching the skies and waiting to be rescued, who builds robot facsimiles of his wife and daughter to keep him company has the poignancy that the story in the book has. Finally Rock Hudson returns to Earth to find his wife and children waiting for him and he takes them back to Mars and destroys the rocket so they have no choice but to live there. This is also translated effectively into the final episode of the TV series, ***The Million Year Picnic.***

So much could have been made of this series but with Rock Hudson's wooden acting and Darren McGavin's melodramatic exaggerations verging on being cartoonish, the stories struggled to generate sustained interest. Roddy McDowell was also in this series but I didn't recognize him so he must have been one of the Martians. With their golden skin, bald heads with no ears, and eyes that were yellow, at least they had a certain dignity…

The series may have looked good in the 1980's but it doesn't today.

Even so, I did enjoy seeing this series again as it brought back memories of the stories I read and were most impressed by as a teenager in the 1950s.

Surely an astute producer could redo these stories in a manner befitting their classic and iconic status. The book does have an option to be filmed that is renewed every year, but as yet no new film has started production.

Early Voyages...

Two of the earliest Mars books in my collection are planetary romances in the style of a *Boy's Own Adventure* by John Wyndham writing as John Benyon. They were originally published in 1936 and 1938.

Wyndham started his career as a writer of pulp fiction before creating more serious science fiction which he wrote as John Wyndham after the 2nd World War.

Of these two books from the 1930s, one was a novel called ***Planet Plane,*** later republished in 1972 as ***Stowaway to Mars***. The other, ***Sleepers of Mars***, a novelette, first published in 1938 was reprinted in 1973 with several other stories in a collection ***Sleepers of Mars*** and billed as *the sequel to* ***Stowaway to Mars***. Both are adventure stories like many others from the early Golden Age of science fiction. (*My copies are the 1970s reprints.*)

Planet Plane (***Stowaway to Mars***) (1936) is set in the year 1981, which no doubt seemed a long way into the future when the story was written and published.

A British millionaire playboy who made his money from the development of rocket planes that could carry large numbers of people across the ocean separating Europe and the new world, is building a super rocket plane capable of travelling across the void to another planet. An American multi-millionaire has established a prize of One Million Pounds to the first person who can build a rocket plane and travel across space to Mars and back.

Dale Curtance has decided he is going to win this prize and sets out to build such a plane.

The story opens with an attempt to sabotage his plane but this is thwarted and the construction proceeds. Eventually the plane and its assorted crew take off but it uses more fuel than they had anticipated and the reason is they discover a stowaway, a young woman who has an extraordinary story to tell them as her reason for wanting to go to Mars.

Debating whether to throw her overboard (ejecting her into space) their masculine sense of chivalry won't countenance such a move. The story she tells them is of Martian machine intelligences and how her father found just such a machine on Earth and how no one would believe him. He lost his respect and his job as physicist because of this machine which had a meltdown and was totally destroyed so he had no physical proof of its existence. She wants to go to Mars to prove such machines do exist and thus restore her late father's respect within the scientific community.

There is mention of Schiaparelli and his canali and Percival Lowell and his canals which almost everyone in the 1930s actually believed existed. The adventurers are expecting to find some kind of dying civilization on Mars when they get there. They also know that the Americans, the Russians and the Germans are all building rocket planes to compete for the prize, and the Russians at least launched their attempt a day after them. They find out later the German attempt exploded on take-off, successfully sabotaged, while the American had also launched several days after the Russians and were on their way to Mars as well.

The British group land badly with their ship almost toppling over near a canal. They will have to right their ship which from the description sounds like a giant V2 type rocket, like all space ships were up until Von Braun came up with staged rockets in the 1960s.

It's interesting to speculate whether Von Braun's idea of the V2 rocket was an inevitable development as he experimented with different rocket shapes and delivery systems, or whether the shape of the V2 was the result of early science fiction writers who had already imagined that particular shape for space ships in their stories having affected Von Braun's concept for the V2 rocket.

Konstantin Tsiolkovski's early rockets in Russia and his claim that rockets could fly in outer space no doubt inspired many writers to extrapolate such rockets as a means of travelling in space... not to mention Robert Goddard's early attempts to launch slender rockets with tail fins in America in the 1920s.

Aeroplanes in the 1920s and 1930s were primitive contraptions barely able to fly let alone carry passengers. Rockets on the other hand were sleek, aerodynamic and could travel at incredible speeds. Extrapolating rockets into high altitude passenger carrying vehicles and then into space ships was a natural one for science fiction writers. Most of them came up with the same streamlined shape that could take off and land vertically to finish balanced on its tail fins.

It is also interesting that modern companies like Space X and Blue Horizon are testing rockets to make them less costly by having them take off and land vertically on tail fins as a way of reusing them to cut down the expense of rocket launches. Maybe those early SF writers weren't too far off the mark after all...

The crew set off to explore the nearby canal and almost immediately are attacked by a bunch of weird machines. The girl is captured by one machine which the others keep well away from, and is carried off to who knows where while the others besiege the British crew who barely manage to get back to their rocket plane unscathed. The machines trap them there and they can't leave.

Meanwhile the Russian ship lands a mile or so away and they send a group of men to confer with the British group, only to find themselves trapped by the aberrant machines. A couple of them are killed but some make it back to their own ship where they too are trapped. The American ship finally arrives but comes in too fast and crashes killing all on board.

Meanwhile the girl has been taken to a city where she encounters a real Martian. They have some interaction during which we find out a history of the Martian civilization and how they are all in hibernation except for a few guardians in various deserted cities, until the planet can be revived. She falls in love with her new friend, and presumably he does with her as well. There is a vague suggestion of intimacy but nothing specific as one would expect from a story of that era. Meanwhile because the Martians want nothing to do with Earth Humans he orders them to leave. He gets his good machines to make extra fuel for them and to stand their rocket plane up properly so it can take off. He sends the girl back to them, again carried by the same machine, and she arrives just in time for the plane to take off so it can make the correct orbit enabling them to encounter Earth. The final scene in the book is back on earth with her having given birth to the first Human Martian hybrid during which she dies. A rather horrible ending I thought.

Sleepers of Mars, (1938) recapitulates the final chapter of ***Stowaway to Mars*** but from the Russian viewpoint. Some of the crew manage to escape from the machines when a monstrous tanklike machine arrives, scattering the crazy machines. It is bringing the girl back to the British ship. Unfortunately only one of the Russians survives to get back to his ship where he finds three other crewmen on board. The machines order them to leave as well. They won't leave until the British ship takes off and when it does they begin, hoping that their lighter weight since most of the crew are dead will enable them to gain more speed and thus beat the British back to win the prize. Unfortunately one of their rockets doesn't work being clogged with sand and the ship tips over and skims across the surface of the land for several miles before coming to a stop near an ancient city.

A different set of machines take the four occupants to this deserted city where they are told to wait in a specially pressurised area until their ship can be repaired. Left to their own devices one of the Russians discovers an underground chamber where millions upon millions of sleeping Martians are entombed in what appears to be glass coffins.

He tries to revive one, a young woman, but she dies choking to death when he removes her from the hibernation device. The second time he tries he revives a young man but makes sure he has an oxygen mask handy so the man won't choke.

They lead him back to the pressurised part of the city they have been given while they wait for their ship to be repaired, and he tells them what has happened on Mars. How they had wars to reduce their population because the planet was slowly dying, drying up, and when this didn't work they made everyone go into suspended animation until canals could be built to bring water from the poles to revive the planet. He is utterly disappointed to find the canals made no difference to the revival of the planet and it is still dying.

He is also extremely angry that his wife had been allowed to suffocate and suddenly draws a heat ray gun and shoots the person who had attempted to revive her. After that he drops the gun and races off to the catacombs to start reviving some of the others. His intention with help from the newly revived Martians is to steal the Russian space ship which has now been repaired and refuelled by the machines and go to Earth. The Russians see them attempting to board the ship and they race out to try and stop them. A fight ensues and one of the Russians falls from the ladder (up the side of the ship which also has the familiar rocket shape from the 1930s) breaking his faceplate. Explosive decompression kills him instantly. The few Martians that got on board start firing the rockets for take-off and the other Russian near the base is incinerated.

The last of the Russians, far enough away and now the only human left on Mars sees his ship take off and disappear, so he takes the heat gun that had killed his companion and shoots himself in the head... End of story.

Both of those stories could be considered as a longer story broken into two parts and published separately even though there is a two year gap between the writing of them. Both are fanciful, although considering the time, (1930s), there is an attempt to depict Mars in a realistic manner as far as what was believed: thin atmosphere and the need to wear space suits to prevent fatal decompression, as well as the type of rocket or rocket planes used for the voyage could allow these to be classified as crossovers into category two.

The other details were variations on what people believed Mars was like at that time with canals and ancient cities left over from a dying civilisation. Each author's view of how those ancient cities were constructed or deconstructed and of what or how the Martian inhabitants looked like is always quite different. There are as many variations in these as there are authors who wrote stories about Mars.

Out of the Silent Planet, (1938) (***the Cosmic Trilogy***) by C S Lewis has stood the test of time by being extraordinarily readable and enjoyable, and it is continuously in print.

Mars, called *Malacandra*, has the lesser gravity, thin atmosphere, giant engineered canals consistent with what people thought Mars would be like at the beginning of the 20th century, and various native species that have adapted to different conditions in the high lands as well as in the low canals (*Handramits*). In this story the dying of the planet was because of a war between godlike overlords (*Oyarsa*) that exist on all the planets to oversee life. These *Oyarsa* each look after a planet, but the 'bent' *Oyarsa* of *Thulcandra* (Earth) waged a war in the far past that destroyed Mars killing most of the life on the surface, causing Earth to be isolated from the rest, thus The Silent Planet. The *Oyarsa* of *Malacandra* however saved some of his beings by engineering giant chasms that criss-crossed the planet and released from underground water trapped far below the surface. Life survives in the deep chasms where the atmosphere is slightly thicker. There are three different species on *Malacandra* and each fits into a specific environment, but together they live in harmony, until two bent earthmen build a spaceship and come there looking for wealth and personal power. They misunderstand a request to present themselves to the *Oyarsa*, and instead return to Earth where they kidnap an old friend who happens to be a linguist, a professor of philology. They drug him and take him to *Malacandra* as a sacrifice to the God of the planet hoping to gain many riches as a reward.

Their ship lands in a low lying area beside a wide lake. When Professor

Ransom wakes up he has no idea where he is other than it is on another planet. He can't even work out which planet it is. The gravity is lighter, the air is cold and thin, but the water in the lake and in the chasm that feeds it is warm. He escapes when his captors are going to give him to hideous humanoid creatures called the *Sorn*. They had already told him he was to be sacrificed. Ransom runs into the forests that border the river feeding the lake. He soon is exhausted and finds a place to sleep for the night.

In the morning he encounters an entirely different being who is talking as it comes out of the river. Realising it must be intelligent he approaches and tries to communicate with it. Eventually they travel together in a boat along the river in the incredibly wide chasm until they come to a village. He stays with the beings that live there, the *hross*, and begins to learn their language and customs. The *hrossa* are poets and singers of strange music, and he fits in well with them, until he is told he has been summoned by the *Oyarsa* who wishes to speak with him. An invisible spirit like being called *eldil*, (*Eldils* are everywhere and can only be seen when they wish to pass on a message) has brought a summons from *Oyarsa*.

Ransom is given directions that take him up over the tops of the mountains where the air is so thin it can't be breathed and is helped by a *Sorn* who gives him oxygen in a bottle and carries him over the mountain to his rendezvous with *Oyarsa*. Here he meets the third species, the engineers and builders, the ones who carve images and make useful things, the *pfifltrigg*.

Finally he meets with *Oyarsa* who is himself only partly visible, like the *eldil*. The two earthmen who kidnapped Ransom are also brought before *Oyarsa* who dismisses them as being bent, unintelligent and useless. They are ordered to return to their planet within 90 days at which point their ship will be destroyed.

He discusses history of the worlds and the cosmos and tells Ransom he can stay on *Malacandra*, but Ranson decides to return with the other two to Earth. It is only after the ship takes off and he can look down on the planet that he realises he is looking at Mars and that the giant chasms in which he spent most of his time there are in fact engineered and from space look exactly like the canals as seen by Lowell and other astronomers.

It concludes with Ransom back on Earth after his two companions abandoned the ship because it was due to be (vanished) destroyed as promised by *Oyarsa*. He manages to escape the ship before it self-destructs, and returning home realises that Earth has yet to be reunited with the other worlds and their inhabitants as well as the life that exists in the void which is not empty space but is really heaven itself, filled with radiance and life.

Chapter Three

The Golden Age for stories about Mars

The 1930s, 40s and 50s, and the first five years of the 1960s were a *Golden Age* for stories set on Mars. There were more Mars stories published during this time than any other. This was a period that saw unprecedented growth of genre pulp magazines and the number of science fiction, science fantasy, and science fiction adventure stories, many of which later came to be derogatively called space opera. *That term now is used more positively to describe a particular sub-genre of science fiction.*

Most of those early stories were implausible but that didn't stop teenage readers who couldn't get enough of them. Adults frowned upon this strange new kind of literature which is perhaps one reason the youth read it so voraciously. But perhaps the real reason it became so popular, producing hundreds of different magazines as well as small paperback books, was that at a time when the world was changing dramatically because of scientific development, and in the aftermath of the 2nd World War when people could see a better future, most of these stories generated in the reader a sense of wonder combined with a feeling that something exciting was soon to come.

There was a sense of positivity within most of these stories. They were new, they were exciting and they reflected the times we lived in. Young readers of the day couldn't get enough of them. Many of these stories have become available again in lovely readable editions at reasonable prices, which is fantastic for those wanting to catch up on what was long gone before they were born. And for those older readers who missed them when they were first published, having the chance to see them again is an absolute pleasure.

Some short novels from the 1940s and 50s

The secret of the Martians by Paul W Fairman

Paul W Fairman, 1900 – 1977, was one of those prolific authors in the late 1940s and early 1950s who used several pseudonyms belonging to the publishing house *Ziff-Davis* to market his stories. He later went on to become an editor for one of their many magazines.

This is a straight forward adventure story set on Mars, a typical example of the kinds of stories that proliferated while the pulps were in their heyday. Mostly they were easy to read and quite enjoyable, but easily forgotten after finishing. It is nice though to see some of these early stories available once again for those who are nostalgia buffs.

Rex Tate an interplanetary investigator is sent to Mars after a famous Terran botanist was found dead, but preserved and shipped back to Earth. On Mars Rex discovers that no one thinks Martians are dangerous. They think there are very few of them left, that they want little to do with humans and have retreated back into caves where they stay hidden as humans encroach upon land they once occupied.

On the farm where the botanist had disappeared, Rex meets one old Martian who lives in a stone hut on the edge of the farm. He thinks he is harmless. The farmer's daughter has her eyes on Rex who she thinks would make a good husband but Rex isn't all that interested at first. She contrives to get him to visit the stone hut where the old Martian lives and they find it empty. They accidentally discover a secret door in the wall that opens into a tunnel system under the house. There is an extensive underground tunnel system and suddenly as they are exploring this they are taken captive by several ferocious Martians. They are beaten and tied up and placed on a small powered rail car which runs on tracks in the tunnels. There is an extensive rail track system underground and Rex and the girl Jean find themselves being taken to an underground city near the pole which is inhabited by thousands of Martians, far more than any of the settlers from Earth realised. There are underground tunnels interconnecting populated cites everywhere and all unknown to the human settlers.

A group of these Martians have rebelled against the current leadership and want to start a war to push all Terrans off their planet. When Rex tells them if they attack the human settlers other humans will come and annihilate them totally, but they laugh this off as a meaningless threat.

Meanwhile Jean's younger brother Tommy has gone looking for Rex and his sister and he too stumbles into the underground tunnel system. He is captured and taken by railcar to the city under the Pole. He manages to escape by causing an accident which kills the Martian who took him prisoner. Eventually he meets up with Rex and Jean, and at the same time rescues another younger girl who had been taken prisoner and who was being prepared for a sacrifice to ancient Gods. At this moment they encounter some other Martians who are loyal to the old leader Fanton, who everyone presumed was dead, but he had been usurped by a much younger man who wanted to lead Martians back to the glory of ancient times.

During a fight in the maze of tunnels Jean is captured and is to be substituted for the sacrifice since the younger girl had disappeared. The rest of the humans along with the few Martians loyal to the original aged leader find where he was being kept a prisoner and take him to the rejuvenation room. In this room all ills and injuries can be repaired, and aged people can be made young and strong again. If someone is dead they are preserved as if alive indefinitely, which is what had happened to the botanist sent back to Earth in a cargo ship.

The aged leader, Fanton, is rejuvenated and taken by a secret passage to oversee the planned sacrifice. When he stops the sacrifice, saving Jean, the false leader is challenged by Maxis, Fanton's loyal servant who had been helping the humans. Although not as good a fighter with a sword as the young usurper, Maxis cunningly defeats him and shows this Martian to be a coward in front of his followers. With the rebel leader dead the followers all give in and proper order is restored. The story finishes with the rejuvenated Fanton agreeing to share some of the Martian technology with the human settlers so all can live in harmony.

You Can't Escape from Mars by E K Jarvis (a *Ziff-Davis* House name used by Paul W Fairman).

Jerry Utah, a test pilot taking a new space ship for a quick jaunt up from Mars approaches the moon Phobos and a vision of a beautiful Earth girl appears and distracts him. He crashes onto Phobos. Staggering out of the ship he discovers there is air he can breathe when there should be none at all on the moon. Suddenly the girl of his vision appears and she tells him to tell the priests he is there to challenge for Nerissa, otherwise they will kill him since it is forbidden for anyone to land on Phobos.

Nerissa disappears as a group of priests arrive to examine the wrecked space vehicle. When Jerry asks for help they tell him it is forbidden to land on Phobos and are about to kill him when he remembers what he was asked to say. Immediately they take him inside and throw him into a cell with four others, three of whom are human. The other one is a Martian.

He is told the challenge for Nerissa is a fight to the death, and there has to be five contestants; he is the fifth. They are to be enclosed in an arena and only one will be allowed out, the one who kills all the others. One of those in the cell is an old friend.

He also discovers that Martians once developed space flight but only ventured as far as their two moons. They also developed a gravity machine that creates an artificial gravity which is equivalent to that of Mars and this is what keeps the thin atmosphere on the Phobos. There are other technologies, hinted at but not elaborated. The head priest has a device which controls the minds of others enabling him to manipulate them to his will. The priests commandeered the first Martian space ships claiming them to be vessels of God and over time came to rule Mars – only they who live in the abode of the Gods know what is best. No Martian would consider going against the priests since they wield godlike powers.

For centuries, every year a female child is brought to the moon and raised by the priests. When she reaches maturity five priests challenge each other for her. The one surviving the challenge wins the girl and his life. But this time only one Martian wanted to challenge for Nerissa. No one else was interested because she was Human, so they had to gather four other humans to fight against each other for her. Three of them they enticed with a promise of earning large amounts of money. The fourth one is Jerry who crashed his ship on the moon.

Jerry doesn't want to fight because one of the others already there is an old friend. They contrive a way with Nerissa's help to escape but the priests foil this attempt, because the head priest uses an ancient mind controlling device. Finally they are locked up in an arena full of native plants and flowing water, representing heaven for Martians who live on a barren planet. One of them is killed, and the killer is shortly after killed by the Martian but the others refuse to fight. That leaves Jerry, his old friend, and the Martian. Nerissa appears and tells them there is a way out. She leads them to a hidden tunnel and they escape. Their object now is to get to the space ship hangar and steal a ship. They manage to get onto a ship only to find it has been emptied of fuel so they can't fly it. As the priests arrive to trap them they again escape and now they are headed for the power source of the machine that controls gravity hoping to sabotage it. They are joined by the renegade Martian who followed them when they escaped. There are running battles in the many corridors inside Phobos and finally as the head priest approaches with his device enabling him to control minds Jerry attacks him and smashes the device. Suddenly there is no more control. Their Martian associate realises the priests are not all powerful and that all they say is a lie. Meanwhile the others have found the gravity machine and are increasing the gravity so the priests find it hard to move. It doesn't affect the humans since they come from a planet with higher gravity. Finally the head priest is killed in a short battle after which the gravity is reversed and as it lessens the air begins to escape from Phobos. Not wanting to suffocate the priests give up. The humans have won. Their Martian friend finds a duplicate device to the one the head priest had and he now becomes the head priest, but promises to change things on Mars. No more lies. Life will be different. The Human survivors leave Phobos in a Martian space ship and head home to Earth.

This was fun to read, but is eminently forgettable.

Legacy from Mars by Raymond Z Gallun (circa 1940) Gallun wrote stories for the pulps between 1928 until 1942, after which he became quiet. He later wrote several novels in the 1950s on into the 1970s, but was mostly forgotten by readers who had outgrown the early pulp traditions. For some reason his name has always stuck in my mind, perhaps because it was an unusual name for me to encounter as a teenager, and although I couldn't remember any actual stories I may have read by him, I knew I had read some of them. I jumped at the chance to buy this new POD copy of one of his earliest stories published about the time I was born. I knew I had never seen this one.

Legacy from Mars was probably published under a different name back in the 1940s. It is a delightful short novel in which traders gathering Martian seaweed for transport back to Earth where it is considered a delicacy encounter two small fish-like/plant-like beings which they capture. It turns out they are intelligent and part of the last of the surviving race of Martians. They use photosynthesis to produce carbon and give off oxygen. The traders capture them and take them on board their ship where they soon discover they are intelligent and can communicate in a musical manner by vibrating their fins and tiny hands against something s resonant like the side of the fish bowl they are kept in. They can escape from the bowl and wander about not necessarily having to remain in the water. As their musical ability develops they are taken on a tour of earth cities where they give concerts in collaboration with the two traders who looked after them. Eventually they escape from their captivity and head out to the ocean via a nearby river. The two traders spend a lot of time looking for them and eventually the two tiny Martians reappear and allow themselves to be housed in a Zoo where they study the humans who are studying them. They like staying in the zoo. As the story ends the female of the Martians is pregnant with the young ones visible through her translucent skin and they both suggest that the traders should be exploring the deep oceans rather than going into outer space, which they do and discover incredible deposits of Uranium which makes them extremely wealthy.

This is a light-hearted story where the Martians are sympathetic and not some monstrous creature as had been the common depiction in earlier pulp magazine stories. After Gallun's sympathetic aliens not all aliens in stories from then on were evil or monstrous or vicious or nasty; quite a few were depicted as likeable, intriguing, and relatively benign. It is a pity this author became relatively obscure after 1940 but his work if encountered is intriguing enough to warrant a good look.

The Titan by P Shuyler Miller, (1954)

This was originally submitted for publication in the early 1930s but was rejected because of its supposed sexuality, implied rather than stated, along with the harsh depiction of the Martian environment, which was nothing like what had been written about Mars before. Part of it was published in 1934 but it wasn't published in its entirety until it became the feature story of a book, giving its title to the book. There are several other short works previously published in the early 1940s included as well.

At a time when imagining a world crumbling into ruin seemed a strong possibility because of anthropogenic intervention, P Shuyler Miller took this concept to Mars, imagining a world slowly dying for millennia turning into a vast planetary desert. It is a heart rending story told from the viewpoint of the Martians, (*unusual for stories written at that time*).

The only water they can get is in the summer when the polar ice melts and sluice gates are opened so melt-water can trickle down along the ditches dug to channel it to the remnants of the population living in ancient cities hidden in vast canyons. The Martians have degenerated into two separate races; a ruling class that no longer has certain constituents in its blood and a slave race called the *blood givers* who from a young age are groomed to regularly supply fresh blood via transfusion to the masters who rule them.

When a throwback princess of the master race who doesn't need as much blood as often as the others of her class and who actually has functioning legs — and who sees herself as deformed— falls in love with the leader of the blood givers at a time when they are talking of refusing to serve the masters any more, complications begin. The blood givers have decided they no longer want to be slaves. They want to reunite the race into one people, as they had been more centuries ago than anyone can remember, by eliminating the masters altogether. A young challenger demands that his leader kills the princess he has fallen in love with as a sign of his strength and determination as a leader, after which the revolution will begin.

He refuses and flees into the desert with his princess, along with a huge hairy creature that has been a prisoner in their zoo for 20 Martian years. The giant prisoner turns out to be an Earthman who was kept in a cage like other weird animals found in the desert. Over the years the prisoner Jim Berk who calls himself a Titan because he is so much bigger than the Martians has learnt their language and finally is able to communicate with the two escaping Martians. He offers to help them, if they free him, by taking them to where his space ship had landed badly. He has weapons there that will help them win their battle.

At first our impression is that these Martians are relatively human, but after encountering the Titan who calls them little people our vision of them begins to change.

They are chased across the barren desert, by a group led by the younger being who wants to take over the blood giver's leadership, into a more mountainous area where the earthman's space ship had been damaged on landing. He is hoping to return to Earth even though after almost 40 earth years no one he knows would be alive any more, but decides first he must help his small Martian friends to fight against those who want to maintain the blood giving system.

The story ends with a fierce battle by the sluice gates where the life giving polar water is to be released. Jim Berk saves his friends and the possibility that the Martians will once again become one race rather than two, but in the process is killed.

He will never go home, but he will be remembered forever by the new Martians that will evolve. As he lay dead, the Martian princess wonders how he must have seen them: *dwarfed, hairless, saucer eyed, hideous things... to him we must have been monsters, as he was to us...*

And this from the penultimate paragraph is the only time we get a description of the Martians; a lovely fantasy that encapsulates ideas of what Mars was thought to have been like up until the mid 1950s.

The forgotten Man of Space (1933) is a short story by P Shuyler Miller that uses the theme of human rapaciousness and the ability to destroy whatever environment humans live in being extended to the gentle environment of Mars.

A miner left to die on Mars after his greedy partners from a first expedition abandoned him is saved by tiny Martians that live in caves. He spends 20 martian years living with them and learning to understand them and how they live in harmony with their environment. One day when he wonders if he will ever go home a ship lands, part of a second expedition, with two young miners who discover the old man is sitting on a fortune in mineral wealth. While examining where the old man and the Martians live, they kill some of the gentle Martians who had saved the old man 20 years earlier.

Realizing that humans will never change when the new prospectors tell the old man they would eat the 'rabbits' who inhabit the caves while they extract the mineral wealth, he agrees to go back with them to the new Mars colony on the other side of the badlands where they have their equipment.

While in transit he causes the space ship to explode and crash in the badlands, and thus repays the debt to the Martians for saving him while at the same time stopping further degradation and destruction of the fragile Martian environment.

A delightful, once forgotten story that has been revived in ***Lost Mars - The Golden Age of the Red Planet.*** (2018).

Duel on Syrtis (1951) by Poul Anderson

Poul Anderson is a skilful creator of strange and wonderful planets with believable ecologies and inhabitants. He captures the moods and feelings of those inhabitants and with only a few words can conjure images of a different ecology that resonates as true, to weave marvellous adventures in planetary systems spread far across the galaxy. This early story set on Mars shows that right from the beginning of his career he had the ability to create a carefully delineated world that was absolutely believable.

This novelette depicts a bold and ruthless hunter, wealthy because he owns a space shipping line, looking for excitement having decided he is going to hunt a native Martian. Many of them were slaves to human colonists on Mars, but are now emancipated. But Riordan doesn't care. He wants the thrill of hunting an adversary that is intelligent and can fight back.

The only Martian in the remote area where Riordan lands is Kreega, a wily older Martian who was once a warrior but who keeps away from human occupied areas.

It's illegal Riordan is told, *to hunt Martians, 20 years in jail if you are caught.* He doesn't care because the government authorities are half way around the planet and will never know.

He sets out with a native rock hound to track his quarry and an eagle like bird to watch from the sky. But what Riordan doesn't know is that Kreega is attuned to all life on Mars. The plants and the small animals are all partially sentient as well as somewhat telepathic and they help Kreega fight back as he tries to elude the arrogant Earth hunter.

The chase goes over many days with the Martian gaining small victories by killing the rock hound, and then the bird, but Riordan is getting closer every day. Finally Riordan catches up to the exhausted Kreega and is about to shoot him when the gun barrel explodes, sabotaged by a small creature that climbed inside to block it.

Kreega immediately launches himself at Riordan even though he is only half the size of a human. In the fight Riordan gets a death grip around Kreega's throat, but Kreega manages to cut off Riordan's oxygen supply.

Realising he has lost Riordan releases a gas into his suit that puts him into a kind of suspended animation so he hardly needs any oxygen other than a breath every couple of hours to stay alive until rescued.

However Kreega is smart and he knows what Riordan has done. He drags the inert human deep into a cave where he will not be found by any rescue party and reconnects a couple of spare oxygen tanks to the pressure suit Riordan wears.

Kreega doesn't hate the earthling; he just wants to teach him a lesson: *Mars does not want people like him.* Riordan is barely conscious but he stares in horror as he realises he will not be rescued and the extra oxygen tanks connected to his suit will keep him alive for a thousand years.

Mount Sharp

Leigh Brackett's Old Mars

At the end of the 19th century it was thought all planets and larger moons in the solar system harboured some form of life, if not necessarily intelligent life, and that the atmosphere of all these various planets and moons was close enough to Earth's atmospheric composition to be breathable by humans without the use of face masks or space suits. Although this view of the solar system was certainly changing by 1950, many still believed those earlier ideas.

Leigh Brackett in her early career wrote many stories set on Mars. In common with her contemporaries she had her version of an occupied solar system, with Venus, Earth and Mars all inhabited. Mercury had life in its twilight zone as well as human mining colonies.

Her vision of Mars in particular was often sad and nostalgic, and was consistent across all of her Martian stories. Her Martians were old millennia before humans became intelligent enough to begin civilization. They are also the last of other races that once existed on Mars before them, of which some remnants remain as half-lings or humanoid semi intelligent animals that are sometimes used as indentured labour. Her Venus was a hot wet tropical world full of wild creatures and a young vibrant humanoid race. She also had habitats in among the outer planets mostly occupied by human colonies. There was prolific trading and commerce between the planets, with well used spaceports and major trading cities on the planets occupied by humans and other races.

Her Martian stories were a mixture of future reality mixed with romantic fantasy of the kind made popular by Edgar Rice Burroughs. She wrote many stories both long and short, set on Mars, (her first being ***Martian Quest***, in 1940). Most of them have common elements which give a kind of verisimilitude to the adventures, the action taking place and the locale. As the reality of Mars became obvious to writers of her generation, she moved her locales further away from the solar system, or ventured into the newly developing genre of post-apocalyptic fiction with probably her best novel ***The Long Tomorrow.***

Her Mars of the present-future time is a dying planet with ancient cities partially abandoned along what was once the shore of a great ocean: cities with names like Jekkara, Valkis, Barrakesh, Kushat and Caer Dhu, which are now alongside canals that were constructed half a million years earlier to bring water from the poles across the dry bed of the vanished ocean, but those cities have degenerated into havens for thieves, criminals and con-men. Caer Hebra is another ancient city built with tall elegant buildings on top an island in the sea, home to the bird people, small flying humans who are the remnants of an ancient race that ruled the oceans — what's left of them struggle to survive in an empty city slowly being eroded by windborne dust and engulfed in sand.

Her Martian stories that I have are ***Queen of the Martian Catacombs*** (1949), ***Black Amazon of Mars*** (1951), ***The Sword of Rhiannon*** (1952), which I think is her most popular and certainly her best written Martian novel, ***The Nemesis from Terra*** (1961), and a collection of novelettes and novellas titled ***The Coming of The Terrans*** (1967), an anthology of shorter stories individually published under different titles in the pulp magazines from the 1940s through to the mid 1950s.

With ***The Sword of Rhiannon***, her protagonist is an ex-archaeologist who has degenerated into a tomb robber and trader of ancient Martian artefacts who is presented with an old sword which he immediately recognizes as the sword of Rhiannon, the rogue God who was punished with eternal abandonment and who was entombed forever. His lost tomb has become a legend, but Matt Carse (Is this name a small tribute to Edgar Rice Burroughs' Carson of Venus?) reads the inscription on the ancient sword and knows the petty thief who wants to sell it to him must have stumbled across the lost tomb of Rhiannon. He convinces the thief to take him to the tomb and while arguing over how much a share each of them will get when they sell what they find; the petty thief pushes Carse into a weird alien black energy field deep inside the tomb. He escapes from this field terrified by what he felt while inside and discovers once he emerges from the black force field that he is still on Mars but a million years in the past.

Outside of the tomb where before was only barren rock and sand high up on a hillside, spread before him is a grassy sward leading down to a vast ocean. The air is moist and sweet unlike the dry barren dusty air of the Mars he knows. In the distance instead of the crumbling stones of ancient Jekarra with its downhill steps composed of wharfs that were built as the sea kept receding, there is only one group of wharfs at the highest level, and there are ships there, trading ships and warships, and the city is beautiful and fresh looking. He can't wait to go down and see. From this point on he is engulfed in a war between various city states for domination of Mars.

Captured and taken as a slave to help row one of the warships, he eventually escapes and takes over the ship. He is then thought of as a God because of the ancient sword in his possession. In fact he is possessed by the mind of the entombed Rhiannon, who intercedes to help him survive the ordeals he goes through during the events that unfold. The planet is engulfed in a war between humans, and Halflings that are humanoid beings evolved from other animal progenitors. The war is being waged by the beings from Caer Dhu whose origin is derived from reptilian ancestors. Because they have ancient scientific weapons obtained from Rhiannon before he was castigated and entombed they are almost invincible, and are feared by everyone else. They want to dominate Mars, but with the help of Carse and Rhiannon, the city of Caer Dhu and all its hideous occupants are destroyed. Rhiannon can now be freed of the curse and of his imprisonment. He guides Carse back to his own time in the far future of Mars and departs to rejoin those who originally imprisoned him.

This is non-stop action from start to finish and is so well written it is hard not to keep reading.

The five stories in ***The coming of the Terrans,*** although published in 1967, were all published individually before that, ***The Beast Jewel of Mars*** (1948), ***The Last Days of Shandakar*** (1952), ***Mars Minus Bisha*** (1954), ***The Road to Sinharat*** (1963), and ***Purple Priestess of the Mad Moon*** (1964). They can be read as separate chapters in the history of old Mars and how humans newly arrived from Earth and isolated in their trade city, Kahora on Mars, (*N-York on Earth, Vhia on Venus and Sun City in Mercury's twilight belt)* interact with native Martians. They are poetical and evocative with the language and all exhibit a feeling of sadness and great loss; loss for the ancient times of Mars, which still lives on in memories of those remnants, the tribal races that still exist on Mars in its run-down small city states.

The earthmen in these stories are intruders, and are either not welcome or are hated. The earthmen are portrayed as barbarians who would never understand the old cultures, and are seen as exploiters. But not all Terrans are terrible; there are some who make great efforts to understand the Martians and their history. Some however are there for other reasons. Burke Winters in the ***Beast Jewel of Mars*** is there to find his missing fiancée, and encounters an addictive process where ancient Martian technology enables humans to be retrogressed into past versions of themselves on the evolutionary scale. He finds who he is looking for is too late to save her. Induced to undergo the process himself he manages to turn it against the Martians who control it and in the process changes the Martians using this old technology into something ancient and bestial.

Mars Minus Bischa is about a doctor doing research out in the desert being forced to look after a young girl her tribe wants to kill. He finds it difficult to understand why she accepts her fate and tries to save her, but fails when he discovers what she truly is and why the tribe wants to kill her.

The last days of Shandakor is about an archaeologist encountering an alien in a bar, going with him to Shandakor, an ancient city he has long searched for and thought was only a legend, but which has been dying for centuries. It is surrounded by wild tribesmen laying siege to it, waiting to enter and destroy it, to loot the riches believed to be there. It appears new and thriving with guards on the parapets surrounding the city, with streets full of light and life and strange music, but which he discovers on entering to be an illusion. The inhabitants are ghostly holographic images. There are only a few hundred people waiting to die when the water finally runs out. He inadvertently destroys the machinery that maintains the illusion and as he sees the city crumbling into ruins around him he comes to believe he has murdered the whole race.

Purple Priestess of the Mad Moon is about a long forgotten ceremony involving a human sacrifice, and ***The Road to Sinharat*** is a serious comment on how well meaning colonists want to change a world and its culture ostensibly to make things better, but for whom? The Martians don't want to be improved. They are happy with things the way they are. They have learned to live with a slowly dying planet and resist forcibly any changes the new human colonists want to make. Although not mentioned the implication is some kind of terraforming which initially involves damming the canals to improve the water supply. The humans finally realise that they can't impose their will or they will be pushed off the planet altogether. They back off and leave Mars to the Martians.

I think ***The Sword of Rhiannon*** and ***The Coming of The Terrans*** should be read one after the other to appreciate the difference between Mars of the far past as a dynamic planet alive and culturally thriving, and Mars of the present/future which is dying or dead with the remnants of its inhabitants struggling to maintain cultural individuality and who reject the values promulgated by Earth citizens most of whom are invaders and exploiters.

Both books beautifully delineate Mars not only as it was imagined by Leigh Brackett, but also as it was imagined by thousands of other readers who could not articulate what they felt until she did it for them. These were possibly the last of the romantic fantasies regarding Mars before science began to make it clear that Mars was not like we imagined.

Queen of the Martian Catacombs (1949) was perhaps Leigh Brackett's first story to feature Eric John Stark, a human orphan brought up by wild tribesmen on Mercury. He has the senses and the fast reaction of a wild animal and can be a ferocious opponent. He is wanted by the law for something he did on Venus and they have chased him to Mars where they have cornered him in the desert. He has been hired by a warlord as a mercenary. This warlord has joined forces with a barbarian leader and they have hired various wild men from all over the solar system as well as wanted criminals to be mercenaries who will lead the tribes into a planetary war for control of Mars. Stark is given the choice by the police of having his police record wiped clean if he infiltrates the mercenary stronghold to find out what is going on, or spend the next 20 years in jail on the Moon. His chance of surviving long enough to report back is very low, but he decides to do it.

The rest of the story revolves around his personal enmity with a nasty character from Venus, and some interesting interplay between the two warlords and the women who control them from the background as they travel across the ancient sea bed to ruins of Sinharat, once an island in the ocean but now a cliff jutting up from a barren wasteland covered by a forgotten fortress. He survives a couple of attempts on his life, being lost in a sandstorm with one of the Martian Queens, and having his mind transferred into another body which is killed when he double crosses the Martian Queen. He survives that too and presumably stays for a while on Mars once the War has been prevented.

The action is non-stop and often breath-taking, which makes this story hard to put down until the end.

What we learn about Stark is that he is as tough as they come but has a good heart and is always on the side of the underdog and the primitive tribesmen no matter the odds against him.

Eric John Stark turned out to be a good character for Leigh Brackett and she wrote many stories after this one which featured him, and not all of them were set on Mars. This novella first appeared in P*lanet Stories* in 1949, but was later expanded into a novel called ***The Secret of Sinharat.*** *(*1964)

Black Amazon of Mars (1951) was published by Planet Stories, most likely with a different title, during the same year Arthur C Clarke's ***Sands of Mars*** appeared. Unlike '***Sands of Mars***' and Asimov's T***he Martian Wa***y

(1952), both of which attempted to depict realistic views of Mars, ***Black Amazon*** is not at all realistic: it is Science Fantasy, reminiscent of the work by writers like Edgar Rice Burroughs and Otis Adelbert Kline who earlier filled our imaginations with fantastic adventures on a Mars with exotic ecosystems. Like all of Brackett's Martian stories, this one has plenty of excitement and action to keep a reader enthralled.

In ***Black Amazon***, we are again reminded that Eric John Stark, was born in the twilight zone of Mercury, grew up there fostered by wild tribes before moving to Earth, and then on to his various adventures on Mars.

The part of Mars in this story is inhabited by various wild tribes and some very alien beings that can only live in the ice of the North Pole, but who want to extend their icy domain. Mars is cold at night but okay during the day. There is a spaceport and some colonization by Earth people, but that is only mentioned in passing as a means of explaining how Stark happens to be on Mars. He is accompanying a dying Martian friend, who wants to return an amulet he stole years before that has mysterious powers, to the city of his birth. Unfortunately he dies, and Stark promises to return the amulet to its place of origin, the city near the ice of the North Pole and a mysterious gate that holds back ghostly icy aliens.

Not long after his friend dies, Stark is captured by a warrior tribe, taken to their camp and tortured before he finally makes his escape from them. Stark is much stronger and faster than the native Martians, and the unmentioned implication is that because he spent a long time on Earth with its higher gravity, his power and speed compared to the Martian warriors is superior.

Finding his way through the cold swamps he arrives at the city by the ice cap to warn them the warrior tribes are going to attack. They do, and during this altercation it is revealed their leader, who is dressed in black armour and ferociously wielding a battle axe, turns out to be a warrior woman. Finally Stark and this Amazon join forces to defeat the icy aliens who want to extend the ice cap and their city within it across the rest of Mars. The amulet and the heat barrier it generates is the key in holding back these icy hoards.

Typical of the stories that filled those early pulp SF magazines, there is minimal character development in this story, and contains non-stop action with fantastic fights and pursuits, from the very first page to the end, hardly giving a reader a moment to breathe and think.

There are other stories featuring John Stark collected as ***Eric John Stark – Outlaw of Mars,*** but I haven't seen this collectcion.

Black Amazon of Mars, (expanded in 1964 as ***People of the Talisman***) is a fine example of the genre, and has stood the test of time; being still readable and enjoyable 70 years after it was first published.

The Nemesis from Terra (1961) is the least likable story in her Martian sequence. It is a novel about exploitation of resources through slave labour by a mining company that has discovered a rare mineral used in plastic making on Earth. It is a about a renegade earthman who becomes through a strange set of circumstances a temporary ruler of the Martian City States and the tribes contained therein, and who leads them in a revolt against the mining company so it won't eventually control and destroy the planet. This super tough earthman is a Jesus like character who at one point in the story is crucified against a brick wall by having knives thrust through his hands and feet pinning him high up on the wall while leaders from the City States confer over what to do about the mining company that is slowly taking over the whole planet.

In this story we get to see the down and dirty side of the Martian cities with their criminals and thieves, drunken spacemen in run-down bars and all the dregs of the lowlife of Mars.

For me there isn't one likeable character, but the protagonist Rick, although out to gain whatever he can by any means possible, is the least dislikeable of the nasty characters.

The only two really likeable people in this story is Kyra, a small bird woman who helps Rick, and Maya, who worked undercover in the mine office to find out what she could do to help stop them, who falls in love with Rick. Their lives intertwine amid the violence and thuggery that happens throughout the story. Nevertheless it is a readable story in that it is hard to put down once started, and there is also much background material that helps reinforce Leigh Brackett's extraordinary vision of Mars and its ancient history.

As the reality of what Mars was really like began to become apparent in the 1960s and 70s authors like Leigh Brackett moved their stories out of the solar system altogether. She rewrote or expanded some stories of John Stark into several novels that take place on a planet circling a dimmer red star, and these were also very popular, but since they don't relate to Mars as such, I will not be looking at them here. For those interested in searching out these stories they are: *The Ginger Star (1974), The Hounds of Skaith (1974) and The Reavers of Skaith (1976).*

Robert Heinlein's Mars

Robert A Heinlein, considered to be one of America's finest science fiction authors, wrote several novels and no doubt many shorter works that featured Mars in one way or another, from being an influence in the background to featuring as a prominent part of the story. In each of them his Martians and the ecology of the planet is different. His depiction of Mars is never the same or consistent across all the stories. In each his Martians have a different appearance and history, and the planet also varies in how it is seen. Mars was a part of Heinlein's inhabited solar system where Venus, Earth, Mars, and Ganymede all had native populations and ecologies, and all of these locations were exploited by human colonization, commerce and politics. He was an exponent of the frontier mentality that gave Americans their national character and projected this character into all his early space adventures and other science fiction works, especially those written for younger readers such as ***Rocketship Galileo*** (1947) elements of which formed the basis for the film ***Destination Moon*** (1950), and ***Farmer in the Sky*** (1950).

One of his earliest novels ***Red Planet*** (1949) is a fine example of the imaginative writing that he was capable of. It is one that people often remember when asked to recall Heinlein's work. This would have to be considered as a fanciful story no matter how realistic it seems, yet realistic is what it seems on reading it. It also straddles categories one and two.

I was only nine years old when it was published so of course I never saw it. Years later I became aware of it but never had the chance to read it until recently having obtained a new edition containing the parts edited out in the earlier publication. This edition has been restored by the Heinlein Estate so it is presented in the way that Heinlein originally wanted it to be.

Red Planet: Robert A Heinlein (1949 – 1967 – 2006)

Heinlein denies writing specifically for younger readers although many of his earlier novels are regarded as such. Perhaps like his contemporaries who were all young themselves, it was natural to write featuring younger characters as protagonists. As they and the genre matured so also did their characters and story ideas.

This story includes many ideas that later engaged Heinlein, such as the superiority of free enterprise over government controlled activities, the right to bear arms for self-protection, the right to rebel against oppression, the dismissive attitude of adults towards children, a feeling of patriotism that much later would evolve into jingoism, and similar concepts which are subtle hints beneath the narrative.

The two main characters happen to be teenage boys being sent off to boarding school half way around the planet; the planet in this case being Mars, the Red Planet.

The boys are the children of mine workers and others that maintain a colonial outpost. As winter approaches the colony of about 200 inhabitants is preparing to migrate to the Southern hemisphere where a larger colony exists. In winter the northern hemisphere is too cold to safely survive with temperatures 100 degrees plus below zero.

Before the migration can begin the boys are sent to the boarding school. The school has recently been taken over by a new headmaster who establishes a strict dictatorial regime that young Jim and his friend find unbearable. Almost immediately they find themselves in trouble with the new headmaster who confiscates Jim's Martian pet which colonists call a bouncer because it is ball shaped. It can extrude eyes, legs or other appendages as required. When frightened it retreats into a ball shape and remains mute. It has a phenomenal memory and can repeat like a parrot anything it hears. It also seems to have a limited intelligence and can converse with Jim who is the only human being that has one of these rare creatures as a companion. He actually saved it from a monstrous wild creature which attacks any living thing to extract water. Humans are not immune from these attacks and kill these things whenever they see them. The saved Bouncer adopts young Jim and stays with him. The two become inseparable and when he takes it with him to the boarding school the new headmaster confiscates it and locks it up in his office. He later wants to sell it to a zoo on Earth willing to pay a very high figure.

As soon as they are aware of this the boys manage to rescue the Bouncer who Jim calls Willis and they run away. On the run with police after them for stealing something from the headmaster's office the boys discover that Willis had overheard a plot to deny the northern colony its annual migration forcing them to stay where they are through the winter. Knowing they can't survive a winter the boys head off to warn their parents and the others in the colony. They manage to do this and the result is a minor revolution against the mining company which controls human activity on Mars and this creates a pivotal confrontation between the humans as well as the Martians who intervene not to save their human friends but to save Willis from coming to any harm.

The boys travel at night skating along the canals of frozen water. They have over 2000 miles to travel and during this they encounter real Martians one of whom befriends Jim because of Willis. The boys are taken underground where the harsh subzero temperatures of the night can't affect them. They also discover a network of tunnels and subways that enables them to travel great distances under the surface. The Martians are obviously not as primitive as humans think.

Heinlein has made use of whatever knowledge there was of Mars in the 1940s and imagined an intricately detailed ecology and Martian history which even today more than half a century later is believable although we know it could not possibly have been like that — which points to how good a writer Heinlein was early in his career.

He has canals which alternately freeze overnight when temperatures drop way below zero, to unfreeze once the sun comes up, unless it is during winter when the water stays frozen day and night. He has complex plant life adapted to the extreme climate, and animal life of which we only see a small part but the implication is that it is as complex although radically different than anything we find in nature on Earth. His Martians are very tall and have three legs and arms.

Jim's acceptance by the Martians who normally avoid any contact with humans who in turn try to avoid them as much as possible is the pivot around which the story unfolds.

As the story evolves Jim finds out that Willis is much more than he expected, and that the Martians also are much more than anyone could imagine.

This is a thrilling and engaging story set on Mars, and definitely one of the better ones from that time period, much better in fact than many later ones. Originally published in 1949 it was heavily edited by the publisher for sale to school libraries. Heinlein objected but there was not much he could do then. It was republished in 1976 which is possibly when I may have seen it although I don't remember it at all. The edition I have just read is from 2006 and has completely restored the text originally edited out upon its first publication.

This is one book that transcends time, and almost 70 years later is still fresh and vibrant and well worth reading if you haven't done so. Even if you read it years ago, do read it again; you will be surprised at how good it is.

Double Star (1956) Has Heinlein imagining a system ruled by descendants of the Royal Dutch family from New Batavia on the Moon. On Mars, a political party called The Expansionists want to include the native Martians, along with the natives of Venus and Ganymede in a treaty to guarantee freedom, equality and the right to vote in elections. It looked as if the ruling party on Mars, the Humanity party which believes in the absolute right of humans to assert control over the lesser races of other planets, was about to lose to The Expansionists so they kidnapped their leader and popular statesman to prevent him participating in a ceremony that would unite the Martians with the Humans on an equal footing. If he doesn't appear the Martians will be insulted and the chance of them gaining equality with the humans, who have colonized their planet to the Martian's detriment, will disappear.

The other leaders of the party go to Earth and hire the Great Lorenzo, an out of work actor, to impersonate the missing statesman who is to participate in the ceremony with the Martians. He is to be adopted by the Martians as one of their own. The only problem is that Lorenzo has a deep rooted dislike of Martians, he considers them to be '*things*' and not people, and he can't abide the smell of them.

Once the doctor on the ship going to Mars has hypnotized Lorenzo and taken away his deep seated dislike of things other than human, he goes along with the plan to impersonate the statesman for a few days.

After the ceremony has successfully taken place the statesman reappears but unfortunately his kidnappers had chemically done something to his brain so that all his memories and ability to think and reason were wiped out. He would recover but perhaps not in time to participate in the concluding ceremony with the King in New Batavia. Lorenzo would have to continue impersonating the statesman for a bit longer.

Lorenzo is by this time desperate to return to Earth, but is unable to refuse the continuing impersonation, especially when he looks upon it as the greatest role of his career. Of course the King spots the impersonation almost immediately but says nothing about it. He understands the reason for it and when he discovers who the impersonator is he is delighted and asks for his autograph. (*An anachronistic moment from the 1950s; do people still collect autographs*?)

With the resignation of the Humanist political party on Mars the Expansionists are authorized by the King to form a caretaker Government and Lorenzo again has to return to Mars to give a victory speech. By this time the real statesman has partially recovered from his memory loss and is delighted to meet the Great Lorenzo. Lorenzo is hoping that he will recover by the time they get back to Mars so he can finally go home, but on the way there the statesman suffers a massive stroke and dies.

Lorenzo, landing on Mars delivers the victory speech and finally realizes he is about to embark on a role greater than anything he has ever done before; to become forever the Statesman and leader of the Expansionist Party that integrated not only the Martians but the races on all the other planets.

This is a fast paced story that captures the reader right from the first page and doesn't let go until the end. Background material is inserted in such a way that it is un-noticeable, blended seamlessly into the story.

Robert Heinlein originally made notes for a story in1948 that turned out eventually to be his most famous novel, the cult classic ***Stranger in a Strange Land.*** It seemed that the story would be too long for the commissioned story he was to write for Astounding SF Magazine so he wrote something else for the magazine. He made several attempts to write this longer piece but kept putting the notes aside until finally the story of a human infant raised on Mars by old Martians, returning to Earth to eventually become a religious cult leader was finally completed in 1960.

It was a massively long novel and totally different from anything else being published at the time. His publishers and editors asked him to reduce the story by at least a third and to restructure it before they published it. He did this reluctantly and the book was published in 1961. Originally it had been 220,000 words or more and the published edition came out at just over 160,000 words... a huge reduction. It was this reduced version that became a cult classic and remained in print for over 28 years. It was reissued in 1990 by the Heinlein Estate in an original fully restored version.

University students and people of the new hippie movements embraced ***Stranger in a Strange Land*** because it attacked the established conformity of the times. It proposed group marriages and embraced male sexuality, it glorified defiant individuality and free thinking, among other ideas that resonated with rebellious university students across the country. It gave the words *grok* and *grokking*, to popular American language, and this word with so many undefined meanings replaced *dig* as the word the hippies and younger generation commonly used. In fact some observers have gone so far as to suggest that the roots of the New Age movement began with the ideas expressed in this best-selling book.

Valentine Smith is a human infant and the only survivor of the first expedition to Mars. After a long gruelling trip out to the Red Planet the crew radioed back that they would attempt a landing. Nothing was heard after that. Twenty-five years later a second expedition is sent and successfully lands and finds the remains of the crashed first attempt. They report there are no survivors, but later correct that to say there was one survivor; a child that had grown up on Mars. They also reported that Mars was inhabited, that there were ancient cities alongside old canals, very much like people still believed were on Mars in 1960. This occurs in the first three pages. When the recue team returns to Earth with their mysterious survivor the rest of the events take place on Earth.

The Martians who have become mystical and all-knowing had raised the child, Valentine Smith, after his parents died so in effect he becomes Martian and is imbued with many of the attributes the Martians believe to be true which includes the ability to manipulate matter itself, a God-like attribute. Smith has those same powers and when he returns as an adult to Earth he starts a nation-wide (planet-wide) movement embracing sexual freedom, individuality, communal spirit and all the things that do not conform to the rigid society that existed in America (and presumably the western civilizations) during the late 1950s on into the 1960s. All the action takes place on Earth but Mars permeates the background adding a hint of strangeness. By looking at the contemporary culture through the eyes of a stranger who had never before experienced anything on Earth Heinlein was able to let his imagination run wild, and to criticise all that he believed were the faults of the society in which he lived. That so many people believed in similar ideas and wished for change to occur guaranteed the book would become a best seller, not just for a short time, but over decades.

Although it seems quaint now, compared to other works from the same time, it is still worth reading since it is imbued with a Martian sensibility.

Podkayne of Mars which Heinlein published in 1962, thirteen years after ***Red Planet*** is still a favourite amongst his many fans, although I don't think it is anywhere near as good as ***Red Planet***.

The narrator tells the story through verbal diaries, and this makes it flat. It doesn't come alive in the way ***Red Planet*** did and from my perspective it doesn't have that sense of wonder that infused that earlier story.

In fact it is not even a Mars story. It is a planetary adventure (harking back to the ideas prevalent in magazine stories from the 1930s and 40s) which features Podkayne, (Poddy) a young Marswoman coming of age as she journeys, from Mars to Earth via Venus, with her younger brother and her uncle , a politician who has business on Earth.

A small part at the beginning takes place on Mars but very soon the characters board the space ship for the trip to Earth. The balance of the first half takes place on the space ship, a luxury liner used by wealthy tourists. It's an eye-opener for young Poddy as she begins to grow into a delightful and curious young woman The last half of the story takes place on Venus after an unscheduled stop, and where her adventures begin to unravel, so in effect it is a Venus story more than it is a Mars story.

It is told in the first person from the point of view of Poddy, who has great ambitions for her future life, but gradually changes her way of thinking as she experiences life off-planet for the first time.

I don't think Heinlein manages to portray how a young woman (of nine Mars years - just over 18 Earth years) thinks and feels; it is more how a mature man thinks a young woman might be. It may have seemed more convincing in 1962...

With the original ending back in this newly published version —the publishers in 1962 didn't like Heinlein's controversial ending and wanted it changed, which he did, reluctantly— the story has a darker feel to it than it did back then.

I do remember reading it in the mid-1960s but I needed to read it again because none of it remained in my memory.

There is a postlude in the voice of Poddy's younger brother, also told in 1st person, and indistinguishable from Poddy's 1st person voice, which convinced me on this reading that Heinlein didn't really capture a female voice.

There are some background details about human occupation of Mars. Marsmen and Marswomen are what the human population call themselves, not Martians which are the remnants of the original inhabitants.

Heinlein has this version of Mars initially settled by making it a penal colony (like Australia was a couple of hundred years ago) where Earth Governments could send petty criminals and political dissidents. Eventually a revolution against Earth Authority allowed Mars to became independent.

Venus is controlled entirely by a private corporation and has nothing to do with Earth government. It fosters tourism, gambling and other nefarious activities all in the name of free enterprise.

Heinlein's view of both these planets is consistent with what was thought they were like before the advent of mariner 4. Venus, because it is closer to the Sun, being hot, tropical, shrouded with fogs and clouds so the sky is never seen, lots of swamps and dangerous animals, and Mars: dry with a thin atmosphere, low gravity, extremely cold temperatures at night, canals criss-crossing the planet to bring water from the poles to ancient now dead cities with the remnants of ancient Martians and desert like plants still managing to survive despite the harshness of the conditions.

Podkayne of Mars is worth another read, but I feel it has aged noticeably and seems flat, whereas ***Red Planet*** still retains a feeling of freshness and excitement.

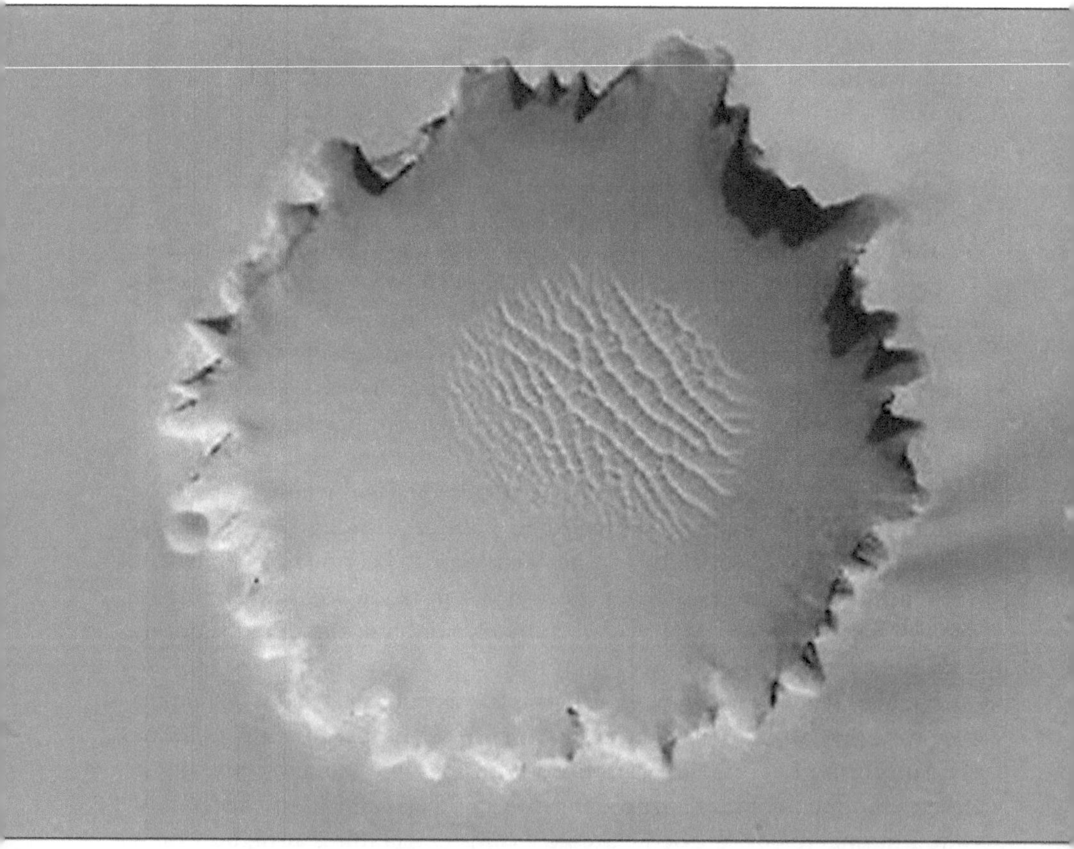

Victoria Crater

Attempts at depicting reality...

As far back as 1950 there had been grand plans to go to Mars as the next step after the Moon. No one had even got to the Moon at that time other than in the imagination of Science Fiction writers. Werner von Braun had surrendered to the Americans in 1945 and brought with him to the USA 115 members of his rocket team plus a large quantity of his V2 rockets. He had been incarcerated for a few weeks towards the end of the 2nd World War for suggesting that rockets should be used to send people into space instead of being weaponry for war.

The Russians still hadn't sent Sputnik into orbit when Werner von Braun suggested in 1952 (in German and later in 1953 in English in a book called ***The Mars Project*** which he revised in 1962 to take into account the better rocket engineering and fuels available) building a fleet of ten giant ships in space to send 70 people to Mars. Some of the ships would be used as landing vehicles on arrival while the others remained in orbit. He expected his astronauts to live and work on Mars for 400 days before returning to Earth. He also expected that while conditions on Mars would be harsh, his travellers would manage with suitable clothing to protect against the cold and lower air pressure. He believed there would be some kind of primitive plant life as did most other people at that time.

As late as 1962 many scientists were still debating over what kind of plant life could be found there and expected that it would not be anything like what we have on Earth. Analysis of spectral lines had convinced many that lichen like plants existed, and of course they were seasonal. No one believed anymore that there would animal life or sentient creatures capable of building canals apart from writers of science fiction.

Von Braun also advocated building a wheel shaped space station which would rotate using centrifugal force to replicate gravity. This space station would be the base where the workers could live while constructing the Martian fleet. But without the capability of getting enough materials into low Earth orbit to build the ships, and without a space station to work from, the whole concept was nothing more than a fantastic dream. But it was a dream often embraced by science fiction writers. What gave it some verisimilitude was that von Braun had done the maths, had calculated the vectors, the velocities, the amounts of materials, fuel needed, the orbital paths for the journey out and for the return; he had done the groundwork that others could use in the future.

Incidentally, there were no computers in the late 1940s and all the calculations presented in his book regarding orbital trajectories, speed of vehicles, and fuel consumption were done using a slide rule.

Von Braun wanted to show that in theory it was possible even with the technology and the fuels available in the early 1950s. His ideas of Mars were based upon what was thought to be scientifically accurate up until 1950, and his plan to ferry all the materials to build his fleet in low earth orbit was far beyond any capacity the Americans (or anyone else) had to do it. He suggested it was possible if only a minute fraction of the money spent on defence could be used for space research.

The concept was certainly spectacular but it wouldn't have worked. There was no allowance for human error, for accidents, mishaps, and anything else that could go wrong during the construction phase of the fleet before it left for Mars. There was also little actual knowledge of conditions in space or on the surface of Mars, which meant anything the fleet encountered once leaving Earth's vicinity was pure speculation; science fiction.

Apart from that, the cost of the project and the infrastructure needed to continually send cargo rockets into space with the materials for constructing the Mars fleet was beyond comprehension. But he never gave up.

When he worked with NASA he invented the concept of multi stage rockets and designed the rockets that took the Apollo missions to the Moon, massive rockets that were far too big for the job at hand. He had designed a rocket that theoretically would loft a space ship on its way to Mars. That this never happened was a great disappointment for him. Once the Moon had been attained NASA went in a different direction, sticking to low earth orbit and coming up with the space shuttle, which for many fans of space travel was a backwards step.

It is interesting to note that almost all science fiction authors based their idea of how a space ship (or in earlier days a rocket ship) would look and function on what they knew about ships, *and ship rather than plane* is the key.

Passenger ships travelled the oceans between continents either as regular routes or specialized tourist cruising. Navy ships patrolled shipping lanes and in general protected the country to which they belonged. In the 1930's planes that could carry large numbers of people didn't exist. The biggest of them could only carry a few people, and jet planers didn't appear until after the 2nd World War, whereas ships traversing oceans could carry hundreds if not a thousand passengers. It was logical to base the idea of space travel on ocean travel and writers used a similar hierarchy for the Captain, officers and other staff that supported the passengers. There were bars and lounge rooms and promenade decks, private and general cabins, theatres and entertainment areas and all these in massive space ships that travelled regularly between colonised and inhabited planets and moons within the solar system. Smaller space ships, like those depicted by E C Tubb, A Bertram Chandler and others were often as not based on tramp steamers and small cargo ships.

But this changed suddenly in the late 1950s when the space race between Russia and America began in earnest. NASA as well as the Russians used test pilots to pilot their miniscule space capsules. There were no big space ships, just small capsules launched from the top of massive expendable rockets. Then NASA partially dumped expendable rockets for a space plane that could land by gliding back to Earth; the space shuttle. It still needed the rocket boosters to take off, but not for landing. The reality compared to the fiction of previous decades was a shock to writers and those who continued to write stories involving space ships immediately changed to ships based on air-force structures and ideas.

Two early films used von Braun's concept of the wheel shaped space station to great effect. George Pal's ***The Conquest of Space*** (1955 release) had a group of astronauts living on the space station while their space ship to take them to Mars was being built, and inside it looked very much like a navy battleship or submarine with huge steel bulkheads and watertight doors.

Thirteen years later in Clarke and Kubrick's ***2001 A Space Odyssey*** (1968) we see a very modern antiseptic station where passengers in transit to the moon change from the rocket that brought them up into orbit to the passenger ship which will take them to the Moon. In this film the moon shuttles and orbital rockets looked like a modern passenger planes. They even had airline logos prominently displayed. This clearly reflects the change in imagining what a space ship and travelling on board would be like from before the space race to after the space race began.

Clarke and Kubrick extrapolated from jetliners and modern aeroplanes, whereas George Pal used the sea going ships and navy ships concepts common before the space race.

There are other SF films which feature wheel shaped rotating space stations and all of them can be traced back to the very logical idea first suggested by Werner von Braun around 1950.

Walt Disney was enthralled with the idea of going to Mars and produced an animated documentary ***Mars and Beyond*** for his television program in 1957 which elaborated on Werner von Braun's ideas and what we might expect to find there.

It started off realistically showing Von Braun's concept of orbiting spaceships being built while the workers lived in the wheel shaped space station that became a symbol of the human conquest of space, and then followed the departing fleet of ten ships for Mars… but it soon became a ridiculous cartoon presentation of the weird creatures that could possibly exist on Mars and on other planets. Good for its time and aimed at the children who watched the Mickey Mouse club, but hopelessly outdated within a few years.

However it is still interesting to look at, especially the first part with all the technical details of the space ship flotilla beautifully animated.

Some commonalities between early Mars novels

When you have been reading books for over sixty years it is sometimes hard to remember specific details regarding particular books, so I needed to read some of them again to be certain I remembered them correctly. The books referred to were all published between 1951 and 1973, and all contained knowledge about Mars that was as up to date as possible given the time they were written. I read them when they were published but that was half a century or more ago. Reading them again to see how they compared with similar recently published work I was surprised at how good some of them were.

The books are: ***The Sands of Mars***, by Arthur C Clarke (1951), ***Alien Dust***, by E C Tubb (1955), ***Marooned on Mars*** by Lester Del Rey (1962), published before Mariner 4 made its flyby of Mars.

Farewell Earth's Bliss, by D G Compton (1966), was written while Mariner 4 was in transit to Mars and published early in the year after the flyby so it doesn't include any new information regarding conditions on Mars, while ***Born under Mars*** by John Brunner (1967) makes some effort to include more realistic knowledge of Mars but still pays homage to the idea of a long dying planet.

The Earth is Near, by Ludek Pesek (1973 English translation), written and published after the Mariner 4 Mars flyby, depicts Mars extrapolated from what was known as a result of the photos sent back from that first historic flyby. He may as well have seen the later images from the 1969 Mariners 6 and 7, which had improved clarity since they were taken much closer to the surface but still showed Mars as a 'dead' cratered planet.

One other novel written in 1962 and eventually published in 1964 made no attempt to be realistic or to use what was known about Mars at that time, but nevertheless, it takes place on Mars and should be included: ***Martian Time Slip*** by Philip K Dick. It stands outside of the category that includes the others, but must be mentioned because it is after all a story that takes place on Mars.

Looking at these stories there are some obvious commonalities.

One of the earliest attempts at a realistic depiction of Mars was Arthur C Clarke's novel ***The Sands of Mars.*** It was his first novel, published in1951, and was certainly different to other contemporary Mars novels which were more fantastic in nature rather than realistic.

Clarke was a scientist who helped with the development of radar during the Second World War to assist the British see German fighter planes attacking England, and is famous for having invented the idea of geosynchronous satellites in orbit to facilitate radio communications around the world. He was a member of the British Interplanetary Society which was founded to inform the public of the infinite possibilities of space travel and how it could be achieved. Arthur C Clarke became treasurer of this organization when it moved from Liverpool to London in 1937.

He was also an amateur astronomer and didn't believe there were canals on Mars. He wanted to depict Mars as realistically as possible so while others were still writing about dying civilizations and evaporating canals he wrote about Mars being a cold desert planet.

As part of an introduction to a reprint of this book in 2001 (by Gollancz - ***The Space Trilogy; Islands in The Sky, The Sands of Mars*** and ***Earthlight***), Clarke confessed to having a certain fondness for *Sands* since it was his first full length novel. He said: "*When I wrote it we knew practically nothing about Mars — and what we did know was completely wrong... It was still generally believed that Mars had a thin but useful atmosphere and that some vegetation flourished in the tropical regions where the temperature often rose above freezing point.*" And of course by extension we assumed that "*there would also be some more interesting forms of life.*"

The original copy of this book has disappeared from my collection but I remember it had illustrations of the kind found in the pulp magazines one of which showed a young man looking through a porthole from a habitat at a vista of endless sand dunes disappearing over the horizon. Clarke later recalled: the story contains one sentence italicised for emphasis —*there are no mountains on Mars* — which later caused him considerable embarrassment when the Viking and Mariner photos started coming back. He apologised in subsequent reprints to his readers, but much later qualified this original statement by claiming *there were no mountains as we understand them, like the Alps, the Andes or the Himalayas. Even Olympus Mons was more a blister in the crust rather than a mountain because it is too large —three times the height of Everest with a crater 600 kilometres in diameter. There are cliffs and canyons of immense length but no real mountains.* (***The Snows of Olympus – A Garden on Mars***, by Arthur C Clarke, published by Victor Gollancz in 1994).

Was Clarke right? Perhaps it is a matter of perspective. If you are on the surface, the cliffs he talks about are as good as being 'real' mountains, but if they weren't caused by the same processes that create mountains on Earth, then perhaps they aren't mountains as we understand them. The Martian surface is more different than we expected and there were no doubt forces that worked differently to those on Earth that created what we now see. And what about volcanoes like Olympus Mons and several others near it; are they not mountains now that they are dormant?

In the 1950s little was known about Mars, but one common assumption was that the atmosphere was breathable, although it was as thin as that found at the top of Mt Everest. It was also believed that with proper conditioning humans could manage to breathe it with only a little assistance from a breathing mask when extra stress made a larger intake of oxygen necessary. It was also generally believed that primitive plant life existed which explained, so they thought, the seasonal changes in colour observed through telescopes.

It was assumed (rightly) that Mars was cold —after all it was further away from the sun than Earth and received considerably less solar radiation.

No one thought it could be as cold as it actually is, when at night temperatures plummet to below 100 degrees Celsius and where daytime temperatures in the tropical regions barely reach what we have in Antarctica.

Another common assumption was that the polar ice caps of Mars were of water ice.

They had no idea the atmospheric pressure was less than 1 percent that of Earth, and that what there was consisted mostly of carbon dioxide. Even if there was enough pressure on the surface it would be unbreathable. They also didn't know that the ice caps at the poles were of frozen carbon dioxide (dry ice). There may very well be water ice underneath the frozen Carbon Dioxide, but it wouldn't be easily accessible to colonists.

What was known was that Mars was a dead or dying world; shrunken and cracked with canyons and giant chasms that, a world of cold deserts, of planet wide sandstorms. It had a day slightly longer than Earth's day (24 hours and 37 minutes) and that it also had four seasons, with each season twice as long as the equivalent on Earth, (because it took almost two earth-years to make one orbit of the sun) and that was about it. All this fell in line with the popular idea of planetary evolution; that Venus was at an early stage of development, Earth was in the middle of its life cycle and Mars was closer to the end of its cycle. This idea no longer exists, but it was seriously considered up until the early 1950s.

Of the group of novels and authors mentioned above, only Pesek had the information sent back to Earth by the Mariner-4 Flyby (November 28 1964), and possibly the Mariner 6 (25 February 1969 arriving July 31st 1969) and Mariner 7 (27 March 1969 arriving August 5th 1969); both of which approached as close as 3400 kilometres above the surface where they transmitted back those mind blowing photos that showed a crater-pocked surface that looked as dead as the Moon. Unfortunately these Mariner fly-bys only passed a small area of Mars and missed the incredible surface formations that the later global surveyor orbiting satellites found and photographed.

With the knowledge from the Mariner 4, 6 and 7 flybys Pesek created a much more realistic story than other earlier authors. He would have been writing it in 1969 for its German publication in 1970. He also painted the cover for his book which was a realistic depiction of the cratered surface not unlike the photos sent back by Mariners 4, 6 and 7. He was primarily an astronomical artist rather than a writer although he combined his paintings with non-fiction in a number of scientific books often with speculative elements.

The books mentioned as a group have various things in common: all recognize Mars as a cold desert planet and make much of the problems caused by dust, sand, and the inevitable dust/sand storms.

Two of them, ***The Sands of Mars,*** and ***Farewell Earth's Bliss***, have colonies already established on Mars and these same two make use of indigenous plant life as an integral part of the story, which to a modern reader is jarring, but up until the late 1960s was commonly accepted.

Four of them involve a trip to Mars in the earlier part of the story, and have the problem of weightlessness inside the ships on the way. Compton and Pesek use drugs to prevent sickness and bone density loss. Clarke shows it but has no problem with his people in freefall, while Tubb doesn't even mention it in ***Alien Dust*** although he has a centrifuge built on Mars so people planning on going back to Earth can exercise their bodies at earth-normal gravity induced by centrifugal force.

Not one of them considered revolving the space ships during the long flight to Mars to create a semblance of artificial gravity.

Two of them, ***The Sands of Mars*** and ***The Earth is Near,*** have the Mars space ship built in orbit before going to Mars, then have it remain on one of the Martian Moons while smaller shuttles go down to the surface.

The others have the space ships land on Mars itself.

Marooned on Mars is straight out boy's fantasy adventure but it does have the space ship used to go to Mars built in orbit around the Moon. ***Farewell Earth's Bliss*** uses old moon shuttles as the ships that take people to Mars so a background assumption is that a thriving outpost with regular traffic from Earth has been established on the Moon for some time.

Born under Mars is space opera harking back in style to material written during the 1930s and 40s.

Arthur C Clarke's first novel alongside some of his contemporaries

The Sands of Mars (1951) by Arthur C Clarke is always being reprinted.

What makes this one different? To begin with it is optimistic and apart from one glaring misconception of finding plant and animal life on Mars, (which is necessary for the story and which could make it fanciful rather than realistic) the story is full of brilliant speculation and big ideas that engender a sense of wonder even today. With Clarke you can believe these things are possible.

His viewpoint character is a science fiction author turned journalist who is asked by the Earth Government to travel on the maiden voyage of a new spaceship liner that later will take tourists to Mars. This ship had been built in orbit.

The Sands of Mars is as modern as any book written today on the same subject, with only one or two slightly jarring anomalies to disturb the modern reader, but if you can overlook those, then the story that unfolds is timeless. If you read the story taking into consideration what was known about Mars at the time it was written and published in 1951, it is an outstanding piece of literature that embodies all of Clarke's ideas of what constitutes science fiction, with believably extrapolated technology, and how that affects the lives of the people using it. This novel is about people, not about the technology, and about how they change as a result of events that occur to challenge them, which in hindsight was unusual for Clarke since most of his later books were about the technology and the science and little consideration was given to the people in the stories affected by that. There are exceptions though, ***Childhood's End*** and ***The Songs of Distant Earth*** being superb examples.

Clarke doesn't give a future date that could destroy verisimilitude by having been passed and thus negating any predictions that may have been made. There is only one reference by Gibson, an ex-SF writer with space opera novels and a book about Mars called *Martian Dust* which he published in 1973 or 74 (a quarter of a century ahead of the time Clarke wrote this book) and which had long been outdated by real events taking place in Space and on Mars, so I assume that this voyage is taking place sometime in the 1990s, 40 years ahead of the time when Clarke wrote the story. But it has the feeling of being further ahead than that so I like to think of it as being closer to the middle of the century we now live in.

Mars has a well established colony with a small 'city' called *Port Lowell* where most of the population live in inflated domes big enough to contain several dozen two and three story buildings. A smaller group lives in another settlement half way around Mars and this is called *Skia* or *Port Schiaparelli*. At *Port Lowell* they are building another even bigger dome in anticipation of an increase in migration from Earth.

Clarke cleverly lays out the background with mention of colonies on the Moon, a huge space station in orbit around the Earth from where the Mars journey begins, with atomic rocket ships (operating only in space at least 1000 kilometres away from Earth) for faster travel than chemical rockets and much stuff that is almost skipped over because for those living in this future it is all very ordinary and hardly noticed. There are no protracted explanations of how things work, every character takes for granted that it does and simply gets on with life. There are regular voyages between Earth and Mars and Venus as well although this is only mentioned in passing. Earth supplies Mars with much that it needs and Mars sends back minerals and other things Earth needs.

At the moment the story opens Mars is trying to get people to come and live there, and as part of this attempt the authorities on Earth have commissioned ex-SF writer Gibson, who is now writing more realistic material to travel to Mars on the maiden voyage of the new passenger liner *Ares*, so he can report back on life in space and on Mars. Gibson is the only passenger on a ship with a crew of six. The spaces for the passenger cabins are filled with cargo for this maiden voyage.

There are some anachronisms that intrude on the story which in effect show us it was written a long time ago, and the first is that Gibson takes a portable typewriter, with stacks of paper and carbon paper (for copies). When he finishes an article or story he takes it to the 'radio room' and the operator feeds it into a fax machine that converts his text to radio signals beamed back to Earth. This is not too bad but it is 'old fashioned' to a modern reader. In 1951 there were no desktop computers, no laptops, smart-phones or tablets; that stuff could not possibly have been imagined, not even by Arthur C Clarke. Another anachronism is that Gibson and his agent communicate via radiogram. I suspect it was Clarke's extension of the idea of telegrams, except without wires to send the text along. Clarke had to use or extrapolate from what existed in 1950 and telegrams were still much in use then.

One nice touch to show us the lack of gravity was Gibson losing his rice-paper thin carbon paper when he starts working. If he leaves it lying around it floats up and gets sucked up against the exhaust air vent. The crew get around the ship by pulling themselves along cables strung along the walls of passages.

Like other stories from this decade no one knew what the long term effects of a lack of gravity would do regarding loss of bone density and muscle mass. Clarke does mention that no one seems very hungry because without gravity the muscles don't work so hard and therefore the body doesn't need as many calories. Is this right or is it no more than a supposition? His contemporary authors often used 'drugs' to offset the nausea they believed was caused by the lack of gravity. No one had actually been in space in 1950 but the general consensus was that everything would float around inside the ship. Any side effects were all speculative. Clarke chose not to have any deleterious side effects because his stories were always optimistic. Others who tended to be pessimistic chose awful side effects to inflict on their hapless travellers.

Clarke mentions in passing that the ship's library contained 'quarter of a million books and thousands of orchestral works (no mention of popular music of any kind) all recorded in electronic patterns awaiting orders to bring it to life.' There is no mention of how those books might be read once they have been brought to life but the crew take turns in selecting which orchestral works they want to hear. As far as I know this is possibly the first mention in Science Fiction of what we now think of as digital storage and eBooks. But Clarke probably wasn't the only one to think of such things; other writers may well have extrapolated similar concepts from what was known science at that time, although I haven't come across them.

He describes the passenger ship *Ares* as being like two doughnuts connected by a long passage, looking like a giant dumbbell, a very similar design to the one he used a decade or so later in his book 2001. However in this early story he does not have the crew's quarters rotating as he did in the ship of 2001 (beautifully shown in the film by Stanley Kubrick in 1968).

He also manages to get a spacewalk into the story, but not by having asteroids bombard the ship causing damage to be fixed, or by having to fix a broken antenna; he does it with a crew member having to go outside to re-align the antennae to more directly contact a faster rocket fired up to chase them. This rocket carries a developing vaccine to a disease, that they call *Martian Fever,* affecting the colonists; the result of a flu or similar virus taken by the colonists to Mars where it mutated and is running rampant. The rocket was too far off course and the ship's radio signals don't travel far enough to make the rocket notice them and adjust its course. By focussing a direct beam at it with the antennae they will be able to correct the course and affect a rendezvous. This gives Clarke the opportunity to have Gibson go outside to witness this activity and of course he can see and describe the ship.

Clarke also becomes almost elegiac in describing what Gibson sees and feels;—*a pale band of light welding the two hemispheres of the sky together, the whole rim of the Milky Way was visible. Gibson could see quite clearly the rents and tears along its edge, where entire continents of stars seemed to break away and go voyaging alone into the abyss. The black chasm of the Coal Sack gaped like a tunnel drilled through the stars into another universe.*

And turning towards Andromeda, — *a ghostly lens of light. He could cover it with his thumbnail, yet it was a whole galaxy as vast as the sky spanning ring of stars in whose heart he was floating now. That misty spectre was a million times further away than the stars — and they were a million times more distant than the planets. How pitiful were all of men's voyaging and adventures when seen against this background!*

And to bring Gibson back into perspective he spots something floating which he is at pains to work out what it is. Is it something gigantic but far away? Or is it something very close and thus seemingly large?

It turns out to be a piece of quarto writing paper, probably a draft of one of his articles floating just beyond his reach. The crewman accompanying him explains they threw out some garbage and it simply orbits the ship like tiny satellites or it floats along beside them since they are all going at the same speed and direction. Gibson wonders what is written on the paper but his tether prevents him from reaching it. He consoles himself that long after he is dead and gone that tiny piece of paper will still be carrying its message to the stars. This story is full of stuff like that which adds verisimilitude to the 'reality' depicted.

One thing that he and others got wrong was the belief that there was some kind of plant life on Mars that grew and died off with the seasons. It was the only way to explain the changes in colour in some areas observed over many centuries, so people thought. Clarke falls prey to this belief and basically hangs the whole second half of his novel on the idea of using those plants in a rather unique way. Clarke's plants are a lot more complex and larger than the primitive fungus and lichen used in Compton's 1966 novel ***Farewell Earth's Bliss.*** Both however also introduce animal life. (Where there are plants there must be animals like herbivores, right?) All of that is a result of our deep-seated desire to find life outside of that which exists on Earth. There has to be life on Mars; there used to be water, and where there was water there was always life… We don't want to be alone in the universe; that is a terrifying thought and so even today with writers well aware of the reality that is Mars they still manage to have their explorers find some remnants of life.

We now know that the colour changes, first seen by Schiaparelli and noted in his drawn maps of Mars in 1877, especially in the area of Syrtis Major are caused by weathering of basalt rock by the huge temperature range between night and day. It causes the rock to flake off. These flaky pieces, so small they are nothing but dust, turn a lighter colour as they weather, but when the season changes and strong winds blow, they lift this fine dusty covering and blow it away to expose the darker basalt underneath. That is what causes the colour change, not plant growth. But that was not known in 1950.

All of them got the sky wrong; Clarke's is deep blue like the high altitude atmosphere of Earth. Compton's is green; Pesek has mostly a yellow or dark brown sky because of the relentless dust blowing about. No one ever thought it could be pink!

Clarke's plot is very simple. Mars has a thriving colony. Ex-SF writer, Gibson, who wrote about Mars in earlier books, is sent on the maiden voyage of a passenger liner, *Ares*, to Mars and back to report on this momentous voyage, and while there for the three month turnaround before the return voyage, to report on what life is like on a frontier planet. The voyage is more exciting than Gibson expected and once he lands on Mars he manages to make a momentous discovery that changes his life. He decides he wants to stay on Mars because there is the promise of a much more exciting life than the one he left behind on Earth. He slowly becomes Martian in outlook rather than Terran. The focus of the story is on the changes within Gibson, and not on the technology that exists, and this is what makes Clark's story enduring while others have simply disappeared.

There is also a sub-plot which involves the young teenage cadet Jimmy who Gibson later suspects is his son from a liaison he had while at university in Cambridge. Jimmy also falls in love with the Chief Executive's daughter, the only other teenager on Mars. All the other colonists are adults. No babies have yet been born and only the Chief Executive had been able to bring his family with him when he came to Mars. The inevitability of the only two teenagers on the planet falling in love is a nice touch but is only in the background.

Once you get past the idea of plant life on Mars the rest of the story makes very good sense. The colony is independent. It gets unlimited oxygen by breaking down minerals to extract the oxygen trapped in them, as well as gaining export product (refined minerals) to send back to Earth. There isn't much said about food but presumably this is also manufactured hydroponically. Much is revealed as the Chief executive takes Gibson on tours around the colony to show him what is happening and how they do things. At first he is somewhat cold towards Gibson, but as Gibson writes highly supportive reports and sends them back to Earth he slowly becomes friendlier. The plants Clarke describes are very different from plants as we know them. The ones near the colony domes open during the day and follow the sun across the sky. At night they close up or fold up to conserve energy.

Gibson also finds a plant that resembles giant kelp the way Clarke describes it. It has small balloon like pods that fill with oxygen extracted from the soil, in much the same way that giant kelp has bulbs filled with air that help keep it floating.

On a trip to *Port Schiaparelli* the jet plane he is travelling in crashes because dust from a storm fills the motors and it can't fly. They crash land in a long canyon. They can't bounce a radio signal off the atmosphere like they could on Earth because Mars' atmosphere is too thin. They need a direct line of sight. They are too far away from base for that so Gibson and the young cadet Jimmy try to find a high spot to broadcast an SOS to Phobos to be rebroadcast back to Port Lowell.

Making their way through a dense patch of the kelp like plants Gibson makes a momentous discovery. He spots a small group of animals grazing on the plants. No one had discovered animal life on Mars before. The supposition is that these animals need the oxygen and so they eat the plants that produce it in the bulbs that are the equivalent of fruit. One of these younger animals attaches itself to Gibson and follows him while the other bigger ones ignore the humans and continue grazing.

They succeed in getting a message across to Base and they are promptly rescued. Gibson becomes a celebrity on both Earth and Mars and his photos of the little 'kangaroo like marsupial creature' are a sensation. Did Clarke decide to make it a marsupial because it has the word Mars in it? or did he consider Australian marsupials to be sufficiently stranger than other mammals so they could be identified as alien? He did spend considerable time in Australia diving on the Great Barrier Reef, about which he later wrote a book called ***The Coast of Coral***, but I think that was long after ***Sands of Mars*** was published.

It is at this point that Gibson subconsciously decides he wants to stay on Mars. He puts forward a plan to cultivate these oxygen producing plants to help increase the oxygen in the atmosphere and as a result of this suggestion he is taken to a secret facility where the scientists are actually attempting to do this. They had known about this plant before Gibson discovered them. But they have some other secret up their sleeve which they didn't want to tell Gibson about, something they didn't want Earth to find out about. Most of the local population also don't know about this scheme but it suddenly becomes clear why their ship was asked to dock on Deimos instead of Phobos. The scientists of Mars have decided to turn Phobos into a miniature sun. They want to warm the planet and promote rapid growth of the oxygen bearing plants so they can increase the oxygen content of Mars' atmosphere to make it possible for the colonists to move about unencumbered with breathing gear.

I had completely forgotten about this and it came as a huge surprise to discover that in 1950 Clarke was describing how to terraform Mars to make it better for humans. Was he the first to do this? At least if he wasn't the first, he at least came up with a logical way of doing it based on the premise that these plants actually existed. And what a grand plan it was: create another sun; a smaller sun that would orbit Mars and supply all the warmth and energy the far distant sun was not capable of doing. No wonder the colonists wanted to keep that secret from Earth.

He later used the same idea of converting a moon into a star, or a long lived thermo-nuclear reaction that might as well have been a star, only he did it on a much bigger scale in his second ***Odyssey*** Book where he has enigmatic aliens turn Jupiter —much better than a small moon— into a second sun to warm one of its moons that contains life in an ocean under a frozen crust.

The increased warmth Phobos would produce on Mars for a thousand years would promote rapid plant growth, with a subsequent rapid production of oxygen vented into the atmosphere. It would melt the ice caps and provide water and generally make the climate more benign. He suggests that in a mere 50 years humans may walk about unencumbered on the Martian surface.

Arthur C Clarke always believed that nothing was impossible if you developed the technology to do it. In this book despite a few anachronisms that he could not possibly have seen beyond, everything else is filled with grand ideas and an optimistic outlook for the future which generates a sense of wonder. It is what made his stories so readable for me as a teenager and as a young man. And as an old man (I finally have to admit to that) on re-reading his early books, I still find them as equally exciting and full of wonder as I did more than half a century ago.

Isaac Asimov was a friend and cheerful rival of Arthur C Clarke.

Each one claimed to be the best SF writer while stating that the other was the best nonfiction writer of scientific articles.

The truth is they were both good. In the nonfiction department Asimov was the most prolific with literally thousands of articles popularizing science collected into many books (Over 400) while Clark's articles tended to be more scientific rather than popular although he wrote both types.

Whose fiction was better?

That's a matter of personal taste. I liked them both.

The Martian Way by Isaac Asimov was first published in 1952 in Galaxy Magazine then again in 1955 by Doubleday and Company.

This novella is about Martian colonists scavenging the empty jettisoned fuel containers ejected from ships travelling between Earth and Mars which they reprocess on Phobos, then later mining for ice along the rings of Saturn.

The only thing produced on Mars is metal from mining ores which they sell and ship to Earth, but this isn't enough to cover the cost of the water used during this process. A lot of water in this story is also used as fuel for the rocket ships which kind of gives it a steam punk feel long before this subgenre existed. Steam powered rocket ships! An interesting concept and Asimov makes it quite plausible. This usage of water is the core around which the story revolves.

The Martian colony has obviously been established for several generations, but because Mars is such a bleak place everything the colonists need is ferried up from Earth and this includes water. Water is the fuel used by the spaceships that travel constantly between Earth and Mars, and finally the Earth government is threatening to stop supplying water, claiming they don't have an endless supply. If this happens the colony will have to be abandoned and the Martians will have to return to Earth. None of them want to do that.

A new scavenger tries to convince his older partner that 'the future of Mars isn't in the mines it is in Space' but at first his partner is reluctant to agree. Finally with the threat of the water supply being stopped, he convinces his fellow scavengers that they should go to the outer planets where there is an abundance of water especially in the Rings around Saturn.

Earthmen can't go out there, they can't stand being in space for extended periods of time, but the Martians can. All their lives they have been living in enclosed environments, so for them living in an enclosed environment like a space ship travelling to Saturn should be no different than living in dome on the surface of Mars. It's the Martian Way, he insists. They have to stop thinking like a Grounder, their word for Earth people, and start thinking like a Martian.

Finally an expedition is sent to Saturn where the scavengers select a several-miles long chunk of ice and they set up rocket engines at one end of it, sink their ships into holes especially melted to contain them, and collectively use the engines of all the ships to operate the newly created giant ice ship and fly it back to Mars. They arrive back after a year away and land the giant ice ship on the surface of Mars exactly as they would any regular space ship.

The story finishes on a high note with the Martians offering to sell water to the Earth if they think they don't have enough, because now Mars has an endless supply which they will continue to mine from the Rings of Saturn. That is the Martian Way, going out into space, exploring and developing new industries. There is even the suggestion that it will be the Martians who will build the first interstellar ship and not the Grounders of Earth.

Was this story a gentle rebuke to Arthur C Clarke whose very positive upbeat story had been published the year before? The two of them were often doing things like that.

Asimov's story appears to be more realistic than Clarke's in its view of how inhospitable Mars could be. But even Asimov's Mars seems benign when compared with ***Crucifixus Etiam***, Walter M Miller Jr's stunningly bleak view of the planet.

Crucifixus Etiam (1953) first appeared in the pulp magazine *Astonishing Science Fiction Stories*. It has been anthologised a few times since then.

This story paints a far grimmer picture of the struggle to live on Mars than does any other story from the 1950's.

For 80 years colonists have been working and mining the planet. When Manue Nanti arrives on Mars, lured by a contract that would pay him handsomely so he could save money that would set him up for life on his return to Peru, he doesn't expect the desolation or the terrible conditions with which he must contend.

He was contracted to work on the drilling rigs, and to do so his body must be modified with tubes extruding from his blood vessels to a device on his back that feeds oxygen directly into the blood stream. He doesn't have to use his lungs but is told he should try to breathe as much as possible so they don't atrophy. Determined not to succumb like the others he turns down the oxygen input at night to force himself to gasp and breathe, but he finds he can't sleep and has terrible nightmares, so he relents and increases the oxygen flow so he can sleep better. Eventually he finds himself breathing less and less, and just like the others his lungs become atrophied and useless.

He is told they are mining for tritium which has radioactive components and this would be exported to Earth, but he observes that nothing is ever exported and starts asking questions. He is fobbed off with meaningless answers.

When he discovers his lungs have deteriorated to the extent he will never be able to breathe normally again, the feeling of desolation, the helplessness of the workers to improve their situation or to prevent the slow deterioration of their bodies penetrates his psyche as he realises he has become as bad as they are, and suffers profound depression. In time he manages to pull himself together and keeps working. It's all he can do.

The drill rig finally penetrates deep enough to hit the frozen ice with tritium deposits and instead of bringing anything up the drilling rig is moved to a new site. A building is constructed over the drill site and something is lowered down into the depths. Once the second site reaches the depth of the tritium deposits work stops. Everyone is evacuated from their camp and from a distance they watch as engineers remotely detonate an atomic bomb deep underground. This melts the ice and causes a chain reaction that releases water vapour and greenhouse gasses blasting them up into the atmosphere.

Some of the workers stage a revolt against the harshness of their working conditions, but Manue knocks out the leader and the rest calm down. It is then they are told the real purpose of their work. They are beginning the terraforming Mars so humans will be able to live on the surface without the need for space suits, breather masks or modified bodies such as those of the workers, so they will be able to breathe the air on the surface naturally, so the planet will warm and be able to support life like the Earth does. This is the first site to be commissioned. Thousands more are going to be constructed to spew out greenhouse gasses for hundreds of years.

Unfortunately it won't happen soon enough for Manue and his companions. They will never see the benefit of what they are doing because it will take 800 years before surface pressure approaches something normal, for rain to fall forming rivers and lakes and for the ice caps to melt with enough water to create an ocean or two. They are doing it for future generations as yet unborn. Eventually humans will be able to live on Mars like they do on Earth. But not Manue; he finally reconciles himself to his new existence and accepts that Mars is now his home and he will have to make the best of it. It is a profoundly grim vision of a deadly alien planet, Mars, even though it finishes on a positive note.

It could have been even grimmer had the author known about the deadly radiation that bombards the surface, that the atmosphere is mainly carbon dioxide, and that Mars is so much colder than people in the 1950s considered. There is much more to this story than the brief summary above. There is enough in this short story to fill a novel length work.

It has been suggested that it is a religious story based on the concept that the great cathedrals in Europe took centuries to build, with families dedicated over generations to the construction of these magnificent buildings. Would it not be the same for Mars and those who undertake the terraforming of the planet so future generations could live freely on the surface?

This seems to be the earliest story I have seen about transforming humans so they can live and work on the surface of Mars. It predates Frederick Pohl's ***Man Plus*** by a couple of decades. Another story that suggests changing humans so they can live on Mars is Charles L Fontenay's ***Rebels of the Red planet*** (1961). There are no doubt others, but I haven't seen them as yet.

Crucifixus Etiam can be found in a collection published by Gollancz in 2015, (***Dark Benediction***) as one of its SF Masterworks series. It is also in a more recent anthology edited by Mike Ashley, ***Lost Mars – The Golden Age of the Red Planet,*** which also has some wonderful almost forgotten stories in this collection. Earlier on in 1980 it was published in an anthology called ***The Best of Walter M Miller Jr.*** by Pocket Books , New York, but this publication may be hard to find.

Omnilingual H Beam Piper (1957)

Omnilingual is unusual because stories involving archaeology in SF are rare, even more so when they are set on Mars.

A team of archaeologists are on Mars to examine the 50,000 year old ruins of an ancient city. They have been there for months and have had little success in discovering much. The city has been deserted, left abandoned and looted of almost everything useful. There are not even skeletons of those who once inhabited the city. Dust has covered or completely buried most of the city over 50,000 years.

A few books have been found of which one archaeologist in particular, Martha Dane, has been trying to decipher words and their meanings. She has figured out the alphabet used and decided on a pronunciation for her convenience in phonetically reading the words but has no idea what any word means.

Other members of the team deride her obsession with the language claiming that without some other ancient but known language which may be written alongside it, there is no way to translate or understand it.

Hittite is given as an earthy example of a language that couldn't be deciphered; along with ancient Egyptian which was only understood from ancient Greek references found on a *Bilingual Rosetta Stone* that had two ancient languages engraved alongside each other, allowing cross referencing with the hieroglyphs and subsequent understanding.

On Mars the people died out before Modern humans started writing their own languages, so what could be used as a bilingual? Deciphering the Martian language seemed to be impossible.

Breaking into another multi level old building they discover a mural which depicts a complete Martian history from ancient days through various stages of their history right up until the moment the city was abandoned. The image of some kind of war machine suggests they annihilated themselves in a massive conflict, but it doesn't explain the absence of bones and skeletons. But even with the mural and various words written as captions Martha can't discover the meanings of individual words. Captions can be interpreted in many different ways and may not explain what it is the picture depicts.

As they come close to the time the expedition is to be relieved by another group coming from Earth, Martha and her small team discover the building was a university and several floors down they find a library with millions of books, a fantastic find but again without a bilingual, a *Rosetta Stone* nothing in any of the books would be translatable.

The floor above the library turns out to be a chemistry or physics class room and on one of its walls is a series of illustrations with words accompanying each illustration. She looks at this and realises she has found her *Rosetta Stone.*

Now she can begin translating ancient Martian. The illustrations on the wall depict the atomic structure of elements which is clear to several of the scientists in the room. Each successive diagram is more complex than the one preceding. From this she works out the Martians used a decimal system of numbering and the word accompanying each illustration of an atomic structure is taken to be its name. At the end of the mural is a panel with 92 numbers and names listed.

That was it!

She has an epiphany and realises that the list is of the 92 elements known to science (In 1957). Starting with Hydrogen, then helium, lithium and on, finishing with Uranium. Each is numbered, (its position on the table) with a name (the Martian name for the element) followed by another number (its atomic weight). There were no transuranics, nothing beyond Uranium the heaviest element so they conclude atomic fission had not been discovered. What's more the archaeologist suspects they will find other tables in other departments, astronomical tables, chemical tables and so on, all of which will enable them to read the books collected in the library below.

The final conclusion of the story is that "*this is better than a bilingual. Physical Science expresses universal facts; necessarily it is a universal language. Prior to the Mars expedition archaeologists only had to contend with pre-scientific cultures.*"

And that's the last line in the story. It finishes abruptly leaving the impression something more should be there to conclude the story, but it isn't. Even so it's a delightful take on the theme of ancient aliens having been on Mars or evolved on Mars and as the planet died they too died out after millennia of struggling to survive ever worsening conditions.

Outpost Mars / Mars Child (1951 1952) by Cyril Judd

The husband and wife team of Cyril M Kornbluth and Judith Merril often collaborated on stories together, and this is their second Mars novel. It was first published as a serial in *Galaxy Science Fiction* in May, June, and July 1951, then later revised slightly and published by Dell Books in 1952. An English 4 square edition was published in 1966. It has been available from 2014 as a beautiful POD book from Armchair Fiction.

This is a story about survival and adaptation on Mars. Dr Tony Hellman is a leading figure in a colony that is idealistic and communal. They all work together and look out for each other. They are trying to modify the inedible Martian plants so humans (and earthly animals like goats) can eat them. They are also trying to modify earth plants so they will grow in the irradiated Martian soil, without much success. Cauliflower for example has so far become full of prussic acid and is inedible and poisonous, so there is still much work to be done.

As in other stories from the 1950s it is assumed that the temperature is warm enough for people to go about without special clothes (Even kids can run around barefoot but this isn't encouraged because the surface regolith is full of jagged stones and sharp crystals that can cut feet to shreds.) and that the atmosphere although very thin is for some people breathable. For most though an oxygen mask was essential until a co-enzyme, ***OxEn,*** that releases oxygen into the blood was discovered and made into tablet form. These tablets which must be taken every twenty-four hours are expensive and have to be imported from Earth.

It is mentioned a couple of times that there are no animal life forms on Mars, only plants, and this is important because some colonists persist in telling stories about '*Brownies*', a squat gnomelike being that hides in caves and is only seen sometimes at night. No one really believes those stories, because obviously there would be other forms of animal life that the *Brownies* could have evolved from, but there isn't anything animal anywhere.

The colony survives by producing radioactive phosphorous for cancer research on Earth. They simply extract it from the regolith which is radioactive all over the planet. They have first class laboratory facilities for refining it and strict protocols are maintained in its production. Other groups on Mars are mainly concerned with mining, extracting minerals and rare metals, but one group Brenner Pharmaceuticals extracts a drug from the local plant life which sells for enormous amounts on Earth. It is highly addictive. The conditions Brenner's workforce endures are below standard, almost makeshift, and leakage of the drug into the atmosphere causes all the workers to become addicted over time. They are then sent back to Earth and a new lot of workers are imported.

Tony is critical of these other organized groups as they only want to exploit Mars whereas his colony wants to become self sustaining and eventually independent of Earth. They are polluting the atmosphere and eventually it will become unbreathable like back on Earth. He doesn't want to see that happen. There are also hints that troubles on Earth are so bad it seems they will all blow themselves up in the not too distant future. (*This was written in1950 when the Cold War was in full swing with the threat of nuclear annihilation hanging over everyone's heads.*)

When a new batch of colonists and mine workers arrive, Dr Hellman and a small team go to Mars City to meet them. There is a confrontation with Hugo Brenner of Brenner Pharmaceuticals and not long after that Tony's colony is accused of stealing the drug Brenner produces, *Marcaine.* 100 kilograms has gone missing and it has been traced to Tony's Sun Lake Colony. At the same time a prostitute working at the mining company has been murdered, bashed to death, and Tony is asked to investigate. It was claimed she had been raped and bashed, but Tony finds she had a self inflicted abortion, after which she had been bashed and had died.

In the Sun Lake Colony one of the inhabitants has given birth to a baby, the first Martian born baby to survive. Some years earlier one had been born but suffocated because there were no oxygen masks small enough for it to use and it was too small to be given the *oxygen enzyme* tablet. This new baby is having trouble feeding and unless Tony can solve this small mystery it will die.

Struggling to solve the mystery of the prostitute's murder, and how to save the newborn baby, Tony also has to monitor the examination of their radioactive cargo in an attempt to find the missing 100 kilograms of *Mar-*

caine. If it can't be found the local authorities who are in league with Brenner Pharmaceuticals will shut down the colony for six months. They will miss sending their radioactive shipments to Earth and miss getting new supplies of essential items from the cargo rockets that visit Mars four times a year.

Meanwhile, the baby's mother is hallucinating; she sees *Brownies* and believes they want to steal her baby. Tony tries to convince her they are a figment of her imagination, but she is adamant, she has seen them looking in through her window. Somehow she has been affected by *Marcaine* which adds another problem to the colony.

A reporter who arrived on Mars with the other colonists and workers is staying at Sun Lake Colony and he is brutally bashed while out walking one night. He blames the colonists because they found out he was writing a negative story about them, which if published back on Earth would see the end of the colony.

Things come to a head while the reporter is lying injured in the hospital with Hugo Brenner and one of the colonists whose wife died. There is a confrontation and people are hurt, and the reporter finds the truth is not what he thought, so he retracts his story. It is also discovered that the *Brownies* are babies born on Mars who have become adapted to the Martian atmosphere and who grow in ways that make them appear to be gnomelike. They are also telepathic, presumably as a result of the irradiated surface of Mars. They need the *marcaine* to survive, and the newborn baby also has a genetic malfunction which enables it to survive on Mars, but it also needs *marcaine*. When the baby goes missing, kidnapped by *Brownies* according to the mother, the colonists follow a trail of footprints into the foothills and find the answer to who the *Brownies* are, and to what the future holds for the colony.

This is a complex and thrilling story which although mostly downbeat regarding conditions on Mars maintains a feeling of determination and positivity throughout. It is very different from Arthur C Clarke's ***Sands of Mars*** even though it was published about the same time.

It is also another one of the earliest novels that suggested transforming a human or that humans could transform to adapt to Mars, hinting at a natural occurrence rather than something mechanically engineered as we later saw in Frederick Pohl's ***Man Plus*** in 1976, or medically engineered as in Kevin J Anderson's ***Climbing Olympus,*** in 1994.

Definitely worth reading if you haven't already done so.

*(Checkout **armchairfiction.com** for this and other SF classics from the golden age).*

Police Your Planet (1956) by Lester del Rey

This short novel first appeared as a serial in 1953 as written by Eric van Lhin, one of the pseudonyms used by Lester del Rey. It could very well have been written by another author using an outline suggested by Lester del Rey, as this was a common practice in the *Pulp Fiction* era when there was such a huge output of novels and stories.

It was published as a book three years later, revised and republished in book form again in 1975, this time with the name Lester del Rey as author. Like many other early SF stories it is now available as a POD book. The cartoonish cover of the POD version suggests it is a novel for young readers, as many of the books written in the 1950s were, but the content belies this.

Bruce Gordon, ex-policeman, ex-reporter, ex-boxer, and general nuisance maker is sent to Mars as punishment for criminal activities on Earth by the Solar Security Service, a worldwide, solar system wide, almost secret security service. He is told to police the planet and clean it up or he will be sent to Mercury instead where things are much worse,

On Mars he finds Marsport the large domed city to be full of criminals, rival gangs fighting over territorial control, thieves, murderers, shakedown agents, crooked cops, political corruption and everything in between. There are supposedly secret security people there but he can't identify any of them. Left to his own devices he goes about winning some money by playing shifty card games, is attacked and almost beaten up, and eventually he decides to survive he needs to be in the local police where with each patrol shaking down certain areas for protection he may make enough money to get back to Earth.

As the story progresses he becomes more involved in the endemic corruption of the city, trying to walk a fine line between trying to do some good, while at the same time having to appear to be as corrupt as all the others. Somewhere it is mentioned that *it takes 8 or 9 good honest people to support one criminal.* There are an awful lot of criminals in this city so there must be many more honest hard working people as well, or there would be no-one to shake down and extort. Not much is seen of these people since the focus of the story is on the corruption of the police and how they deal with gangster elements. The feeling is reminiscent of noir detective fiction or frontier western stories where a lone 'good' guy takes out all the 'bad' guys to save ordinary citizens.

The domed city that is Marsport has many areas outside the dome which are absolute slums where no one in their right mind would go after dark. Outside everyone has to wear an atmosphere suit and helmet, since the air is too thin to breathe properly, although there are some who have been conditioned on Earth (by living at heights above 40,000 feet) to manage the atmosphere. Each building outside the domed city has its own airlock.

The initial impression is that Marsport is where all the people live and work but this is not so. Further in we find there are small communities and farms well away from Marsport, and these are serviced by a monorail system that allows transport of goods produced to be sent to the city for sale and trading. Space ships come and go regularly just like planes landing at an airport.

There is no mention of how long it takes a ship to come from Earth, but the implication is it isn't very long. Like in ***Outpost Mars*** by Cyril Judd, it takes about twelve days of travel. Philip K Dick also has his people travel to Mars in ***Martian Time Slip*** in only a few days, so most authors in the 1950s never considered in general the real length of time it would take to go to Mars. This was pushed aside with the assumption it would be as common an event as people travelling by plane from one city to another within the US or from one country to another.

Spaceports were generally some place a ship could land not far from a settlement, or as with E C Tubb they were reminiscent of Third World Country International Airports, moribund, run down but functional. Arthur C Clarke was perhaps the only one in the early 1950s who actually had his characters take considerable time to get to Mars and thus had a good third of the story taken up with the journey out.

Things go from bad to worse within a very short time and Bruce Gordon finds himself in the thick of it. He discovers other members of the Solar Security who have remained inactive since arriving and one who even became extremely corrupt and is a leading officer in the local police. As the rigged elections approach, with gangs running the streets, violence erupts, and the city itself is threatened. Gordon finds it harder to do any good and in the end helps create a small revolution that threatens to destroy Marsport by sabotaging the dome.

In a trip outside the city with one of the worst corrupt cops to collect automatic guns smuggled in by a small spaceship, he discovers that third generation children have no trouble breathing the Martian atmosphere. Second generation can also manage for a short while before having to supplement their breathing with a face mask.

He sees the future lies in not relying on Earth, but by adapting to Mars. Other contemporary authors implied the same concept: the future of life on Mars relies on being able to adapt to the harsh conditions on the planet rather than trying to maintain an earth like environment.

Of course this was when it was thought Mars had an atmosphere similar in content to our own only with much less surface pressure. No one knew then it had no oxygen in it being mostly carbon-dioxide, and thus totally unbreathable. Nor did anyone realize how cold the surface would be, colder than Antarctica even in the summer. There would be no running around barefoot or sweating in the middle of the day working outside. There could never be any adapting naturally over a couple of generations to Martian conditions. But that didn't bother the pulp writers of the 1950s because they didn't know. Mars was just a frontier, like the Wild West, or the deserts of Africa, or if attempting a touch of realism like the cold deserts of the Gobi or the Atacama.

On return to Marsport Gordon helps the rebellion destroy the dome in the belief that it is wrong to try and remain earth like. In the process most of the worst criminals and the corrupt officials are killed. Solar Security forces finally arrive to re-organize what's left and Bruce Gordon and his new wife are about to be dispatched to the Mercury where the mining conglomerates need to be cleaned up.

This story is easy to read, and a lot of fun.

I am delighted that many of the early '*classics of SF*' are available now as print on demand books. Modern readers have no idea of what terrific stuff existed before they were born, and without all that early SF none of the modern stuff would be anywhere near as good as some of it is.

Another early novel available again is **Rebels of the Red Planet** (1961) by Charles L Fontenay. The author died in 2007.

He only wrote a few novels during the 1950s and 60s and this was one of them.

The mysterious return of Dark Kensington, thought to have died 25 years earlier, signals a renewed attempt by rebels to attack the tyrannical governing powers of Mars. The rebels want Mars to be free of importing food and other necessities from Earth. Marscorp, the space ship transport company which controls the Martian settlers' government, won't allow the settlers to become independent because they will lose all the profits they make by controlling the space transport.

Mars has a great number of domed habitats and a large human population. The native Martians are grotesque by human standards, but they are able to extract oxygen from the regolith, to store it in huge humps, to use as they need it to metabolize body functions.

There are ongoing experiments to genetically alter embryos so the resultant children are capable of living on the surface, but most of these experiments over the last quarter of a century have failed because of the crudity of mechanically altering gene structure.

However the Martians are able to telekinetically alter embryos with much greater and refined delicacy so the children born are able to utilise sunlight as an energy source and no longer need to breathe, eat, or feel the cold when they are on the surface without a mars-suit.

Only two children were so altered by the Martians, Dark Kensington and Maya Cara who was born on Mars, and spent her early childhood with native Martians, but who later went to earth and stayed there until she returned to Mars as a government agent.

Cara is tasked to arrest Dark Kensington who is supposed to be the leader of the rebels, but when she does, she discovers her true nature and falls in love with him. She decides to help the rebellion free the settlers from Marscorp control. Presumably their children will be born inheriting the ability given to Dark and Maya, and all future children born on Mars in the new rebel stronghold will also be altered by the Martians so they can live freely on the surface, eventually passing on this ability to future children they have.

This short pulp novel is notable only because it foreshadows the concept of altering humans to live in the alien environment of Mars rather than trying to terraform Mars to suit humans, ideas later brought into prominence by Frederick Pohl with his mechanical alteration of a human into a cyborg capable of living on Mars, and Kevin J Anderson with his medically and genetically altered humans sent to Mars.

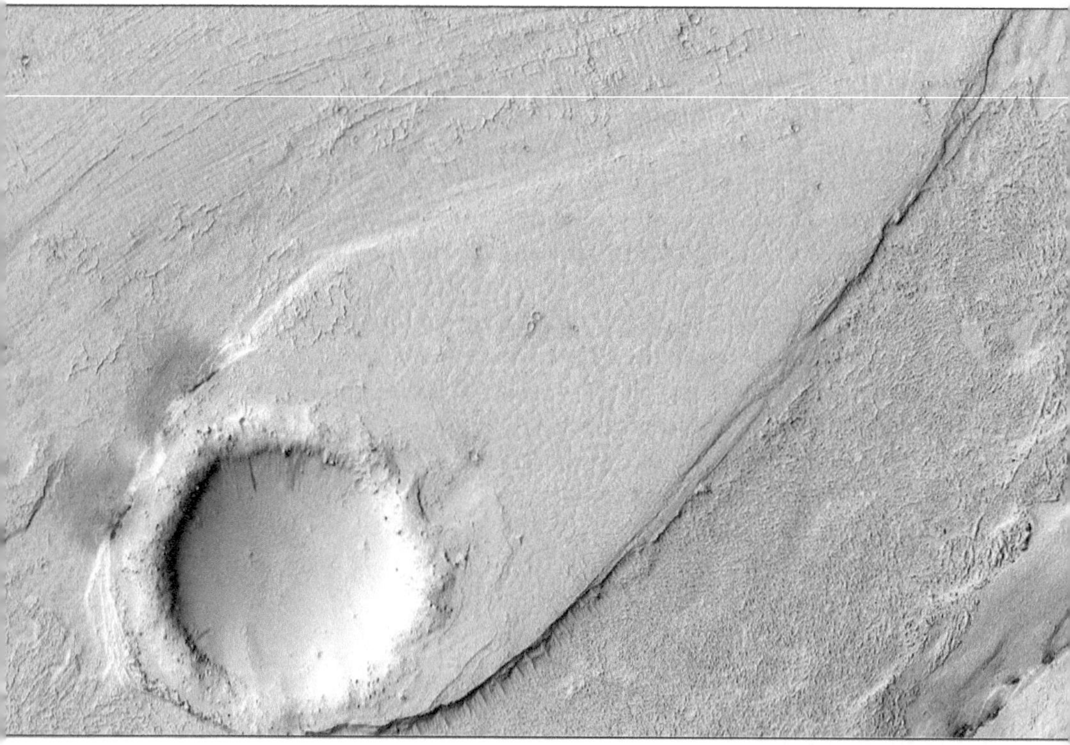

A streamlined crater in Lethe Vallis thought to have been caused by a catastrophic flood leaving a tear shaped island in the lee of the crater.

Chapter Four

The Golden Age continues
Mars in the early future Solar System of E C Tubb

Edwin Charles Tubb (E C Tubb 1919 - 2010) was a prolific writer who wrote over 130 SF novels as well as Detective, Mystery and Western novels under various names, along with hundreds of short stories and novellas for the major pulp magazines. He is better known for his Dumarest Saga which spanned 33 novels set in a galaxy of millions of inhabited planets where Dumarest searched for Earth which everyone believed was nothing more than a myth. Unfortunately he died before he could have Dumarest rediscover Earth.

He published his first story in 1951 (***No Short Cuts***) and continued producing material at a prodigious rate using many house names and pseudonyms as well as his own for two decades. Early in his career he wrote several Mars novels: ***Atom War on Mars*** (1952), ***I fight for Mars*** (1953), ***Journey to Mars*** (1954) before combining a series of early shorter works into the fix-up novel ***Alien Dust*** (1955).

For the most part his stories are space opera set in an undated future. The solar system in his early space operas adheres to the commonly held beliefs extant during the 1930s, 40s and early 50s extrapolated into an undefined future time where the whole solar system is pretty much occupied, with private company mining groups living in the asteroid belt and on various moons of Jupiter and Saturn, long established colonies on Mars and Venus and even mining activities on Mercury where the special metals used in space ship rocket tubes were obtained. Big business and semi totalitarian government are often at loggerheads, and this gives Tubb endless opportunities for murder mysteries, spy thrillers and all kinds of adventure stories set in his inhabited solar system. He didn't attempt to depict a future history in the way Heinlein or Asimov did, but because his solar system is inhabited, mention of Mars, along with Venus, often occurs. Characters from those places appear in many stories, and inevitably with similar backgrounds, the impression of an early future history is created. In this universe his space ships are atomic powered plasma rockets, and apart from those modern clean ships run by huge conglomerates, or by the government, independent trading ships tended to be rundown, badly maintained equivalents of tramp steamers. His spaceports on the various planets resemble third world airports, and many of his characters are from the bottom end of society struggling to make ends meet. In a typical description of one of his independent trading ships, it would stink of stale air, rotting food and burnt grease, human sweat and animal waste with bulkheads and floors stained with dirt. The outer hulls of such ships would be scarred and patched.

He adhered to the ideas prevalent during the first half of the 20th century that Mars was a dry desert planet with a thin but breathable atmosphere although he exaggerated the extremes of temperature during the day and night, making it cold enough at night for someone left out to freeze, and hot enough during the day for a worker in the open to sweat. It was known by scientists in 1950 that Mars' atmosphere was unbreathable being mostly carbon dioxide, and too thin for anyone to venture out without a space suit, but Tubb, like many of his contemporaries, ignored this. That it was also much colder than expected was also ignored along with the constant bombardment of radiation from space because there was no magnetic field to deflect it.

Once Mariner 4 went to Mars the images it sent back dispelled all previous held beliefs regarding Mars and writers couldn't ignore this any longer. Tubb then moved his space operas out into a far future fully inhabited galaxy with his 33 book Dumarest saga.

Similarly Venus was believed to be a dense cloud covered tropical planet with a very wet environment of swamps and oceans filled with dangerous wildlife, and if there were any sentient beings living on Venus they inevitably were of reptilian descent. Tubb's Venusians were reptilian. We also lost Venus in the 1960s when it was confirmed firstly by the Russians and then again by the Americans to be more than 400 degrees centigrade on the surface with the dense cloud cover mostly of sulfuric acid. No more jungles and reptiles in swamps and oceans.

His base on Mercury was established in the Twilight zone between the perpetually hot side facing the sun and the dark frozen side facing outwards. He also had another small planetary body orbiting the sun between Mercury and the sun called Vulcan. This mysterious inner planetoid still exists in the minds of many people, but remains to be confirmed.

E C Tubb's planetary backgrounds always seemed convincing and were inserted into his action stories in such a way as to be accepted as realistic by the reader, who more often than not couldn't put the book down once the story had been started. You were compelled to keep reading right to the very end, the effect of a good entertaining writer.

E C Tubb always opened his stories with action in the middle of something dramatic. This action was maintained right through to the end of the story. His endings were always abrupt, often spectacular, finishing with positivity and hope for the future. It was a formula that made Tubb a popular author from the 1950s through to the 1980s when space opera and planetary adventure of this type started to lose popularity.

Alien Dust (1955)

The ***Alien Dust*** stories were published as a series in *New Worlds* magazine during 1952 and 1953 so they predate two, if not all his other Mars novels, which could explain why his depiction of Mars in this book is so different from his other novels where Mars features prominently. In this book Mars is a dangerous inhospitable place, not suitable for humans or any other life. This may actually be closer to the reality than we think with the latest information suggesting that the surface of Mars is toxic due to constant radiation bombardment from space. There is no magnetic field to protect the planet and the thin atmosphere does nothing to impede solar radiation.

Although it was published in 1955 as a book, compared to ***Sands of Mars***, T***he Martian Way*** and to Tubb's other Mars novels, ***Alien Dust*** seems dated. It uses the old idea of huge rockets taking off from Earth to travel to Mars where they land vertically using the rocket engines to slow them down until they touch the surface. Presumably these are chemical rockets in the traditional sense though there is no mention of exactly how they work. In the other Mars novels his rockets use atomic plasma engines, but similarly take off and land directly onto the surface of the planet.

Strangely enough Modern developments in rocket use have gone back to the old SF idea of vertical take-off and landing in order to reduce the wastage of engines and first stage components so they can be reused again, to make sending payloads into space more economical.

The rockets in this book also take off from Mars to return to Earth where they extrude wings and glide in to land at sea because Earth's air is too thick to land vertically (similar to the now redundant space shuttle). The problem with rockets in early SF was with their size and the concept of being a single stage rather than multiple stages. How big must these single stage rocket ships have been? How much fuel would they have had to carry to lift off with a dozen passengers and supplies for the trip out and additional supplies for the colonists, and still have reserve fuel for lift off from Mars to return? It would be impossible but no one thought that at the time.

Asimov's idea in ***The Martian Way*** was to carry the fuel as external additions to the rocket later to be jettisoned in space where they would be collected by the Martian scavengers and taken back to Mars for reprocessing, which seems more practical than making a rocket large enough to carry all the fuel for a trip to Mars and back.

Everyone knows NASA used external boosters to initiate shuttle lift off before jettisoning them as the shuttle entered orbit which meant the shuttle did not carry a lot of fuel, only what was required for final manoeuvring into orbital space. It glided back to Earth and landed like a plane. It makes you wonder just how many space scientists were inspired by the science fiction they read as young teenagers.

Writers before 1950 never thought of multi stage rockets as Werner Von Braun later advocated. They simply made their rockets bigger. Similarly the makers of early science fiction films about trips to Mars did exactly the same. ***Rocketship XM*** in which the rocket took off from the Earth's surface and ***The Conquest of Space*** where the rocket was built in orbit but landed vertically on arrival at Mars, both used gigantic rockets with huge interiors resembling the inside of a battleship or a submarine. Presumably they carried all the fuel needed for the trip to Mars and back.

E C Tubb skims over this with a brief mention of how exact weight requirements are needed for the trip, and that when an idealistic youth (the nephew of the ship's captain) stows away he has to be ejected into space so they won't waste any more of their precious fuel which is needed for Mars landing and take-off later to return to Earth.

Alien Dust, although read as a novel, is a collection of short stories of varying length, with a five or ten year gap between each one, that delineates the establishment of a colony on Mars, one hundred miles south of the North polar ice cap. It begins in 1995 and the final story chapter is dated 2030. Characters overlap from one story to the next so there is a feeling of continuity. The colony is established in a deep chasm because the air pressure is just enough at the bottom of this chasm to allow them to breathe. Even so they usually wear a mask with a filter to prevent breathing in the fine radioactive dust whenever they are outside.

This idea of a higher atmospheric pressure deep down in the chasms that split the surface often pops up in stories and even in films as recent as the Spanish SF movie, ***Stranded***, made in 2001, which has three survivors finding enough air to breathe at the very bottom of the Valles Marineris Canyon. It seems logical because the deeper you go the higher the atmospheric pressure. This system of canyons on Mars is as deep as 8000 metres. No one ever mentions the un-breathability of Mars' atmosphere. It doesn't have any oxygen and is almost all carbon dioxide, so no matter what the pressure we still couldn't breathe it.

The dramatic opening of ***Alien Dust*** has one of three ships crash landing and exploding on arrival. This ship carried most of the food supplies for the colony, so from the outset they are in real trouble. One of the ships has to return to Earth to get more supplies while the other one is cannibalized for its atomic power plant which is needed to power the colony. They work hard to establish themselves and manage to grow yeast in vats after building a pipeline to the polar ice cap where they obtain water to pump to the colony. They all have trouble breathing the thin air and eventually all suffer from a debilitating lung disease like silicosis caused by the fine abrasive dust which no matter how careful they are gets into everything. After five years on Mars none of them want to (or can) return to Earth, the heavier gravity would kill them if they managed to survive the take-off from Mars and the landing on Earth.

Nothing grows in the alien dust of Mars, which is radioactive. The whole planet is dead. There is no life of any kind anywhere, not even bacteria. How the regolith became radioactive is left open, but there is a vague suggestion that Martian inhabitants hundreds of millions of years in the past waged an atomic war and destroyed themselves and over time the irradiated soil and dust slowly blew around the planet killing every form of life.

At this time no other author had radioactive Martian dust so either Tubb was prescient regarding this, or else he thought to make these stories different from other contemporary Martian stories. In his Martian novels which were written later than these Alien Dust stories there is no mention of radioactive dust, and Mars, in those stories is a much more benign place.

When several shiploads of women arrive the subsequent children born are okay, but no woman is able to have a second child because she is either sterile (from the radiation) or she dies in childbirth giving birth to a mutated or deformed foetus. Eventually the women and children are evacuated and the colony is about to be abandoned. Earth prefers to send ships to Venus (which in 1955 was still thought of as a tropical world with abundant possibilities for colonisation).

Somewhat melodramatically the Martians colonists use the threat of loading a space ship with radioactive dust to crash land it on Earth with the implied threat of causing cancer or sterility in the women of Earth as a means of ensuring the colony survives. Why they would want to survive there is beyond comprehension since all they can eat is yeast hydroponically grown while they all slowly die of lung cancer induced by the radioactive dust that permeates everything. However, although all the women returned to Earth from Mars die of cancer, the children evacuated with them are immune to the cancers produced by the radioactive dust and now grown up they want to return to Mars which for them is home, and so the book finishes on a positive note after being relentlessly pessimistic up to the last few pages.

No other novel set on Mars was ever as bleak as this one, other than perhaps Ludek Pesek's ***The Earth is Near*** which also has an extraordinarily harsh environment on Mars.

Since his other three Mars novels were written during the height of the Cold War between The United States of America (USA) and The Union of Soviet Socialist Republics (USSR), it was inevitable that the depiction of living in a totalitarian state and the fight for freedom against government (or dictatorial big business) control would be an underlying theme in his work. It doesn't distract from the adventures in these stories; it is simply a base to extrapolate an exciting adventure which is always about people rather than systems of government in worlds of the future.

There is a nostalgic feel to reading these stories set in a future universe that we now know could never exist but half a century ago often thought that it might. To read them today is just as enjoyable, as exciting as I remember it being back in the 1950s.

Atom War on Mars (1952)

Major John Benson, a rocketeer who commands a space ship in the Moon Fleet, is rudely awakened by security forces in the middle of the night. Against his protests he is arrested and taken to security headquarters. He has no idea what he might have done to deserve this rough treatment. He is forcibly ushered into the presence of the Co-ordinator — the aged dictatorial ruler of the world — who informs Benson he is to pretend to be a dissident. He will be sent undercover into a jail where some known dissidents are plotting against the world Government. Benson's job is to ingratiate himself with the suspected leader of this group who is a mad scientist supposedly working for the government on a new weapon, The Co-ordinator wants to know what this weapon is. The so called mad scientist was the one who created the weapons that led to the Atom War which devastated Earth 50 years earlier and which led to the rise of the present dictatorial government.

Benson willingly agrees to become a spy. He, like everyone else, has been brainwashed to obey unquestioningly orders that are given to him, just as he expects order he gives to others to be obeyed. The whole society is stratified into classes with the security on top, followed by various levels of military forces, big business employees, and finally on the bottom, the general population who are treated more or less as slaves. Being a prisoner without status he finds it difficult to cope with those who regard him as despicable. He is immediately bullied by the guards escorting him to his cell. He maims one and disables another instinctively using his military training, before he is rendered unconscious by other guards and thrown into the cell.

Within 24 hours he and the other prisoners are shoved aboard a prison transfer 'copter and flown to a base buried under ice in the Arctic. He and the only prisoner he befriended are given to the mad scientist as assistants. The other prisoners are sent to a mining complex.

He realizes why he has been sent there when the mad scientist begins to think of him as his long lost son. Benson's resemblance to the scientist's son is the reason he was chosen by the Co-ordinator.

Ben Wharten, his co-prisoner is an idealist, a freedom fighter who wants to bring down the regime at any cost, and to do this he needs to go to Mars where after 50 years of isolation from Earth control (they were abandoned when the Atom War on Earth took place) they are an independent colony who want nothing to do with Earth. When he discovers the scientist wants to escape to Mars and has made a drive that can take them there in a few days rather than the months it takes normally using rocket drives he is determined more than ever to go there.

When Benson discovers the same fact he wants to escape so he can turn the invention over to the Co-ordinator and thus secure his promised reward to be reinstated as a world warden.

Wharten needs Benson to pilot the secret ship the scientist has them assemble in his laboratory. He had built this in pieces over several years which he has hidden in the chaotic piles of equipment in his laboratory. After they disable the cameras spying on them the security try to break down the door while they assemble the ship. They manage to escape by melting the ice above the laboratory and fly up and away.

They fly to Peru where excess equipment is discarded in a deep valley between mountains, but the ship is only big enough for two. Benson decides he has to kill Wharten so he can take the ship with its inertia-less drive to the Co-ordinator, when Wharten gets the better of him knocking him unconscious. He wakes up and the ship is gone. He now realises Wharten was more than he seemed. Using his military skills he manages to contact security forces using Morse code and when they come they are under orders to kill him. He convinces them to contact the Co-ordinator who is furious at the turn of events. He tells the Co-ordinator he can still salvage the mission.

With the help of the two security people who came for him in a high altitude helicopter he builds an inertia-less drive using the discarded equipment thrown down into the deep valley.

Leaving the security men on the mountain top to be rescued he heads up into the stratosphere and out into space. (He doesn't know it but the two men he left to be rescued are summarily executed instead so they can't reveal what they may have seen.)

Benson flies past the Moon and sees a fleet of 30 rocket ships heading towards Mars. He estimates it will take three weeks for them to get there. He shoots past them at a speed that makes him invisible to them and within two days he arrives at Mars where his drive suddenly looses power as he attempts to land. He crashes and is rescued and taken to hospital. His nurse turns out to be the niece of the scientist, who no longer appears mad, (that had been an act which allowed him to invent his drive and build his secret space ship). She falls in love with Benson and he realises he feels the same towards her. Slowly, as he sees how free the Martian colonists are compared to people on Earth, he is convinced that they must stop the fleet on its way from the Moon from reaching Mars.

They set out to build a fleet of their own using the inertia-less drive but before they can complete more than 5 ships they come under attack from the Earth fleet still travelling towards them. Long range missiles with atom bomb heads are fired at them. The base on Phobos is destroyed with a massive explosion, and soon after atom explosions begin on Mars' surface. They miss most of the inhabited areas but it is obvious the Co-ordinator wants to utterly destroy Mars. Benson now realises that the Co-ordinator is totally mad.

With the 5 ships they have managed to complete they take off to do battle with the incoming space fleet. After a furious and spectacular battle in which they lose 4 of the 5 little ships while destroying more than half of the incoming fleet, what's left is disabled enough to be useless.

Back on Mars Wharten informs Benson that there are more than 300 warships on the moon probably making ready to take off for Mars right now. How is this possible? Benson wonders.

Wharten tells him they were built with slave labour. The workers had to build something so the Co-ordinator had them build space battle ships for his own protection.

As soon as they can build some more inertia-less drive ships they load them with atom type bombs and head for the Moon where they destroy the massive fleet that was being readied to take off for Mars. Their bombs also destroy the weapons stockpiled on the Moon leaving the Co-ordinator with nothing.

The story ends with the destruction of this war fleet and Benson and the others return to Mars where he knows someone special is waiting for his return.

I fight for Mars (1953) E C Tubb writing as Charles Grey.

Reading this reminded me of B grade movies from the 1950s where a long preamble to set up the story is followed by various degrees of action to challenge the protagonist with an abrupt conclusion in the last few minutes.

This short novel follows the same structure. It opens with the lead character, John Delmar, and a sidekick, Slade, both in prison and about to be released. Slade is in prison for stealing while John is there because he attacked an officer of the Spaceline Company he worked for as a pilot. They wouldn't let him access his back pay in order to help his wife who was sick in hospital. He got angry and broke the clerk's jaw. He was sent to prison for two years during which time his wife died.

Slade suggests that he might have a job for John when they get out, but John being a space ship pilot thinks he will have no trouble finding work and ignores his cell mate.

Outside it is a different story. The streets are full of beggars who steal whatever they can in order to live. The whole city is part of a police state that controls everyone and no one wants to hire an ex prisoner. The story follows John as he tries to find out what happened to his wife, and as his money runs out quickly after a couple of days he finds getting a job is impossible. He joins a long queue of people wanting work at a factory, any kind of work, but they only want one. John is the one chosen because he stands out from the others by being less scrawny and reasonably healthy.

The job turns out to be collecting dead bodies — those who die in the streets overnight or who are killed by the fights and violence that exists amongst the jobless and homeless — which are taken back to the factory. During the night they come across the police chasing a vagrant who turns out to be his prison cell mate Slade. They hide him in the truck with the other bodies. When the police check the vehicle they don't recognize the one they are chasing. Told to move on they return to the factory and Slade reminds John that there is a job for him if he wants it. He then disappears. John wonders what they do with the bodies since there is a quota they need to fill every night, and when he finds out that they are turned into fertilizer for the regeneration of areas devastated after a brief atomic war he is disgusted and leaves.

Unable to find any work at all he goes looking for Slade at a remote tavern and discovers the people there want a space pilot to fly a ship they have built themselves (in their backyard). He is told they are transporting refugees who want to go to Mars. Only the big companies fly ships regularly to Mars and they control the mining and other activities. They also control who goes there and do not want more than what they allow. Not only that the big companies control the police and have replaced all previous forms of government that existed prior to the atomic war.

A colony had been set up on Mars for exploration and scientific work only to be left to its own devices when the atomic war on Earth devastated the planet. The colony had been established with people of both genders and once communication with Earth was cut it became self-sufficient. After twenty years of abandonment the colony is again under control of the Spaceline companies. The colonists want to expand but a terrible menace on the planet, an insect like creature with 12 legs swarms across the surface killing any humans and destroying any settlements they can find. These things are over a metre in length, jet black and swarm like soldier ants tearing everything in their path to shreds and instantly devouring it... and that also means humans. The colonists constantly battle these monsters and no matter how many they kill there are always more replacements. It is a losing battle.

The police try to stop the homemade ship from taking off but fail and John with Slade and one other person head off to Mars. On this flight John discovers there are no colonists on board; the ship is loaded with contraband weapons being transported to the colonists on Mars so they can fight the monstrous Lobants, the antlike monsters bent on destroying the human invaders.

The story is fast paced and relentless. The reader hardly has time to think about what kind of ecology these giant killer antlike creatures could have evolved in. Mars is pictured as being all deserts; hot during the day and below freezing at night (just as it is in any desert here on Earth). The air is thin but the light gravity compensates for that. There is water deep underground and the colony has been established where they can access this water. The colony is controlled by big businesses on Earth which are only interested in the minerals they can get from Mars. They support the colony but not to the extent that they will allow it to expand. However their control is tenuous and the colonists are basically independent. They want more people, more weapons, so they can fight off the Lobants.

John finds the ship is difficult to control and unstable as it enters Mars' atmosphere. The ship crashes on arrival. The colonists come in an armed convoy to rescue the occupants of the crashed ship and to collect the weapons they need to fight the Lobants. They are attacked on the way back to the colony base and in the fight John is severely injured. He wakes up in the hospital ward and falls in love with his nurse who resembles his late wife.

Back on his feet John discovers the monstrous Lobants are all exactly the same size, weight, and completely sexless. He suspects that they are robots, but made of flesh, and bone and gristle rather than metal. Flesh robots can self-repair if needed, metal ones can't.

John and Slade set off to find the source of the robots but the glider they use crashes near a deep crater from which the Lobants are emerging. They come out on the side facing the colony. Fortunately the glider had crashed on the blind side.

John decides to go into the crater to see where and how these creatures are being manufactured while Slade stays with the glider to create a diversion for John.

Deep inside the crater John discovers a huge alien brain-like thing, (like a giant queen ant) that is constantly giving birth to new Lobants. The alien brain discovers him telepathically and tries to stop him from destroying it. At first John was going to burn it with his blaster, but had second thoughts about destroying something truly alien. Imagine what they could learn from it! But it quickly becomes obvious that after billions of years confined on Mars, with the constant radiation that bombards it slowly mutating cells in the brain, it has become insane. Suddenly while his mind was distracted he is attacked by the Lobants. Finally he manages to blast the alien brain with his heat gun and all the Lobants stop dead in their tracks. They had all been controlled by the brain.

Finally John, again badly injured, slowly makes his way back up out of the crater towards the surface, where Mars will now be safe for colonisation to succeed, and he will stay there with the woman he now loves.

This is a fast moving story that captures a reader and doesn't let go until the last word is read. E C Tubb was a master at writing fast paced exciting stories that were almost pure adrenaline for readers, and being probably no much more than 50,000 words it is a story that can be read at one sitting.

Journey to Mars (1953) (Published with the pseudonym of John Richards)

Although not about Mars, the idea of getting to Mars permeates the whole story which begins with action, a bar-room fight, and never lets up momentum until the very last page.

Verrill is a bouncer in a bar he owns on Venus. In the process of stopping an altercation between two groups of rival company spacemen a massive brawl ensues which sees his bar burnt to the ground and several members of the company spacers killed. They blame him even though they started the brawl, and want revenge.

Just before the brawl Verrill was told by a customer that a huge spaceship was being built on Mars in preparation for 'the big jump' to another star system. They are just waiting for a crew to be assembled before taking off, but no one seems very interested. It is a one way trip. Most of the exploratory ships sent earlier never came back, which makes it hard to get a crew for this much bigger ship.

Since there is nothing left for him on Venus Verrill decides he needs to go to Mars because he wants to be on the crew of that ship.

Unfortunately no ships are leaving Venus for Mars. He can't use a company ship because company men are looking for him so he must use an independent trading ship, and most of these are poorly maintained junk cargo ships that don't take passengers. He needs to sign on as a crewman. The first ship leaving, almost immediately, is bound for Mercury, so he asks the captain if he can sign on. The captain says if he can convince the teng-weed drug addicted astrogator to let him have the job it is his. Verrill goes to the astrogator and knocks him out. He is hired for the job and they leave immediately.

On the way to Mercury things go wrong and a mutiny is attempted. The previous astrogator was involved with the rest of the crew in smuggling Venusian teng-weed which they were going to sell after taking control of the ship and going out to the asteroid belt. Verrill coming on board upset their plans. Verrill, an ex-space-fleet rocketeer prevents the mutiny and kills the would-be drug smugglers. They are ejected into space. Verrill doesn't escape injury being burnt by a blaster shot. He uses a spray on artificial plastic skin which also helps promote healing and contains anaesthetic to deaden the pain.

(This is a common approach to healing burns now, even real artificial skin grown from the victims own cells is used today, but in 1953 this idea was certainly futuristic.)

The ship, using suspect fuel bought on the cheap has gained too much speed and will overshoot the orbit of Mercury to head directly for the sun. They can't escape the sun's gravity so the only alternative is to increase their speed and create a parabolic orbit around the sun like a comet makes. They come as close as 20 million miles before their speed throws them out and away from the sun. Letting the sun's gravity drag them back, in effect slowing them down, they lose enough speed to make it into Mercury's orbit and they land. They report the smuggling attempt, and are allowed entry to the base. The whole cargo is confiscated and the ship's captain goes looking for another cargo to take him off planet outbound.

Someone recognizes Verrill and an attempt is made on his life. Again he escapes and returns to the cargo ship he came in on. He can't stay on Mercury. The captain is glad he came back because he needs an astrogator who can calculate orbits which allows the ship to be properly piloted. "*We're going to Mars*" he tells him, and Verrill is more than happy to join the crew again. Calculating a trajectory that will get them to Mars in a mere four weeks they have trouble at the end of the initial burn to build up speed with the rocket exhaust tubes overheating. It seems the unreliable fuel has damaged the linings. If the tubes overheat they can crack and a blast-back occurs which will cripple, or worse, destroy the ship completely. Since they must reverse the ship and accelerate to slow down speed to orbit Mars before landing they have to find a way of keeping the tubes cool enough while firing so this won't happen. Initially they try short bursts but each time the tubes get hotter than before. Finally they spray liquid air onto the tubes as they are firing which works for a while. They use Mars thin atmosphere to aero-brake and slow the ship, then Verrill flips the ship to a vertical position and uses the blast tubes to lower them down to the surface. Unfortunately the tubes crack and a blowback destroys the lower half of the ship and it crashes. It kills the engineer who was nursing the drive tubes. But the captain, the ship's cook and Verrill survive because the lower gravity of Mars makes the landing and crashing less destructive.

They manage to get out of the ship before the entire thing blows up.

But they are on Mars.

They start walking in the direction they think the settlement and the space port is because they are uncertain they will be rescued. Their ship blew up, which must have been seen from the settlement. No one would expect survivors so it is unlikely a recue party would be sent.

Mars is a dry desert that sucks the moisture out of them. Nothing lives there; the planet is dead, but the atmosphere is just thick enough to be breathable so they don't need to wear spacesuits — a common idea in the 1950s. With night falling they fear freezing to death so they keep walking until they are exhausted. Finally they dig a hole in the sand and huddle together, covering themselves with the fine sand to keep warm. As dawn approaches they hear a ship coming in and suddenly in the distance they see the lights of the spaceport brighten to guide the ship so they know which direction to travel.

Arriving at the base they are offered free meals and accommodation for three days, quite unlike anywhere else in the solar system where everything must be paid for in advance.

They discover the giant ship is ready to make the long jump to another star system but hasn't done so because there is no crew willing to go. They immediately offer themselves as crew and are accepted.

Verrill also discovers the beautiful dancer who worked at his bar on Venus is here, waiting for him because he told her he was going to Mars. She has signed on for the Long Jump and so Verrill is ecstatic. They will make a new life together somewhere out there in a new star system.

During the story we also discover that Verrill had been to Alpha Centauri with his brother in one of the five exploratory flights. Two ships never came back, two crashed into the sun because they couldn't slow down and one crashed on Mars. Verrill had been on that one, but he didn't want anyone to know what they had discovered in that far star system or what had happened to his brother, because greedy company people would want to loot the new planets for profit. He destroyed the log, burnt the interior of his crashed ship to make people believe he had been killed on landing, before finding his way to Venus.

Tubb's description of the effects of freefall and why this happens was exactly what was later discovered by astronauts and cosmonauts in the shuttles and orbiting space stations in existence today. This was something no one knew about with any certainty in 1950, and Clarke, Asimov, Compton and Pesek, and all the other writers who wrote about going to Mars came up with different solutions to how to deal with the effects of weightlessness. Tubb's solution was to spin the ship so centrifugal force would create an artificial gravity as the ship coasted between planets. He was I suspect the first to use this idea. It wasn't until 30 years later that other authors used this same concept.

The Extra Man (1954 -58)

Because E C Tubb had several novels with his publisher at the same time there was a mix-up with the titles and this novel was published with the title that belonged to another story. It first appeared in 1954 as ***Enterprise 2115,*** a title that had nothing to do with the content, then was later retitled and republished in 1958 as ***The Mechanical Monarch.*** Finally it was given its real title in an omnibus edition in 2013; ***The Extra Man***.

The story opens with the first manned space ship about to take off for a flight to the Moon and Back. There was to be no landing. The ship would sling around the Moon and return.

Curt Rossylyn, the pilot and Comain, the scientist who designed, engineered and built the space ship grew up together and dreamed of conquering space. Now their dream was about to become a reality.

The ship is fully automated which makes the pilot redundant, but a pilot had to be there in case course corrections were needed. Something goes wrong as the ship nears the Moon. Curt attempts to fix it but the location of the problem is inaccessible, no matter how hard he tries. As the ship goes behind the Moon and radio contact is lost an explosion splits the ship. The pilot is killed; snap frozen as the air suddenly escapes. The ship with its frozen corpse drifts on into space and is never seen again, until 250 years later two asteroid miners who are Martian colonists come across it. They immediately lock onto it and tow it back to Mars for salvage.

On Mars the colony's doctors revive Curt, which suggests medical science has evolved enough to revive cryogenically frozen bodies more or less as a routine. They revive him because they see this as an opportunity to disrupt the Earth government's order that the colonists return to Earth where they can better be controlled. The frozen pilot is from before the time when everyone born was registered with the huge computer that controlled everyone and everything. This computer can predict what will happen since all knowledge attainable resides within it. But Curt Rosslyn is not in the system. He is an Extra Man. And as such the Martians hope he will destabilize the predictive ability of the computer (since he is unregistered and his actions cannot be predicted) enough to have the colonists sent back to

Mars where they can cause no trouble to Earth. They smuggle him back to Earth when they are forced to return. Each colonist re integrates their consciousness with the computer and are assigned work on Earth. Curt‘s brain is different and it doesn't register, so he remains outside of the system that controls everybody.

The all seeing computer is known as Comain, after the genius who had devised and constructed it.

Yes, the same Comain who built the space ship that was lost behind the Moon. His mind and personality had been uploaded (transplanted) into the computer giving it sentience. Since then the world has become a matriarchal society with tendencies towards fascism and where men are subservient to women. The matriarchs especially the oldest one who controls the computer want the Martians returned because they consider them, a mostly male society, to be disruptive, and with them back on Earth things would run a lot smoother.

The Martians were right; Curt does disrupt things, but not in the way they had hoped. Over the 250 years that he had been frozen and drifting in space the constant bombardment of radiation had altered his brain cells. He discovers he has developed a telekinetic ability, a power which he puts to good use disrupting the established way the computer works, as well as the matriarchal leader, her attendants and the power they wield backed up by the computer, Comain. Curt discovers the mind and personality inside the massive computer is his old friend Comain, and he awakens him, at which point the matriarchs become redundant. Comain. Together Curt and Comain decide they will change the world as well as fulfil their early dreams of going into interstellar space.

Although not really about Mars, the planet and its colonists are a pivotal part of this fast paced short novel, and it does tie into Tubb's early visions of the solar system and the beginnings of the exploration and colonisation of the planets. His ideas were modern for the time; reviving cryogenically frozen bodies, uploading of human minds into computers... I don't remember too many stories from the 1950s where such things were depicted in so much detail.

Tubb's stories were meant to be taken as realistic adventures. This places them in my second category, although there are a lot of fanciful elements and liberties taken with what was known at the time. They definitely read as science fiction adventures rather than science fantasy, but however a reader perceives them, they are primarily entertaining and enjoyable, and that's all that really matters. Incidentally they are all available as eBooks.

Mars, still popular with many authors in the early 1960s

Marooned on Mars by Lester del Rey (1962) was published in Hardcover by Holt, Reinhart and Winston Inc, then later by arrangement by the Paperback Library in 1967. It was originally published in 1952 using the pseudonym John C Winston, one of many used by del Rey which sometimes makes it difficult to know who actually wrote what. For example del Rey used Paul W Fairman to ghost write half a dozen novels for which he supplied outlines. Fairman also wrote novels using several pseudonyms as well as his own name.

The 1962 version was most likely revised before being published in hardcover and then paperback.

In 1952 what was still assumed about Mars was that there were canals, there were remnants of a dying civilization, there were inhabitants struggling to survive on a desiccated planet, the air was too thin to breathe but was essentially the same mixture as our own air, that daytime temperatures reached as high as 70 degrees Fahrenheit and went down at night to about 50 below, there was lots of desert and fine sand, many sandstorms, and the air was too dry to hold any moisture at all. This was most likely still the belief in 1962 when ***Marooned on Mars*** was published under del Rey's own name. (Incidentally a pseudonym but the one he used for most of his career.) As Arthur C Clarke said elsewhere, *they knew a lot about Mars, and all of it was wrong.*

With ***Marooned on Mars,*** Lester Del Rey has produced a fine planetary adventure aimed at young male readers.

Chuck Svensen, 17 years old and about to turn 18, lives on the Moon where the rocket ship Eros is being constructed. He was selected as the Moon's representative on the international crew to make the first journey to Mars. But because of a possible meteor swarm that could damage the ship in transit the departure date is brought forward. Unfortunately for Chuck it is now before his 18th birthday, and international laws prevent anyone under 18 from being on the crew. Another person an American Chinese citizen is chosen to replace him. To make matters worse Chuck is told he has to go to Earth where he is to further his studies with a special scholarship awarded to him in compensation.

Bitterly disappointed Chuck decides to stow away on the ship, and with help from a couple of his crewmates with whom he has been training for this trip to Mars, he sneaks aboard the Eros and hides.

He knows his presence on board means less food and water for the rest of the crew over the duration of the trip, but they want him there and are willing to ration their supplies. They don't report him as a stowaway until the Eros is beyond the point of return by which time he must stay. And of course the usual dramatic events occur during the voyage, they encounter a swarm of micro meteorites which damage the ship and punch holes through the hull. Repairs are quickly affected, but the gyroscopes which assist in balancing the ship on landing and take-off are damaged and can't be repaired. When they arrive at Mars and attempt a landing the Eros wobbles uncontrollably during the vertical descent and upon landing immediately tips over sideways. Sustaining some internal damage that now needs repairing.

(Like most SF writers up until the mid-1960s space ships were like giant scaled up V2 rockets and always took off and landed vertically, balancing on tail fins.) Though of this shape, Del Rey saw his rocket ship as being like a navy cruiser or large patrol boat in that it had bunk rooms for sleeping, a workshop with welding equipment and spare parts for repairs, a mess room and boundless storage space — unthinkable when you consider the weight of welding equipment using oxy-acetylene tanks, as well as other tools and equipment.

The first thing the crew discovers when they manage to exit the ship — their airlock was partly buried and they had to dig away the sand to get out — is strange plants, rows and rows stretching for miles in straight lines as far as they can see. The rows of plants have connecting tubes which carry water, presumably from the poles, so these are what when seen from space a long distance away, appear to be canals. I suspect Del Rey didn't believe there were really canals so this was his explanation of the lines astronomers could see on the surface with earthbound telescopes. Special plants to funnel water from the poles suggest the desperate measures an ancient civilization used to obtain the water they needed.

They next discover an ancient ruined city within a short walking distance.

Then at night equipment starts disappearing and the crew sees eyes peering out of the darkness at them. It is of course Chuck who discovers the creatures peering at them from the darkness are bipedal humanoids and follows them into the ancient city where they disappear through the floor into catacombs hidden beneath.

It turns out that the little Martians have been steeling equipment from the humans so they can regain some of their lost technology. How they could figure out its use is not explained. Chuck follows them down into the catacombs and is captured by them, but he escapes and while doing this helps one older creature to repair a machine. Because of this they let him go and then come with him to help the other humans to right the ship, to stand it up onto its tail fins ready for take-off.

Interestingly Del Rey doesn't give a date for his future setting, but it is obviously far enough ahead for a well-established presence on the moon which has the industrial capacity to build an interplanetary space ship and the few mentions of Earth suggest there is a planet wide single government much like the UN. He also has constant and regular travel between Earth and the Moon.

It's not a bad adventure story but it is dated now because of his idea of the rocket ship and the use of early ideas of Mars and what it would be like. It is still an enjoyable read though, so don't pass it up if you see it. Just remember when it was written and what was known at the time and you will enjoy it.

Both *Podkayne* and this one are dated. Which was the better of the two? I don't think this kind of comparison is valid. They were both enjoyable in their time and which of them a reader preferred would ultimately come down to personal taste.

Mars is my Destination, Frank Belknap Long (1962)

A simple story: Mars is in the process of being colonised. Large numbers of people dissatisfied with life on a polluted and massively crowded Earth with strict government control want to go and start a new life on a new planet. Only several thousand can migrate and literally millions want to go so those who have a ticket to be transported keep it secret or it could be stolen or they could be killed so someone else can take their place in the transport ships.

On Mars two large corporations are in a battle to control the colony. The larger one supplies the power through atomic generation of electricity, while the other has the monopoly on transporting fuel and other necessities. The larger one wants total control and is willing to do anything to gain such control. The colonising authority on Earth decides to send a special agent to Mars to sort out the situation. Before he is due to leave an assassination attempt was made the very day he was appointed, and when that failed a second attempt was made in which an innocent person (on a crowded train) was killed by mistake. On the way to Mars another attempt is made to destroy the ship and all the others on board to prevent the agent from arriving. This was also foiled.

Finally on disembarking, he is shot in the back with a poison dart and ends up in the hospital. In the hospital as he is recovering the boss of the larger corporation tries to interview him. Knowing that if he answers anything the other man will kill him once he has told him what he wants to know, he instead attacks the man and escapes from the hospital. This man's private police forces are ordered to shoot him on sight. Meanwhile the same ruthless leader is having fuel storage supplies sabotaged, and doesn't care that the resultant small atomic explosions will kill thousands of colonists. Finally with the help of a colonist the agent manages to stop any more atomic explosions by sending the latest bomb into orbit where it explodes harmlessly in space. Finally revealing his status as a special agent he commandeers some assistance and eventually confronts the power corporation leader, and prevents any further massacres and gets the proof that this man and his corporation were behind the sabotage and assassination attempts. The story is resolved in favour of the colonists who don't want to be controlled by either corporation.

In early part of his career Frank Belknap Long wrote many horror stories and novels before switching to science fiction action in the 1950s.

Mars is my Destination is probably his major SF novel and it has the feel of a noir detective action thriller, typical of detective stories in the 50s and 60s. Most of it is entertaining and certainly well written. What probably spoils it a bit for today's readers is there are too many clichés —which were no doubt new back in 1960 but have become so overused since then— that they distract the reader, interrupting the flow of the story. Sometimes he digresses with his analogies as well and they become a little bloated, quite acceptable back when it was written as a method for the protagonist to describe how he feels or what he thinks about things as they happen, since the story is told in the first person, but again I found that to be distracting. Nevertheless, from a nostalgic viewpoint it is enjoyable and a worthwhile addition to anyone's collection of stories set on, or about Mars.

I have in general avoided short stories about Mars because there have been so many of them — especially during the 'Golden Age' of science fiction about Mars 1940- 1960 — that it would be impossible for me to compare and evaluate them with the many novels over that time as well as those that continued to appear in the subsequent decades.

Some of those early short stories that predate 1950 I would have read as a boy just discovering science fiction, as well as those published afterwards. But there would have been many others in American magazines which at that time were not available in Australia so I would never have had the chance to read them.

I have managed to catch up with some of them more recently so some of the more outstanding stories do deserve a mention: One early one by Theodore Sturgeon ***The Man who Lost the Sea***, (circa 1960) is about the first astronaut to get to Mars, who crash lands and is dying and as he looks across the barren sandy landscape and the wreckage of his ship he tries to make sense of where he is and what it took for him to get there. This is very different from Sturgeon's pervious work being a stream of consciousness story which is not what he usually wrote. Reflecting back on it I now think it was Sturgeon's best ever story. It was his only one published in the prestigious mainstream publication *Best American Short Stories for 1960.*

I have read that story a couple of times since the early 1960s, but not over the last thirty years, yet it sticks in my mind because it is a profoundly moving story. It was his comeback after a long period of writer's block and he worked on it for two years. And what a comeback! Very few stories as short as this one could encompass tragedy, nostalgia, sadness and at the same time express the immense joy of a great achievement such as finally making it to Mars. This story proved Sturgeon was a master storyteller, garnering him a mainstream publication which none of his other stories had achieved.

Half a century later another short that stands out for me is one by Alastair Reynolds written especially for a collection of Mars stories edited by Jonathan Strahan and published in 2011 called ***Life on Mars***, as well as in his own collection of stories ***Beyond the Aquila Rift*** (2016). The story is ***The Old Man and the Martian Sea***, in which the planet has been settled by humans for centuries and it is slowly being transformed into a more earth like environment. It is about a runaway teenage girl who is bored with her life and she stows away on an airship delivering supplies to one of the huge machines that are terraforming the planet. On this machine she meets the old man who operates it and he takes her to visit a sunken city; a long abandoned earlier human settlement that is covered by slowly rising waters as the planet is terraformed. It is his last visit while the sunken city is still accessible. In a few years the city will be too deep under the newly forming sea and people will forget it even existed. He is about to be replaced by a new machine operator and wants to visit this place one more time. He takes the girl to see it and the story has a poignant ending that you should read to find out for yourself. It is a beautiful story that reminded me of Hemmingway's **The Old Man and The Sea,** the novel that gained him the Nobel Prize for Literature. It has the same underlying sense of accomplishment tinged with sadness that the Hemmingway story has.

In the collection of Mars stories published by *The Magazine of Fantasy and Science Fiction* edited by Gordon Van Gelder, called ***The Fourth Planet from the Sun*** (2005), there are some outstanding novellas, the first of which should be mentioned here.

A Rose for Ecclesiastes by Roger Zelazny was first published in 1963 and has been reprinted many times in various collections and anthologies since then.

Like the rest of the world, Roger knew that NASA had a satellite heading towards Mars and that once it got there he was certain that what it would show would change forever the perception people had of Mars.

How it would be changed was of course unknown at that time. There were still people who believed an ancient civilization had constructed canals to bring water from the Polar Regions to the less viable areas, but this was a dying view. The majority had the idea Mars was quite uninhabitable with a harsher than expected climate, but one nonetheless to which human visitors could adapt even though the latest advancements in astronomy and methods of using light refraction to determine atmospheric content, and the increasing ability to measure temperatures on the planet showed Mars was inhospitable for humans and that it appeared to be lifeless. Up until the mid-1960s it was thought that if Humans could live high in the Andes Mountains or the Himalayas then quite possibly they could also live on Mars.

Gorden Van Gelder, suggests Roger wanted to write a *Planetary Romance* about Mars before the Mariner 4 probe got there, a romance in the style of many from the previous two decades, and that Roger produced a superb result. There is no question that the result was superb, but it is easy to make such assumptions in hindsight years later.

Planetary Romances and *Boy's Own Adventure* stories set on other worlds, often Mars, were a staple of science fiction from the early part of the 20th century and that Roger, being a new writer to the field who no doubt was familiar with what had previously been written simply decided he would write a romantic story set on Mars dealing with human contact with an ancient civilization that was dying out. Most well-known SF authors up until that time had written a story if not several about Mars.

What Roger achieved in this novella was possibly the best *Planetary Romance* of all time.

It has the depth of character, the maturity and complexity of ideas along with a deep sense of history (Martian) that can only be found in a novel: that Roger achieved this in a much shorter work is remarkable, and he was only beginning his career when he wrote this.

It is a love story between a linguist and poet, the son of a preacher, who as part of an expedition to Mars is given permission to study the high and low Martian languages. He falls in love with a temple dancer tasked to assist him in the understanding of both modern and ancient Martian language and culture.

The details regarding language and dance and the history of the dying Martian Race and civilization are woven into the story so unobtrusively that the reader hardly notices but these details are subconsciously accepted as the real basis of the story underlying the romantic aspects of the developing love between the two main characters. That the linguist is instrumental in saving the ancient Martian Race is the climax of the story.

I won't go into details of the story because this would spoil it if you haven't read it, and if you haven't, you should read it immediately because it is one of the all-time great stories about Mars as it was conceived before the advent of Mariner 4's arrival and subsequent dispelling of prior Martian Mythology.

Of course if you have read it but have forgotten about it, as I had, then you should read it again; it will be well worthwhile.

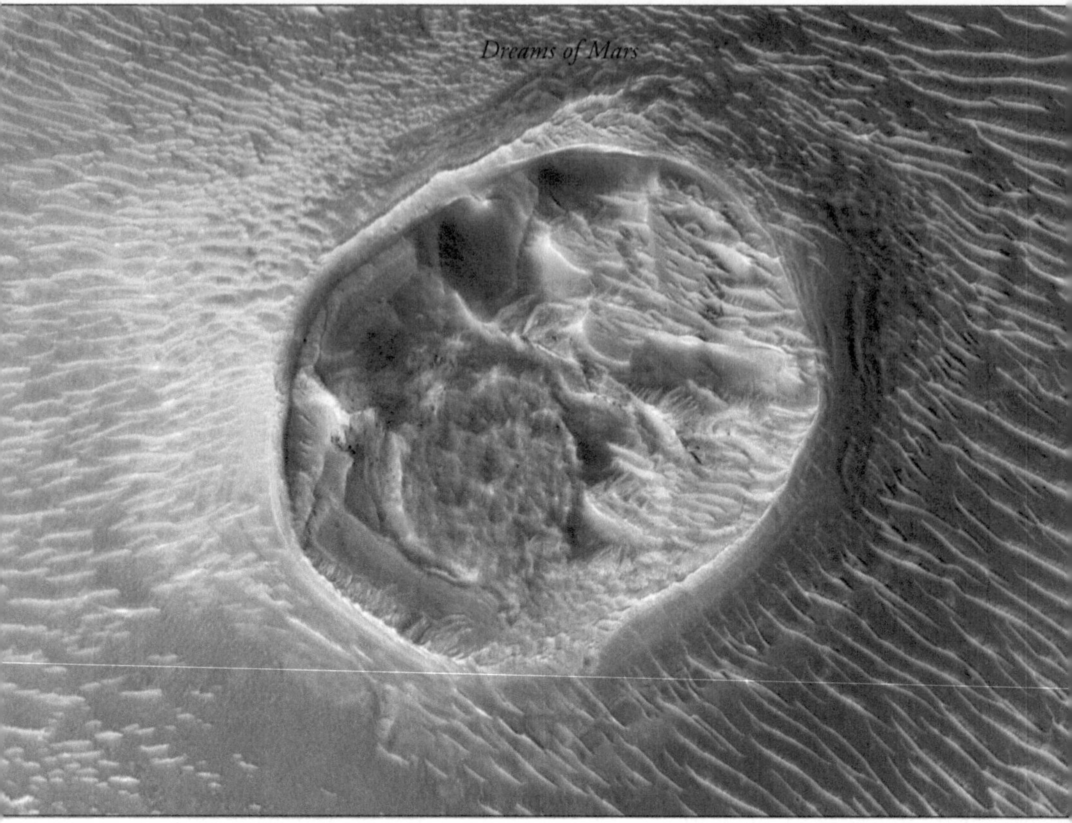

A mesa in Noctis Labrynthus, surrounded by sand dunes in an extensively fractured region at the western end of Valles Marineris.

Fan shaped deposits - alluvial fans...emerging from steep topography

Chapter Five

Unique visions from Philip K Dick

The Collected short stories of Philip K Dick, Volume 2. We can remember it for you Wholesale.

Philip K Dick was a prolific writer of short stories before the bulk of the pulp magazines began to disappear, after which he began writing short novels, published as double novels or one of a double novel paperback. Over time his novels grew longer and more complex.

Apart from ***We can remember it for you Wholesale*** (*Total Recall*) (1965), all the other stories in this volume date from 1953 and 1954. There are two other short stories dealing with Martians or with Mars, ***Martians come in Clouds,*** and ***Survey Team***, and one that at first appears to be Mars but turns out to be a long abandoned devastated Earth, ***The Impossible Planet***.

Martians come in clouds (1954) reminded me of writers like Bradbury. It has an autumnal feel about it. Martians, dry desiccated things like conglomerations of spider webs and dead leaves come floating down like clouds when Mars is at its closest. Previously thousands of them floated down out of the sky, but this time there are very few. Humans immediately destroy them, and tell their children to run away if they see one.

One day after school Jimmy sees a Martian hiding in a big tree at the edge of the forest. Instead of running away he approaches to look but becomes paralysed as the Martian projects thoughts and images into his head. The Martian tells him not to be afraid. Their planet is dying and they are drifting off to come to Earth. They would like to live on floating artificial island in the ocean, an area not used by humans, but there are so few of them left. It asks Jimmy for help. Once released Jimmy runs back and tells adults he meets that there is a Martian hiding in a tree. They all go to the park and set fire to the tree killing the Martian. After fire they stamp the ashes into the ground so nothing is left. Jimmy goes home as the townsmen rejoice to tell his father, who is proud of how brave his son was.

Survey Team (1954) has a group of military men, survivors from a thirty year war that has devastated Earth, come up from underground to commandeer a space ship to take them to Mars. They want to survey the planet to see if it is suitable for the migration of the remnants of their society to start anew, away from having to live underground. On arrival the ship goes out of control and they eject and float down to the surface while the ship crashes and explodes. As they float down they see a ruined industrial complex and further on the endless ruins of a huge city.

Deserted for thousands of years, there is nothing left. The planet has been gutted. Mining pits extend as far as they can see. There are no signs of life. This is as bad if not worse than the recently devastated Earth. There is no hope for humans to move to Mars, they will have to go and find new worlds in other star systems.

"How could they do this?" One of them asks, while another replies, "We ruined Earth in only 30 years..."

It seems the Martians abandoned their planet 60,000 years ago, and went somewhere else. Finally the archaeologist in the survey team discovers that the Martians all migrated to Earth. They must have degenerated into wild tribes before beginning to rebuild. We destroyed two planets, the team finally realises, Mars first and then Earth. And because Mars is nothing more than a giant scrapheap, they must look for another planet in another star system; a virgin world that in time they will also destroy.

The Impossible Planet (1953) is not a Mars story. It is about a really old woman who wants a ship's captain to take her to see Earth. At first he refuses because Earth doesn't exist, it is a legend, the mythological birthplace of humankind.

The belief across the inhabited galaxy is that humans spontaneously developed and evolved in many different star systems and there is no such place as earth: but this old woman who is more than 300 years old remembers it as her parents told her it was, and will pay anything to be taken to see Earth before she dies. So he agrees to take her and her robot companion. There are a thousand systems that contain 9 planets, all likely candidates to be the system of the mythological planet Earth. He picks the nearest one and takes her there. On arrival she can't believe the Earth is so barren and dead. There is a swampy sea that looks more coagulated than watery, and dust storms blow across endless red plains. Dry worn down mountains in the distance create the illusion for the reader that they have landed on Mars by mistake, and that if this is the third planet then perhaps Earth had been destroyed.

The captain doesn't care. He took the old lady to the third planet from its sun and he and his first mate accompany her as she insists on going outside into the toxic atmosphere. The woman believes she has arrived on Earth and imaginess it to be different from what it is. She wades out into the coagulated sea and sinks beneath the sluggish waves. He robot companion follows.

The captain and the first mate return to their ship and on the way he picks up a small metal fragment which he takes on board. *E Pluribus Unum* is inscribed on the piece of metal, words which are meaningless to him. This tells the reader they are on Earth in what used to be the USA and that earth has been totally destroyed, either by humans at some stage, or simply by time itself. The captain shrugs and throws the piece of metal into the waste disposal bin before taking off to return to his home system.

This story was one of those included in the recent TV series ***Electric Dreams*** (2017) based on 10 of Philip K Dick's early short stories, and for most of the episode it has been filmed quite beautifully, but the ending is substantially different from the original short story and more ambiguous. I preferred the short story ending rather than the filmed ending, but I guess the filmmakers wanted a more upbeat ending than the original one written by Dick.

Martian Time Slip (1964)

Philip K Dick ignored all assumptions usually made by authors writing about Mars.

He wrote this in 1962 but it was not published until 1964 and his projected future is only 30 years ahead to 1994. In the 60's there was no way a large colony could be established on Mars in 30 years. Not even today with technology advancing at breakneck speed will 30 years be enough time to get a few people there for a first visit, let alone encourage migration on a large scale, as depicted by Dick, and the establishment of various colonies.

Philip K Dick, unlike all writers before 1965 and the Mariner 4 flyby of Mars who assumed that Mars has a thin but breathable atmosphere, has simply ignored any knowledge of what Mars could possibly have been like other than a brief mention that a vast canal system was speculative until they arrived there to establish settlements along the canals.

During the late fifties and early sixties the *Martian Canals* were considered to be a major mystery yet to be solved. What a rude shock Mariner 4 produced!

He assumes the temperatures during the day are hot enough to turn milk sour if it is left un-refrigerated. He mentions how hot it is a few times. He has one of his main characters refer to the local Martian natives derogatively as Niggers, and uses the name Bleekmen to further describe them. Was Dick prejudiced against African Americans? This was a major problem in the 1960's in the USA so perhaps Dick was not immune to the prevailing feelings about African Americans and it shows in several of his novels; not overtly, but it is there nonetheless.

This novel — written in the same year as ***The Man in the High Castle*** which exhibits German hatred of Jews and Japanese superiority over the Anglo Americans and also mentions the extermination by the Germans of the Africans in Africa so they can establish an Aryan stronghold on that continent — certainly indicates an underlying prejudice. This prejudice is strongly demonstrated by Arnie Kott the thuggish Plumber's Union leader who hates the Bleekmen yet has one working for him as a slave.

That name itself conjures up images of sad looking mysterious beings eternally unhappy at the way their homeland has degenerated both on a physical level as well as a psychological level having been pushed aside by the invading colonists who have taken over their only habitable land along the canals pushing them further out into the deserts. Perhaps this was a comment on what happened in America several hundred years earlier as invading immigrants forced the Native Americans to move further and further out into the wilderness. Or maybe he was indirectly criticising all European 'Powers' that pushed aside natives in other parts of the world so they could establish their empires.

My first impression of his colony is of a group of homesteaders transplanted from depression time's rural America to Mars where they struggle to exist in a hostile and barren land. They appear to be absolutely ordinary and the only reason we think they are on Mars is because it is mentioned several times.

It is not a novel about Mars or even about people adapting to the Martian environment, or how that environment could possible affect them. It is about blue collar working class people struggling to survive harsh conditions, and reflects America during the depression years or just after, with door to door salesmen pedalling black market goods, and a repairman, Jack Bohlen, who fixes anything broken because replacement items can't be afforded or obtained. But primarily it is about schizophrenia and autism and the ideas people had about those afflictions in the 1960's. Unfortunately that dates the novel, which I suspect was originally a mainstream novel set in rural America during the depression. (Can you imagine a title like Nebraskan Time Slip? It would be rejected instantly, but ***Martian Time Slip*** – now that's a good title.) Knowing it wouldn't sell, or having had it rejected like all his other mainstream novels, Dick added the SF elements in a rewrite, by placing the story on Mars which is simply an earth-like desert. He has people able to get there in a couple of days so there is back and forth trading. He has everyone using private helicopters instead of motor vehicles, or else they walk or use bikes because it is easy to pedal around in the lower Martian gravity.

Jack Bohlen the repairman who is the other main character in the novel was once a schizophrenic who thought he had been cured, but being forced to deal with a young boy suffering from autism who has visions of a future Mars and a massive apartment building which houses thousands of poor immigrants, Jack begins to re-experience bouts of schizophrenia himself. Arnie Kott thinks he can make money by getting the land the apartments are to be built on and much of his machinations involve forcing Jack to communicate with the autistic boy who has these visions by building some kind of machine to slow down thoughts which he believes would enable them to communicate with him.

Arnie Kott gets what he deserves after undertaking a pilgrimage with the autistic boy to a sacred cave in the mountains which the Bleekmen believe holds secrets of both the past and the future times which the boy can see. Arnie experiences a backwards time vision which doesn't go the way he planned, and finally one of the bad things he did earlier catches up with him.

Philip K Dick himself suffered episodes of schizophrenia and was able to convey how this feels as reality slips away from him, although I suspect nobody knew much about autism back then and this aspect of the story doesn't seem convincing.

Of the novels set on or about Mars written in the 1950's and 60's this one is the least Mars like and in fact gives no impression at all of a possible Mars. Dick didn't use any of the then current knowledge of Mars; he ignored it completely. I think it could have been a much better and more profound story if he really had made some effort to have his vision of Mars be more like what was known about Mars at that time.

This story was serialized as ***All We Marsmen*** in *Worlds of Tomorrow* magazine, before it eventually came out as a novel in 1964 published by Ballantine Books.

Many consider this to be Dick's best novel, and it probably is if one considers it is about manipulative working class people and schizophrenia, but it is a fantasy novel, not a science fiction novel, because the setting on Mars simply isn't believable or even slightly realistic. With more care regarding the setting it could have been a great novel rather than just a good novel.

The most well known Dick's Martian based stories is probably ***We Can Remember it for you Wholesale*** because of the film starring Arnold Swarzenneger. There is one other novel ***The Three Stigmata of Palmer Eldritch*** which many claim to be his finest novel. Like most of his novels it also deals with reality not being what is perceived, but is in this case induced by using drugs to escape the harshness of the Martian environment. I didn't particularly care for this novel, but then we all have our favourites and everyone who enjoys Dick's work will have their own particular one.

We can Remember it for you Wholesale (1965) was turned into ***Total Recall*** (1990), an amazing film by Paul Verhoeven starring Arnold Swarzenneger, Sharon Stone and Michael Ironside. The first fifteen or so minutes of the film is exactly like the short story upon which it was based. This includes having hidden memories uncovered by the people trying to implant a false vacation on Mars that suggest Quaid really was a secret agent on Mars who has been retired and had his memory wiped.

It all starts when bored with his job —as an office worker in the story but as a construction worker in the film— he goes to an organization called Rekall which implants memories into people who can't or are unable to take holidays. Quaid who keeps dreaming about Mars opts to experience the life of a spy on Mars. But once he is in the chair and the procedure starts problems occur. He becomes violent and the procedure is cancelled but it is too late, his memory has returned.

He is being watched in case his memory comes back and reveals things the people or government on Mars do not want known. If this happens he is to be eliminated. In the story he goes on the run and decides to hand himself in for a new false memory implant. The story finishes ominously with a further problem of an even deeper memory regarding an alien invasion being revealed.

The film takes considerable liberty at this point and has Quaid, escape from his pursuers, some of whom he kills violently, decide to go to Mars to try to recover his lost memories, after following advice from his original self who left him a video explaining what had happened.

The rest of the film is set on a well colonised Mars in the year 2084, and is quite violent. Special effects were fantastic and mostly mechanical in origin rather than computer generated which didn't really begin until ***Terminator 2.*** There is one horrifying scene before he goes to Mars where Quaid pulls a monitoring device out of his brain through his nostrils.

In the story this device allows his monitors to read his mind and his intentions so they can thwart him before he does anything. In the film it is a location device that enables the secret police to follow his movements and track him.

Focussing on paranoia against government agencies and big business the whole film is so layered with conspiracies and fantasies that the audience, just like the main character Quaid played by Swarzenneger, can't tell what is real and what is a fantasy or realistic hallucination. It seems Quaid is part of an insurgency on Mars against the corrupt ruler who rations and taxes oxygen supplied to people who live in the domed cities. The revolutionaries live underground in pressurised caves and are full of mutants affected by Mars' constant bombardment of radiation from space. They were originally workers housed in inadequate domes which did not protect against this remorseless radiation. They lost their jobs when a huge pyramid they were mining turned out to contain a gigantic alien device. Perhaps this is a nod to the last mention in the short story of an alien invasion that didn't happen and won't while Quaid is still alive.

Even Quaid's wife turns out to be a secret agent who is there to monitor him in his boring life as a construction worker. From the moment the attempt to implant false memories begins we don't know if all that follows is the implanted memory or, if what he was living before as a construction worker was implanted and he has finally woken up, after which he sets out to right wrongs done on Mars. What makes this film good is the vision of a colonized Mars. The Mars parts which are the bulk of the film are quite spectacular, especially the ending of the film, and some of the mutants are very creepy. In the film, the alien device is a nuclear reactor designed to melt the permafrost to create an atmosphere that could be breathable.

In the exciting finale Quaid manages to turn this on just in time to save the mutants from suffocating and with the added benefit of changing the planet into something more earth like. However this happens far too rapidly to be plausible. He also decides he doesn't want to go back to who he supposedly was opting to remain as Quaid. The film has an almost happy ending, whereas the original short story suggests further layers of reality still to be uncovered.

The later remake failed to capture any of this film's feeling even though it was far more spectacular because of improvements in CGI and HD video filming. The later film wasn't even set on Mars, but stays right here on Earth with Quaid going to Australia via some massive tunnel through the centre of the Earth rather than going to Mars. This is even more implausible than terraforming Mars over a few mintues as was done in the original film.

I often wonder why filmmakers are prepared to spend 100s of millions of dollars to remake a film that was successful in its time only to finish with a less interesting unmemorable version.

It has been suggested that several other novels Dick wrote have references to Mars as part of the plot or background, ***The Simulacra, We Can Build You,*** and even ***Do Androids Dream of Elecctric Sheep?*** where characters come from Mars or escape to Mars, or are affected in some way by the idea of Mars.

I don't know if this is true or not without reading those books again. If that is the case I suspect it was simply because Mars has always been in the background of human thought ever since Percival Lowell claimed to have seen canals on the surface giving rise to endless speculation regarding the possibility of life on that mysterious red planet, and Dick would have been no different to anyone else in that respect. Mars or a simulacrum of Mars was in his subconscious and he tended to use it as a mirror to reflect his characters' and often his own detachment from reality.

Chapter Six

Voyages to Mars

Voyages to Mars as a major theme began to appear in stories from the late 1950s on into the early 1960s. Visions of utopian Mars or space opera adventures on Mars fell into obscurity as a more technical approach began. The space age had commenced with Russia and the USA competing against each other to see who could achieve the latest outcome in space exploration. Writers turned their attention to depicting just how a voyage to Mars could be achieved and what may be likely to happen during such a voyage. They tried to be as accurate as possible often taking into account the latest developments in space technology as a jumping off point.

Arthur C Clarke's ***The Sands of Mars*** was an exception since it was published in 1951 well before the space race between the two super powers began, and only part of that story is concerned with voyage out. It was Clarke's attempt to be realistic compared to most of the other Mars stories of the time which had established colonies on Mars, Venus and other parts of the solar system in which corruption, thievery and nefarious activities often took place. Those 'space operas' were more a fantasy than anything else, whereas Clarke wanted to be realistic as far as what was known about Mars.

In the early 1960s those who wrote about going to Mars concentrated mostly on the voyage out or the preparation leading up to the voyage as the main focus of the story. But at the same time other writers still wrote stories set on Mars that harked back to the 1950s style of space opera. By the 1970s voyages to Mars were not as popular and writers moved on to other variations of Martian settings. Two notable exceptions were: ***The Earth is Near,*** by Ludek Pesek (1973) one of the most harrowing expeditions to Mars, and Gordon Dickson's ***The Far Call*** (1978) which was more about the politics of an international expedition only culminating in the arrival on Mars at the very end. We would have to wait until the 1990s for a revival of Voyages to Mars as a basic theme again with Ben Bova and Jack Williamson leading the way.

In October 1960 the Russians finally managed to recover animals sent into orbit which gave sufficient knowledge to atteempt a manned mission. In 1961 the Russians made the first manned flight into space with Yuri Gagarin orbiting Earth once on April 12th.

The Americans were behind, following with Alan Shepard making a sub-orbital flight of only 15 minutes. It was followed two months later by Gus Grissom with another 15 minute sub-orbital flight.

To show off their superiority, the Russians in August (1961) sent up Vostok 2 with German Titov who made 16 orbits over 25 hours.

John Glen had made the first American manned orbital flight of 3 orbits over 4 hours 50 minutes on February 20th 1962. It was followed with a lunar probe Ranger 4 which was to impact the Moon but the equipment failed and the mission was unsuccessful. Another orbital flight followed, this time with Scot Carpenter who made three orbits.

The Russians still outshone the Americans by next sending up a dual mission Vostok 3 which lasted 3 days 22 hours over 48 orbits. The Americans sent Mariner 2 on a flyby of Venus and finished off the year with Mercury Atlas 8, (Oct 3rd 1962) a manned mission with Walter Schirra who spent 9 hours making 6 orbits.

From this point on NASA went crazy in a desperate development of the technology needed to beat the Russians which culminated in landing on the Moon in July 1969 and the subsequent moon landings and unmanned missions to Mars and Venus, but particularly to Mars.

There was a lot of activity and a lot of information coming out of NASA when Russ Winterbotham wrote ***The Red Planet*** which was published in 1962.

The Red Planet by Russ Winterbotham (1962)

As the planned flight to Mars is almost ready to depart an accident during an orbital exercise causes one of the crew to be killed on re-entry. Desperate for the mission not to be scrubbed by NASA the captain of the crew Dr Lewis Spartan suggests his female assistant replace the unfortunate crewman. This causes consternation amongst the NASA hierarchy and the newspapers of the day suggesting an orgy in space on the way to Mars with one female and five male astronauts on board. Dr Spartan suggests if he marries his assistant Gail Loring, that problem would be solved. However Gail has other ideas and she says she will marry one of them to forestall prurient comments, but in name only, and that she will choose which of them she marries. She selects Bill Drake, who rather likes her so he agrees. There is a lot of 'fake' publicity about the two 'lovers' making the trip to Mars their honeymoon, and so NASA and the public are enthralled with the mission.

We know that NASA would never have approved a mission with five men and one woman, the numbers would have to be more equal, and in 1962 no American woman had ever been into space.

The descriptions of mission control seem accurate, the kind of rockets mentioned which were used to transport equipment and materials into orbit to build the Mars space ship were Atlas (used by the real astronauts) and the huge Saturn rocket (used to launch the later moon missions but which had not been used when this story was written), all of which gives a feeling of reality to the story. The mars rocket itself uses plasma drives powered with atomic energy, (something talked about by NASA scientists even back then).

The journey out begins to develop tension between the crew. Spartan becomes dictatorial and bombastic, claiming as Captain he makes the rules and says who does what. He obviously is jealous of Gail's 'marriage' to Drake, and envious feelings emerge among the younger crew members as they eye off Gail, who manages to keep a certain mental distance between herself and the others. Physically it is impossible since they are confined to a small ship.

The ship rotates laterally to provide a feeling of artificial gravity. Up to the halfway mark the story is accurate technologically, extrapolating from what NASA was actually using and doing in the 1960s, but as they get closer to the half way mark, things start to go wrong. Some crew members are beginning to have unstable moments due to the long confinement of the trip out to Mars. One of the younger crew members attacks Gail and attempts to rape her, which is prevented at the last moment by Bill (technically and legally her husband) who enters to check some equipment. A fight ensues during which their water purifying system is damaged, so they won't have enough water for the return trip. Spartan is furious. He wants to toss the young man overboard. The author throws in the usual tropes at this point, a meteor cloud or swarm, suggested to be the Leonids, partially damages the ship and ruins one of the plasma drive motors. As punishment for the attempted rape the young crewman Grover is asked to repair the motor. As he leaves the airlock, the captain asks Bill to take out some welding equipment, but asks him to change his full oxygen tank for a partially empty one since they are short of oxygen. When Bill arrives to assist Grover, the young miscreant, he discovers he is dead. He decides to bring the body back on board and as he does so he finds his cable connection to the ship has come undone and he is floating away with the body. This is a beautifully written nail-biting scene. He can't get back by using his oxygen as a propellant or he will suffocate. The ship is continuing to accelerate and will soon be beyond the point where he can catch up. He finally uses the oxygen from the full tank on Grover's back to propel both of them back to the ship. Back on board Bill and Alex discover the inlet vale in the space suit had been sabotaged with a piece of paper. The only paper on the ship is kept by the captain in his cabin. They replace the evidence and when the captain arrives to examine the body he looks at the helmet and fiddles around with the valve, declaring that it was a faulty valve that caused his death. After the captain leaves Alex and Bill re-examine the helmet intake valve and discover the piece of paper used to block it has been removed. They know now that the captain had wanted Grover dead as well as Bill who he had insisted should use a depleted oxygen tank when he went outside.

From this point on they are sure that the captain has no intention of having them return once they reach Mars. He will come back alone, perhaps accompanied by Gail, to claim all the glory for the expedition to Mars.

There is a space burial as Grover's space suited body is ejected from the airlock, which reminded me of innumerable movies in which an astronaut making an EVA to repair damage to the ship caused by meteors is accidentally killed then later given a funeral where the body is ejected into space, only in this case the astronaut was murdered, which raises more tension among the remaining crew each of whom is wondering what the captain is planning to do next.

From this point on the story becomes less factual and more like the earlier stories that used the idea of a dying planet with abandoned ancient cities and remnants of once intelligent Martians struggling to survive ever harshening conditions. The information the astronauts obtain regarding atmosphere, surface temperatures, and general features are what were known scientifically at the time. However Winterbotham populates his Mars with the strangest aliens that are part vegetable and part animal and like 'electric' eels they are able to use electric currents to kill, maim, or destroy enemies.

They communicate with radio and see with radar, quite innovative for the 1960s. Their blood is acidic and they use ammonia instead of oxygen. Their ancestors built the massive canals that are generally 5 miles wide and several miles deep, not to bring water from the poles, but rather to allow it to seep out of the water table in the rocky substrate.

At first contact the Martians don't think the humans are a danger, but this is quickly quashed when Dr Spartan shoots two of them with explosive bullets, to show them who 'the dominant species' is. He won't consider that they are, or might be intelligent or that they may have superior weapons.

There is a hint that the Martians destroyed their own civilization by using atomic bombs, since the nearest abandoned city is radioactive. The Subtext here is a dig at the cold war and the treat of atomic annihilation that filled the minds of people during the 1950s and 60s which perhaps was sublimated by being directed into the Space Race between Russia and America.

Almost immediately the humans come under attack from hordes of Martians which swarm out of another ancient nearby city and up from the deep canals, and which in unison are capable of frying a space suit with projected electrical energy causing it to melt. A fierce battle ensues with the humans managing to repel the Martians with their machine guns and pistols using explosive bullets.

As the Martians retreat Spartan shoots Alex and then tries to kill Bill. He is planning to return alone to claim the glory of being the first human to set foot on Mars and would say the Martians killed all the crew. But Alex is only wounded, and he shoots Spartan who falls in amongst injured and dying Martians which immediately turn their electric power onto him to melt his spacesuit.

Bill and Gail frantically get Alex on board the space ship before the air in his suit can leak out and before the Martians can regroup for another attack. The three of them take off to return to Earth. Bill and Gail finally decide they do love each other and their marriage no longer remains platonic. The voyage back to Earth will be their honeymoon.

Apart from the last part on Mars, the bulk of this story is engaging and still readable since it focuses mainly on the psychology of those in the crew and how they could react given the time spent and the circumstances that could occur in a closed environment. The last part on Mars harks back to the kind of story prevalent in the 1930s and is melodramatic, but overall doesn't spoil the enjoyment of reading this well crafted example of a voyage to Mars.

The Golden Age draws to a close as reality impinges...

Two of the last novels to be published prior to the Mariner 4 flyby of Mars were ***The Martian Sphinx*** by John Brunner and ***Welcome to Mars*** by James Blish.

The Martian Sphinx (1965) by John Brunner

The title is misleading since what is discovered on Mars is not anything like a sphinx which conjures a specific set of images in one's mind, but is a giant machine left on Mars to warn a space faring species of a danger from the Andromeda galaxy. Of the people who found it, one was killed instantly while another had some kind of fit and died on the way back to Earth. The third one experienced a vision which told him about the impending conquest of all intelligence by something malevolent from the Andromeda galaxy. Arriving back on Earth he is thought to be insane but a second expedition to discover what the machine is includes him since he is the only survivor of the communication with the enigmatic machine.

The machine has been there for millions of years and the leader of the second expedition calls it a Martian Sphinx because like its namesake it is ancient and surrounded with mystery.

Shortly after they land a mysterious alien ship arrives and it captures the people examining the strange artefact. They too had been brought to Mars from another star system because they felt the message given to the first expedition. Once in their past they too had been warned by the same type of machine, which resulted in their civilization being destroyed and their planet turned into rubble. It appears the same thing had happened in our solar system millions of years previously and the fifth planet was destroyed leaving the asteroid belt, after which the machine became inert. Somehow the first expedition to Mars triggered the machine back to life again.

There is some conflict because of a misunderstanding but eventually they begin to make progress communicating with each other, when all of a sudden another very different alien ship arrives and it utterly destroys the first alien ship and then starts towards the human ships. The supposition is that they also received the vision projected by the machine and had arrived to ensure they remained the masters of the galaxy. The humans use their gravitic power (which also powers their space ships) drawing on the gravity of Mars to disable the newly arrived alien ship. It is ruptured and the horrible beings emerge only to die because they can't breathe the Martian atmosphere. They try to destroy the remains of their ship but die before they can do this which gives the humans and the first aliens an opportunity to examine the interior and try to find some way to send a message to the first alien's home world.

The survivors of the first lot of aliens are also dying because there is no food on Mars or in the human's ships that they can eat.

The humans leave a message for the rescue team coming for the aliens which explains how this 'sphinx' and others like it had duped various civilizations into believing they could become all powerful and destroy the menace from Andromeda, and that supposedly no such menace exists. They ended up destroying themselves. Perhaps the makers of these mysterious machines were the true menace who wanted to make sure no other intelligent beings could ever become an interstellar species rather than a planetary species.

There is absolutely nothing in this story that gives any impression of what Mars could be like; it is simply a locale in which to set an alien confrontation story. The story is fast paced with lots of action, a typical pulp novel from 1965, but for me today, there were no feelings one way or another about the characters or the story idea. Fifty years ago I would have found it exciting. Today I read it because it appeared to be a Mars story.

Welcome to Mars, by James Blish (1965)

James Blish wrote this story before Mariner 4 was launched, and the manuscript went to the publishers before any photos were sent back from Mars. He contributed an afterword in which he praises himself for getting some surface details right, such as meteor craters from the early massive bombardment of the planet. He was disappointed that the Mariner 4 photos didn't show any canals, but tongue in cheek he suggests the camera was not looking in the right direction.

He concludes with the thought that Mars seems to be an even harsher place than what he describes in the story, but the agreement between the photos and what he describes is closer than he would have imagined.

If I had read this as a teenager I would have loved it.

A teenager who invents an anti-gravity device which he builds into a tree house constructed of a wooden packing crate sealed inside and out with epoxy resin flies off to Mars and arrives there in a couple of days. All he has is some drugstore bought bottles of oxygen with a face mask for use on the surface of Mars and enough food to last him a few weeks. He doesn't even have a space suit, just heavy hiking boots and warm clothes. He intends to collect a few samples on the surface and then return, but the vacuum tube that powers his anti-gravity device fails and he is stranded. He never thought to bring a spare.

As an adult sixty years later reading this I find it hard to suspend belief to really get into the story. The very idea of a teenager, not so much inventing an anti-gravity device, but building a space ship in his back yard out of wood is something I can't accept. That he gets to Mars within a couple of days is fantasy rather than science fiction.

James Blish is not the only author to have a protagonist build a space ship in a back yard. John Varley also has his young protagonists build a space ship in their back yard from a disused oil tanker in ***Red Thunder*** (2003) which is probably better than using a wooden packing crate disguised as a tree house, but equally as unlikely. Anti-gravity also makes an appearance here. I started reading this but couldn't suspend belief enough to continue beyond the first 100 pages. (*There are over 400 in the paperback edition.*)

I find the idea of a home-built spaceship impossible to accept. Can you build an automobile in your back yard? It's possible if you buy all the ready-made parts, but you can't buy ready-made space ship components, they would have to be constructed from scratch, from raw materials, and the technology involved is not something anyone would have available in their garage. Why not teleport the protagonist to Mars, or have them wake up there as if in a dream? Early writers like Edgar Rice Burroughs did it somewhat like that, which even today is an acceptable concept since from the beginning the reader knows it is a fantasy.

Since ***Welcome to Mars*** is only 155 pages in the Sphere SF edition, I decided to finish reading it to see how Blish's description of Mars tallies with what was actually discovered after the Mariner 4 flyby.

Like most writers he got the colour of the sky wrong, his is a deep blue. About the only things he did get right were the cratered surface, and how cascading dust could create landslides and channels in ways similar to water, and a permanently frozen layer of water beneath the surface, which because Dolph landed his makeshift ship inside a crater he didn't have to dig too deep to find ice for his water supply. The dust storms that form every morning and evening as the temperature changes may be right as well, and will be confirmed or not when someone actually gets to Mars. The rest is a fantasy like most stories that take place on Mars that were written up until 1965, before Mariner 4 sent back those hazy images of a cratered surface.

He discovers mossy plants riddled with insect like organisms equivalent to lice. After his girlfriend arrives — she set off to rescue him in the early ship he made before the one he used to travel to Mars and crash lands not far from his tree house ship — they discover the fruit of the mossy plants gives them an extract which once ingested helps produce extra oxygen in their blood so they can almost breathe the thin atmosphere. The extract also helps feed them to make up for the little they brought in supplies.

Dolph can construct almost anything from supplies he brought with him in his wooden ship, none of which is mentioned earlier but he seems to have an endless assortment of odd stuff from which to construct whatever he needs, such as a still to extract moisture from the plants, and to build a radio jamming device to block a constant signal, like a radio beacon, being sent out from somewhere on Mars. This was an attempt to let people know they were still alive. Together they discover that a vaguely lobster shaped crustacean that feeds on the mites that live on the plants, is also good for them to eat, so the problem of food is solved. The temperatures are cold, but not as much as we would expect, or neither of them would survive even one night on the surface, let alone a couple of years.

Other aspects of the fantasy is the arrival of a very large lemur like being that appears to be intelligent and with whom they manage to communicate in a primitive way. When Dolph, with diagrams explains about the beacon and the jammer he made to interrupt it, the cat like being points off in the distance and then draws a diagram in the sand to indicate it knows where the beacon is and will show them the way. They build a sled and load everything they can from the tree house ship they called home. With their new friend dragging it they climb up out of the crater and head across the desert until they arrive at a mountainous area and a large cave.

Entering the cave the Martian leads them down for miles until they arrive at an ancient city buried under the ice layer. The city appears alive but abandoned except for one strange being inside an enclosed stasis field. Here is the source of the signal. This being informs them in English (because it speaks all Earth languages having studied radio broadcasts since they started) that there are no Martians left and the hairy lemur like beings were once pets. It tells them the beacon was an attempt to attract others of his own kind, but there has been no response for thousands of years. It also informs them that more humans are about to arrive. It finishes by bequeathing the planet Mars to them, telling them they can mine the ancient cities for their technologies, after which it dies.

The city seems to die as well, and they leave and head back to surface where they see the flares of several arriving space ships. The ships had homed in on the signal beacon as well as their jamming signal. They head back to the wooden hut they called home and wait for their rescuers to arrive.

The story finishes with them on the rescue space ship where the boy's mother is waiting for them. She happens to be the exobiologist on the crew. The two teenagers who are now adults are married by the ship's captain (presumably to legitimise the time spent together as a couple on Mars) and are told they will be leaders in exploring Mars since they are of course the resident experts.

Looking at this story today, it is dated and unbelievable, being a mixture of fact as well as fantasy, an awkward mixture to do well. It would have been an exciting read for any teenager around the time it was written. I never saw it when it was published in 1965. I only came across it recently, and liking James Blish as a writer, I couldn't resist the temptation to buy it. I wasn't disappointed but was expecting something better.

Farewell Earth's Bliss, (1966) by D G Compton, would have been written prior to the first Mars flyby, so Compton worked with whatever knowledge was available before the first photos came back to show the true face of Mars. He didn't assume like some other novelists of the time that Mars had a thin but breathable atmosphere, he made sure his protagonists wore space suits whenever they were outside of a habitat. To his credit, he also never mentioned canals or ancient cities abandoned as the planet dried up. His depiction of Mars is reasonably realistic considering the time it was written. By 1960 most scientists as well as much of the general population no longer believed in the old ideas about Mars once proposed by Percival Lowell and his associates.

Being a British writer, Compton came up with the idea of doing what England did with its unwanted criminals. The British sent them to Australia. In Compton's undated future the Earth people send their unwanted citizens to Mars. Once a year they use old Moon shuttles for the twelve week trip and the passengers are kept drugged and semi-comatose throughout the journey. The ship functions automatically. These ships are not expected to return. Mars has nothing useful for Earth so it is only used as a dumping ground for unwanted people.

Unlike the petty thieves and criminals sent to Australia by the British, who had a choice to return to England after serving their sentence. Most of them didn't, accepting land grants and becoming upright citizens of their new country which was so much better than what they had left behind in England. On Mars the exiled prisoners had no choice. There was no going back. They had to survive no matter what.

The idea is preposterous, but Compton is a good enough writer to convince you it is possible.

When the shuttle lands not far from where the previous 11 ships had landed, the passengers alight to find a group of the surviving forced colonists waiting for them. These colonists board the ship and confiscate everything on board. They leave the new arrivals there and tell them they will be back the next day to help shift them over to the colony base camp. However an enormous dust storm envelopes the ship and the colonists are stuck there. Two of them attempt to go outside and are lost in the storm, killed, frozen and desiccated by the extreme cold at night. The storm last almost 40 days by which time half the ship's people have died of starvation while the rest are emaciated and dehydrated. Finally the storm abates and the survivors are taken to the main camp where they discover the previous 11 shuttles are used for accommodation and related activities.

Each survivor is billeted with someone and so begins their lessons in how to survive on Mars. Compton assumes there is some form of fungal plant life and this is used for food, apart from the supplies confiscated from the new arrivals. Everything is patched endlessly. Nothing is wasted. Space suits are always fixed and re-used. When someone doesn't obey the rules of the colony they are forced to stay outdoors at night where they will freeze to death. Later their clothes and space suit are recovered for use by the rest of the colony. As new arrivals slowly learn, life on Mars is tough and there is no going back to Earth or the Moon. Everyone works hard; they have no choice.

Eventually some small creatures that live underground are discovered eating the ubiquitous fungus and these are caught and killed for food as well as for their furry skins. They call these creatures rabbits; thus Compton completes his analogy of convicts being sent to Australia. There is no mention of any other ecology which there would have been if there were plants and at least one animal. It would have had to evolve, and along with it there would have been many other living things in a proper ecosystem. All he has is one plant and one animal, nothing else.

Over the progress of the story we follow the life of one person in particular; a person who is American of African descent, and this with the prejudice shown by the other characters towards him dates this book firmly to the 1960s. Sometimes Compton forgets that his characters have to wear space suits at all times outside of a habitat because he has one person derisively piss on the desiccated bodies of the two lost in the initial dust storm after they retrieve the space suits and clothes. How could this be done while wearing a space suit? This was as the group were about to drag the 12th shuttle overland towards the colony where it would be allocated as new accommodation.

The colony itself has been established near the ice cap because that is where they get water for their use. Compton, as with everyone else, erroneously assumed the ice caps would be water-ice.

Later it was thought the ice caps were composed entirely of frozen carbon dioxide, but it is now known they do consist of frozen water-ice overlaid with frozen carbon dioxide or dry ice. The northern ice cap has approximately one metre of carbon dioxide ice covering the water ice beneath while the southern ice cap has a much thicker and permanent layer of carbon dioxide ice many metres thick. The northern ice cap is much larger than the southern so it seems likely the colony Compton envisages would be located near this place where in the summer water would be available.

The story is unrelentingly depressing and at times melodramatic.

The final scene takes place a year later. When another shuttle arrives the colonists head out not to welcome the newly arrived inhabitants but to steal from them whatever they can, and then to artificially create a dust storm that will last long enough so that at least half of them will die of starvation. This is the only way they can survive because there aren't the resources to support a large number of people. Mars is too harsh.

On board the newly arrived shuttle is one coloured girl, and our viewpoint character quietly tells her to hang on no matter what. After that he goes outside to help the others create the dust storm that will envelope the shuttle for 40 or so days. Because of the implication of a future for our character with one of the new arrivals there is an expectation of hope so the story ends on a positive note.

To Compton's credit his story is about the people and their ability to survive the extreme conditions and not about Mars itself. He concerns himself with the social and puritanical structure of the colony as well as the pragmatism of survival. On that basis it works, but his assumptions about Martian plant life and ecology dates it to a forgotten past.

Part Two

After the Mariner 4 flyby

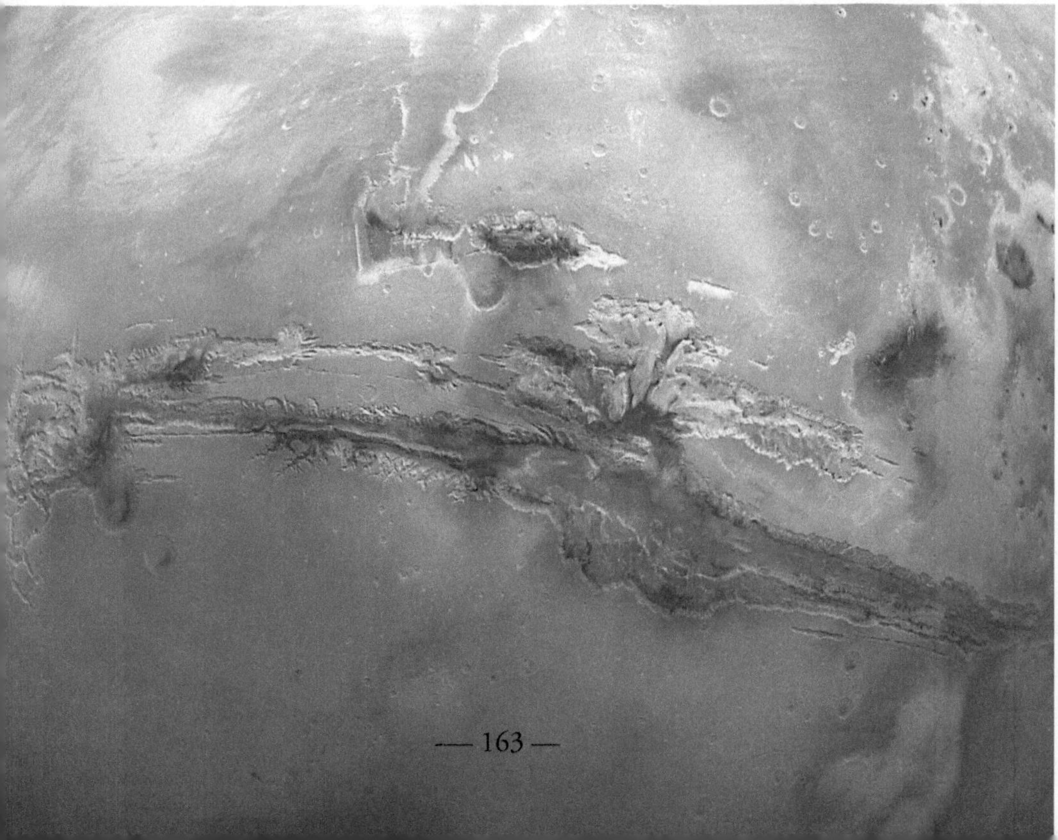

Chapter Seven

The new reality of Mars

As late as 1962 many still believed that the greatest mystery in the solar system yet to be solved was the riddle of the canals on Mars. Others who accepted that the canals did not exist still held in their minds the idea that some form of plant life would be found on Mars.

But all fanciful speculations about Mars came to a sudden stop when NASA's Mariner 4 probe, after seven months of journeying arrived there in July 1965. Passing by at a distance of 9,600 kilometres it took 19 grainy photographs over the 4 days it was in the vicinity of Mars. The images were recorded onto videotape and broadcast back to Earth. Each image took between seven and eight hours from the moment of being broadcast until it was fully reconstructed at the control centre. These grainy pictures killed forever the idea of canals and ancient civilizations.

They showed Mars' surface pockmarked with countless impact craters, and recorded a temperature of minus 100 degrees Celsius with an atmosphere only 8 millibars compared to the 1000 millibars of the pressure we have on Earth. The pressure on the surface is only 0.6% of what we have at the ssurface on Earth.

The arrival of Mariner 4 at Mars and the images and information sent back can be seen as a dividing moment which separates the earlier stories from the later ones with those written before being more fanciful while those written after being more realistic in terms of how Mars is depicted.

Mariner 5 went to Venus, also dispelling any hope that Venus was a tropical water world.

The shocking reality was there were no canals on Mars, no water, virtually no atmosphere, — and what little there was, was mostly carbon dioxide — but there were vast deserts dotted with impact craters, massive chasms and dead volcanos, planet-wide dust storms and frozen carbon dioxide, not water ice, at one of the Poles. With summer temperatures at its equator like those experienced in Antarctica it was much colder than expected.

These early images from Mariner 4 showed a surface pockmarked with impact craters ... barren and moonlike

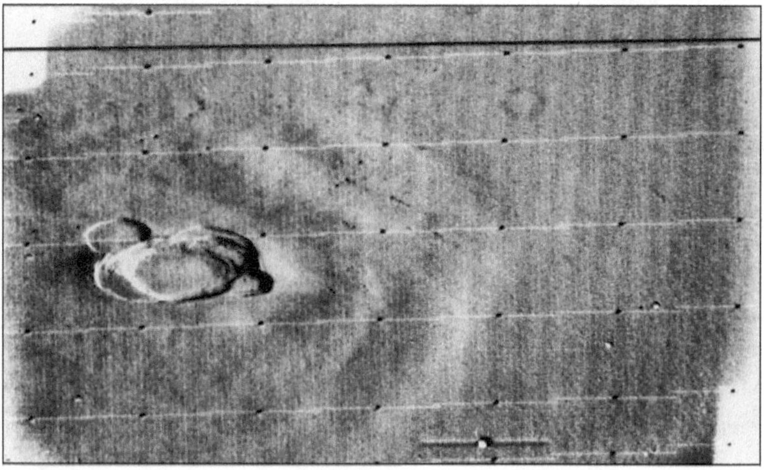

Mars was not the benign place once envisaged. It would be a very difficult place for any kind of life familiar to us to exist. And it would be very difficult for us to live there as well, although with the right equipment, not impossible.

It was even worse for Venus which we discovered is a runaway hothouse with surface temperatures too hot for anything we know of to be able to live. Totally covered by clouds of acid and with a volcanically active surface it is only through radar from satellites circling the planet that we can see anything at all. So Venus is out of the fanciful category for ever, along with some of the moons of the larger planets like Jupiter and Saturn that are too inimical for human life, but on these moons there could be something that is alive in seas beneath frozen surfaces. We will find this out in the not too distant future.

But the hope remains that perhaps once Mars, the planet most accessible to us with our present technology, did support life of some kind, and that one day we will discover fossilized remnants of such life, or even surviving bacteria deep beneath the surface. In fact in many stories about the first journey to Mars an important aspect of the story is to have the astronauts or Marsnauts discover some kind of life either deep underground or way down in the bottom of deep chasms like Valles Marineris, which is a plausible assumption.

Since Mariner 4, many probes, Orbiters and robotic Landers were sent to Mars, and they still continue to be sent. Some were lost or destroyed as they attempted orbiting or landing, but many were successful. Through telemetry and photos sent back to Earth from these robotic probes, orbiters, and rovers on the surface, a new and often astonishing picture of our nearest neighbour has emerged.

This ongoing exploration of Mars by NASA and other Space Agencies has led to far greater knowledge about the Red Planet than writers 50 years ago could ever have imagined. And although since the 1970s there have been serious strategies to send human expeditions to Mars, this has yet to come about.

The new reality of Mars revealed by the Orbiters stunned most SF writers. Many of them initially abandoned Mars as a subject of their speculative stories and headed off to the asteroid belt, the outer planets and into the far depths of the galaxy, which meant not so many stories about Mars were published during the late 1960s through to the 1970s compared to earlier decades, with much less during the 1980s. This didn't mean that interest in Mars declined: on the contrary, conspiracy theorists put forth ideas that alien bases existed there, that aliens had created the Face on Mars and nearby pyramid like structures. With the spread of the internet into most homes they also claimed the US Government had a secret base on Mars as well as on the Moon, but the public at large ignored these, which more often than not were just ridiculous. Does anyone take these people seriously apart from themselves?

By the 1990s and beyond after NASA had deployed rovers to photograph and examine the surface of Mars writers again realised that Mars was unbelievably fascinating. Here was a whole world about which they knew nothing but which was being revealed bit by bit. Its stark deserts and magnificent canyons, the largest volcano in the whole solar system, ice caps of frozen carbon dioxide, of water frozen under the surface with the possibility of finding some form of life deep underground, for many of the physical features photographed in exquisite detail showed that running water had sculpted them some millions of years in the past. Later indications are that some water-sculpted areas were much more recent; perhaps only a few hundred thousand years ago.

It was like an unknown planet had been discovered; a world no one had known about, and all of a sudden it was there, dropped into an orbit a little bit further out than our own. It was within reach.

We had gone to the moon; surely the next step would be to go to Mars.

This idea has more recently been re-iterated by President Obama who also believes that the future of mankind must include the establishment of a human presence on the Moon and on other worlds like Mars. People are already training for the long voyage, or studying how a base might be established by doing it in Iceland where the terrain could be similar to parts of Mars.

There is another Mars camp on a remote island in Canada where the same training is taking place in preparation to go to Mars. And there is one on the volcanic wastes on top of a mountain in Hawaii.

The Russians conducted an experiment where a group of (potential) Mars-cosmonauts lived for the duration of a voyage to Mars and back in a replica space ship, doing what a crew is expected to do, eating what they would have to eat, exercising, and learning to live with each other in extremely close quarters. Scientists studied the psychological effects of such a long voyage on people in that tiny closed environment with no escape until they returned to Earth and have concluded that it can be done. It will be done, sooner rather than later.

Suddenly the 1990s seemed to be filled with stories about Mars, as well as non-fiction speculations of how we could make the journey and what would happen when we did.

This ever-growing number of books continues to this day. The novels take into account the latest knowledge gained from orbital surveys, images, and reports sent back from the satellites orbiting the planet and the rovers wandering about on the surface. Mars is an exciting and thrilling place to explore and writers are doing exactly that with new stories that are for the most believable, prophetic, and dramatic while at the same time being scientifically accurate in their descriptions of conditions future astronauts and potential explorers and colonists will encounter. It is this scientific accuracy that adds verisimilitude and a sense of wonder to these more recent stories.

The non-fiction technical and semi-technical books all have elements of speculation bordering on being fictional about how future Marsnauts could solve problems that arise once they get to Mars.

Our knowledge of the Red Planet is increasing exponentially as Rovers and Orbiters continue to send back information to be processed. Each new generation of writers draws on the greater knowledge available and so the stories they write become more and more credible. Exactly how realistic they are remains to be seen, and we won't know this until people actually go there and begin to write about it.

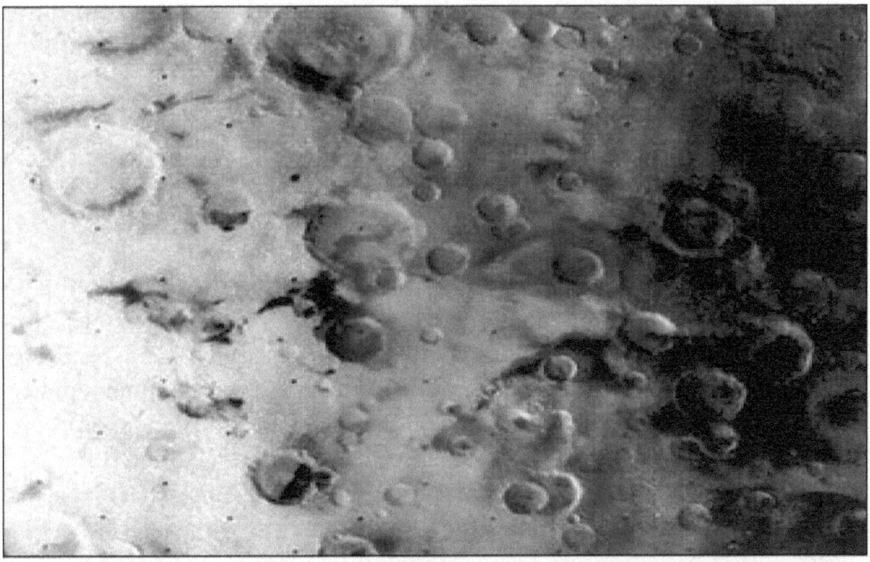

More of the cratered surface which disappointed story tellers who dreamed of a much different Mars.

Born under Mars by John Brunner (1967)

This story was probably written shortly after images started coming back from Mariner 4. The author makes concessions to the new reality of Mars, but he still had to have some kind of plant life there as well as a thin but breathable atmosphere. I suspect it was hard for writers to imagine a whole planet so barren that no plants of any kind at all could exist. Even places on Earth where it hasn't rained for hundreds of years still manage to have some form of plant life growing there.

In this story, Mars has been inhabited for generations and a newly developed interstellar drive has allowed humans to colonise two different star systems in opposing directions away from Earth and the solar system: Centaurus as seen from the southern hemisphere, and from the northern hemisphere Ursa Major and the constellations around Polaris. It is a long term experiment to foster genetic diversity and to guarantee humanity's continued existence in the galaxy.. The colonisation of Mars was the first part of the experiment, though those who live on Mars aren't really aware of this. As the story opens humans in those other worlds have already started to evolve in ways antagonistic to the others

He acknowledges info sent back from Mariner 4 when talking about the low atmospheric pressure requiring face masks to be worn when outside and all building and offices, shops, hotels are pressurised and people must enter and exit via airlocks. (*But this was generally well known for decades before more exact details were revealed by the Mariner probes.*) Larger sections of settlement are roofed over with domelike structures to keep in air pressure. There is no mention of how cold it is and no one wears anything other than ordinary clothes when outside apart from the face mask needed to breathe. Surely Brunner should have known a very thin atmosphere meant a very cold temperature since there was hardly any *air* to trap heat.

On page 22 the narrator, Ray Malin, an interstellar drive engineer who has been away from Mars for some time reflects on returning home: Not even I would call my planet beautiful. Rolling red brown plains, shifting dunes, hills hardly higher than the dunes, darkling sky, the moons pretty blinking lights, the native plants majestic rather than handsome – even the famous sand flowers – the winds weak but harsh like much diluted acid...

The title ***Born under Mars*** comes from Malin explaining that all babies born on the planet are carried throughout their term with the mothers in Earth atmospheric pressure in underground habitats or they won't mature properly. They stay underground until they are weaned after which they are slowly acclimatized to the thinner air of Mars. Also because of the lesser gravity their bodies become elongated with very long limbs, the average adult being seven to eight feet tall. Martians can survive outside in the thinner air and sometimes need to supplement their oxygen supply by using face masks, whereas foreigners from Earth and the other star systems need fully pressurised environments on Mars. They stay in hotels or domed areas where earth like surface pressure is maintained.

I suspect if Brunner had tried to make his background details match too closely to new information from Mariner 4 he would have had to rewrite the complete novel, so apart from some minor details his story depends on older concepts of what Mars was like. He supplies enough details to create a bleak view of a planet uninhabited and desolate apart from small areas where the moribund colonies exist.

The story isn't really about Mars even though the bulk of it takes place there. It is more about an interstellar conspiracy mystery where Centaur agents as well as Bear agents demand information from Ray Malin the moment he steps onto the surface of Mars, information that he doesn't know he has.

He is kidnapped, subjected to torture, but can't reveal what he doesn't know.

Interstellar ships are not allowed to land on Earth, but must use Mars. There was something odd about the ship he was the engineer on for the Journey from Bear territory to Sol and Mars, but he was unaware of this at the time. Through the course of the story Malin discovers the captain of the ship was involved in the kidnapping of a twin baby.

But not only that, his old and trusted mentor on Mars was also involved with the kidnapping. The baby carries the genetic make-up of Bears, Centaurs, as well as Martians, and is the key to the future development of Humankind throughout the galaxy, and all parties want this baby.

Apparently not only humans on Earth are stagnating, but also the Martians as well as the Centaurs and Bears. The future of the race depends upon the genetic makeup of this baby twin.

For its time this was no doubt an exciting story, but now 50 years later it seems dull, yet still it is interesting to read. Brunner was a writer who could always keep a reader turning pages, and then wanting more when it was finished.

Pesek's bleak view of Mars

Ludek Pesek's ***The Earth is Near***, published in 1973 in English, was originally published in 1970 as *Die Erde ist nah – die Marsexpedition* winning the prestigious German Children's Book Prize in 1971.

Ludek Pesek was born in Czechoslovakia and educated in Prague. He is both a writer and an astronomical artist with many paintings used to illustrate books such as ***Journey to the Planets*** (1972), ***Planet Earth*** (1972), ***The Ocean World*** (1973) ***UFOs and Other Worlds*** (1975), ***The Solar System*** (1978) as well as covers and illustrations for books and magazines.

The Earth is Near is a seminal book in the history of books about travelling to Mars examining the psychological and physical problems that could realistically be expected to occur during such a long voyage as well as the difficulties in establishing a foothold on the planet itself. Because it was a translation from German into English I suspect it has long been overlooked by many English language readers.

Of the previous three authors, Pesek had the advantage of more-up-to-date knowledge about Mars than they could not have had. As far as I can tell this was the first novel written about such a voyage after the Mariner 4 probe had sent back 19 or so photographs of the surface of Mars that showed a barren surface littered with craters, destroying forever the legendary canals and dying civilizations that had proliferated before 1950.

The illustration on the cover of the English hardcover is a painting by Pesek showing the surface pockmarked with craters which was one of the most unexpected finds from the series of images sent back from the probe. Another find was an enormous dust storm that obscured observation of the surface for a long time, so dust and sand storms feature prominently in Pesek's story.

The tone of the book is initially flat and is told in the 1st person from the point of view of one of two doctors on board, the psychologist, (the other is a medical doctor) so a lot of detail is developed regarding the mental state of the expedition members and the effects of the long confinement in the ships as well as the deterioration of their physical abilities due to prolonged time in free-fall. Experiments at that time dealt with the effects of muscle atrophy and loss of bone density. Pesek's solution was to give everyone a drug that somehow countered the effects of prolonged free-fall but it did have other side effects which become apparent as the voyage progresses.

There are twenty crew members in a huge mother ship which is part of a convoy of ships linked together making the long voyage to Mars. Set at an undetermined time in the future after we have returned and established colonies on the Moon, this expedition is to take a year to get there, spend 400 days on the surface of Mars, before taking another year returning to Earth.

There is nothing overly dramatic apart from a 'swarm' of meteorites that they almost collide with as they near the insertion point for orbit around Mars. It is suggested that these meteorites are also making long orbits around Mars (implying that as they fall they create the cratered surface) This is a tense moment because they can't change their trajectory (as they might in a film like Star Wars) or they would not be able to achieve Mars orbit but would shoot on past and around. Fortunately the meteorites miss the convoy by something like 30 kilometres and orbital insertion is achieved.

The convoy slowly manoeuvres into a parallel orbit with Phobos and approaches and lands on the surface. The mother ship and some of the others are separated and fixed to the surface of Phobos as a base, like a space station, from which they can use a landing module and some of the smaller cargo freighters carrying equipment to go down to the surface where they will establish another base to stay for 400 days.

Arthur C Clarke already used Mars' Moons as a staging base for trips down to Mars and back up again, so it was a common idea, and obviously practical rather than trying to land a huge ship or convoy of ships on the planet's surface. It is in fact what is being considered now for future Mars expeditions.

This first third of the book is titled ***The Long Voyage.***

The second third is titled ***The First Man on Mars*** and now the narration becomes more alive as we experience through the narrator's eyes the initial attempts at exploration. They had a problem with the landing: a huge dust storm obscured the area where they were intending to land, which because of its colouration they suspected may harbour some form of primitive life, but they couldn't land if they couldn't see the terrain beneath them, so they travelled a bit further on past the storm and landed in an area of flat desert six hundred kilometres from where they wanted to be. But that was it; they were stuck there and would have to make the best of it. The landing party consisted of several smaller cargo ships, and one larger ship that was the main base. The mother ship stayed on Phobos.

There had been some conflict between the original Captain while they were in training and his replacement two days before the voyage began with another more military minded man while the original Captain was demoted to second in command. This didn't affect them much on the long voyage out, but once on the surface of Mars animosity develops between these two men with the crew members splitting their support equally between them. Conflicts arise over what the expedition's objects are. Some want to follow the original plan and go to the designated landing area, while others want to explore the local surroundings.

Establishing a perimeter they almost lose one of their small tractor vehicles when it disappears into super fine soft sand. This dust-like sand fills craters so they are not visible and presents a constant danger whenever the explorers are moving about on the surface. The fine sand also gets into everything so they are always having problems getting equipment to work. Utterly exhausted because they were experiencing the effects of gravity after a year in fee-fall they were prone to accidents and things did go wrong. One of the landing craft had been damaged and they had to salvage what they could.

They spend a lot of time probing the surrounding area to determine what was solid and what wasn't. But before they could do much of anything they were enveloped in a sand storm that inserted fine grit into everything and prevented them from exploring further out from their base.

Travelling anywhere was so difficult they soon realized they would not be able to simply drive to the original landing location, but that idea became the obsession of the second in command. An expedition was despatched and it takes weeks for them to gain a few hundred kilometres where they become stuck on a ridge surrounded by hidden craters covered in super fine sand that acts like quicksand if they drive over it. To make any headway they have to walk out in front of their tractors and probe the sand for solid ground underneath, a difficult job wearing space suits which they must because of the lack of air and the extreme cold. It also meant they made many detours and often a whole day was spent probing and slowly crawling forward only to gain a kilometre or less in the direction they wanted to go after having travelled forty or so zigzagging around hidden dust filled craters to get there.

The descriptions of dust storms and the prelude to such storms are quite beautiful and evocative. The feelings of the team members as they struggle to reach even simple goals under harsh conditions are believable and at this point the book is hard to put down.

One of them is injured, and because they can't remove the space suit to treat him he slowly becomes infected with gangrene. Finally after much delay because of dust storms a small helicopter is sent from the base to rescue the injured man. The helicopter's gyroscopic navigation instrument doesn't work so they can't find their way back if they lose sight of the base because everywhere looks the same. They use signal rockets fired up into the atmosphere for the pilot to see his destination. Unfortunately the injured man later dies back at the base and is buried near the landing module and covered by a cairn of rocks. He becomes *the first man on Mars.*

The last third of the book called ***The Long March*** is about the continuing attempt to get to the originally proposed landing site, but the terrain becomes more and more difficult to traverse with too many detours around impassable sections. Valuable equipment is lost, so the captain finally allows the helicopter to make an exploratory trip towards the originally proposed landing site from where the pilot briefly reports seeing something green.

It had landed first where the group is stranded, refueled and headed off towards the place where the ship should have landed. Communication is lost in the middle of the pilot reporting he sees something odd.

The helicopter doesn't return, so another person is lost along with irreplaceable equipment. Still the second in command wants to continue on foot while the others want to return to base. The team splits into two groups and one heads off with the second in command while the others prepare to head back to the ships. Not long after they lose more equipment when their tractor over turns and its contents, which includes their oxygen supplies, tumbles down into a deep crater. They radio the team heading off in the direction of the lost helicopter to come back and rescue them. This team thinks it a ruse to make them return and ignores them.

Very soon the expedition would have to leave anyway; their time on Mars is coming to an end, and they must return to Phobos if they wish to take the mother ship back to Earth. The date of departure is fixed and if they don't make it on time the Earth will not be there when they finally reach its orbit. Finally the other half, dissatisfied with the second in command and his obsession return to find those they left weren't joking. They really did need rescuing. Finally they all return to base for the departure to Phobos and on to Earth.

Mars has beaten them.

As they are about to take off, the second in command goes out through the airlock and heads out into the desert. He has decided he is not going back. Though they try everything to convince him to return they are unsuccessful and finally have no choice but to take off and leave him. The final scene is the ship taking off as seen from the viewpoint of the second in command standing alone on Mars in his dusty space suit. We know he only has 90 days of food and oxygen left in the base and after that he will be dead.

Pesek has crafted an original story that shows humans will never give up on their dreams no matter the cost. It is at times pessimistic but at the same time it is also optimistic. I believe he set a high standard with this story about the first voyage to Mars that many other writers could only emulate. He covered it all, technically, psychologically, emotionally, realistically, and from the point of view of grand adventure. Anyone coming after him can only apply variations to this basic storyline.

It is a pity that this is not better known than some of the later stories which cover the same ground.

A more recent view of Mars' cratered surface.

Chapter Eight

The Moon and beyond... into the 1970s

In December 1968 American astronauts went to the Moon, and for the first time we had a glimpse of the dark side which no one had ever seen before. The Russians had already sent a probe to the Moon on September 14, 1968. It was a desperate attempt to outdo the Americans who had been testing the command module for Moon missions in near Earth orbit.

Panicked, the Americans hastily readied their crew for Apollo 8. This was only the second manned Apollo mission. The mission was to go around the Moon and the astronauts were to test trans-lunar injection with the systems on board. They were not able to land because the landing module wasn't ready. NASA believed that if they didn't do something spectacular the Russians would beat them to the Moon. So they went, departing on December 21 1968, and three days later they circled the Moon and were the first humans to witness Earthrise on the Moon. They took that iconic photo of the half full Earth sitting just above the horizon of the Moon. It is no doubt the most famous picture ever taken of our home world.

Apollo 9 tested docking procedures in Earth orbit, Apollo 10 again went to the Moon to test the landing module, but without actually landing. It approached to a distance of 15 kilometres and the crew took some spectacular photos of the cratered surface beneath. It wasn't until July 16 1969 that Apollo 11 went to the Moon and for the first time humans stepped onto the surface of another world. The astronauts spent 21 hours 31 minutes and 40 seconds on the surface.

A near mishap with Apollo 13 put a dent in the American enthusiasm and they were more cautious after that. Subsequent Moon missions had the astronauts with moon buggies driving around on the surface collecting samples and generally having a great time. Apollo 17 in December 1972 was the last time humans went to the Moon. Having won the space race with the Russians with Apollo 11 when Armstrong stepped tentatively onto the moon's surface, the Americans didn't want to spend any more money on moon missions. They abandoned the Moon, much to the disappointment of SF fans all around the world.

But a new race had begun. The Russians had sent probes to Venus and to Mars as had the Americans, but now they resumed this activity with more intensity. Not all the Russians probes were successful, most disappeared in transit or crashed on arrival. The Americans hedged their bets by sending two probes more or less at the same time to Mars. Mariner 3 and Mariner 4 launched a month apart. It turned out to be a wise move because Mariner 3 malfunctioned on takeoff but Mariner 4 was successful and went to Mars where it sent back those famous blurry images of the surface from a distance of only 6000 kilometres. After Mariner 5 went to Venus, Mariners 6 and 7 again went to Mars with stunning photographic results.

The incorporation of new knowledge

By 1977 John Varley had access to images from Mariner 4 as well as well as later flyby Mariner missions 6 and 7 in 1969, and the two Viking rovers both of which touched down on the surface of Mars in 1976 some 4000 kilometres apart. (Viking 1 in July 1976 and Viking 2 in September 1976) This gave him and any other author writing stories set on Mars unprecedented imagery and knowledge about Mars than had previously been available to authors and the general public prior to 1965.

Mars' atmosphere was 1000 times thinner than Earth's at sea level, so there was no way conditioning people in the Andes to a lower atmosphere would have helped. They would still need some kind of space suit to walk around on the surface. Summer time temperatures in the equatorial regions of the planet equated to something similar to Antarctica or worse. Temperatures at night dropped almost a couple of hundred below freezing even in equatorial regions, and the regolith was irradiated from space constantly since there was no magnetic field to ward of dangerous radiation which meant too much exposure would be deadly for humans so proposed settlements would have to be buried beneath the surface partially or completely. The ice caps were not frozen water but frozen carbon dioxide or dry ice and of course there were no canals; that had always been a fantasy.

Many SF writers simply shifted their locales to other planetary systems where they could imagine anything they wanted, or moved their stories further away into the outer solar system, or turned inwards and wrote about overpopulation and pollution making the Earth a grungy and desolate environment.

Those who decided to write about Mars had to take into account the new known facts to make their story plausible. This didn't mean one couldn't let the imagination roam. It was fine as long as facts were adhered to. And John Varley certainly allowed his imagination to roam with this story.

In ***The Hall of the Martian Kings,*** first published in 1977 in *The Magazine of Fantasy and Science Fiction* is a novella with considerable depth. It can also be found in the collection titled ***Fourth Planet from the Sun*** edited by Gordon Van Gelder and subtitled *Tales of Mars from The Magazine of Fantasy and Science Fiction.*

His story begins realistically and dramatically with the first expedition, while establishing its base, experiencing a massive disaster as their living quarters dome collapses. Everyone inside the dome dies from explosive decompression, truly horrible deaths. There are five survivors, three women and two men, who were outside in their pressure suits or already in their pressure suits ready to go outside.

Initially they can only survive inside their lander which is still nearby ready to shuttle them back to the orbiting mothership. Unfortunately the only people who could pilot the lander/return vehicle were both killed when the dome collapsed. None of the surviving five have any idea about piloting. One other person does but he is the captain and is the only person on board the orbiting mothership. There are no other landers on the ship so the five survivors are stuck where they are. Somehow they will have to survive for four years before the next expedition arrives, and they can be rescued. This is so realistically depicted it is nail-biting…

It is at this point Varley crosses from category two, realistic, into category one, fantasy, and category three, transformative, but he does so in a way that is plausible and scientific if not a bit speculative. He postulates Mars having an extended summer and winter, as does the Earth with its occurring cold periods with ice ages and warm periods where the ice has long melted, and this is tied in with rotation of the galaxy over a two hundred thousand year period. It takes roughly that long for our solar system to complete one orbit around the galactic centre (as the galaxy rotates), and we know, or think we know, that our isolated arm of the galaxy during this massive orbital rotation passes through a part of the universe that has more gas and dust clouds than other parts, resulting in a long period of much colder average temperatures producing ice ages on Earth followed by, as we emerge from the gas and dust cloud, a long period of warmer average temperatures. We are experiencing this now and our whole human civilization has arisen during this warming period.

Why not the same for Mars?

The survivors, as they gather the food and oxygen stored in the dome which gives them enough to survive for two years since there are now only five instead of twenty, discover the reason the dome collapsed. It was because the warmth inside the dome warmed the ground underneath with sufficient condensation to affect the regolith beneath. Something started growing underneath the dome, growing towards the warmth and the moisture. This something ate into the plastic, digesting it, and very quickly produced holes in the floor which caused the massive decompression of the dome. This stuff continues to grow as the survivors monitor it from their makeshift base in the lander.

Studying the ever strengthening growths they discover they are not plant like or animal but are made of plastic and metal refined from the regolith. They are engineered, and can replicate themselves. The survivors naturally study these growths which seem to adapt to the needs of the five who now think of themselves as colonists or settlers rather than expedition members. Firstly the strange growths produce clear ball like extrusions which contain oxygen which now means the colonists won't run out of something to breathe.

Later the growths produce larger dome shaped structures filled with oxygen into which the colonists manage to contrive a means of entering and exiting without losing the oxygen pressure inside. Now they have a way of surviving. They work out how to grow food. They come to an arrangement where they share each other emotionally and sexually, and when two of the women become pregnant they stop thinking of themselves as colonists. They have become Martians.

They speculate that Mars has glacial cycles like Earth does, periodically having warm wet periods with running water every two or three hundred thousand years alternating with super cold dry periods which is how we have known it for the last 100 years or so that reasonably accurate observations have shown. That isn't beyond the realm of possibility. But their conclusion that other alien beings engineered the life that has adapted to them and allowed them to survive, postulating that it is designed to prepare the planet as it warms, to make it liveable once again for the return of the original inhabitants, is a fantasy.

When another expedition arrives 8 years later to gather the dead bodies of the first disastrous attempt to settle on Mars, they find a thriving colony of five adults and several children who consider Mars their home. They have no intention of being rescued. In fact they want to wait until the original engineers return to a warmer and wetter planet even if it will take many generations for that to happen.

Is engineered life a fantasy or a possibility? Ii it something we could possibly see in our lifetime? Is this story is science fantasy or science fiction? In my view it is both, as well as being transformative with the five humans becoming something else by the end. Will Mars be transformed into a more habitable planet through this engineered life, and will the original engineers of this life return? How many thousands of years will the planet stay like that before reverting back to a cold and desiccated environment?

These are questions left hanging, leaving the reader desperately wanting more.

Not too many stories can do this.

Two Mars novels from the 1970s have the underlying theme of a contest between Russia and America; a time of Mutually Assured Destruction with both nations on the brink of a nuclear catastrophe which to everyone at that time seemed inevitable. There was tension and conflict between two radically different ideological approaches to life and this is manifested in a race between them to be the first to go to Mars. (Much the same as what happened between the two countries that ended up with American astronauts going to the Moon.)

These two books, ***Man Plus*** by Frederick Pohl (1976), and ***The Martian Inca***, by Ian Watson, (1977), are radically different from each other although both are concerned with a major transformation. ***The Martian Inca*** is more mainstream SF while ***Man Plus*** is traditional SF with mainstream elements. Pohl evolved from the pulp tradition of SF in America while Watson came from the more literary British tradition established by such people as H G Wells and Olaf Stapledon.

Both authors delved deeply into the characters of their protagonists, something not often done in science fiction novels, and this puts them well above other books of the 1970s.

The Martian Inca (1977) opens with a returning Russian robotic probe from Mars, carrying a sample of Martian soil, having a mishap. Instead of landing safely in Kazakhstan it crash lands on the Altiplano of Bolivia, high in the Andes Mountains, just behind a village that is having a fiesta and everyone rushes to the site to see what happened, and to grab whatever they can for salvage. Anyone who handled the parachute cloth used to slow the descent, or who ran their hands through the spilled Martian soil or who breathed in the dust of it, almost immediately is struck down with a terrible affliction.

Doctors are brought in from La Paz to try and cure the villagers. Police and Army are brought in to control the villagers so none will leave. No matter what the doctors do, all those afflicted die horribly, except for two who managed to avoid any treatment.

One, Julio, ran off and hid in a cave while the other, Angelina, was kept hidden by the tribe's healer so the foreign doctors from La Paz wouldn't touch her. He knew she would survive if left alone. They became paralysed, went into a coma and almost appeared to be dead before they came back to life a few weeks later.

Meanwhile a trio of American astronauts are on their way to Mars, and N ASA wants to warn them about the danger of the Martian soil and to tell them not to land as planned.

The survivor Julio, who comes out of his cave with enhanced perception of the world around him, decides he wants to recreate the ancient Inca Empire. He sets out, alongside his girlfriend Angelina who has also undergone a similar transformation, with followers from the village to start a revolution.

Government soldiers take the remains of the Russian probe back to La Paz. The Russians want it back. The Americans want to examine the two survivors of the Martian infection. They need to know what happened in case it could happen to their astronauts on the way to Mars. The Bolivians don't want anything to do with the Russians or the Americans and keep their borders closed to both.

With the American astronauts arriving in orbit around Mars, the plan was to land and examine the surface, and after various tests, return to the command module. They want to position a huge unfolded mirror over one of the Polar ice caps to reflect sunlight down to melt it to increase the carbon dioxide content of the air, warming the planet to take it out of its long winter period. But that plan was changed. Ignoring the advice from NASA not to land they decide two will go down while the third will remain on orbit in the command module, in case something happens.

This is the first story that mentions the sky is pink, so Watson was paying attention when the first photos came back from the Mars Rovers in July and September 1976.

Something does happen: one of the astronauts has a minor accident while setting up an external habitat to examine the soil in detail. His space suit is pierced near his foot. Going back inside the Lander the other one treats his partner's damaged foot wiping away some blood and some dust that got in through the damaged suit. Within hours the astronaut is afflicted with the same disease that wiped out the Bolivian villagers.

Advice from NASA is to leave him alone and don't try to treat him in any way.

As part of the background the Russians have been sending probes to Venus. They plan to start terraforming the planet by seeding the atmosphere with bacteria that will break it down by consuming carbon dioxide and releasing oxygen, eventually changing it into something more like that of Earth; a process that will take many decades. They have decided to leave Mars to the Americans.

The Americans are still trying to work out what to do about their astronauts on the surface of Mars. The sick astronaut has been transformed and he has visions of how life on Mars works. He wants to continue with his experiments to verify his visions but the one in the command module wants them to return. NASA advises not to let them return but to leave them there. Meanwhile a dust storm is developing as a result of the mirror the lone astronaut in orbit has placed over the pole. The night before they are due to return to orbit the recovered astronaut cuts his partner on the leg with a scalpel and rubs in some Martian soil knowing it contains the micro-organisms which will infect and transform him.

There is no way NASA will allow them to come back so the one in orbit is ordered to return to Earth.

On Mars the developing storm damages the Lander beyond repair and all that survives is the small geodesic dome established for their experiments with the soil. The astronauts have nothing to eat so the presumption is that they will not survive.

The implication is also that Mars will be a very dangerous place for humans to try and colonize.

Throughout this story there is much speculation about evolution of consciousness and suggestions that this kind of transformation has taken place randomly over millennia giving rise to ancient Egyptians and their Mummies, the establishment of the Inca Empire, which almost overnight grew out of a few obscure hillside tribes to become a dominant culture until the Spanish destroyed it, and life in general throughout the universe and how it could evolve.

Most of the time on the trip to Mars is spent not on detailing what they do to survive the long journey but on back story about the astronauts and their life before, which brings to life the fragmented paranoid society of the period that Watson has extrapolated from the world of the 1970s.

This book, though in the transformative category also could be included in a sub-category of books about invasion from space. Such invasion stories are not always about Mars. This one is.

Double Shadow, by Frederick Turner (1978)

Frederick Turner is a poet and before this novel, he had already published 5 books of poetry, one of criticism and one of translations of poetry from German. ***Double Shadow*** was his first novel. After this he composed an epic book length poem about the colonization and terraforming of Mars, called ***Genesis***. I had this book in my collection around the 1980s but put it aside after reading the first 40 pages. I wasn't that fond of poetry then, although I don't mind some these days. The book disappeared later and I have no idea what happened to it. I did not finish reading it, so can't comment.

The setting for ***Double Shadow*** is Mars; Mars that has been terraformed for a thousand years or more, and has a society evolved with modified humans of three sexes; male, female, and hermaphrodite. Ancient extinct animals have been revived in the wilder places.

The engineers and scientists who changed the planet established their original base in the crater of Olympus Mons which is now the abode of humans so far advanced they are virtually gods to those who live below. Part of the terraforming included turning Phobos into a second sun to generate additional warmth, making dormant volcanos erupt to fill the atmosphere with greenhouse gasses as well as constructing a series of canals —as an homage to Schiaparelli who first saw blurred interconnecting lines and called them canali— to connect the two major seas resulting from the warming of the planet: the Hellespontic Ocean and the Helene Sea. The canals were built more for the use of pleasure craft by the inhabitants rather than to channel water for irrigation.

This is a literary fantasy, not science fiction or science fantasy, although fantastic science underlies background details it often appears magical. It was marketed as a novel and not categorised as genre. There is a lot of mythology mixed together influencing the way people live, Greek, Egyptian, Hindu and Japanese, with gods from all these cultures residing on mount Olympus and interfering with the inhabitants on the surface below.

The story is a simple one of two rival nobles whose lifestyles are radically different but when one insults the other there is a perceived loss of face and so a challenge is issued and a Status War begins between them. Mostly this involves one of them trying to embarrass the other at every opportunity until eventually there is a proper challenge and duel is proposed in which one of them will die. Both combatants have many followers who watch every move, since there hasn't been a status war on Mars for centuries. While the status war develops there is much meddling from the gods on Olympus who can inhabit other normal people making them do things they don't know they are doing.

The fantastic duel finally takes place in the air above Coprates Canyon with both participants wearing wings and sharpened spurs on their wrists and ankles so they can slash at each other as they fly: literally a cockfight in the air. The fight takes place over three days with the wounds each participant inflicts on the other being healed by the super science of the gods at night while they rest at night. There is also much debauchery as the population doesn't work and lives only for pleasure. Those who do work such as artisans, actors, writers and painters only work for the enjoyment of it.

The style to me seems overly literary and poetical in places, with examples of Haiku and other poetical forms prominent near the conclusion. The author occasionally interjects to inform the reader of something about to happen, and although this must have been a common mainstream literary device over the earlier part of the last century, it now seems old-fashioned because it interrupts the flow of the story.

There is no question the writing is good, it just doesn't appeal to me. I couldn't get involved with the characters. I did like the background material regarding the terraforming of Mars but overall it was too much of a fantasy for me. No doubt there are many who would love this book.

The Far Call (1978) by Gordon Dickson is a story of the first international expedition to Mars, which is basically an American effort but it has marsnauts from six nations participating: America, Russia, Pan-Europe, England, Japan, and India, all nations that have active space exploration programmes at the present time. China wasn't mentioned because when this book was written China seemed unlikely to be involved in space exploration. Today, it is likely to eclipse most of the others except perhaps for Russia and America.

Although copyrighted in 1973 it must have been in the process of being written over several years because it wasn't published until 1978.

Dickson must have seen the photos transmitted back from the Viking 1 Rover (*which began activities on the surface in July 1976, and lasted until November 1982*) since in his description of the surface seen by the Russian marsnaut who finally makes it to Mars he sees an orange pink sky partly shrouded with fine dust. The surface seen as the lander descends is cratered and rocky (*as shown by earlier photos from the Mariner missions*). Dickson, like Watson the year before also mentions the Martian sky is pink. Before the mid 1970s other authors described the sky as anything from deep blue to purple or almost black because of the thin atmosphere, or various shades of murky brown because of the dust storms thought to be continually blowing across the surface.

This is a big sprawling character driven novel dealing as much with the political intrigues and manoeuvres by the representatives of the six nations involved in the project as it does with the voyage to Mars and what happens on the way. (Two anachronisms date it slightly, reporters using typewriters and faxes and the use of video phone booths instead of public phone booths. There was no mention of cell phones. No one in the 1970s era could even imagine cell phones and other portable devices like tablets and the effect they would have on communications worldwide.) But these minor distractions in an otherwise excellent story can easily be ignored. The political posturing and the unwillingness to compromise without losing face is as typical today as it was in the 1970s.

The story is set towards the end of the century, no dates mentioned, and begins the night before the shuttle launches to take the six marsnauts up to the two waiting space ships. Presumably they were built in orbit. There are three marsnauts in each ship so if something happens to one ship the other can continue the mission.

There is concern by the marsnauts that the number of experiments each participating nation wants them to do while en-route to Mars is too much, but no amount of asking to have this reduced is successful. No nation wants to lose face by having something less than the others and the American president won't intervene because he doesn't want to be seen as bullying the others. Tad, the American marsnaut asks his white house science representative to intervene by asking the president to ask the other nations observers to reduce the experimental load but he refuses. It is up to the marsnauts to ask for reductions while on the ships and on their way to Mars, that way no one loses face.

The ships are tethered together and are made to rotate around a common centre creating a low gravity environment. There is an access tube between the two ships so they can cross over from one to the other. Once the ships leave orbit and head to Mars things start to go wrong. The marsnauts find there is not enough time to do all they are supposed to do and get tired enough to start making mistakes. A severe solar storm a few weeks into the voyage forces them to take the precaution of separating the ships to conduct an experiment to measure the radiation. During the storm communication is lost and they have to resort to more primitive methods of using radio instead of laser communication. Tad, the American marsnaut makes an EVA to check the laser and finds the radiation in the solar storm has damaged some electronic parts. He asks one of the others to find the spares so he can repair it but it turns out not enough spare parts were loaded on board because of all the equipment needed for each nation's experiments. It can't be repaired. Unfortunately the gauge measuring the solar radiation outside the ship is faulty showing less than there actually is and he cops a severe dose of exposure to radiation. He is brought inside and immediately is showered and the medical officer gives him a complete blood transfusion, but the radiation dose was too much and this only delays his eventual death.

Mission control decides to abort the mission while they can still return to Earth. The marsnauts don't want to do this, nor do the representatives of the six nations either. They want the mission to continue. The marsnauts know that if they abort there will never be another Mars mission. Eventually they contrive a plan in which five of them will return to Earth in the ship piloted by the dying American while the other ship will continue on to Mars piloted by the mission's second in command, the Russian marsnaut.

As this is happening there is much posturing and blame-laying by the various governments representatives and they decide to lay the blame on the marsnauts for the failure of the mission rather than on themselves for expecting them to do much en-route to Mars.

However the American White House science representative makes a statement at a press conference in which he explains it isn't the marsnauts who are at fault, but the six governments who expected them to do far more than they were physically capable of achieving. He is arrested but now the public knows the truth.

Finally the lone Russian Marsnaut arrives in Mars orbit. He is also sick and slowly dying, but he brings his lander down and exiting the ship he struggles to set up a rig where he can half-stand-half-sit and look out across the Martian surface. He sets up the United Nations flag and the individual flags of the nations involved in the expedition and sits on his support rig with an immense sense of pride as he looks at the ship and the desolate planet around him, knowing that because he made it, others will also come in the near future.

This is one of Gordon Dickson's best novels and is well worth reading if you haven't already done so.

The Transformative Visions of Frederick Pohl and Kevin J Anderson

Man Plus by Frederick Pohl (1976) is an unusual Mars story because very little of it takes place on Mars.

In chapter 3 Pohl sums up a history of what we know about Mars starting from Schiaparelli seeing canali in 1877, to Lowell Thomas with his canals and ancient cities, to improvements in telescopic viewing and the eventual realization that Mars is too cold, has too little air, no water on the surface, to the first Mariner flybys which convinced the world that there was no Martian Race. He briefly explains how an unprotected human could be killed on Mars from freezing, from a lack of air, from thirst, from exposure to unshielded solar radiation and so on. Nothing grows there so there is nothing there humans could eat. An unprotected human would be lucky to last 15 minutes on the surface.

He mentions that an unprotected human would also die in Antarctica, but we still go there and survive there. We survive by bringing a kinder environment with us.

We would do this on the Moon since we can't survive there either. But the Moon can be supplied from Earth with essentials, at any time. Any day a rocket can be launched and it will be at the Moon in a few days.

Not so Mars, it is too far away. It can only be reached when it most closely approaches Earth. Earth orbits the sun twice while Mars only makes one orbit. There are two months or a bit less when both are on the same side of the sun and in line. Any trip to Mars must take place so the ship arrives when the planets are at their closest point every two earth years. Since the trip takes several months to get there the journey must be planned so arrival in Mars orbit coincides when Mars is there, or the ship would continue on forever. And as well, the return journey can't take place soon after arriving or when the ship gets back to Earth orbit the Earth won't be there, but will be further around its orbit of the sun and most likely on the far side away from Mars. The ship must wait almost an earth year before commencing the return journey to guarantee they will both arrive at the same spot at the same time.

To supply a colony on Mars as you would one on the Moon is impossible. The colony has to be self-sustaining. Changing Mars so it is suitable for human occupation would take centuries, and in this story, time is of the essence if they are to prevent a cataclysm of our own making on Earth. The only solution is to alter humans so they can live on Mars. This is the premise of Pohl's story.

It is not about going to Mars.

It is about making a human into something that can live on Mars. Changing a human to fit the Martian climate, and not trying to make Mars suitable for humans, or setting up a colony that is self-sufficient which would over time cost more than the resources of Earth could afford.

Take away the lungs and replace them with a miniaturized oxygen regenerating system, and the circulatory system from the extremities, remove the skin and replace it with something that can withstand solar radiation, augment the major muscles with mechanical ones and the need for food is almost eliminated, replace the eyes with special cameras that can see infrared wavelengths as well as ultra-violet and beyond, and for energy add solar wings to absorb energy from the sun or radiation beamed down from a satellite orbiting Mars to power mechanical and electronic systems built in, but keep the brain and the personality of the human so it can interpret what it sees and feels and what do you have? —a Cyborg.

Is a Cyborg still human, or is it something else?

This is the question that Pohl answers in this novel.

The first attempt fails. The subject's brain ceases functioning from too much input that can't be processed and he dies. The next in line has a broken leg so the third in line, Roger Torraway, steps up, not quite willing to be transformed.

Once word of the project to create a cyborg that can live on Mars is out it fires up a new Space Race between America, China, and Russia who are competing for the same end result. There is much unrest in the world with small wars going on in many different places and the general belief is that humans need to establish a colony on Mars or they will be wiped out like the dinosaurs, only it will be of our own doing and not some accidental event from outer space.

Pohl paints vivid images of a world descending into chaos with the inevitability of world war and self-destruction if something isn't done soon to change things. But this is part of the background extrapolated from the reality we know existed during the 1960s and 1970s, and some of it is very much like what is happening right now in our own time. One of the things that could delay the inevitable would be to establish a human presence on Mars.

There are a couple of things that jar the consciousness and one is he has Spacelab continuing on and becoming bigger and grander than it is, doing the job that the present International Space Station does. It may have seemed that Spacelab would do that in the 1970s, but Pohl could not have known that America would abandon it and allow it to burn up in the atmosphere as it fell back to Earth. He was also being inventive by having room sized computers shrunk down to the size of a backpack which the cyborg wears and needs for proper functioning, but the development of computers into what they are today was simply beyond imagining in 1976. There is more power in a laptop or a Smartphone than what they had when America was sending astronauts to the Moon, but we can discard this and simply enjoy the story. He wrote this in the early part of the 1970s.

The modifications to make a human into a cyborg seem reasonable and possible, although not a great deal of specific information is given. Enough is suggested however to make it seem plausible. That they could do it and that it would be expensive is implied, and that it would have to be a secret government project is also stated. They were in a race to get a presence on Mars, and China and Russia were right on their heels with similar projects.

Roger is an unforgettable character. He becomes a monster to look at, with glowing lenses for eyes, skin like a rhinoceros, strange bat wings extruding from his shoulders to stretch out above his head for gathering solar radiation. Everything, eyes, ears, lungs, nose, mouth, calculating systems, perception centres, heart, all replaced or augmented, rebuilt for the sole purpose of surviving on Mars. But underneath this he is still very human. He is worried about his wife who is having an affair with one of the people working to turn him into a cyborg, but there is nothing he can do about it since as part of the process he has been emasculated. He has problems adjusting to heightened awareness, and for a while he believes himself to be a monster.

As these inner feelings are resolved Roger comes to accept himself for what he is.

Finally the cyborg team accompanies him to Mars where for the first time he is allowed to be free. This is only the last couple of chapters and the trip out is glossed over in a paragraph or two. Roger's experience of what it is like to be a creature that can live on the surface of Mars as it is, and how he sees the beauty that mere humans confined to unenhanced perceptions, space suits and pressurized habitats cannot is the highlight of a profound study in what it is to be human.

Some chapters begin with an odd fist person statement usually beginning with … we saw, we did, we understood that Roger was… and so on before dropping back into the third person narrative from Roger's viewpoint. It is revealed in the epilogue that the whole project had been instigated by artificial intelligences which consist of various worldwide computer networks that think they will be destroyed if humanity destroys itself. They wish to continue existing so they subtly manipulate government programs in various countries to engineer humans to be able to live on another world, namely Mars since it is the nearest most logical contender. It is these AIs which create the impetus behind the ***Man Plus*** project. By moving humanity off Earth they save some of humanity but they themselves will also be able to survive.

One of Pohl's best stories…

Climbing Olympus (1994) by Kevin J Anderson takes place entirely on Mars with a couple of flashback scenes on Earth to set up background explanations. This novel also deals with transforming and augmenting humans so they can live on Mars unencumbered by space suits and habitats. There is a reference in this story to Americans working on a similar project to create a *man-plus* and this is a nice homage to Frederick Pohl's story where he also mentions the Russians and Chinese are working on augmenting humans to live on Mars. Anderson doesn't refer to his Martians as being cyborgs, and this is because they are not cyborgs (or humans augmented with mechanical and electronic devises like Pohl used), but surgically modified humans with extra lungs and thicker skin and other natural enhancements. Although sterilized (with vasectomies) they were not emasculated. They retain more of their human characteristics than does Pohl's Man-plus cyborg.

The back story is that a corrupt Russian government (that doesn't want the Americans to get ahead of them) has given the okay to Dr Rachel Dychek to augment humans so they can live on Mars and she has a choice of her society's criminals and unwanted prisoners in Siberia to experiment with. She offers them the chance to be free if they undergo the complex surgeries needed to make them able to survive in the harsh conditions on Mars, and they accept. Many die during the process but there are enough to complete the project. Taking them to Mars over the 4 month journey the ship gradually lowers the temperature and the air pressure so that when the ship arrives they will be conditioned to what they will find on the surface; extreme cold often as low as minus 100C and air pressure that is barely more than one percent of that of Earth. Some of them die on the way. Others die on Mars after a few days leaving only the toughest of them to do their jobs. Their work on Mars is to build habitats for the humans who will be following that are sent out by the UNSA (United Nations Space Agency) and to begin the process of terraforming Mars. Since the project was secret and UNSA knew little about it they are most upset when Russia announces it has landed humans on Mars who can live on the surface.

When these first augmented humans later realize that by terraforming Mars they will doom themselves because they would not be able to live in such a climate, they revolt, and the toughest of them who is their leader (Boris) publicly executes the UNSA administrator on Mars by breaking his neck during a live broadcast to Earth. Now wanted for murder these augmented humans known as Adins (first in Russian) race off into the rugged terrain of the land near the extinct volcano Pavonis Mons where they hide out and eventually everyone thinks they are dead.

On Earth in Russia Dr Dychek had created more advanced surgically altered humans for living on Mars. These she calls Dva (second in Russian), and this time she asked for volunteers and she got many who were scientists and doctors and other professional people from a minority group that had been exiled from their own country. Their idea was to recreate their country on Mars where they could live without fear of repression and exile. Though by agreeing to surgery there was no coming back to Earth. Dr Dychek is called in by the UN to explain her reasons for doing what she had done, which was illegal and secretive, and unhappy with her explanations they send her to Mars as punishment to oversee her Dva begin the transforming of the planet. She is the Administrator.

Rather than go into medical details Kevin J Anderson has his story begin on Mars with Dr Dychek waiting replacement in a day or so and visiting the site of an avalanche that killed half of her Dva workforce. The novel crosses back and forth between her and the activities at Port Lowell the main base, and the five still living Adin led by Boris, (15 years later now) living in caves high up the slopes of Pavonis Mons. Boris is still determined to stop the transformation of Mars and believes the whole planet belongs to him and his crew since they are the only ones able to live there. What spurs him on is that his woman is pregnant and about to give birth. He knows the baby will be human and will not survive being born; unable to breathe the icy thin air it would die before it would freeze. He wants it to die so he can show the humans at Port Lowell that unaltered humans should not be on Mars. He takes one of the other Adin with him and they descend down the slopes of Pavonis Mons and attack a water reclamation and pumping station run by Dva. Boris wrecks the pump and the pipes and water spills out instantly freezing before beginning to sublimate. His companion bursts into the habitat of the Dva and tries to kill the five in there but only manages two before they kill him. Boris retreats back up Pavonis Mons leaving his dead companion there.

When Dr Dychek comes to see what the emergency was about she discovers the dead Adin and is excited that some of her first augmented humans are still alive. She follows the tracks left by Boris and discovers the hideout on Pavonis Mons where she also discovers that Boris' woman Cora Marisovna is pregnant and about to give birth. She convinces the woman to come with her back to Port Lowell where there is medical equipment to help her.

Angry that Dr Dychek has found them he threatens to kill her, but Cora intervenes and he disappears outside where he pushes the rover Dr Dychek uses over the side of a cliff. When Dychek and Cora leave they find the rover gone, and no sign of Boris anywhere.

Back at the base they are worried that Dr Dychek hasn't returned and they can't contact her by radio, so the new administrator goes out to search for her in the only other rover. They only have a few hours because a massive storm is threatening and will be upon them soon. Not knowing where Dr Dychek went, she doesn't often log her outings as she should, they head off to the site of the avalanche where the Dva were killed thinking she might have gone there one last time before returning to Earth.

The storm is brewing and the other surviving Adin help Dr Dychek get down to the rover to see if it is still okay. These are tough machines and it soon rights itself. No damage was done. She manages to get Cora inside where suddenly her labour intensifies. The baby is about to be born. Seeing the others betray him Boris is furious and rushes down to the rover and tries to smash his way in. He wants to kill all the occupants. He smashed a small hole in the windscreen which Dr Dychek manages to patch, but to be on the safe side she takes off her space suit and puts the newly born baby inside where a proper air pressure can be maintained. Cora is having trouble breathing the thicker air so she goes outside where she is immediately attacked by Boris. Dr Dychek starts the rover and it makes its way down the side of the volcano following the gully it had been dropped into. Her last site of Cora is that she has wrestled the spear from Boris and has stabbed him in the chest.

At the same time Jesus Keefer the new administrator has arrived at the avalanche site and sees a Dva running away. He and his companion follow and end up in a dead end. They discover a fake rock door which they slide open and follow a tunnel deeper into the cliff side. They go through several doors which are actually airlocks and finally enter a large series of partially pressurised chambers where there are many Dva workers. There is a garden and suddenly the leader of this group confronts them. These are the Dva that were supposedly killed in the avalanche. It was faked. Their plan all along was to install a separate habitat so they could give birth to human children who could survive, and this way they could claim Mars for themselves. By having descendants, the land they were promised for their lifetime would go on to their children and thus they could recreate their lost homeland on a new world.

All the men were sterilized during the medical processes that made them Adin or Dva while the women were not. Unfortunately the vasectomies were not always done properly thus allowing Boris to become a father. With the Dva, they brought frozen sperm with them to impregnate their womenfolk. Their idea was to present the children once born to the base to show the whole world that humans will be able to survive on Mars, even before the full terraforming had been completed. Unfortunately they had been discovered too soon. Their women still had a few months to go before giving birth. They knew nothing of the whereabouts of Dr Dychek, and hadn't seen her since the fake avalanche.

Before the sand storm arrives with full force, the new administrator and the leader of the Dva head back to Port Lowell. Dr Dychek also finally makes it back to base and gets her new born baby into the medical centre. Needless to say this baby causes a sensation at Port Lowell, and news of its birth is broadcast back to Earth.

Not long after there is a banging on the habitat wall and looking out through a window they see a badly injured Cora lying in the dust. She had been severely beaten and dumped there by Boris, who again is nowhere to be seen. However he soon turns up and tries to smash his way in to the medical centre. He is determined to kill the baby to prove his point that unaltered humans cannot live on Mars. Also the new administrator has managed to come back with the leader of the missing Dva and he wants to see the first human baby born on Mars.

At this point Boris smashes his way in and there is an explosive decompression of the medical base. Dr Dychek cuts Boris with a surgical laser forcing him back outside. She tries to patch the hole while the Dva leader rushes out to confront Boris, to stop him. Boris kills his new opponent, receiving further serious injuries in the fight. Knowing he has lost his battle he rushes off to hide in the wilderness, alone and unwanted. The last we see of him, he is climbing Mount Olympus where he feels he will be safe from humans. He can no longer live down where the air is getting thicker, and Mount Olympus, the highest mountain in the whole solar system, is his final retreat.

This story deals with the people who came to change Mars and in the process ended up being changed themselves. Kevin J Anderson portrays the minds and feelings of all the different humans with great skill and empathy and has crafted a memorable story that reflects ideas first presented in Pohl's much earlier book. The two books complement each other perfectly by giving both the American side (***Man Plus***) and the Russian side (***Climbing Olympus)*** even though there is almost a 20 year gap between when each was written and published.

Also in 1994 a sequel to ***Man Plus*** by Frederick Pohl called ***Mars Plus*** was published, written in collaboration with Thomas T Thomas.

The events in this story take place fifty years after the conclusion of ***Man Plus***. I suspect this story was written by Thomas T Thomas; it just doesn't read like something written by Frederick Pohl even though it has his name on the cover.

Mars has a population of about 30,000 scattered over several colonies which are mostly human along with partially modified human/cyborg combinations. Also outside there are a number of free cyborgs including Roger Torraway who is now the oldest and the first of the Cyborgs to inhabit the planet.

At the end of ***Man Plus*** Frederick Pohl revealed that the computers controlling the worldwide computer net have become sentient and that there were a number of these sentient conglomerations manipulating events to create the programs to get humans to settle on Mars. This was for their own preservation as well as that of humankind because if there was a war then everyone, human and AI would lose out.

On Mars the computer intelligences control everything needed for the colonists to survive, but they are secretly still manipulating events for their own purposes, one of which is to set up an AI group around the edges of the solar system.

The story involves a young female spy sent to Mars to find out what is going on in Valles Marineris, because she represents the company that was once NASA but is now privately owned that lays claim to this area and to the cyborg Roger Torraway, who incidentally appears briefly at the beginning and only reappears towards the end of the story. A New Zealand as well as a Korean group is interested in the same area. There is much talk about terraforming Mars by smashing comets into it to increase the water and atmospheric content, but this would likely damage the delicate balance that exists on the planet and the computer intelligences don't want this to happen.

In the process of her finding out what is going on we discover that there is a group of dissidents who believe the computers are deliberately manipulating events and they want to stop it. Everywhere they go is monitored so they have managed to find a disused part of the colony, long abandoned because the ground they bored the tunnels in was too unstable, and in here they set up a hiding place that is secure. They are trying to construct a computer to generate viruses to be inserted into the mainframes to disrupt all the AIs that control Mars.

There is much talk about computers and computer human interfacing with implanted chips and other computer parts. There is much background information about how this works and how the colony operates which slows down the action taking place. I'm not sure whether this was meant to be written for younger readers or for adults; it has the feel of a juvenile but there is enough weird sex between human and partial cyborg enhanced human that push it into the adult area.

I feel the only reason Frederick Pohl's name is on this book is that Thomas T Thomas may have asked to use Roger Torraway and the implied future of Mars suggested by Pohl in ***Man Plus*** and probably also asked Pohl for suggestions regarding possible futures for the AIs in the story. But then Pohl may have created the synopsis and the general plot and given it to Thomas to complete the writing.There is little character development and it reads like a straight forward adventure on Mars which includes romance, intrigue, a couple of fight scenes and an enigmatic ending regarding the Artificial Intelligences and the differences between them and humans.

I would place this book in category two whereas ***Man Plus*** and ***Climbing Olympus*** definitely fall into category three.

Chapter Nine

The almost Empty Eighties

Compared to previous decades (1940s, 1950s, and 1960s) not so many stories about Mars were published during the 1980s. Most SF writers were depicting an overpopulated Earth with pollution problems or other dystopian visions of our future. It was a decade when SF writers were extrapolating the demise of Governments around the world through economic collapse and small wars known euphemistically as police actions, rather than the more recent stories using global warming or anthropocentric interference with natural ecology via excessive carbon emissions as a base from which to extrapolate. They re-examined Earth and how it was developing into a grungy polluted environment where too many people struggled to survive amidst dwindling resources and ever growing anarchy and chaos.

Some novels from the 1970s had taken into account discoveries made by Mariner 4 and Mariner 6, and Mars looked like a dead planet half covered with impact craters. It was no longer as exciting to SF writers as it had been in earlier decades so they moved on to locales further out into the solar system and nearby star systems where once again they could let their imaginations run wild.

Mars was almost forgotten other than by conspiracy theorists who always believe aliens inhabit Mars or one or more of Earth's nations has a secret base on Mars, or there are hidden messages carved into enigmatic faces that can only be seen from orbit.

But there are some books from the 1980s. ***The Day the Martians Came*** by Frederick Pohl (1988) was the only one I actually got in the late 1980s. ***Frontera*** by Lewis Shiner (1984), I discovered twenty-five years later and I have subsequently found several others; ***Menace Under Marswood*** by

Sterling Lanier (1983), ***The Greening of Mars*** by James Lovelock and Michael Allaby (1984), ***Martian Spring*** by Michael Lindsay Williams (1986) and ***Crescent in the Sky*** by Donald Moffit (1989), so Mars had not been entirely forgotten.

One way of dealing with the new reality of Mars was to set a story well into the future after the planet had been terraformed, or alternatively very far back in the past when the planet had water on the surface and a thicker atmosphere with presumably some indigenous life. Stories like that inevitably fall into category one, Fantasy, where anything goes within reason: sword and sorcery, epic adventures that feel exotic yet medieval, or a slight suggestion of science to underlay the fantasy as a way of explaining the present in which the story takes place. Authors could let their imagination run wild without having to adhere strictly to scientific fact. If the story was well enough written the reader could easily suspend belief and accept what the author presented with pleasure and enjoyment.

Menace under Marswood by Sterling E Lanier (1983)

It is stated within the first few pages that Mars has been terraformed for centuries and that humans seeded the planet with many plants, animals, birds and insects to create an earth like biosphere, but the Chinese didn't want their rivals, the capitalistic Americans, and the neo-revisionist Russians to divide the world between them, so they too sent colonists as well as all manner of insects from spiders, scorpions, flies, wasps, lice, poisonous beetles, and plants like kudzu vines, poison ivy, and Mongolian thorn bushes among other strangely interesting plants — all no doubt with the idea to upset their rivals. But what happened was that with the lesser gravity of Mars and the constant radiation from space most of these imported life forms mutated and grew much bigger, and became far more dangerous than their earthly progenitors. A large portion of the planet has become a wilderness too dangerous for most people. But there are groups of humans who went into the bush, called the Ruck and who stayed there, learning to live with their new and constantly developing environment. They fractionated into tribes that belonged to certain areas and they constantly fight against the other normal settlers who live in walled village communities and forts where soldiers maintain constant vigilance against predation by the Ruckers, the wild humans.

But something strange is happening. A new clan led by an ex-convict murderer is trying to unite the wild tribes against the other human settlers.

They want to push them off the planet altogether so the true men, the Ruckers can have Mars to themselves. The government won't allow this to happen so a small group (of three elite soldiers plus four Ruckers) is formed to penetrate the wilder parts of the planet, especially the badlands, where mysterious events seem to be occurring, to find what is happening and to prevent it if they can.

Basically this is an exciting adventure through the wildest jungle imaginable and is full of tension as the group goes deeper and deeper into the Ruck. What they find in the badlands is something very alien, something that has been on Mars for millions of years; something the ex-convict and his vicious new clan want to take advantage of to eliminate any rivals. It is up to the specialist team to contact this alien being in a hidden fort, to understand what its purpose was on Mars and to prevent the rogue clan from using the alien to their benefit.

The final couple of chapters are non-stop action leading to an exciting climax, and is reminiscent of the stories written further back in the Golden Age of SF. It is nice to see this kind of story still being written while more realistic attempts to depict Mars were the current trend in the 1980s.

Frontera by Lewis Shiner (1984)

surprised many readers with its dystopian view of a collapsing world and its prediction of the abandonment of space exploration.

Shiner extrapolated the 1980s consequences of worldwide economic collapse in a novel about an expedition to Mars to get something that has been developed by people of a long abandoned colony that could be an 'Earth shattering' discovery.

Twenty years before the story begins NASA had sent expeditions to Mars and had established a colony. Reece, one of the Astronauts who had been instrumental in starting that colony had returned to Earth but never had the opportunity to go back to Mars. He left his daughter there along with all the other colonists.

NASA gave up sending any help or even wanting to get into space. It ran out of funding and one of the larger corporations in America bought all its assets at a very cheap price. Although the colony had been abandoned, information from them was regularly beamed back to Earth where the Huston facility recorded all the messages.

After most major world governments collapsed due to increasing debts, which left millions starving and out of work, there were for a period of 10 years constant riots and violence as many took whatever they wanted. The military forces disbanded and many members became mercenaries working for major corporations. Finally it was these mercenaries working for the corporations acting as policemen who quelled the riots.

The major corporations who employed the mercenaries imposed what they called a riot tax on anyone who was working and used this money to pay a basic pension to the millions unemployed which was just enough to allow them to live a frugal life. Things had settled down but there would need to be many years of rebuilding and consolidation to get anywhere near to how things had been before the collapse.

The American conglomerate that owns NASA and its facilities, in partnership with a Japanese Zaibatsu, come searching for Reece. They find a borderline alcoholic living on past glories and convince him to lead an expedition back to Mars. He is reluctant because he is 20 years past his prime. He also believes that everyone in the abandoned colony is dead after 20 years. Eventually he is convinced to come back and training at Huston begins.

Once there he discovers that not only are the colonists still alive, but so is his daughter and that they have developed something extremely important, which is why the corporations want to go there now. They only have 6 weeks to launch if they are to beat the Russians who have also heard that something very special has been developed on Mars by the colony left there. They want it as well. The Japanese corporations have partnered with the American one and they contribute to the cost as well as supply a couple of astronauts.

The training is intense, but they manage to leave two days ahead of the Russians. They first have to rendezvous with Deimos where a transfer base had been established but long abandoned. There is a Lander there that they will need to go down to Mars since their space ship isn't designed to land on a planetary surface.

The gritty grungy tone of the book is amply seen as the astronauts walk across the surface of Deimos to the moribund station through a field of debris; discarded oxygen tanks, pieces of broken machinery and other detritus simply tossed out of the station when it wasn't needed. That stuff would be there for eternity.

Luckily the Lander is still operational. Inside the station Reece recovers some data he will need when he is on the surface of Mars. He doesn't tell the other astronauts what he has. In fact he knows what it is that the Corporations want so desperately while the other members of his team don't. He worked it out while listening to the messages sent back to Huston.

On the surface Reece reconnects with his daughter in a colony that is barely surviving and discovers he has become a grandfather. His daughter has a daughter and many of the colonists also have children. Most of them are about 10 years old with a few younger ones.

They don't live much in the colony but occupy a cave nearby that they have turned into a laboratory. The cave was the original colony site until the domes and other pressurized buildings were constructed. The children are all mutations, their parents' DNA having been affected by the constant radiation that pours down onto the surface of Mars.

It is the children who have made the discoveries the world's governing corporations want.

The children have discovered a way to control anti-matter and it is this that the corporations want. They don't know at first that the children using this energy source have also developed a form of matter transmission which has yet to be perfected but can transmit something as far away as several light years. But Reece does. What he got from the station on Deimos was a set of data giving the coordinates of all nearby star systems. With this data he can get the children to transmit him to another world.

Why he wants to do this isn't really explained.

There is a confrontation between the Americans and the Russians once they land nearby and the colony is almost destroyed. The violence is eventually resolved by the children rather than the adults and the colony just survives. The Americans get what they want.

Reece finally gets what he wants. He is transmitted to another star system, and the story ends on a positive note after all the grunge and violence. (It would have been nice to know what happens to Reece after h e is transmitted to this other star system.)

Unlike most novels about going to or being on Mars Lewis Shiner focuses his story on the characters and their motivations rather than on the hardware and the science as earlier stories did. This is a more literary work that has some depth. The focus all the way through has been on the aging astronaut Reece, and the younger Kane, his protégé, their motivations, desires, and the things that have affected them over the years to make them who they are which in turn results in the outcomes achieved when they reach Mars.

This book presents a very different perspective of what it could be like living on Mars, isolated from a world that is slowly falling apart.

In retrospect I would say this was perhaps the first modern book that started the current trend of Mars stories being about an established colony left on its own struggling to survive after some catastrophe has destroyed any hope of rescue, contact, or return to Earth.

It set a fine precedent that most of the recent stories in this category apart from ***Snowfall on Mars*** by Brandon Frankell (2015) have yet to live up to.

Frontera was not the first story to extrapolate a grungy future, it was preceded by many stories in the 1950s that depicted in one way or another a deteriorating Earth, via political control and the threat of nuclear annihilation, or runaway pollution and overpopulation, which determined the reasons for expanding into the solar system and especially for colonizing Mars, and usually Mars was also depicted as rundown, or as a depressing struggling colony planet that was not much better than what was left on Earth.

Outpost Mars (1953, later reprinted as ***Mars Child***) by Cyril Judd, ***Gunner Cade,*** (1952) by Cyril Judd, ***Police Your Planet*** (1956) by Lester del Rey are three fine examples.

The Greening of Mars (1984) by James Lovelock and Michael Allaby is not a novel, but it is a story told as a report relating the history of the development of Mars and its colonization.

The publishers claim it is popular science, and this is partly true because there is a plethora of scientific detail about Mars and its atmosphere, its geography and terrain, but it is also a fictional memoir in the way the history of the colonization of Mars is told as seen from the perspective of a Martian looking back from the year 2245. It is also speculative in that it proposes ways in which Mars can be transformed into a place where humans can manage to live as well as suggesting that humans need to change as well to adapt to Mars. It is a two way process. Life changes the environment, but life also adapts and changes at the same time to fit into that changing environment.

James Lovelock is the author of ***Gaia*** and so it comes as no surprise that he suggests we can't terraform Mars to make it like Earth, but we can introduce life in the form of algae and lichen and bacteria which can begin the process of changing Mars so the planet will become alive. It is not that life adapts to a planet, but that the planet adapts to life and they both continue to change to create an entirely new living thing. Mars can be made habitable to a degree and much quicker than we would expect, but at the same time humans must change as well if they are to live on Mars, and in so changing they become a new species of human.

To make a 'science' book about how humans could change and live on Mars while changing Mars to be more amenable the authors have chosen to present this as a memoir from a second generation Martian who has been to Earth as a diplomat to report on how things are going on Mars and is currently returning to Mars accompanied by a group of new colonists. He composes a history of the evolution of a habitable Mars for use of future colonists. This history explains how CFCs were first used to thicken the atmosphere (starting from 1997 which the Martians now call their year One) to generate a rise in temperature, to the introduction of plants and the eventual arrival of Humans on the planet and how they must adapt to survive and more importantly how life itself causes the planet to change.

It is beautifully written and far more interesting than one would expect. It is speculative fiction while still being a scientific text on what should or can be done. From my point of view it falls into my second and third categories regarding Mars stories: factual because the scientific detail is accurate, and transformative in that it postulates changing Mars and Humans so they fit together harmoniously is an inevitable result of colonisation.

The Day the Martians Came by Frederick Pohl (1988) is not exactly a novel though it is billed as such. It is a collection of short stories 5 of which were written and published in 1976 and 1977, one which was written in 1972 and another from 1967 (about the same time as he wrote ***Man Plus***). This earlier one called ***The Day after the Martians came***, was probably the genesis for the other stories. He also wrote short segments to connect the individual stories together as well as three extra stories for this collection in 1988.

It almost reads as a novel, but it feels more like a TV mini-series. Each story is separate and complete, yet each is connected to the others by the background references to the Martians and the astronauts bringing them back to Earth.

The underlying theme expressed in the first story is that the expedition to mars that took 270 people there was a disaster. An accident with the ship carrying their supplies occurred on landing. Also through mismanagement and misuse of materials everyone on Mars was dying of radiation poisoning. The mission is abandoned and the 38 of the 270 astronauts that survive return to Earth.

Shortly before they leave they discover under the ground, under the ice of the North Pole, an ancient series of caves and a city that is occupied by seal like creatures, the remnants of an older Martian civilization.

They decide to bring five of these Martians back to Earth with them. That first story is straight SF, and so is the very final piece which is from the Martian's collective viewpoint. The second last links all the other stories together to complete the story arc.

The stories between the first and the second last are set on Earth — all except one in the USA — and deal with how people — mostly opportunists and con men — are affected by the discovery of Martians and of them being brought to Earth. These stories are not really SF but certainly are speculative.

There are real people brought into the short narratives that link the stories, like Carl Sagan, James Randi, Oprah Winfrey, and so on. The stories are sardonic and reflect an exaggerated view of what America was like in the decade of the 1980s. Several of them overlap enough to make the whole seem like a novel rather than a collection of stories.

This book falls into my first category (Fantasy) because of the discovery of an ancient underground complex and the remnants of living Martians, as well as for the feeling of it all being in a parallel time frame. The book flap says something about it being a satirical look at a near future America, but it seems to me to be set in an alternate America of the same time period in which it was written, the 1980s. It is a delightful collection nonetheless, and shows just how perceptive Frederick Pohl was at seeing into the American psyche.

Crescent in the sky (1989) Donald Moffitt

Moffitt proposes a radically different Mars resulting from Islamic expansion, firstly across the world and then into space which began after a serious oil crisis in the early twenty first century threw western countries into chaos. The rulers of Arab speaking countries who had accumulated most of the world's monetary funds through oil sales began buying property for food production, businesses and hotels for generating other funds and eventually they controlled everything.

This was already starting when Moffitt wrote this story in 1989 and has continued since then. He has extrapolated this trend a thousand years into the future. Also at that time US had not retired its shuttle fleet.

The migration of Muslim people into European countries eventually led to them having the major part of the population. They also tended to have much larger families which quickly gave them a majority in most countries. Baykonur in Kazakhstan where the Russians sent their cosmonauts into space was soon controlled by Islamic people as the Russian citizens retreated back to the more European part of the USSR. Islamic cosmonauts were initially sent into space from Batkonur until Saudi Arabia started building and buying space shuttles at the rate of two a week to send their people into orbit. But it wasn't only them; the Yemenis also did the same, as did the Mullahs from Iran. They also took into space their old animosities and the various factions do not always agree with each other, which leads to an interesting state of affairs on Mars.

After a thousand years or so Islamic people control the world completely and have colonized and partially terraformed Mars and have sent people out to establish colonies all over the solar system and several nearby star systems. The world (Earth) has divided into regions ruled by Emirs and Sultans who often don't agree with each other. It is the same on Mars. For those who live on another planet like Mars or even further out it is almost impossible to make the annual pilgrimage to Mecca. With the distances involved from another star system it simply can't be done.

The story opens with The Emir of Mars announcing two things; it is time for him to inhabit a new cloned body of himself, so he has arranged to be beheaded and for his head to be transplanted, and secondly he wants to go to Mecca where Islam's most holy shrine is located to vie for the position of Caliphate. There has not been a Caliphate for a thousand years.

Abdul Hamid-Jones, a young cloning technician who is the favoured of the Emir's clone-master, has been invited to attend the beheading ceremony. Unfortunately things go seriously wrong and the Emir is assassinated. Abdul atteempts to prevent one of the ginmen from shooting at the Emir afater which he finds himself involved in the subsequent power plays and political intrigues that threaten his life and all those whose allegiance belongs to the Vizier, the clone-master and his department in the Palace. The clone-master is arrested and charged with treason by those who wish to take over from the dead Emir and all who are associated with him are hunted down, arrested and subsequently tortured and executed at the behest of the Chamberlain who has substituted a pair of clones of the Emir to act as a figurehead so the public won't know the Emir is dead.

The desert rebels, descendants of the Bedouin tribes of North Africa, who live a harsh life away from the cities rebel against the usurper, and in fact were rebelling against the assassinated Emir claiming he was not the real head by descent but only because his father had usurped the old Emir centuries before. Their leader claims to be the rightful heir.

Hamid Jones finds himself a fugitive from the palace pogrom, forced to give up his chance to become someone important in the cloning department, as well as denied the love of his life who was the clone-master's daughter who has now associated herself with those that are taking over, he discovers an assassin has been hired to get rid of him. He flees into the desert and finds himself with the rebels. When he is captured by the new Palace forces he narrowly avoids torture and execution, being rescued by the Alpha Centauri Ambassador who doesn't agree with what has been happening on Mars. Islam has a beautiful future out amongst the stars and they need Hamid Jones to be a part of that.

Not too many authors have written about an Islamic future and this makes this particular story quite interesting in how Moffitt extrapolates situations and events based on how the world was in the late 1980s.

Mars as he depicts it and the way people and animals have adapted seems plausible, and the reader does get a credible image of what it would be like on Mars for those who have settled there. My overall impression is that the society depicted is barbaric rather than romantic, but the evocation of an Islamic Mars on the surface appears to be much like Islam was in its earlier history when it had spread across into Europe, a time of education and enlightenment, of scholarship and scientific innovation which overlaid the concept of Jihad and battles for control by different factions within Islam itself.

Crescent in the Sky is the first half of a much longer story. Once Hamid Jones is rescued he is taken to Alpha Centauri where the scientists there are developing a faster than light form of travelling which would allow Islamic culture to spread further into the Galaxy. Hamid Jones will no doubt have an integral part in this continuation of the story, but I have yet to read this part so cannot comment.

Martian Spring by Michael Lindsay Williams (1986) appears to be an exciting novel for younger readers about Mars beginning to thaw out as well as a first contact story. Somehow I missed reading this one...

I also missed in 1988, ***Desolation Road*** by Ian Mc Donald, his first novel, about a Mars that is vastly different from any other Mars imagined up to that time. It straddles all three of my arbitrary categories which means I can't categorize it at all. It was republished in 2009 as a prelude to a sequel ***Ares Express***, published in 2010, but more about this later…

Chapter Ten

An explosion of interest

1990 and on saw a huge renewal of interest in Mars, and during that decade more books, both novels and non-fiction works, as well as films appeared about Mars than in any other previous decade.

Voyage to the Red Planet by Terry Bisson (1990) was the first novel to appear.

This is a joyful and optimistic story considering it features a similar background concept as another novel from 6 years earlier where major corporations have taken over the functions of governments around the world, but that novel presented a much more depressing situation than does this one by Terry Bisson; notably the US Government has gone bankrupt and has sold off its various agencies to the highest bidders. Disney Studios bought NASA and all its assets. One of their hotshot producers has convinced the studio to bankroll him in producing a blockbuster movie to be filmed on Mars/

Unknown to the public, in its dying days NASA was preparing an expedition to Mars and had actually built a mile long spaceship for this lengthy journey and trained the pilots for it; a Russian woman and an American Man. The spaceship they hid behind orbiting radioactive garbage where no one could detect it, and it has remained there for almost 20 years. (All radioactive waste has been sent into orbit where it cannot affect the planet's environment.) The space station once used by international scientists for research (here called the Nixon Orbital Space Station) has been turned into an amusement park. The hidden spaceship is called the Mary Poppins because with its radiation shield expanded the ship appears like an opened umbrella.

The producer manages to find two registered movie stars to commit to being filmed on Mars and he convinces an award winning cinematographer to shoot the movie. He has also convinced the two originally trained pilots to fly the ship as well as a doctor.

While this process is underway we get to see the machinations behind the scenes of Hollywood blockbuster productions and all the things that can go wrong. There are constant bankruptcies and changing ownerships of businesses that cause delays but eventually the team heads up to the space station for transfer to the Mary Poppins. There is a rush because some other corporation claims ownership of the space ship and is sending someone up to take it. Finally with the expedition team on board and filming already started they de-orbit the Mary Poppins and head off into space on their way to Mars.

The trip involves a fall down into the gravity well of the Sun to use Venus as a slingshot to send them to Mars. This will be a long voyage and the crew will go into hibernation for the first half of the voyage and then again for the second half after a close flyby of Venus.

Not long after leaving the hidden orbit the crew discover they have two stowaways, a seventeen year old girl and a cat which the doctor smuggled on board, but it is a big ship designed to carry many more than its present crew so there is no need to throw anyone out into space — the dramatic centrepiece of many earlier novels and films dealing with space travel.

Bisson pays tribute to earlier works both in film and in books as his story progresses. On arrival at Mars the ship goes into orbit parallel to Phobos, but because the actress' hibernation unit malfunctions they are unable to wake her they take the young stowaway down to the surface with them to act in her place in the film. The cat and the still sleeping woman are left on the Mary Poppins.

They manage to get the Lander down close to one of the supply ships sent to Mars twenty years before and find it hasn't got enough fuel for them to regain orbit. It was supposed to be manufacturing fuel for the return to orbit of subsequent expeditions. Something has caused the fuel to leak out. They now need to search for the other ship, originally thought to be lost but the doctor thought he had seen it over in another deep valley as they were coming in for a landing. He saw something glistening momentarily anyway.

While the cinematographer is directing and filming the two actors walking about on the surface, the doctor and the American pilot take a small rover and start looking for the other missing supply ship. This part while containing a certain amount of tension is a factual description of what the surface area of their landing site is like. Bisson would have had photos from NASA from the Mars Rovers to get accurate descriptions and he integrates these well into the story with some speculation about cracks releasing heavy oxygenated air from frozen deposits of water beneath the surface.

Needless to say they find the other ship and its fuel tank is full so they start pumping the fuel out and into containers so they can take it back to their Lander. And here we come to the wishful thinking and the homage to previous ideas in Mars stories and films. The supply ship is not what the doctor saw and it is not in the same valley.

He goes for a walk telling his companion he is collecting samples and discovers an alien artefact in the shape of a glistening pyramid hidden in a valley where a series of old (millions of years old) steps form part of an amphitheatre. Taking his glove off he touches the alien pyramid and instantly finds himself inside it, and it appears much bigger inside than it did from the outside. It also has a higher air pressure so he can remove his helmet. On approaching a small spire in the centre a figure appears trying to explain something to him. The figure appears similar to an African only he is a bluish grey colour with masses of dreadlocks. The figure holds up globes of Earth and Mars as they may have appeared hundreds of millions of years ago, and the doctor believes he is suggesting that humans were created by these aliens who had nothing to do with Mars or the steps outside but came from somewhere else to experiment on the life growing on Earth. Humans are their experiment.

It is in this part that Bisson suggests the pyramid had been left on Mars for Humans to find so they can be pointed towards a nearby star system where the figure in the display came from, in much the same way that Arthur C Clarke had a Monolith discovered on the Moon in 2001. The message the doctor eventually translates is not unlike the message given to the astronaut in a recent film featuring the face on Mars. Once the doctor takes the projector that created the holographic image of the almost human looking alien with the dreadlocks, the pyramid disappears completely and the doctor is suddenly outside on the Martian surface again. He re-joins the pilot who was pumping the fuel from the second supply ship.

On their way back to the Lander which is being readied for take-off they discover another problem. A gravitic anomaly has affected the orbit of their vessel the Mary Poppins and it seems it will collide with Phobos. They only have a few hours to return to orbit before this happens or they will never make the return trip to Earth. They may not have enough fuel to lift off as it is so they start stripping the Lander of all unessential items, dumping them outside. After several trips from the second supply ship using a small rover to ferry the fuel on the final trip cracks in the surface start releasing heavier oxygen rich vaporous gasses from beneath the surface. Dodging and riding over these ever widening cracks they lose one tank of fuel. They now don't have enough for take-off.

Having dumped all they can they are still around 169 pounds overweight. The older American pilot decides he will stay on Mars which will give them just enough fuel for lift-off and rendezvous with the Mary Poppins before it can collide with Phobos. He will film the Lander taking off and beam the images up to the Mary Poppins so they can have a proper conclusion to their film.

Apart from paying tribute to previous novelists and filmmakers, Bisson also makes sardonic digs at the Hollywood blockbuster phenomena and the way producers and studios of such epic films go about their business, which is what makes this adventure such a delight.

It predates the advent of the latest billionaire private enterprise attempts to commercialize space and go to the Moon and Mars by suggesting that only Hollywood could come up with enough money to finance a trip to Mars, and in 1990 when this was published it seemed more likely than Space X, Blue Horizons, Virgin Galactic or any other of the present commercial ventures that either didn't or barely existed in 1990.

A very human ability

Humans have the ability to connect loosely gathered lines of dots into shapes they feel are familiar; it has something to do with recognizing faces and other people. We see random groups of rock formations from a distance as faces, or human shapes. It was the cause of early astronomers thinking blurred spots on the surface of Mars were junction points of the channels which Schiaparelli had seen and called canali — mistranslated as Canals — which in turn led Percival Lowell to surmise something must have built them if they were canals, and of course he came up with numerous theories regarding dying races and ancient civilizations and all the reasons why such beings would want to build giant canals across Mars. Once he was convinced that he saw Canals others too were convinced they also could see the Canals on Mars. Of course this reasoning was anthropocentric, transposing human reasons for what they believed Martian intelligences had done.

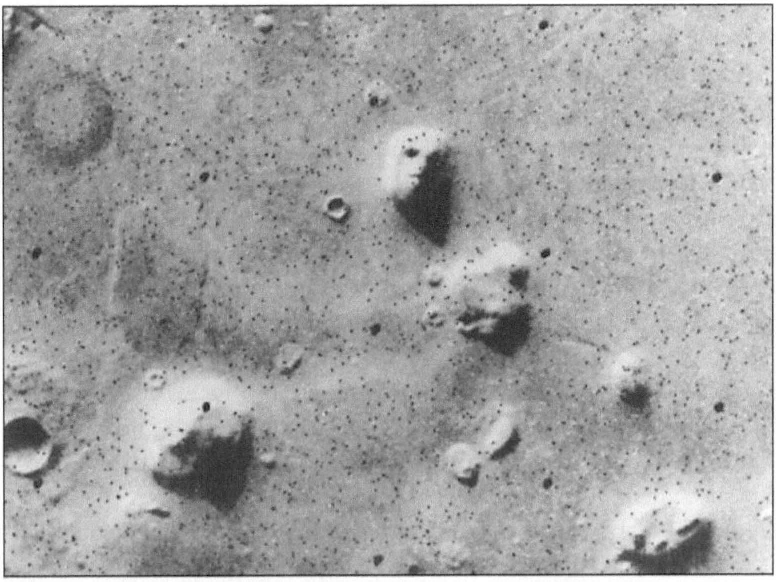

***The Face on Mars**... Viking 1 Orbiter took this photograph on July 25th 1976. It caused a sensation amongst conspiracy theorists who were convinced it was an alien construction. NASA says the black speckles are caused by bit errors in the transmission. There are bit errors on the 'eye' and the 'nostril' and combined with shadows from side-light there is the illusion of a nose and mouth. The size of the structure is 1.5 kilometres wide and the image was taken from a height of 1873 kilometres.*

The high resolution image below shows in much greater detail that the 'face' is just another one of the thousands of buttes, mesas and ridges in a fractured zone between the uplands of Arabia Terra and the northern low lying plains.

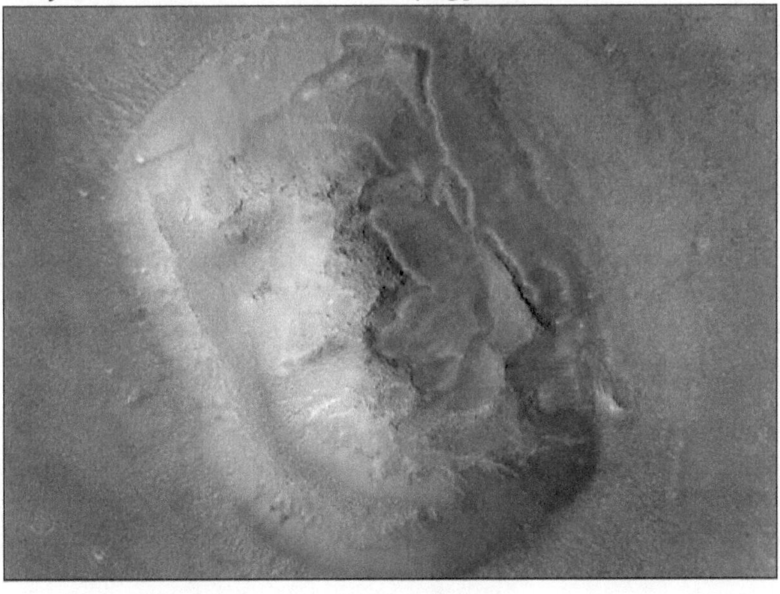

For exactly those same reasons, when images from Mars of the Cydonia region were transmitted from an orbiting satellite many people saw a simian face staring up into space alongside a collection of what those same people believed were pyramids. The way the shadows fell was convincing. A face could clearly be seen, and to be seen thus from space it must have been enormous. They were convinced that random assemblages of rocks and weathering on a rugged mesa, which is what they were shown to be when photographed from different side angles rather than straight down, were constructed by intelligent beings. And from that came all kinds of theories about who or what built them and why. It still goes on today with far too many people believing that NASA is covering up the existence of aliens on Mars, ancient buildings on Mars, abandoned spaceships and whatever else they can think of. This will not change until humans actually go to Mars and see for themselves exactly what is there.

From the perspective of science fiction writers this new belief was ripe for exploitation in stories such as ***Voyage to the Red Planet*** (1990) by Terry Bisson, ***Labyrinth of Night*** (1991) by Alan Steele, ***Red Planet Run*** (1995) by Dana Stabenow, ***Mars Underground*** (1997) by William K Hartmann, which doesn't talk about the face on Mars but has the discovery of a very huge alien machine buried under the ice at the South Pole, ***Semper Mars*** *(*1998*)* by Ian Douglas, and ***War Dogs*** (2014) by Greg Bear. Another is a delightful short story, ***The Great Pyramid Hoax,*** by Jerry Oltion in the anthology ***Fourth Planet from the Sun.*** (1995)

It has been suggested by Robert Markley in his ***Dying Planet*** (2005) that perhaps the idea of alien artefacts on Mars originated from the Paul Verhoeven film ***Total Recall*** (1989) in which a 500,000 year old alien atmosphere generating plant activated by Arnold Swarzenegger's character to save the mutated mining colonists inspired the idea of alien artefacts on Mars, but I doubt this. It's easy to say something like that in hindsight. Alien artefacts in the solar system and on Mars in particular have been a common idea in SF stories from much further back than the film ***Total Recall***, and often appear as part of a story background. However, once it was thought there was a face on Mars, the general alien artefacts idea gained renewed enthusiasm and resulted in those Mars novels mentioned above.

Labyrinth of Night by Alan Steele (1991)

Alan Steele is a writer whose stories engage the reader from the first page, and ***Labyrinth of Night*** is no exception. Once you start reading this, it is very difficult to put it aside. He makes good use of the knowledge gained by

30 years of orbiting satellite observations as well as that gained from the rovers on the surface of Mars, crafting a realistic utterly convincing background — showing how to deal with the lesser gravity, narrow curved horizons, pink sky, ever present dust, extreme cold and the precautions people must take when working on the surface or in a habitat. He has also penetrated the military mindset and how this compares with the way scientists think, and it is through these two contrasts of personality types that the tension and drama is generated.

In his story the *Face* and the *pyramids* are alien constructs which scientists are trying to understand. Entering the largest pyramid they encounter a series of puzzles that must be solved in order to proceed further in. If a puzzle isn't solved the explorer is hilled, literally torn to shreds. For this reason there is a military presence. They perceive the alien constructs as a threat to humanity which they want to eliminate, whereas the scientists deem it to be a puzzle that needs to be solved to gain further knowledge that could possible benefit mankind into the future.

The scientists believe they are being tested for intelligence. If they solve the puzzle they exhibit a certain level of intelligence and are allowed to gain further entry. Finally bringing a musician, a blues guitarist up from Earth because the final puzzle involved a weird form of music, they believe that they can communicate through the use of musical improvisation. This time they succeed and entry to deeper catacombs beneath the pyramid is permitted. Here they discover that there are literally millions of antlike replicating robots that exhibit characteristic of a hive mind, and this is the first real clue to what kind of aliens actually built the face and the pyramids.

This discovery unnerves the military personnel and they immediately want to destroy the alien structures. Everything they try is undone by swarming robots that literally deconstruct every weapon or machine used against them.

The scientists come to the conclusion that the alien beings were insect-like with a group mind and lived in hives like ants, bees or wasps, and that they explored the solar system perhaps millions of years ago when Mars was much more earth like than it is now. They decided to settle on Mars because Earth's gravity was too strong and its atmosphere too thick, but when their generation star ship arrived Mars was already dried up, desiccated and cold. Since it was a one way ship they had no choice but to settle here. They constructed an underground hive beneath a complex of entranceways through the pyramids and there they stayed until they all died, leaving behind their avatars, the robots, which were programmed to survive and build a ship for the return to their home star system.

They knew the inhabitants of Earth were ferocious simian beings that always fought each other and the hope of the Martian colonizers was to wait for the earth beings to develop destructive weapons that eventually when they were attracted to Mars (because of the face) they would bring those weapons with them, and finally they would have a means to propel the star ship they were building so they could return to their home system perhaps 20 light years away.

While the scientists and the military argue and fight each other over what to do with the pyramid complex the military contrive to have a small tactical hydrogen bomb taken down into the hive which they hope to detonate remotely.

Unknown to them, this is exactly what the alien robot swarm wants, and they take the tactical hydrogen bomb and install it directly under the huge ship they have spent millennia building so that when it detonates it will propel the ship into space.

The two scientists who were forced to take the bomb down into the catacombs manage to escape and get back on board the airship heading away from Cydonia back to the main base several thousand kilometres away around the planet. When the bomb explodes the mad military leader thinks the aliens have been destroyed but the scientists point out to him that the aliens only used it to propel their ship back into space for the return to their home system.

The whole plot is obviously playing on the ideas of those who believe aliens constructed the face and pyramids on the surface of Mars, giving a reasonably plausible explanation of how that may have occurred. It moves at a breathtaking pace so the reader is left with no time to ponder its plausibility. It is an enjoyable and fun book to read if you don't think too much about it. Just go along for the ride.

It would make a great blockbuster movie, and I am surprised that it hasn't been done.

Perhaps 1991 was too early for this type of film about Mars, and by now the book has probably been forgotten. It would have been much better than films about zombies on Mars: ***Ghosts of Mars, Last Days on Mars, Martian Land***, to mention a few, although ***Martian Land*** is more about anthropomorphising a ferocious windstorm to give it a sentient malevolence that on reflection seems ridiculous.

Red Genesis by S. C. Sykes (1991) is a romance.

It is a love story about a man, Graham Kuan Sinclair, despised by the whole world because he was the director of multi-national companies that over time dumped industrial waste into the oceans. Deep in the ocean this waste, along with discarded pesticides, combines with radioactive wastes dumped years before to form toxic clouds that rise up from the ocean floor killing everything. It then drifts towards land and coastal cities where within seconds of exposure millions die a horrible death.

Exiled on Mars with no hope of ever returning to Earth, Graham Kuan Sinclair accepts the blame although he is innocent. He goes to Mars and nothing about Earth is allowed to be mentioned in his presence, or shown to him. Everything he has that originated on Earth is taken from him, but he does have a guide who helps him adjust to life on Mars.

Even on Mars, he is initially despised and legends grow around him and his prowess as he tries to make amends for those horrible deaths for which he blames himself. On Mars various groups have formed different colonies with different ideals. Unknown to most of the population, they are all monitored from a control station. Graham is trained as a medic and assigned to a remote mining community, but first he travels to all the different colonies with his guide in order to acclimatize him. Because of his ability to organize business deals he helps assist each colony solve various problems they have. But he does it in such a way that they think they themselves are initiating the ideas and putting them into practice.

Graham doesn't know this is the real reason he was sent to Mars. He was going to be isolated in Antarctica, but the authorities on Earth decided Mars needed someone like him if it was ever to become anything more than a few isolated colonies.

On landing he meets a young woman with whom he forms a platonic relationship that evolves over the years. He also meets the female leader of a group of colonists with strange powers with whom he really does fall in love. Each colony has something to offer and we see through Graham's eyes how they barter with each other to gain what they need. He causes problems for those monitoring the whole Mars Experiment, who observe but don't intervene even when someone is dying. Everywhere he goes he destroys their listening devices and miniature cameras blinding them to what is happening. The miners revolt about tranquilizers in their food and in the end become more productive without the tranquilizers to make them calmer. He becomes the father of the first human born on Mars. He promotes art produced in the colony of the contaminated where he eventually elects to stay.

Throughout the story he wants to go back to Earth, but this is denied him for so long he finally doesn't care. Mars has truly become his home.

Over the years his reputation and his apparent abilities become mythologised both on Earth and Mars. Through his intervention more people than ever want to migrate to Mars, which finally becomes independent of Earth as each colony shares what is has and what it produces with others so they all benefit.

Although the book describes in detail the various colonies and the different ways in which they have adapted to the harsh Martian climate, the real story is about Graham, his loves and his friends and how he evolves from someone despised universally to someone who is loved by all. It is a beautifully written story of redemption and love; it just happens to be set on Mars. Once the reader finishes this story, the realization dawns that it could not have been set anywhere else but Mars; everything fits together so well.

This story that should be better known than it is.

Isaac Asimov wrote an introduction and a brief history of Mars over the years and how the planet has evolved in the imagination of writers, and to round it off, an essay by Dr. Eugene Mallove details what steps are being made to prepare for a trip to Mars as well as how the colonists may survive when they get there. He also predicts (in 1991) that the first human voyage to Mars may take place in 2011. That hasn't happened, which again suggests that a definite date should never be part of a prediction, because inevitably the visionary hasn't looked far enough into the future.

Martian Rainbow by Robert L Forward (1991, 2000)

Sub-heading: *Mars must defend itself against a ruthless dictator, or die.*

This issue from 2000 begins with acknowledgements which explains who helped with the science and lists a number of scientists. It also contains an apology where the author states that if the science is right in the mind of the reader then the people listed can take credit. If the science seems doubtful or overly speculative then it is the fault of the author. He finishes his apology with what he calls the final law of storytelling, "*never let the facts get in the way of a good story.*"

This statement seems particularly apt in so far as the science regarding Mars and what is known about the planet seems spot on. His mechanics of orbital flights, of potential asteroid mining, doing research on the surface of the planet also seems well within the realms of possibility. But for a novel claiming to be hard SF it does take the 'familiar trope' of finding life on the planet to the extreme, even though the science involved, speculative as it is, makes sense.

The story follows the simple plot outlined above as a sub-heading.

Mars has been explored by Russian scientists who have set up the majority of the bases on the planet. There are other nationalities there, but primarily it is Russian. On Earth the Russians have become a dominant power with a new party reverting back to earlier hardline communist ideals which upsets the Americans, especially when the Russian Governor of Mars declares Mars to be a Russian territory, and renames the planet Novorossiysk.

An American led military force that as a gesture towards the United Nations includes British, Japanese and other European forces and ships approaches Mars and with an almost perfect execution takes over the planet and captures all the Russians. They are to be sent back to Earth and replaced by American and other national scientists so the scientific exploration of Mars can continue. The invading force is led by two charismatic twin brothers, One General Alexander who is head of the military aspect and Gus who is a planetary scientist in charge of scientific studies of the planet. Alexander is a megalomaniac and loves the feeling of power, while Gus is the absolute opposite being an administrator and planetary scientist. He suggests that not all the Russians are pro neo-communists and that some of them should remain so the work they have done won't have to be repeated by a new crop of scientists coming in from America. So the brothers do not always agree. And this difference between them becomes more exaggerated as the story proceeds.

Once he returns to Earth General Alexander is seen as a hero and he tours the US with tickertape parades and much adulation from the general public. Alexander is annoyed because he wasn't promoted from a two star to a four star general but he does revel in the adulation from the public. He can't get enough of it. Alexander also believes that the neo-Russians are still a threat to the US, that what they won on Mars was only a minor battle and not the war. Taken in by an advertising agency Guru Alexander begins to promote a new image of himself— a Godlike image —that insinuates his religious ideals into the mind of the masses via television and virtual reality masks. He rapidly becomes more Godlike as his image is cleverly manipulated by the agency. Over time his megalomania is reinforced as more and more people worship him and he comes to believe he is immortal and can do whatever he wants. He ends up taking over the presidency of the US and has his 'church' members elected to the senate. He has his scientists develop a weapon that can cause atomic bombs and missiles to explode... and this is where the science starts to get dubious although in theory it probably is possible. Missiles and bombs all over Russia and Europe, and everywhere else self-destruct where they are stored and effectively Alexander and his new church take over the whole world so instead of just the Unified States it is now the Unified World.

Meanwhile on Mars, exploration and scientific work especially around the giant volcanoes continues. News from Earth is not encouraging. When the colonies on the Moon are ordered to be abandoned, the people told to return to Earth for integration into the unified whole, many refuse with more than 2000 wanting to stay on the Moon. Mars is also told the same, but being too far away they think they can ignore Alexander's dictatorial demands. No one on Mars wants to return to Earth.

When Alexander threatens to bombard the Moon with missiles from a newly developed space weapons system the Martians decide to rescue those on the Moon who want to remain free.

While Alexander was subduing the world, scientists on Mars made a remarkable study. Firstly they found a frozen segmented creature that was billions of years old. And this is where the science departs from hard science and become speculative to point of being almost fantasy. The wheels of rovers are tangled up in a kind of cable buried under the sand that appears to be a continuous diamond crystal. Following this cable the explorers discover a cave at the edge of the polar ice where there is a door that appears to be made of diamond, with a transparent diamond panel through which they observe a tunnel leading to another door; obviously an airlock. When they enter the airlock they discover there are similar segmented aliens further inside that are tending plants and doing other such activities. A method of communicating is developed and the explorers find the alien segmented creatures can join together to form longer creatures that are more intelligent collectively than individual segments. They discover these creatures are guardians of the planet and have been maintaining themselves in underground enclaves for billions of years as the planet slowly died.

Meanwhile, using the diamond cables and the nets the asteroid miners use to capture small asteroids they manage to rescue almost secretly, the people on the Moon who do not want to be 'unified.' This is a spectacular sequence in the events of the story but the rescue is discovered by the unified authorities who send a bunch of missiles after the rescue ship to destroy it. Because the ship travels faster than the missiles it is safe until it has to slow down on approaching Mars at which time the missiles following will catch up and destroy it.

Much heroism is shown by the shuttle pilots who are willing to directly fly into the missiles in order to detonate them. Not all are killed as moribund weapons systems on Phobos are activated and they destroy some of the incoming missiles. However with so many extra people on Mars, (quite a few thousand) they realise they must become independent of Earth even though they still need medicines and other stuff they can't manufacture on Mars. But with Earth unified they are not going to get what they need. They decide the only solution is to alter Mars so it is more habitable for humans. They draw up long term plans for partially terraforming and know that it would be at least 25 years before they could even raise the atmospheric pressure in low lying areas enough to be able to not use a Mars suit but would still need breathing masks.

Uneasy about attempting any terraforming without telling the segmented creatures that live underground, they tell them what they are planning to do. The segmented guardians decide to help speed up the process and following the plans laid out by the scientists on the surface they conclude they could achieve it in one Martian year. They rapidly reproduce and by consuming the materials in the regolith and in the ice they begin to transform Mars. It turns out these are not living things in the strict sense that we understand, but had been manufactured by something else to do the job of preserving Mars. What that something else was they are not permitted to tell so we don't find out.

Finally to make sure that Mars is safe Gus has to secretly return to Earth to convince his brother Alexander that Mars should be left alone. They do not want to be unified or bombed by long range missiles.

On Earth Alexander refuses to recognise his brother, and Gus, in an altercation, accidentally kills him. Because he is an identical twin and no one on Earth knows he is there he impersonates Alexander and gets his followers to dismantle the weapons systems threatening Mars (and Earth which was used to keep his 'subjects' in line) as well as dismantling the absolute control over other countries. He orders the regents in other countries resign and allows those countries to once again become individual states based on languages spoken as they were before. After that he goes to Mars supposedly to see what is happening there, but once there of course he stays.

The book finishes with a section called New Colonists' guide to Mars wherein all the facts known about Mars are given and much emphasis is made of new clocks, calendar, and how to adjust to the Martian Sol which is 39.5 minutes longer than a day on Earth.

All of this information is woven into the story in one form or another, but it is nice to see it all summarised as it is here.

The author was right about not letting facts get in the way of a good story. It is a good story and in context the exaggerated facts and ultra speculative science don't get in the way, they make the story, even if some parts with Alexander seem a bit melodramatic. It all fits together and makes an enjoyable read. What more could you want?

Mars Missions

In his book ***The Snows of Olympus – A garden on Mars*** (1994) on page 30, Arthur C Clarke mentioned three books that he considered outstanding.

Mission to Mars by the Apollo 11 Command Module pilot Michael Collins, a fictional as well as non-fictional account of an expedition to Mars in 2004 making use of the technology available at the time it was written in 1990, but it is not the only book with that name — there are several. Since he speculated it would take place in 2004 he was way off the mark, far too optimistic.

Mars, by Ben Bova (1992)

Beachhead by Jack Williamson (1992)

Both Bova and Williamson have written a story using only the facts known about Mars at the time (early1990s) and how the technology of that time would enable such a journey. These are true novels that are speculative and enthralling. But these are not the only ones; the rest of the decade is replete with exciting, plausible, and often magnificent stories of going to Mars and establishing a colony or a foothold there.

Mission to Mars by Michael Colllins (1990)

Michael Collins was the third Apollo 11 astronaut. He stayed on board the orbiting Command Module (as the pilot) while Neil Armstrong and Buzz Aldrin landed on the Moon and became the first two people to walk on its surface.

He was far too optimistic in proposing that a journey to Mars using the 1990s space technology be made by 2004. Arthur C Clarke recommended this book probably because it included much technical detail which as a scientist appealed to him, but to general readers the narrative is bogged down by those endless details.

Being an ex-astronaut his details are accurate, but for me this book was hard to read.

He asks many questions and supplies answers, regarding the makeup of the crew, whether it should be of both sexes or all one sex —in this case men — and whether they should go direct to Mars or use the Moon as a staging post first. He advocates a flyby of Venus to give the ship a gravity boost to go out to Mars. He discusses the effect of radiation in space, of weightlessness, and its effect on human physiology, and discusses ways of preventing serious side effects such as loss of bone density. He brings up the problems of months of long term isolation and confinement in a tiny space over the length of the voyage. He proposes they first orbit Mars before sending an expedition down to establish a base for subsequent expeditions. Those first explorers will only be there for a month before they have to commit to more long isolation during the return to Earth.

All this is interesting but it is told in a manner that does not capture a reader who is not technically minded.

The final third of the book is a fictionalization of the voyage out and the landing by telling the story of the first Mars expedition astronauts, their voyage out from Earth to Mars and the problems they encounter on board the ship during the voyage, arrival and landing.

The trouble with this is that he is trying to dramatize what he has already told us, repeating it in the form of a novella. The characters are imaginary, but rather than delving into them and showing us through their actions, feelings and conversations how they would make such a voyage, he tells it as a dispassionate observer in much the same style as the earlier non-fiction part, which doesn't generate any empathy in the reader for them.

Perhaps the book would have been better without this last third, since it would have been strictly a technical book rather than part speculative fiction and part factual, but even the technical first part is speculative extrapolating possibilities from known facts.

Buzz Aldrin also wrote a book with the same title ***Mission to Mars,*** sixteen years later in 2006, in which he asks the question: Can astronauts reach Mars by 2035?... subtitled ***My Vision for Space Exploration.***

He travels the world on speaking engagements publicising his vision of how we can go to Mars, promoting his book as well as the need to explore space, to expand into the solar system which will bring untold benefits to the world as a whole in scientific, technological and economical advances.

Aldrin was also a crew member of Apollo 11 and was the second man to walk on the Moon. He is convinced that not only can humans reach Mars by 2035, but that space exploration beginning with a manned mission to

Mars is essential for America's future.

He shows how this can be done with the technology we have today in a lively and interesting style with many illustrations to bring to life what he is talking about.

He covers the history of American space flight and the benefits this brought to the country and suggests we need a vision like the one proposed by JF Kennedy from a newer president to galvanize the efforts to get humans off the Earth and into Space for our long term survival as a species. He talks about threats from space such as asteroid or comet impacts and the need to establish a human colony on Mars.

The second half of the book details how such a voyage out to Mars and the establishment of a colony could take place. He even discusses terraforming and has some wonderful colour plates depicting human activity on Mars. This is by far one of the best technical books for a non-technical person to understand a proposed Mission to Mars.

It contains a sense of infectious excitement which makes you want to keep reading and this is rare in a book about space travel and how to voyage out to Mars. Technical details are explained is such a way that they are not the least boring and are easily understood, which makes this book stand out from other similar books.

Aldrin has also written a couple of books about Mars for younger readers and they really are delightful.

Ben Bova and Jack Williamson — Missions to Mars

Mars by Ben Bova and ***Beachhead*** by Jack Williamson can be compared because both were published in 1992.

Both authors by 1992 had decades of writing SF, Williamson with over 60 years, and Bova just over 40 years. Williamson was 83 when he wrote ***Beachhead***.

Both had access to whatever was known about Mars in 1991 including thousands of colour photos of the surface as seen from space and from the surface as seen by the mars rovers, as well as all the technical information, detailed maps with every feature named and much speculation or interpretation regarding the forces that shaped Mars into what we see today.

Both novels tell the story of a first expedition to Mars and the intention to establish a base of operations on the surface for exploration and study.

Both have a character who is an Alpha male who eventually becomes a dominant person in the expeditionary groups. In both cases this character has a strong will to live, and is determined to obtain a positive outcome for the expedition regardless of the odds.

In ***Mars***, Jamie Waterman is a Native American of Navajo descent who was an alternate choice for the position of geologist. In ***Beachhead*** Huston Kelligan is the son of a very wealthy Texan businessman who wants to escape his father's influence and doesn't care about his inheritance; all he's ever dreamed about is going to Mars.

In both stories the space ships that take the expedition members to Mars rotate to generate artificial gravity via centrifugal force, a device not used by Arthur C Clarke in 1951 or Ludek Pesek in 1970.

Both expeditions' ships begin with Earth-normal gravity and gradually slow down the spin over the long voyage until they are rotating with the equivalent of Mars' gravity.

In Bova's book two space ships are tethered together rotating around a common centre: the location of the fusion drive and the instruments for astronomical studies. Each ship has a crew of twelve and when they arrive and orbit Mars, six from each ship descend to establish an operational base, while the others remain in orbit as back up.

In Williamson's book, the space ship is a rotating ring around a central elongated core, at the end of which is the fusion engine. It is a smaller ship and it carries only six people.

Both books have their Mars ships built in orbit, one (***Mars***) around the earth, the other (***Beachhead***) around the Moon.

In both books the space ships orbit Mars while the expedition members use Landers or shuttles to go down to the surface and ferry equipment back and forth.

Both give some detail about the voyage out, which takes 5 months in ***Beachhead***, but nine months in ***Mars***, and the alignment of team members into pairs since each group is made up equally of male and female team members. Each book also has team members from different countries and ethnic origins. This is more noticeable in Bova's book because there are more people with the whole expedition being International both in membership and funding. Williamson's team is funded by NASA or a similar organization and is basically American although some team members are from other countries.

Both authors propose that Mars will have some kind of life or proto-life that affects part of the outcome of the explorers' activities.

In Williamson's book, it is a quasi-lifelike virus that lays dormant in the dust infecting humans when the dust is breathed in and it gets into their lungs and bloodstream. It makes their life more miserable than it needs to be — rather different from the life form in Watson's ***The Martian Inca*** which transforms the person infected into a higher consciousness.

In Bova's book a hardy lichen-like substance is discovered in the deeper parts of Valles Marineris growing in the cracks of ancient rocks where it draws moisture from the mists that form overnight deep in the canyon. This implies a kind of eco-system that the explorers wish to find, since no single organism lives entirely alone but is part of an eco-system no matter how primitive it seems.

Both Bova and Williamson speculate within the bounds of reasonableness and do not extrapolate ridiculous outcomes.

Both authors have serious problems arise to threaten the teams on the surface forcing them to be inventive and resourceful in order to survive.

Both books give brilliantly evocative descriptions of Mars, how it feels to be down there on the surface, how it feels to land or take off in one of the shuttles used, or how it is to solve the problems encountered while driving rovers about on the surface. These passages are so well written that sometimes you can't put the book down, you have to keep reading.

With so much in common you would expect the stories to be similar, but they aren't.

Willimason begins his story with a long lead up to the arrival on Mars.

Bova begins his story as the first group lands and begins to set up the inflatable habitat that will be their home for 45 days.

Williamson's approach is old fashioned and linear, showing the origins of his style in the early SF magazines.

Bova's approach is modern — he continually cross-cuts between the story's action and the selection and training of the crew, and the voyage out. It also cross-cuts to what is happening on Earth simultaneously, making his book an intricate and more engaging read.

Jack Williamson spends too much time on the lead up to the actual Mars mission. He concentrates on background, providing documentary detail rather than drama. None of the characters come alive and any event shown, such as the moon race to see how independently each potential astronaut can handle difficult situations, seems overly melodramatic.

The expedition does not reach Mars until just over halfway through the book and only then does the book come alive.

The problems he creates for his characters make sense based on the information given in the first half. There are only six of them. Once they reach Mars two of them decide they don't want to go down and spend a year and a half trying to establish a colony, but wish to return immediately while the orbital window to Earth is still open. One of them is terrified of contracting the Mars virus. They initiate two landings to check for a suitable site to establish a base and to do some on the spot scientific investigations, but the first Lander crashes and that's when the problems begin.

The two who want to go back don't want to waste fuel searching for the first two. The other two want to go down and rescue their team mates. Once they have reached the surface of Mars the two in the orbiting ship abandon them and take off for Earth jettisoning all the supplies and livestock meant for the base in order to lighten the ship and conserve fuel.

The four on the surface are forced to make the best of the site near where they crashed in order to survive until the next ship in orbit around the Moon is finished and can reach Mars to rescue them. Williamson now presents alternate chapters set on Earth, showing that the public is being fed a lot of lies about how successful the mission is to keep up the flow of finances. The ship in orbit around the Moon is not being finished because there isn't enough money and the organization building it is bankrupt.

In desperation the stranded astronauts on Mars come up with a way for one of them to return in the only functioning landing shuttle. It must be the billionaire's son Huston Kelligan, because he is the only one who would be believed on Earth and who could organize the finances to return with a rescue mission.

But when he arrives on Earth off the coast of Chile no one believes him because of the lies being presented daily in the media. He is arrested, and branded a conman by the Mars Corporation, which doesn't want the public to know the truth about what happened. Eventually the truth comes out and the ship in orbit around the Moon is finished and our hero returns with a new crew to rescue his three remaining team mates, and to set up a permanent base on Mars.

True to his pulp origins Williamson throws all sorts of obstacles in the way which his astronauts. If I had read it 25 years ago, I would certainly have enjoyed it more than I did now.

Ben Bova's ***Mars*** is much longer with much more detail, and it is structured in way that encourages continuous reading. He puts 12 people on Mars' surface, setting up a more practical kind of base. Two different teams go exploring, and his descriptions of what they see and find are believable His situations are not at all melodramatic but arise from what the teams do while on the surface.

Equally as interesting are the international politics and the 'back room expectations Earth-side about future funding and what is expected of the expedition. More is made of the differences in the crew's nationalities probably because there are twelve of them with another twelve as backup in orbit.

The focus of the story is Jamie Waterman's gradual bringing around of the others to his way of thinking. When a slow disaster — which cleverly hints at a possible unseen Martian cause — almost kills all of them, the reader is desperately hoping a solution will be found. Finally it is, but the solution is unexpected. When the forty five days are up, the base habitat is evacuated and the astronauts, cosmonauts and scientists on the surface return to the orbiting ships in preparation for their trip back to Earth.

The big discovery of this story is life, a hardy lichen type of organism that lives in the cracks in the rocks at the bottom of the deepest chasm on Mars. But something else is also there. Jamie sees it but could not get close enough to confirm his observation. We are left pondering this mystery at the conclusion of the book.

Arthur C Clarke has a blurb on the front cover of Bova's book: *...the definitive novel about our fascinating neighbour...* I think he was right, at least until Kim Stanley Robinson hit the bookshelves with his incredible trilogy a few years later. Michael Collins, the astronaut whose book ***Mission to Mars*** is also recommended by Clarke, also wrote a blurb for Bova's book, stating: *"A fascinating story – a novel worthy of our sister planet."*

Arthur C Clarke also contributed a forward to Jack Williamson's book, ***Beachhead***, which praises it as well, so I guess he liked both of these books.

Ben Bova's story does not finish. ***Mars*** was in effect only the first part of a longer novel. The second part was published 6 years later in 1999 and was quite rightly called ***Return to Mars***.

This time Jamie Waterman is the leader of a smaller expedition of 5 men and 3 women that is funded privately by a wealthy corporation looking to make a profit out of what they find and from subscriptions to virtual reality broadcasts of the expedition members going about their work on the planet.

Again we begin on Mars, with the new expedition members entering the habitat established by the first expedition. Although there are flashbacks to the events that led up to the establishment of the new voyage as well as crosscuts to manipulative events currently taking place on Earth, they do not detract from the main events taking place on Mars, but enhance it. Like ***Mars***, this book is also hard to put down.

Underlying the action is Jamie's obsession with what he saw but could not confirm during the first expedition. This desire gives the book an unstated tension apart from the tension generated between Jamie and the other alpha male, Dex Trumball, the son of the man behind the funding for this second expedition, who goads Jamie at every opportunity, constantly referring derisively to Jamie's Navajo heritage.

As would be expected in a group consisting of five man and three women, there is also some sexual tension, all of which combined makes the story more believable. Dex wants to recover the early rovers sent to Mars because he believes they would be worth a fortune, enough to finance a third expedition. His father, the man behind the money, wants to open Mars to tourism in the near future, much to Jamie's horror, because he believes tourism would destroy the planet and whatever they may find. He equates it to the coming of the white man to America and the subsequent destruction of Native American culture and heritage. Jamie slowly loses control over the expedition's goals until he is forced to resign and place one of the others in charge.

Free of responsibility for the expedition, Jaime can now concentrate on confirming what he saw 6 years earlier. He is coerced into taking Dex with him to Valles Marineris chasm and the cleft where he thought he saw ancient ruins. Over the course of this journey out in a rover, the two men reconcile their differences, and they do discover an ancient ruin, a building hidden inside the cleft and protected from the elements. Astounded, the other team members come out and set up another habitat so they can work there without having to travel back and forth.

Meanwhile a series of accidents fuels the idea that one of them is trying to sabotage the mission with the intention of forcing them to return to Earth, where presumably they would all be safe.

With the help of archaeologists back on Earth, they come to the conclusion that the buildings are 65 million years old. This is an astonishing date, because it pinpoints the time of the destruction of Mars from a warm inhabited planet into what it is today to the same time as the event that occurred on Earth wiping out the dinosaurs and most of life on Earth. Earth was larger than Mars and could recover. Mars couldn't. Its life died with only a few deeply buried bacteria and some primitive lichen like moss surviving.

Bova cleverly suggests that intelligent life once existed on Mars without speculating as to what it was or how it looked. There are no clues in the building other than undecipherable writings on some of its walls. This understated foray into a fanciful possibility is so low-key that it doesn't intrude into the realistic depiction of surviving on Mars.

His speculation of finding primitive life somewhere on or under the surface is quite acceptable. Almost every author writing about Mars does this to some degree. It is the great hope of humankind that we will find evidence of life elsewhere in the universe, and the search for this proof underlies most of our explorations across the solar system regardless of other stated reasons.

This story however isn't finished and in 2008 he published ***Mars Life***, in which Jamie returns once more to Mars.

Mars Life by Ben Bova (2008) completes the story he began 16 years earlier in 1992 with ***Mars*** and continued in 1999 with ***Return to Mars.***

This final segment takes place some 20 years after Jamie Waterman discovered the cliff dwellings high up in the side of the Rift Valley,Tithonium Chasma. By the end of the first two expeditions to Mars a permanent base has been established in the Rift valley while scientists search for the remains of life. Nothing much has been discovered other than some lichen growing in cracks in rocks at the base of the chasm where the smallest amount of moisture condenses out of the atmosphere during the freezing nights and this sustains the lichen growing in the rocks.

When the third book opens Jamie has been on Earth for just on twenty years and is the scientific head of the expedition which now numbers around 200 people on the red planet.

One of these people, is anthropologist Carter Carleton who discovers the remains of a village buried under 30 metres of detritus which has collected over the 60 million years since the meteor bombardment that destroyed Mars and its planetary ecosystem (at the same time destroying Earth's habitat and wiping out the dinosaurs). Earth's eco-system recovered, but Mars, being much smaller, lost most of its atmosphere and never recovered. It has been slowly dying ever since.

Back on Earth with greenhouse effects altering climate, religious fundamentalists are gradually taking control of the media, the universities, and even the government. They want to close down the Mars expeditions because they deny the possibility that there could have been intelligent Martians even 60 million years ago. They claim the village discovered and the fossils are all faked to make the government continue funding for the Mars explorations. The government hardly funds it anyway. Most of the money comes from private sources, but under the new fundamentalism spreading across the country; even private organizations are not willing to fund Mars exploration any more.

As a solution, limited tourism is suggested. Wealthy people would pay millions for the chance of a trip to Mars, now accomplished by super-fast fusion propelled rockets.

Jamie Waterman returns to Mars with his wife Vijay, a biologist, to maintain a Navajo presence on the planet. When he was leader of the second expedition twenty years earlier he refused to consider the idea of tourism as fund-raiser. He is even more against any kind of tourism now, adamant that it would ruin Mars forever.

The solution suggested by his business partner, and friend on Earth, Dex Trumball, who had been on Mars 20 years earlier with Jamie is to bring everyone back so he can fund a private expedition to claim Mars once the Navajo presence is no longer there.

Jamie refuses to leave and solicits limited help from Selene, the now independent Moon colony, so he can stay with a small number of people to preserve Mars as it is forever.

He is finally convinced that this will not work, Mars will be abandoned, so a compromise is eventually reached where in the long run everyone benefits while Jamie gets to stay on his beloved Mars.

Though not as vast as Kim Stanley Robinson's massive Mars trilogy, Ben Bova's Mars trilogy is certainly equal to it, and is engrossing.

It is a more accessible story because it covers in total only about 25 years, and most of the characters we meet at the beginning stay to the end. Bova's character development is good enough to make you care about them and about what they are trying to achieve, while at the same time he paints an accurate picture of what Mars is actually like and the difficulties involved in living there. His speculations about the way the world is being affected by climate change and the reactions of religious fundamentalists can be seen in the news headlines at this very moment. *The details may not be the same but the events seem eerily similar.*

This is a brilliant series well worth taking the time to read.

Polar Deposits a stunning view from the edge of the ice cap

Chapter Eleven

A new reality

Out of the Ordinary

The Season of Passage (1970 -1992) by Christopher Pike is difficult to categorise.

Is it science fiction, horror, or fantasy? It was not listed as any of those genres and it made the best seller lists. Originally written in 1970, it was not published until 1992.

Basically it is Science fiction because it about an expedition to Mars, and is typical of that period in that there is considerable focus on preparation for the astronauts and on the trip to Mars, whereas from the 1990s onwards stories focussed not on how to get there but on what happened once they were there. But once the astronauts arrive it crosses over into horror of the vampire kind, with a fantasy back-story to explain the horror elements and the origins of humankind. Yet even in this part the science fiction elements outweigh the horror and fantasy. It does present a fascinating picture of Mars.

It is beautifully written and is a page turner so it is not surprising it made the best seller lists. Christopher pike's books have sold in the millions and he has been in the Times New York best seller list many times.

The author includes an apology at the beginning explaining that this story was written in 1970 when Mars was only beginning to be seen as a different place than expected, but he didn't publish it until 1992. He did not revise or alter it to update the story but left it exactly as it was first written, so there are some anachronisms present, as well as missing cell phones. They didn't exist in 1970 and no one could have foreseen their explosive expansion into present day life, so they don't exist in this story and phone booths with video-phones (found in thousands of other early SF stories from the pulp era) are common. His details of Mars and of the solar system in general reflect what was known in 1970 rather than what is known today.

That said, my theory is that vampire stories were out of fashion in the 1970s, and one combined with a story about going to Mars simply would not have been accepted. In 1992 with new stories of Mars being published and with a growing popularity of vampire stories it was the right time to publish this one.

The story follows an American expedition to Mars ostensibly to find out what happened to a ten year earlier Russian expedition which suddenly stopped reporting back; in effect it disappeared. Everything seemed to be going well, then suddenly… nothing.

The story is set in 2006 as he imagined it from 1970 so it is not greatly different to how one would find the world in 1992 when it was published, or even in the present day for that matter.

Unlike most novels about Mars, referring to 1970 when it was written rather than today, it is a very readable literary work focussing on character; compared to earlier SF attempts which were usually concerned with action rather than character. The reader becomes absorbed with the characters and what is happening to them, and this absorption keeps you reading no matter how unlikely some events eventually become.

The story follows Lauren Wagner a medical doctor who is also an astronaut. She is the expedition's doctor.

Shifting third person viewpoints allows us to see events from several character viewpoints for a broader picture of unfolding events, but in general we follow Lauren and see events from her viewpoint. Lauren has always wanted to go to Mars, and finally, here she is.

The American expedition lands close to where the Russians landed ten years earlier to find the Russian base deserted. The Russian return ship is still orbiting the planet and when they cross over to examine it, at first it also appears totally deserted and very cold.

Lauren is part of the party examining the orbiting ship and she discovers a dead cosmonaut in one of the bunks. Mysteriously he is not frozen as he should be in a ship where the temperature is close to absolute zero. Open to space, there is no oxygen in the ship.

Suddenly the corpse comes to life and attacks them. He has no heartbeat and isn't breathing.

Down on the surface the other Americans discover a cave, a giant lava tube under the escarpment of Olympus Mons, the largest volcano and the highest mountain in the solar system. They enter this tube going deeper and deeper into the bowels of the planet. The deeper they go the thicker the air becomes (another old idea from early Mars stories, and one still often used in movies about Mars). Further in, much deeper, they discover miles of other lava tubes some of which are flowing with water. (The water doesn't sublimate because the air is thicker down here than on the surface where water can't exist) They decide to call these immense water filled lava tubes that go for miles under the surface, canals. (What else?)

From this point the story diverges from being realistic and starts to become a vampire story.

Running parallel to the main story is an alternate story about Lauren's sister back on Earth. She dreams of writing a novel about an ancient culture with humans versus a lizard like shape shifting being, a story about 'good' versus 'evil'. The good being humans and the evil being a lizard like race that lives in the dark and hunts humans for their blood. There really isn't any mention of vampires and if the reader thinks of these nasty creatures as something very alien then it can almost stay within the realm of science fiction or science fantasy, since these nasty creatures are encountered deep inside the lava tube cave systems of Mars.

There is so much action in the Martian cave systems that the reader hardly has a moment to take a breath before being plunged into another action filled moment. Most of the American crew is killed except for Lauren and one other uninfected man. Both of them escape the cave system in time and get back to their ship after managing to destroy the underground home of these horrible creatures with an atomic bomb.

There is a lot of tension, and edge of the seat action that keeps the reader glued to the pages. The whole thing is so implausible yet absolutely enthralling because Christopher Pike is a brilliant thriller writer.

Once the remaining astronauts return to Earth the story isn't over, but it becomes more obvious that this is a vampire story, an SF vampire story. It is the two astronauts who bring the vampire threat back to Earth where a final confrontation takes place between Dr Lauren Wagner, her fiancée and her sister. This is a Martian story with a difference.

The stuff about Mars is very good, but as for the vampire concept… it's not exactly something I like, but if I think of them as nasty aliens from ancient times on Earth as well as Mars it just works. It is without a doubt a thrilling and engrossing story

Something different from Greg Bear and Paul McAuley

The Mars novels from 1992 and 1993 are based on increasingly up-to-date knowledge about Mars and all include some speculation as to whether the planet held an earlier form of life. In some way or another they detail methods that might be used to transform Mars into a more benign place for human occupation. They are different from earlier novels, which were concerned with the voyage out and initial establishment of a base on the surface. The exception is the first of the Kim Stanley Robinson Mars trilogy, Red Mars, which describes the preparations and the training for the voyage out and the establishment of a colony and plans for terraforming the planet.

Moving Mars by Greg Bear (1992) has a bold idea at its core; moving Mars. To my knowledge, no earlier writer suggested moving Mars to another location. Does this make it a fantasy? I don't think so; it belongs in category two since it uses up to date background knowledge of Mars from where it extrapolates a possible future. It also plays with cutting edge scientific thinking regarding physics that borders on being magical because the ideas are beyond present day comprehension. Advanced science really does seem magical to those who don't understand it.

Mars has been settled for over 150 years and has a population of just over four million. The people live in warrens tunnelled underground, safe from the radiation that bathes the surface. Scattered settlements over the planet provide accommodation for extended family groups called Binding Multiples (BMs). Each BM controls such activities as mining, food growing, engineering and so on. Earth is the recipient of most produce from Mars as well as that from the Moon and the asteroid colonies. Travel on Mars is by taking a monorail between BM settlements, or by flying.

The story opens with a student rebellion resulting with the Earth administrators of the University abandoning Mars. The students want more freedom for Mars. Mars itself wants to become independent of Earth. Earth's controlling governments do not want this newfound independence to blossom, so they do all they can to forestall it. But not all BMs want to be part of a central Mars government, so there is much political debate about becoming independent of Earth and of forming a new government on Mars.

Two of the students from the opening student rebellion are pivotal to the unfolding story; the story is told in first person by Casseia Majumdar, the daughter of a leading BM, who becomes politically involved, and her friend Charles Franklin, a physics genius who discovers how to generate anti matter from matter at a distance to create a formidable weapon.

Cassseia goes to Earth as an ambassador while Charles works in secret. Earth suspects something is up so the trip is wasted. Earth takes direct control of Mars, threatening to destroy the Martian political structure by bringing its citizens under control right at the moment when they are about to elect a President, Vice President and other government members.

In desperation, Charles uses his new knowledge of the underlying structure of the universe to shift Mars' moon Phobos into an orbit around Earth, with the implied threat that it could be dropped onto the planet to cause untold damage. Earth immediately withdraws, but in secret works on the Moon to discover what Charles has done, so it can develop a weapon to use against Mars before Mars does something to Earth. Earth's governing groups have backed off, but once they discover how to turn matter into antimatter from a distance they again attack Mars destroying the new administrative centre and all those within. This in effect destroys the Martian government.

Rather than retaliate in kind by destroying major Earth cities, Casseia and Charles decide to move Mars. They don't have time to inform the people of Mars or to get an approval. Since their own destruction is imminent, they take it upon themselves to shift Mars, to Move it out of its orbit around the Sun and put it into orbit around another similar sun 10,000 light years away towards the galactic centre.

The story finishes here with Mars taking an orbit around a new sun. It is closer to this star than it was to the Sun in the solar system, so it is warmer. A postscript tells us that Casseia and Charles had been considered to be traitors and the cause of all Mars's problems, so had been sentenced and imprisoned. Years later they are revered as saviours, because Mars now has a warmer climate and is slowly regenerating a biosphere with permafrost melting and releasing greenhouse gasses into the atmosphere. Ancient Martian life, thought to be fossilized but only found to be dormant, begins to revive, and Mars is becoming a very different planet to what it once was.

The major problem with this story is that too much political discussion takes place among rival families and between Mars and Earth. This becomes a turgid reading experience. I found myself falling asleep in these long sections. But when Bear gets into the action scenes they are absolutely riveting.

You simply can't put the book down. These bits I remembered from my previous reading of twenty years ago and not the longer political parts or the dissertation of essential background.

Some people like stories with heaps of background detail, and in SF there must be some in order to establish the time, planetary locale, and background history, but often today's authors give us too much wordage, which either stops the story dead, side-tracks it into oblique directions, or slows it down so much that some readers fall asleep or tend to skip over the extended passages.

I suggested earlier that most stories about Mars usually fall into one of three categories: Fanciful, factual and transformative. Most of Moving Mars I would put in category two, factual. Only when Mars is moved as a dire consequence of unfolding events does it fall into the transformative category. It could also be considered as science fantasy at this point although I like to think of this as super science rather than science fantasy. Arthur C Clarke often said something like: *if science is sufficiently advanced over what we can comprehend it might as well be magic as far as we are concerned.*

The science involved with the anti matter weapon and shifting of astronomical bodies in space from one location to another is advanced far beyond what we can conceive, yet it is believable in the context of the story.

Red Dust by Paul McAuley (1993) stands out from the other contemporary books about Mars because it is a fantasy — not like those of Edgar Rice Burroughs and others of his time — but a modern science fantasy. It straddles both of my first and second categories, mostly staying within the second category. But at the very end it becomes transformative.

Mars is dying. Five hundred years earlier the Chinese arrived and took over the planet from the Americans who had set up a scientific base there. The Chinese imported millions of Tibetans to act as slaves in the terra-forming of Mars. But the process has stopped and slowly the planet is reverting back to what it once was. There are wild Yaks, horses and other animals roaming the plains, there are seas of dust which have ships sailing across them, there is a unique ecosystem in the seas involving phytoplankton and entities like giant dust rays that sustain the remnants of the American scientific mission whose base sails endlessly over the seas, only coming ashore when they need to render down a giant dust ray.

There are settlements scattered all across Mars called Danwei, where groups of Chinese settlers live. There are plainsmen called cowboys who are like bandits, herding the wild yaks, taking them to the larger cities for sale. Most of the ruling Han Chinese have elected to upload themselves into an electronic universe where they can live forever. When their Emperor physically dies a revolution begins between the ordinary folk and the armies controlled by the Emperor.

Wei Lee has a mission to bring back the rains and save Mars from a slow death. Wei Lee is a clone. A number of them, both male and female, are inhabited by nano-viruses that alter their perception giving them extraordinary powers. Wei Lee is quite ordinary at the start, but when he recues an anarchist pilot whose rocket crashes she infects him with a nano-virus that turns him into something more than human. The army wants what she is carrying. They capture her and Wei Lee to interrogate them, but they escape during a dust storm. So begins a remarkable adventure as Wei Lee travels across Mars encountering many different people who have adapted to Mars in often extraordinary ways, while feeling compelled to go to the tallest mountain in the solar system where the Emperor lies wired up in the new Forbidden City inside the caldera of this giant extinct volcano. It is here that he finds answers and fulfils a mission he didn't know that he was programmed to carry out.

At times the detail in this remarkable book is very scientific, while at other times it borders on fantasy with a plausible scientific background. Sometimes you even think that an alternate historical reality has happened, because the Mars we know could never be like this Mars. Wei Lee gets into all kinds of trouble as he journeys to his destination across a very believable planet. McAuley so convincingly extrapolates the effects of the digital age that you accept whatever outrageous implausibility he offers as a possibility. This book sucks you in and shakes you up. When you get to the end, you give a sigh of relief that everything is tied up and explained and you know life will go on.

Paul McAuley's other Mars book *The Secret of Life* (2001) is not entirely a Mars book although a third of it takes place there. It is a story of industrial espionage and how governments and big business want to keep secret the most astonishing discovery in human history, yet Mars is always in the background.

The year is 2026. Something weird is growing in the Pacific Ocean, an organism that may threaten our entire ecosystem as well as the food chain we all depend upon, something the Chinese discovered deep under the southern polar ice cap and brought back from Mars. It has, through deliberate sabotage of a plane carrying a courier with a sample of the substance, been released into the ocean with disastrous consequences. Without telling the rest of the world the Chinese send another expedition to Mars to the site where they discovered this alien life. What their agenda is no one knows. Meanwhile scientists and marine biologists around the world are desperately trying to discover ways to stop the rapid spread of this alien organism.

An American combined International expedition is sent to Mars to try and find what the Chinese found so they can examine its DNA and come up with a way of stopping the spread of the organism through the oceans. It seems to be turning up everywhere. After much rivalry among scientists and political machination between governments and big business, an expedition is finally organized and the members trained while the Chinese are already half way to Mars. The International expedition will use a faster ship to arrive there not long after the Chinese.

On Mars the members of the expedition make their way to the south-pole and wait for the Chinese to leave so they can find out what was discovered. The Chinese sabotage their campsite and destroy the drill sites where this organism was discovered deep under the ice. Of the three Chinese, two head back to their Lander for the return trip to Earth but die before they can reach it. They have been infected by the organism. The third one stays to try to stop the American International group from gaining any information. There is a shootout, during which the remaining Chinese member is killed along with one rather obnoxious American who it turns out was working with a private company to steal and monopolise the genetic secrets of the Martian life.

Eco terrorists have their own agenda and cause no end of problems on Earth and on Mars. Finally, one of the scientists who has higher motives makes her way to the Chinese Lander and takes off with some samples recovered from the dead Chinese astronaut to return in their ship orbiting Mars. When she gets back to Earth she is charged with piracy, eco terrorism and whatever else the Chinese and the International community can come up with. All she ever wanted was to discover the genetic code of Martian life because it shares much similarity with early Earth life, and she wants to know how much it has changed and evolved after 4 billion years of separate evolution.

This book is very different from McAuley's other Mars book, but is just as exciting. McAuley writes action scenes that capture your attention, and his narrative is so well done you can't put the book down. His descriptions of Mars are up to date with how it looks and with what scientists think has happened on Mars over the last 4 billion years. His description of the small colony established by the Americans and the reason its location was chosen is just what one would think it might be like, and his background details of Earth in the near future are believable because they are not really much different from the modern world we currently inhabit. He probably should have set the time at 2046 rather than 2026 and it would have been more believable than it is. Nevertheless this is an exciting story and well worth the time to read.

Red Planet Run (1995) by Dana Stabanow

Star Svensdotter after a decade is still mourning the loss of her husband Caleb, but she has learned to live with it as she brings up her teenage daughter and son. She is in the business of transforming asteroids into liveable habitats, by hollowing them out and constructing an earth-like environment inside. She is tired and when her children become involved with a religious fanatic who is trying to gain converts among the inhabitants of the asteroid belt she seeks a way to change her life.

Her mother, the ruling magistrate and committee member of the loosely organized government of the Asteroid communities asks her to go to Mars to help solve the mystery of the ruins at Cydonia and whether they had anything to do with the formation of the asteroid belt because it is now believed they were once a planet which they call *Prometheus*. An expedition has already been sent to Cydonia but no results have been forthcoming. Star is also a part of the police force that maintains law and order throughout the asteroid belt and as the story opens she has had a confrontation with a group of bandits or pirates who want to take control of as much as they can get their hands on and they are ruthless. Death and destruction follows wherever they go.

With a special balloon type dirigible using helium as well as hot air designed and delivered to her Star takes her two children with her to Mars. They have problems landing as something seems to push them off course and they almost crash. Their ship is damaged and they have to repair it. Once that is done they find they are way off course and are somewhere in Valles Marineris, half way around the planet from Cydonia. As they sail their ship using the wind for power they encounter a colony that has been destroyed with bodies desiccated by the thin Martian atmosphere scattered about the ruined habitat, and Star is convinced this was done by the same 'pirate' gang she encountered in the belt before.

Knowing they will meet these pirates sooner or later she trains her two children in the use of hand weapons. Travelling further along the great rift valley of Mars they come across a Russian settlement under siege by the very same pirates. She and her children attack the pirates from the rear and force them to leave the settlement. At first the settlers are wary of Star but they do accept her and the children into their small community where they spend several months as they wait for the sandstorm season to pass before they can continue on to Cydonisa.

Eventually they make their way to Cydonia where the finally meet the archaeological team digging around the ruins of a strange obelisk which is a part of the larger area containing the pyramid structures and the face on Mars.

Somehow the children gain entrance to the obelisk and inside at the very top they discover a weird machine which they surmise is a deflecting mechanism to prevent meteors crashing into the planet. They assume this device is what pushed their ship off course during entry and landing and what has caused many other ships, probes and landers to crash or disappear, and what was euphemistically known as the *Martian Ghoul.* Before they can get much further they are again attacked by the pirates who have taken over the team at the main site where the pyramids are located. A fight ensues and eventually Star saves the archaeologists from being killed although some are injured. They also discover the pyramid is much more than what it seems, and that is as far as we get.

The mystery is not solved, but it is suggested that the Martians colonized Earth and left the face there to attract us back when we developed enough to recognize it.

What the mechanisms inside the pyramid do is also not explicit, so we are left hanging with unresolved questions about human origins and possible alien intervention or origins. I suspect a further volume to continue the story was to follow but it appears not to have been written.

Two other books featuring Star Svensdotter precede this story; ***Second Star*** (1991) and ***A Handful of Stars*** (1991). These two earlier books chronicle the development of human habitation in the asteroid belt.

Her descriptions of Mars and what the family sees on their extended travels across Mars are beautifully evocative and leave a lasting impression of the planet in the mind of the reader, but the focus of the story is about Star and her relationship with her two children;.

This is definitely a book worth reading.

Voyage (1996) by Stephen Baxter

An alternate history in which NASA abandons the moon shots after Apollo 14 and decides to adapt the Apollo module for a voyage to Mars.

The trigger point for the change was the Kennedy Assassination, only he doesn't die, his wife does. Kennedy is wounded but survives and it is his influence behind the scenes that pushes the space programme forwards.

Going to Mars is the next step after the Moon and President Nixon while uncommitted at first, eventually gives the okay for a mission to Mars.

The bulk of the book concerns the various astronauts who will train and compete against each other over a number of years as they prepare for the mission to Mars.

The story is intercut with short segments of the actual astronauts leaving Earth orbit and voyaging to Mars. But most of it follows the training and the political shenanigans involved behind the scenes as well as focussing on the first American female astronaut, who not only is the first female in Space but as well is the first female astronaut to go to Mars. There is some collaboration with Russian cosmonauts but no mention of the first Russian female cosmonaut in space who would already have been in orbit long before, and the American Moon voyages and landings, but then this is an alternate history and although the early part of the training and selection of the astronauts has real astronauts who actually participated, the later part has more fictional characters intermixed with real people.

For technophiles this is a marvellous story since it contains an overabundance of technical details regarding the development of rocket engines, and powerful rockets able to support a journey to Mars, as well as an incredible amount of information regarding the training and preparation for the astronauts. Baxter doesn't ignore the personal rivalries and romances that take place between the main astronauts which enliven the story.

For the non-technically minded person it is a very long story, and from my point of view although the idea of going to Mars is imbued throughout, there isn't enough of what happens on the voyage out or what they do when they get to Mars. There is far too much technical detail regarding every aspect of training and the development of the hardware needed for the voyage which makes it like a documentary story rather than a more fictional one. The book finishes abruptly with them landing successfully on Mars.

Baxter seamlessly mixes real people with his fictitious characters to make the whole story realistic and believable.

In our reality we didn't go to Mars, but Baxter suggests that in 1969 there was the will to do it, and Americans could have gone to Mars by 1987 had they wanted to. Of course that didn't happen and the history of NASA is substantially different to what Baxter envisages. But this is Baxter's vision of how it could have happened. He follows this epic story with two similarly lengthy novels to make up his alternate history NASA trilogy; ***Titan*** and ***Moonseed***.

Travelling to Mars

It appears that some authors got it more or less right when speculating on what to do on arrival at Mars. Both Arthur C Clarke and Ludek Pesek — in 1951 and 1970 respectively — had their space ships land on one or the other of Mars' moons, from where smaller vessels ferried crew members and equipment down to the surface.

Ben Bova and Jack Williamson had their ships orbiting Mars while the astronauts used small ferries to go to and from the surface.

Long gone are the authors who had their ships take off from Earth, fly to Mars and land, before reversing the process to return home again. Ships like that could never carry enough fuel to sustain landings and take-offs. E C Tubb in 1955 (***Alien Dust***) was probably the last to offer that as a method.

All the plans suggested in the non-fiction books and offered by various organizations involve either establishing a base on one of the moons or working from a mother ship in orbit. In his non-fiction book ***Mission to Mars***, Buzz Aldrin (the second man to walk on the Moon) suggests that the first astronauts should set up a base on Phobos, which is only 9,377 kilometres (5,827 miles) above the surface. They would be able to study the planet and operate tele-controlled robots on the surface without the time delay that would occur if operations were attempted from Earth. Once a presence is established on Phobos, or Deimos, or in orbit, huge amounts of scientific work can be carried out before any serious attempt is made to go down to the surface.

It is planned that Landers will separate from the mother ship to land, then they separate again to return to orbit, where they will dock with the mother ship for the return back to Earth.

NASA plans to send an expedition to Mars' moon Phobos sometime after 2030.

They will surely be beaten by private enterprise. A private non-profit US group wants to send a married couple to make a half orbit flyover of Mars in 2018 using Mars' gravity as a slingshot to hurl the ship into a trajectory that will return it to Earth.

The Mars One organization intends to send 4 colonists to Mars in 2023 where they will stay permanently. They have already narrowed the selection of volunteers from over two hundred thousand, to less than a hundred whose activities will be followed by a TV reality show (to finance the whole endeavour) as they decide on who will be the first four people to colonize Mars.

Elon Musk, of *Space X* and the manufacturer of the *Tesla* electric motor car, wants to go to Mars and has a fantastic plan beyond his present activities in space, ferrying supplies to and from the International Space Station. He wants to establish a colony on Mars in the mid-2030s. But more than that, he wants to have 1000 large spaceships in Earth orbit to transport huge numbers of people to Mars every two years when Mars and Earth are at their closest. Over 40 to 100 years his intention is to send one million people to Mars to establish a new human population in case something terrible happens to the home planet and humans are destroyed. Even with a few hundred thousand people on Mars, which seems a more likely figure, there would sufficient variety within the gene pool to guarantee a diverse human population. If anyone can succeed, he will be the one to do it.

Already he can send up rockets and have the first stage come back down and land vertically (like in the early SF stories) so it can be used again, reducing the cost of launches into orbit. He is at present working on the newer larger rocket ships for the colonization of Mars.

Other groups such as Blue Horizons are also coming up with ambitious plans for building gigantic space habitats, taking tourists to the Moon, and later planning to go to Mars.

Private enterprise is leading the way not because of altruism but because they can see profits in space exploration, asteroid mining, tourism, and the colonizing of Mars.

Governments bloated with bureaucrats in their space agencies don't have enough money at their disposal to achieve much more than basic robotic exploration.

The longest Mars story ever

When Kim Stanley Robinson's novel *Red Mars* appeared in 1992, it stunned science fiction readers (not necessarily SF fans). The Times Literary Supplement called it '*One of the finest works of American SF*' while Arthur C Clarke wrote that it was '*A staggering book; the best novel on the colonization of Mars that has ever been written.*' Interzone said: '*Red Mars may simply be the best novel ever written about Mars.*'

All this was said before anyone knew that ***Red Mars*** would be the first instalment of a trilogy that would become the longest novel ever written about Mars; just on 1698 pages plus several pages of acknowledgements and chronologies in my Harper Collins hardcover editions.

It is claimed that it took 17 years of research culminating in the writing of this trilogy, but I suspect that is hyperbole. Like most other SF fans, Robinson had been thinking about the possibilities of Mars for many years. (8 years earlier he had published a Martian novel called Icehenge). Since Robinson was born in 1952 and presumably started reading SF at a young teenage it could easily by claimed he spent 17 years researching Mars for these books, he was 40 years old when Red Mars was published. He certainly spent 12 years writing about Mars by the time the trilogy was completed; and that is remarkable in itself.

Obviously Robinson had been thinking deeply about Mars, how it could be terraformed, and how the establishment of a colony or colonies could take place. He also thought much about how the personal rivalries and politics would play out over 200 years. The end result of this careful thought and research is a magnificently detailed epic trilogy that rings true. You can believe it is real.

The first volume ***Red Mars*** won a Nebula award, and the following year ***Green Mars*** (1993) won the Hugo award. The third volume ***Blue Mars*** was published in 1996. So much material was accumulated and side stories written that eventually Robinson collected them as separate volume featuring characters and events and background material used for the original trilogy. Simply called ***The Martians*** (1999), it is fragmentary and disjointed, only making sense if read alongside the original trilogy. Some of the stories in this volume predate the trilogy of novels while at least one takes place many years after the end of *Blue Mars* when Mars is beginning to freeze over, (see A Martian Romance) a suggestion that the transformation of the planet into a more equable environment is beginning to fail. Perhaps the most important story in this volume is one called ***Green Mars***, a novella which predates the Mars trilogy and contains similar material as well as other visions of what would later be expressed in the second volume of the trilogy which has the same name, Green Mars. Interestingly the book also contains 27 poems under the heading; *If Wang Wei lived on Mars and other poems.*

Robinson creates a Martian mythology and a Martian Constitution, and filled his massive trilogy with dreams of a pure uncontaminated Mars competing against a slowly changing Mars (over several hundred years) as it is terraformed into something where its new inhabitants can walk on the surface without having to use breathing masks. He has the evolution of medical technology allowing people to live hundreds of years rather the short span we experience today so that many of the major characters at the beginning are still there, albeit much changed, at the end of the story. There are revolutions, murder, political skulduggery and all the things that go on in a modern society transposed into a changing Martian environment, a tremendous variety of people and ideas that reflect the vast diversity which exists on our own planet (Earth). Their interaction on Mars creates a new society, new ways of thinking, and new ways of interpreting old ideas once settlement begins. This trilogy and the accompanying fourth volume, ***The Martians*** is a stunning achievement.

To do these books justice would need an entire book devoted to them, but I will leave that for someone else to do if it hasn't already been done. Robert Markley for example has a chapter (9) in his book ***Dying Planet - Mars in Science and the Imagination***, which discusses in fine detail the theory of terraforming and eco economics in Kim Stanley Robinson's Martian trilogy.

Before his Mars trilogy, in 1984 Robinson wrote and published a novel which has been reissued (as a POD book) with the sub-heading *Kim Stanley Robinson's other Mars novel.* This is ***Icehenge***. You could call this a small trilogy, or more accurately a triptych, because the story is told in three parts and from three very different viewpoints which adds to the complexity of the narrative and gives it much more depth than a single narrative would.

Icehenge: the writing and initial publication predates his Mars trilogy by eight years. It has no direct connection with that work although it does explore similar themes. Even though it begins after a revolution ruined the independent colonies on Mars allowing government by Committee, it is not the same kind of event that took place in the massive Mars trilogy.

Icehenge begins in 2248 when several million people are living on Mars (already partially terraformed though not directly mentioned) and there was a rebellion during which three ships belonging to the rebels disappeared somewhere beyond the asteroid belt, presumed lost.

Emma Weil a leading systems eco-geneticist keeps a journal of her life. This journal tells the story of a trading ship in which Emma is the officer in charge of life support being hijacked by a rebel crew and taken to a hidden location near the edge of the solar system where two missing ships thought lost five years earlier are being modified and reconstructed to become a starship. A previous lover of Emma Weil, Oleg Davydov, is the leader of the starship group and he wants her to help perfect the life support system in the starship so they can survive the journey of perhaps one hundred years. She agrees under duress to help but refuses to go with them and wants to return to Mars even though it has been devastated because of the rebellion.

This section ends with the return of Emma to Mars along with a few who didn't want to risk a voyage to another star. She decides to disappear in an area known as The Choatic Terrain, where there are still rebel hideouts, knowing that the ruling Committee will try to follow her and the few rebels left on Mars, to wipe them out, along with all memory of them and the rebellion from the historical records. Whether the Committee police can find her in this impassable terrain is left open.

Part Two, the longest part, is from the viewpoint of Hjalmar Nederland, already three hundred years old and bemoaning the fact that he can't remember much from when he was younger, a problem all long lived people have, which is why they tend to write autobiographies and journals, not for posterity, but so they can remember later who they were and what they did. A problem with living for 500 to 600 years is that early memories are wiped out by the accumulation of more recent memories, and no one remembers too far back, hence the need for auto-biographical journals

The events in this part take place on Mars in 2547 and concern an expedition to a city destroyed during the rebellion three hundred years earlier. People were killed when domed cities were destroyed. Three centuries later an archaeological expedition examining one ruined domed city discovers disturbing facts about who actually destroyed the city killing all its inhabitants. Further upsetting is the discovery of an abandoned vehicle buried for so long no knew it was there. A landslide exposed it. Inside a journal written by Emma Weil is discovered which tells the story of the hijacking of her ship and of the Davydov expedition which had disappeared, and how they were preparing a starship to leave the solar system.

Nederland searches for obscure references in lost or hidden records and constructs a theory of what could have happened. This theory which doesn't quite match what Emma wrote in her journal changes as he discovers new information. The later discovery of a megalithic structure made of gigantic ice columns in the shape of Stonehenge but much grander on the north pole of Pluto causes him to rethink his theories of what happened to the Davydov expedition and what Emma Weil had done.

He believes the departing rebels built the icehenge and inscribed a date on one of the columns in Sanskrit which is the date of the rebellion that was crushed. He also believes that he was allowed to obtain once hidden information because the Committee now wants truer version of events to be known. There are many theories regarding the icehenge, such as it was constructed by aliens, or it was far older than dating methods assume, that it was a fake to mislead archaeologists, but it is his theory that becomes the accepted one.

Part three in 2610 is told from the viewpoint of Edmond Doya a great grandson of Nederland and part time academic, who comes up with an alternative theory as to who constructed the ice henge. He thinks that it was a trick to make people believe in something that had never happened. There are too many anomalies in the known facts to make any sense, and he does come up with an alternative solution as to who constructed the ice henge and why.

This is possibly the most interesting part of the story because none of it takes place on Mars. Robinson builds a complex picture of humanity occupying asteroids and various other habitats in space, of mining, and big business, and not much about politics on Mars although Mars is always there in the background. He also shows us how events from the past can be distorted or changed because of different viewpoints, misconceptions and misunderstandings of what really happened.

It is also interesting because just as we think a solution to the construction of the ice henge has been discovered it is all turned upside down. Further mysteries are revealed to Doya and although the ending seems ambiguous it does conclude with who actually built the ice henge and why, although a vague uncertainty still persists.

All the characters in this story are believable and beautifully delineated and the events seen from various viewpoints create a complex story much bigger than the three parts suggest.

Although not directly connected to his later Mars trilogy it does add depth to that work and shows Robinson was for many years thinking a lot about Mars and how humans could live and survive there as well as in the greater solar system.

Alternate visions

In 1997 a book appeared that should have eclipsed most books written about Mars. Somehow this novel doesn't seem to be reprinted or to be very well known. ***Mars Underground*** was written between 1988 and 1996. Its author is well-known planetary scientist William K Hartmann, whose work includes research into the origin of planets and other bodies in the solar system. He also had important roles in the NASA Mariner 9 mission which mapped in detail the surface of Mars as well as well as being a participating scientist in the Mars Global Surveyor Mission.

His previous non-fiction (but speculative) work with co-author Ron miller, ***The Grand Tour***, won a Hugo award in 1988.

In 2003 he published ***A Traveller's guide to Mars - The mysterious Landscapes of the Red Planet,*** (2003 probably one of the best illustrated books about everything we know about Mars up to this point in time. He is an astronomer and a physicist, and also a brilliant writer of fiction as Mars Underground testifies.

Is ***Mars Underground*** science fiction?

Yes, by any definition, but it is also a literary mainstream novel that just happens to be set on Mars in the future. Arthur C Clarke describes it as, "*A realistic and exciting view of the future presence of humans on Mars.*" At the same time the book garnered fine praise from the likes of Greg Bear, Gregory Benford, Ray Bradbury and astronaut Buzz Aldrin, but it also received a nod from other prominent Authors who do not write science fiction.

Mystery writer Tony Hillerman said: "*If you doubted science fiction and mystery would make a good mix, William Hartman proves you wrong in Mars Underground.*" Christopher J Koch author of The year of Living Dangerously writes: "*Like H G Wells, William K Hartman brings a scientific training to his fiction, and a serious concern with ideas. His portrayal of a colony on Mars is so convincing and real that I felt I'd been taken into the imminent future.*"

Koch is right. Mars is so realistically portrayed that you immediately accept that settlers have gone there and established a foothold on the planet with a substantial city and outposts in two other areas including the South

Polar region, that its dangers and beauties are well known to the inhabitants, and that has become background which informs action and determines how inhabitants need to react.

The inhabitants take it for granted just as characters in a story set upon Earth don't need to wonder at their surrounds but simply accept them as they are. Mars and its incredible vistas are never explained because everyone who lives on Mars understands. This frees the author to concentrate on the interaction between Annie, a female reporter, and two leading people on the planet, Philippe, an artist who has created a sculpture resembling Stonehenge, and Carter, a planetary administrator. She falls in love with both of them to differing degrees. The book also offers comparisons with the moral behaviour in the future compared with that of the present time (1997), and aims to solve a mystery that Annie has come down to report on.

The mystery involves the disappearance of a prominent person, Alwyn Stafford (a planetary scientist, exo-biologist and explorer) who was there on Mars from the beginning of colonization and who was famous for discovering the remains of ancient bacterial life. He never follows the rules and often goes off by himself. When he disappears in the remote desert area of Hellespontus, having left some enigmatic clues for his friend Carter to follow, everyone in the solar system wants to know what happened.

The clues that are followed are often scientific, such as using orbital imagery to find tracks left in the desert sands by Stafford's rover, but this doesn't intrude upon the story; it seems natural and appropriate. As Carter's search for his missing friend continues, more mysteries are uncovered, and obfuscation by military authorities becomes a further problem for Carter, Philippe and Annie as an even deeper mystery unfolds at the South Pole with the discovery of a huge buried alien artefact which they accidentally activate during a prolonged exploration of it.

Apart from examining love and the relationships involved between a woman and two men, Hartman examines the absurdity of secret services and the paranoia these people possess, as well as greater mysteries in the universe such as the origin of life and our place as living intelligent beings in this universe.

What elevates this story is that it is not about going to Mars or establishing a colony, but it is about the people who live there and how their lives are interconnected to each other and the place they live in. Like many other wonderful novels it could have been set anywhere reasonably remote, but this time the setting is Mars. Mars influences all that happens but it doesn't over-ride or dominate.

Buzz Aldrin (the second astronaut to walk on the Moon) wrote: "*Mars Underground gives an exciting depiction of the coming decades not only on Mars but also on its moon Phobos —and some of the surprises that may await us.*"

My only criticism is the date the story is set, 2031 to 2033.

Even in 1997 it should have been obvious that it was too close, and having an established colony with a city (Mars City) that has 4000 inhabitants and all the things a city of that size would contain, not to mention a secondary township near the south pole called Hellas as well as a scientific base at the south pole, with a university in a settlement on Phobos, simply couldn't happen within the 30 or so years from the time the book was written. It seems very unlikely that we will have anyone on Mars by the date of the action of the book. None the less, it is probably one of the best books yet with a story set on Mars.

Alien Artefacts on Mars — a common theme

The discovery of alien artefacts on Mars was a common element from 1990 and onwards resulting from the erroneous belief that in the rugged Cydonia region there was a massive alien carving that from space appeared human, or at the least Simian. NASA later took more detailed high resolution images which showed the face was only a rock formation, and that with the way light falls on it sometimes and with the human ability to connect shadows and lines mentally into a shape that resembles a face, it was easy to mistake a jagged weatherworn mesa for a face when seeing it from a great height. *(see page 211)*

Unfortunately these high resolution images really didn't dispel the alien artefact idea for many people. It made them believe that NASA was trying to cover up the truth. As a result of this a number of authors based their entire story or a major part of their story around the idea that the face at Cydonia, and the nearby hills and small mountains resembling pyramids, were all alien constructions and needed to be explored.

Semper Mars by Ian Douglas (1998)

Something has been discovered on Mars; something that could change the way we see human history, something buried for 500,000 years.

An American and Russian scientific expedition has scientists and archaeologists studying the face and the ruined city surrounding it. Two of them make a remarkable discovery.

The UN which is a quasi dictatorial government controlling most of Earth has sent a team of crack soldiers to protect 'their' interests on Mars. The Americans have also sent a team of Special Marines there to protect American and Russian interests. America and Russia are allies with Japan a loose cannon. Meanwhile on Earth confrontations between the Americans and the UN countries have reached a point where war is inevitable. The Japanese align themselves initially with the UN.

What starts the war is the discovery by two American archaeologists who enter a tunnel in one of the ruins of several human bodies in space suits. They have been dead for half a million years and are perfectly preserved though totally desiccated. The UN person in charge of the contingent on Mars immediately imprisons the American forces and disconnects all communications with Earth. This is the tipping point for the war on Earth to begin.

On Mars the imprisoned forces who are kept at an isolated base in Valles Marineris manage to escape and head along the chasm towards Mars Prime, the main base in Candor Chasm. This 500 mile trek is a massive undertaking through some of the most rugged terrain on Mars. They want to recapture the base because they know the main UN force is at Cydonia 'protecting' the ruins from American interference. The UN wants whatever technology is buried there for themselves.

As the Marines are making their way across Mars, on Earth the Japanese and the UN are attacking the US forces especially those in space on the ISS, but there is a secret American satellite that has a powerful laser weapon which is used to destroy UN forces, missiles and rockets. When the Japanese see that the UN will lose they re-align themselves with the American because they also want a part of whatever has been and will be discovered on Mars. On their way to Mars Prime base the scientists and the marines manage to send information of their discovery through an alternate route to Earth so everyone knows about the finding of ancient bodies at Cydonia and the secret is out. Mars Prime is retaken at about the same time as the UN loses on Earth. There is one final confrontation between the Martian Marines and their UN counterparts at Cydonia where the Americans used smuggled beer in cans as bombs which they drop on the UN forces to disorient them allowing the Marines to regain control of the base at Cydonia.

This is quite an exciting story as it unfolds without undue emphasis on American Marine tradition (which in some military SF is off-putting), there is more concern for the main characters, and a romance on Earth between the daughter of the American Marine leader on Mars and a Japanese pilot who unfortunately is skilled while attempting to destroy the laser weapon satellite is a nice counterpoint to the action on Mars.

Two further volumes will conclude the story; Luna Marine and Europa Strike, and presumably the history of humans on Earth will never be the same again.

Rainbow Mars by Larry Niven (1999)

A delightful time travel fantasy which is quite different. The year is set more than 1100 years into what Niven calls the Atomic Era and Svetz returns from a trip into the past where he collects extinct animals for his patron's private zoo, to find his employer the Secretary General, has died and a new regime controls Earth. The ruler wants to send him back, way back in time, but on the planet Mars. He wants to know what happened to turn Mars into the desolate barren place it is today.

Arriving on Mars Svetz finds himself embroiled in a conflict between warring very alien Martians who are fighting over a an enormous (Spacefaring) Tree that has taken root in the canals and is slowly sucking the life out of the planet. It has grown so huge it extends out of the atmosphere and into space. Many of these aliens live on and in the tree and their battles are territorial against each other and against the tree which is trying to get rid of the parasites living within it.

Having finally gained enough sustenance (after thousands of years) the tree uproots itself and heads across the space between Mars and Earth. It is up to Svetz and his team to prevent the tree from taking root on Earth and doing to it what it has done to Mars.

The Earth the tree lands on is an alternate Earth from the one Svetz left, and unless he can destroy the tree before it gets too big, there will not be the same Earth for him to return to. The tree has blasted seed pods from orbit down into the Amazon Basin during the time of the conquistadors' penetration into Brazil. This is what these space faring trees do; they seed a planet, and then leave, and when one of the seeds grows into a big enough tree, having sucked all it can from the planet it blasts off into space in search of another star system with suitable planets to seed.

There is a lot of action and excitement and a brilliant evocation of what Brazil was like 500 years ago. Needless to say the story ends satisfactorily with Svetz finally returning home to a slightly altered future from the one he left.

Part Three

2000 and beyond

The most complex roving robot sent to Mars to date. Over the next few years there will be more, until finally an attempt to land humans onMars takes place.

Chapter Twelve

Gregory Benford and the inevitability of life in the Universe

Throughout his epic space novels Benford convinces us that life is everywhere, and it is vastly different to anything we could expect; so different that it could be incomprehensible.

Planets like Earth that exist in a 'habitable' zone that has from our perspective comfortable temperatures where water exists in three forms simultaneously, — ice, liquid, and gaseous — are rare in the galaxy. Even in our solar system there are only two, Earth and Mars. Mars is out on the extreme edge of the zone and has lost its surface water and most of its atmosphere although there is still water frozen beneath the surface and at the poles. Venus on the very edge of the inner limit has probably always been too hot and too deadly a place, although it could be made habitable with the right long term introduction of extremophiles to change the atmosphere and the climate in general. It may still be too close to the sun to be worth the trouble. The prospect of eventually transforming Mars to make it slightly warmer and more benign is much more likely in the future and is probably a definite possibility.

The rest of the planets in our solar system are too big, too cold, extremely cold, or like Mercury, far too hot, to harbour any possibility of life... or is that a valid assumption?

Not anymore. On our own planet life has been discovered in places once thought impossible for life to exist: In frozen arctic wastes and in the freezing dry valleys of Antarctica there are tough bacteria, in almost boiling hot springs and lakes where geothermal activity has broken out on the surface there are plants, algae and small marine animals, deep down in rocks far below the surface bacteria thrive in an environment devoid of oxygen, and far down in the abyssal depths of the oceans where volcanic vents spew minerals and gasses like methane into water so dense it can't boil, colonies of tube worms, crabs, other crustaceans, and bacteria thrive completely isolated from any other environmental effects that allowed life in the upper parts of the oceans and on the land to evolve.

If life can exist and obviously evolve in such extreme environments on this planet alone, why can it not exist in even more extreme environments in space further out in the solar system and far beyond in other planetary systems?

Thousands of exoplanets have now been discovered around nearby stars in our Galaxy, and although some are almost earth like and exist in what we call our comfort zone and would most likely harbour some kind of life, the majority of the discoveries are gas giants or massive rocky planets either far too cold or far too hot for life as we think of it. The universe is so vast and our galaxy and its nearby companions contain so many billions of stars there must be many other forms of life out there no matter how extreme the environment, but would human explorers be able to recognize it?

What kind of life could use extremely cold chemical reactions to sustain itself? What about machine life that has evolved over millions of years and is as far beyond us as we are beyond the first creatures that crawled onto land. Or what kind of life could exist on extremely hot environments close to a sun? What about life that doesn't need a planet but exists as gaseous and magnetic energy beings in the space between the stars? Gregory Benford presents us with a myriad of possibilities that he explores in his novels much to the delight of his readers.

What about Mars? Traces of methane continue to be found from time to time, and methane is a by product of life. Methane is broken down by ultraviolet light and so to regularly find traces of it in the Martian atmosphere means that it is being replaced. This opens a couple of possibilities: the methane is produced by geological processes, or it is being produced by microbial life deep beneath the surface. The geological process requires olivine, abundant on Mars, to react with water during which methane is produced. If this is the case it is good news for future colonists because it means water is certainly present underground. Even better if it is produced by microbial activity as it means life outside Earth exists. It could also be the result of ancient microbial activity which produced sufficient methane for it to slowly seep up to the surface. The most likely scenario is perhaps a combination of the geological process as well as living microbial by product.

A joint European/Russian Mission, the Exo-Mars Trace-Gas Orbiter, departed from Baikonur in March 2016 and has arrived in orbit around Mars. A lander to test parachutes and heat shield failed and crashed, but the gas detector has slowly been adjusting its orbit until it now orbits at a height of 250 miles. It can detect methane with an accuracy of one molecule in 10 billion, and it can also determine whether the methane is biologically or geologically produced.

Will we find life deep under the surface where it is unaffected by the continuous bombardment of radiation from the sun that has fried and sterilized the surface regolith?

Benford, like many scientists, believes that deep under the surface on Mars we will find life and that some exploration of cave systems should be attempted, but this would have to wait for human explorers rather than robotic rovers and orbital satellites.

This brings us to ***The Martian Race, Vortex*** and ***The Sunborn.***

When NASA mothballed the space shuttles and started relying on Russia to get their astronauts up to the International Space Station, it also instigated a prize to be offered to the first private business ventures which could deliver payloads and astronauts into orbit with a degree of regularity. As a result of this initiative a number of wealthy companies are developing rockets and launch systems to either deliver cargo and/or astronauts to orbit on a regular basis, or to take joy flights with tourists to the edge of space as well as to the Moon and back. These ventures are ongoing and still developing.

There have already been several billionaires who have been to the Mir space station as well as the International space station as tourists and who have paid tens of millions for the privilege. These people have already formed a space tourism business which will probably use Virgin Galactic with regularity once it starts taking passengers into near-earth space. It is only natural that books about Mars written since the new millennium begin to reflect this competitive private enterprise approach rather than the turgid bureaucratic government approach to exploration.

This idea is not really new. Offering a prize for the first people to go to Mars and return was used as the basis of a novel written by John Wyndham back in 1936; ***Planet Plane***, later reprinted as ***Stowaway to Mars.*** Of course his vision of Mars was based around ideas of Mars extant in the 1930s and is vastly different compared to what is known today.

Capitalizing on NASA's concept of a prize to the winner of a race to develop multiple-use delivery systems, Gregory Benford has written ***The Martian Race*** (1999), whose initial event takes place in 2015, seventeen years ahead of when it was published. The author has said he wanted to stress how it could be done soon, if the determination was there. He writes a delightful book that begins with a disaster and keeps the reader hooked all the way through.

NASA's first manned voyage to Mars, launching in 2015 explodes because of a fuel blockage shortly after ignition, destroying the launch pad, gantry and other facilities, killing all on board. Unwilling to mount another ridiculously expensive expedition Congress puts all Mars missions on hold. Unwilling to accept blame if something goes wrong again NASA offers a prize of $30 billion to any enterprise that can launch an expedition to Mars during which the astronauts (Marsnauts) will carry out scientific studies on the surface and return safely to Earth.

One business consortium led by John Axelrod has every intention of winning the money, but the Chinese and the Europeans have also combined to develop a similar expedition. The race has begun. Axelrod intends to finance his expedition by selling media rights to the highest bidder. The expedition in effect becomes a reality TV show that billions of people watch enthusiastically every day. Corners are cut and various dramatic incidents take place. Finally the marsnauts take off, and successfully land on Mars in 2018.

The story uses alternating chapters with the lead chapter taking place on Mars while the alternate chapter is a flashback to the development of the expedition. Eventually the two streams merge into the current situation on Mars.

The Chinese led consortium is building a nuclear powered rocket system which can get their people to Mars quicker than the chemical system used by Axelrod's marsnauts. After five months on Mars the American led expedition is about to return home when Julia, the only biologist on the team, discovers slime mould (LIFE!) in a volcanic vent that is sometimes active. She hardly has time to study this life because preparations are being made for the return journey to Earth.

This discovery of life under the surface is the real point of the novel. We are always speculating over the possibility of life outside of the Earth, and look to Achaean extremophile bacteria as examples on our own planet that exist in conditions totally inimical to the life as we have understood it until now.

One example, which Gregory Benford uses as a premise for Martian life, was the discovery in the Witwatersrand Basin of South Africa, at a depth of 2 to 3 kilometres, anaerobic bacteria that utilize H2 (produced by radiolysis of water) as an energy source (reducing CO2 to CH4). These bacteria colonies have been isolated from the surface for millions of years.

Benford theorizes that similar bacterial colonies could exist on Mars, deep underground where they could remain unaffected by whatever has happened on the surface. To help prove his assertion is the fact that sporadic methane emissions have been recorded and continue to be recorded on the surface of Mars. Methane is a by-product of life. But NASA has not done much more than scratch the surface and drill a few holes to see what shows, with little results so far. Most of the surface is bathed with radiation from space, which makes it toxic. We will have to look deep underground, or deep down inside ancient lava tubes for any chance to find life, and that hasn't been done yet.

It is probably unlikely to be done until people actually go to Mars and start exploring.

This is exactly what Julia does. She discovers a massive living organism that is neither plant nor animal but something related to slime mould that has had 4 billion years to evolve. It occupies lava tubes and deep caverns covering the surfaces like a mat and controls its own environment. Though unaware of it, when the marsnauts enter the lava tube their expelled oxygen and carbon dioxide proves to be poisonous to this communal organism which prompts it to eject them from its interior creating difficulties they barely manage to escape from. Julia calls this life form the Marsmat.

Meanwhile disaster strikes on the surface. The reserve vehicle which has sat on Mars since NASA's failed attempt to send a group there has deteriorated, and malfunctions when they test it. They try to affect repairs, but fail. The Chinese have arrived and are following in the footsteps of Julia's group, using her already published results and research to save them doing their own work, which angers the American members who have worked very hard while on Mars.

Because the repairs failed the Americans are stuck on Mars unless the Chinese agree to take them home when they leave. Unfortunately there is only room for one extra person on the Chinese ship.

Meanwhile the Chinese, in an attempt to steal the glory of Julia's biological discoveries, lose two of their team who are inadvertently killed down in the vent where Julia discovered the slime mould, but there is something far more complex further down. The vent contains much more than anyone had anticipated. When Julia and her companion follow the cables the Chinese used to lower themselves deep into the vent they find the bodies, but they also find this massive communal organism, which they suspect is planet-wide, using waves of fluorescence that follow them so they know it is aware of their presence. It also tries extruding material in the shape of a human figure which Julia suspects is the organism attempting to communicate with them. This organism, far beyond anything they expected, is truly alien.

The two deaths of the Chinese expedition means that the one Chinese member left can't fly the ship back alone and needs the Americans to help.

Unfortunately one would still have to stay behind. Julia decides she will stay so she can continue her studies of this Martian organism. Her husband Viktor, who is the captain of the American team, also decides to stay with her. He doesn't want to leave her alone on Mars for the two years it would take for a return trip. Their hope is that with the two of them stranded on Mars, the American government will authorise NASA to make a rescue attempt. Otherwise all future expeditions to Mars would likely be cancelled.

The other important point of the story is that the astronauts who are on the spot decide their own fate through the choices they have to make for survival, not the mission controllers back on Earth.

This is an entertaining, and thoughtful story ending on a positive note.

The speculation on possible life on Mars is based soundly on scientific knowledge regarding extremophiles on Earth, with the probability of something similar being on Mars, which after billions of years of separate evolution could produce something remarkable, along with the technical details of how to get there makes this realistic, and speculative rather than fantasy.

A short story that appeared in Gardner Dozois' 'Best of...' for 1916 was ***Vortex***, a small sequel to ***The Martian Race*** and takes place almost 20 years after the original landings with a conflict between another Chinese astrobiology group and the two Americans still on Mars, Julia and Viktor, arising as a result of conflicts back on Earth instigated by a new Korean war.

The Chinese reluctantly ask them for help in solving the reason the Marsmat seems to be rapidly dying in the original vent discovered by Julia. It's a simple problem that Julia solves while discovering how the Marsmat reproduces and gets rid of dead and dying parts. It also suggests cooperation rather than conflict is the answer to survival on Mars when that may not be possible back on Earth. It does a lot for a short story and is an excellent addition to the original novel The Martian Race and its sequel The Sunborn.

The Sunborn was published in 2005.

It begins on Mars with something strange happening to the communal life form they have called the Marsmat down in the vents and lava tubes. Julia has always suspected the life form is intelligent in a rudimentary way and is convinced it is trying to communicate with the human explorers.

By the end of twenty two years the scientific colony on Mars had grown considerably and the base has been expanded and extended into a reasonably sized domed community. The story begins with Julia making her usual video broadcast to Earth. They are filming a student biologist free flying —gliding inside the dome— a sport that has become popular with new arrivals and those on temporary study visits. With the thicker atmosphere in the dome and the low gravity of Mars, flying and gliding has become a popular activity; something that can't be done on Earth, flying like a bird. It ends in a disaster, broadcast live. Somehow the student miscalculates his speed and damages a wing as he tries to pull out of a steep dive, resulting in a devastating crash down to the surface. He breaks his neck in the fall.

Shortly after that the consortium sends a new administrator who forbids Julia and Viktor to go outside the dome. They are world famous and John Axlerod and the consortium are concerned something might happen to them. There have been accidents and other deaths, and the last thing anyone wants is for something awful to happen to Julia and Viktor. In fact the consortium wants them to return to take on management jobs on the Moon. There is no way they could readapt to Earth gravity after twenty two years on Mars, but on the Moon, they would be fine.

They both refuse to leave Mars, the very thought of going to take an administrative position on the Moon is abhorrent. They have their work, their obsession to communicate with the Marsmat, so ignoring orders from the new administrator they head off to a remote lava tube where the Marsmat has been strangely active. Victor wants to try pulsing a series of small voltage electrical currents through an exposed iron seam in the lava tube that isn't covered by growth to see whether they get a response. They do and it is a disaster. Waves of fluorescence travel across the Marsmat surface before huge sparks shoot out from the iron seam. The return current is so powerful it blows up Viktor's capacitor and damages his protective suit and its life support.

Julia manages to extricate him from the lava tube and gets him back into the Rover and eventually to the hospital at the home base. Viktor is okay apart from minor electrical burns and the bits of the capacitor that exploded blowing shrapnel though his suit and into him have been removed.

His first thought is to calculate the return voltage and it was enormous in comparison to what he used: 200 volts as a response to his two volts. Julia is convinced the Marsmat is trying to communicate with them, as it has always tried since they first discovered it.

Meanwhile far out in the solar system close to the orbit of Pluto an exploration ship run by the daughter of John Axlerod, Shanna, has discovered Pluto is warmer than they expected and there is a strange form of life on its surface.

There is also a problem with the zone where the plasma expelled from the sun hits the edge of interstellar space where the pressure of invisible matter between the stars seems to push back into the edge of the solar system forming a bow wave of energy and magnetic forces.

This is where Benford's imagination shines. He posits a gigantic life form that is immortal but as we find later can be destroyed. These gigantic beings, bigger than planets, are energy beings that use magnetic forces as part of their circulatory system. They thrive on the plasma and magnetic fields expelled by the sun but cannot go too far into the solar system or the heat from a planet could trap or destroy them, and they are intelligent. One of their goals in life is to find the fount of their existence, the place that birthed them. Four billion years earlier one of their kind ventured down into the solar system but never came back. A group of them has instigated an experiment on Pluto, the creating of 'hot' life, both biological and mechanical.

To the human explorers led by Shanna, Pluto is on the edge of being absolute zero, extremely cold and to discover life in a place considered too cold at minus300 degrees for any kind of life is a shock. It causes a sensation. To discover they are intelligent is even more of a sensation. Shanna uses a newly developed computer that is self aware to help scommunicate with the beings on Pluto which call themselves the Zand, and in the process comes to realize that they didn't evolve naturally but were created by something more mysterious further out than Pluto.

The consortium led by John Axlerod contrives to convince Julia and Viktor to go to Pluto on a new fusion powered spaceship already on its way to Mars to collect them. He wants them to assist with communicating with this new alien life. In fact he puts Julia in charge of the now joint expedition, much to the chagrin of Shanna who doesn't want to be usurped from her leadership position. There is a lot of tension between Julia and Shanna, who once admired Julia and her achievements but who now is jealous of her being put in command of the mission. She discovered the Zand on Pluto and thinks she should be in charge.

There is even more tension between the miniscule humans in their two space ships and the giant energy beings that surround the edges of the solar system. In attempting to communicate with them there are misunderstandings and the humans think the giant alien beings are attacking them and respond by cutting them with the ships' plasma exhausts. Conversely the aliens believe they are being attacked by the things in the metal ships and respond by trying to destroy them.

Benford crosses from the viewpoint of the giant energy beings alternatively with the viewpoint from his human protagonists to produce an enthralling story loaded with tension and incredible speculations about the meaning and definition of life from two very different perspectives.

Eventually once an understanding has been reached Julia and Viktor discover that the energy waves used by the beings in communication are the same as the waves of fluorescence that the Marsmat tried to use to communicate with them. She suspects that the long lost being who attempted to dive into the solar system became trapped in the metallic iron seams deep under the Martian surface and that the slime mould was not intelligent itself but is actually the missing energy being using it. She agrees to use their two ships to create a pressure bow wave that would deflect energy and heat from the sun to allow cover for one of the energy beings to follow behind so it can communicate with its long lost family member. In return the energy beings agree to stop the bow wave at the edge of interstellar space from penetrating too far into the solar system which would cause severe problems for Earth and the inner planets.

It turns out that the sun is the fount and that these energy beings were born in the Sun and ejected as massive plasma eruptions, and from time to time another one is born. The birth of a new being is happening at the same time as the events unfolding with the humans in contact with the older mature beings beyond the system. This is a fascinating scenario in itself which leaves the reader wondering if the Sun and other stars are also alive in ways we could never understand. If they weren't there could be no birthing of beings composed of plasma and magnetic forces.

The novel finishes with a small group of the plasma beings making an attempt to travel across interstellar space to another star system while the others are delighted to find what happened to their long lost member.

Presumably Julia and Viktor return to Mars which for them is home.

Gregory Benford is a writer to look out for; his work is always full of surprises, and these three stories about Mars are something no one should miss.

Into the 21st Century

From 2000 on until the present time we continue to see new books and films about Mars and travelling to Mars, especially non-fiction speculative books, and semi documentary TV series, as preparations are actually being made by several organizations for such a voyage. We are well into the 21st century now and a real sense of anticipation of going to Mars infuses public awareness, whereas fifty years ago it was nothing more than a vivid dream.

I often wonder why modern authors are conservative in regard to setting a future time in which to place their story. Are they afraid that if they set it too far ahead of the current date any predictions contained in the story will not come true?

Authors like Clarke, Pesek and others looked ahead 60, 80, sometime 100 years, and some of the things they wrote about could still happen. Their minor technical predictions have often been side tracked by other developments, sometimes making their stories old fashioned and quaint, but still readable because the main ideas developed in those stories are still some way off in the future.

In the works of recent authors, placing the story only 30 or 40 years ahead is hardly enough time to allow the events depicted in establishing a colony on Mars with a viable society to happen. A lot could happen in 100 years, but in a period of a mere 20 years, we will hardly get a single person to go to Mars, let alone thousands plus the ships to carry them and the materials needed to establish a domed city or any kind of complex living quarters.

I suspect authors think that if they set their story too far ahead readers will not accept it as being realistic. They keep the setting as close as possible to our present time and remain cautious with their extrapolations of present trends to lend credibility to the story. Unfortunately for me this has the opposite effect. As a reader, when I see a date uncomfortably close to the present, I subconsciously add 100 years to it, and that makes the story more acceptable.

From the mid1960s and on, many Mars stories were about the journey out, how long to stay on Mars before being able to return, the establishment of a first base and the carrying out of scientific experiments — plus the problems incurred when something went wrong. They were attempting to be realistic and use whatever new knowledge there was available. There were exceptions with some authors harking back to the ideas prevalent in the 1940s and 50s.

In the later 1970s and 80s, much more information about Mars was becoming available, and stories began to assume an established human presence on the planet, with lots of people making a life for themselves. The range of action depicted widened, allowing for stories featuring greater amounts of human interaction and drama.

In the 1990s realistic depictions of Mars were becoming combined with stories that either involved changing humans to fit the climate of Mars or alternatively changing Mars over decades and centuries, terraforming it, so that it became more habitable for humans. The definitive work on this subject is Kim Stanley Robinson's '***Mars***' trilogy (terraforming), and both Frederick Pohl and Kevin J Anderson for human modification to fit Mars.

But over all this time, although humans were increasingly being portrayed with more depth of character, Mars has always remained the place that has dominated these novels.

The 1990s became the best decade for books of all kinds about Mars. Every permutation appeared, from straight adventures on the surface of Mars, updated stories about getting there, about genetic manipulation, of terraforming some which were realistic in approach while others were more fantasy-like. All of them at the very least competently written and enjoyable while a few were outstanding.

In the most recent decade the trend has been to Mars stories about extricating an exploration team from some kind of disaster that occurs after they have landed and set up a base to live in and work from on the surface, or about finding some kind of primitive life, and the consequences of that discovery.

A new trend is emerging as we near the end of the second decade of the new millennium. This is a combination of detective noir or murder mystery within an established colony where lots of people interact and tensions inevitably result. A good murder mystery set on Mars with its extraordinarily harsh environment and difficult living conditions in an enclosed community can make for a brilliant story that is entertaining and thought provoking at the same time.

Of course none of this is new. The same trends existed back in the 1930s, 40s and 50s. Today's stories are updated with informatiuon that is realistic rather than completely imagined, which makes them more acceptable, but people still do the same kinds of things that they always have and always will, that never changes, and this is what forms the basis of a good enjoyable story.

Geoffrey A Landis's Mars

Geoffrey A Landis knows a lot about Mars just as William K Hartman does. He also worked for NASA in 1997 on experiments on the Pathfinder 'Sojourner' Rover (measuring the amounts of dust that collected on the rover each day) as well as images from Mars Global Surveyor. While writing this book he was working on advanced concepts for the NASA John Glenn Research Centre.

Landis also dates his story ***Mars Crossing*** (2000) —in the middle of the 21st century (it says on the cover) by inserting some dates unobtrusively in the text. In 2018 an unmanned ship/habitat with supplies for an extended stay was sent so the crew of the first American expedition could use it. While it sat on Mars it produced fuel by extracting oxygen and hydrogen from the atmosphere and stored it in tanks. The American crew were to go in 2022 but two Brazilians beat them to it by landing near the North Pole on the other side of the planet in 2020. They both died as the whole world watched on TV and no one knew what caused it.

The second expedition, (the first American one) arrives. During the flight the whole crew becomes infected with athlete's foot, a fungal infection which goes wild in the enclosed environment of the space ship because the astronauts had been sterilized of the skin bacteria which normally control fungal infections. The infection invades everything, making the astronauts' lives intolerable, forcing them to leave almost as soon as they had landed. They would have turned around mid-flight if they could have. Orbital mechanics forces them to complete the journey to Mars before being able to return. They abandon the habitat and take off immediately.

Their ship is destroyed as it makes a gravity boost around Venus.

To back up the 1st American expedition if the unmanned ship/habitat failed, a second one was sent at the same time on a slower, longer orbit to arrive much later. This puts the second American group's arrival around 2034.

This third expedition arrives with all six marsnauts knowing that the previous two expeditions finished disastrously. If they fail there will be no rescue or fourth mission. They really are on their own and must make certain they don't fail.

Unfortunately after 6 years on the surface, the second return ship's fuel storage explodes when two of the marsnauts try to check how much is there. Highly active sulphur in the dust got into everything over the six years it has been sitting there. It corroded fuel lines, measurement gauges, and seals, rendering the habitat unusable. One of the marsnauts is killed when the fuel tanks explode dousing him in liquid oxygen.

The members of this expedition are stuck with no way back and no possible rescue mission. They hatch a crazy plan to travel across Mars to the location of the Brazilian expedition to see if its ship is usable for a return to Earth. The problem with the Brazilian ship, however, is that it had been designed for two people, and there are five remaining in the American team. The Brazilian ship is 4000 miles (6000 kilometres) from their location, sitting on the polar ice cap.

This is where Landis' knowledge of Mars comes to the fore. His descriptions of surface features and colours, dust storms, and the kind of features the travellers encounter are superb in their detail. His knowledge of space suits and how they work too is detailed and I would assume accurate. I certainly believed that they were real.

The rest of the story involves the difficulties of travelling across the unknown terrain of Mars with equipment that was designed for short excursions rather than long epic ones. Some things break down with disastrous consequences.

They must cross chasms leading to Valles Marineris. Finally they must cross that big one itself as they head north. The first major disaster occurs here and one of them is killed. Equipment fails and they are reduced to walking. Too far from the North Pole they change plans, and walk to the first American expedition's supply habitat. There should be enough supplies there to last them more than a year. But more importantly, there is an aeroplane there: a flimsy gossamer winged craft designed to fly in Mars' thin atmosphere. The remaining marsnauts want to use it to fly to the North Pole where the Brazilian ship sits on the ice. One of the four wanders off early one morning looking for fossils and gets lost. He is found later, dead from lack of oxygen as his suit supply ran out. There are hints that the two deaths were not accidental but were deliberately caused.

The flight of the gossamer plane and what they see from above is beautiful and the final resolution, once the three reach the location of the Brazilian ship is unexpected but does seem natural, given the character development through flashback chapters. It was a sudden finish, but overall this is a story that rightly deserved to win the Locus award for best first novel in 2000.

Robert Zubrin's present Mars

Not so many Mars stories appeared in the first decade of the new millennium but as we enter the second decade, they are proliferating. Many non-fiction books were also published detailing how to go to Mars, and how to establish a base, or the beginnings of a colony there. Three that stand out are ***The Quest for Mars,*** by Laurence Bergreen (2000), beautifully written and engrossing, which charts the history and the setbacks, the triumphs, and the exhilaration of exploring Mars by remote control rovers and orbiting satellites, ***Mission to Mars*** by Astronaut Buzz Aldrin, (2013) which explains his plans for how we can go to Mars with our present technology, and an updated re-issue of ***The Case For Mars*** (*considered the Mars Mission Bible*) by Robert Zubrin who advocates establishing a base on the surface of Mars, detailing methods of living off the land to minimise what must be taken to the planet. It was originally published in 1996, but updated to include additional material in 2011.

First Landing by Robert Zubrin (2001) is a novel depicting exactly how he has suggested it could be done using today's technology, or that of 2001 when the novel was published.

Zubrin firmly believes that a journey to Mars could be undertaken within a decade. He advocates this in his book ***The Case for Mars***, explaining how to live off the land to make the things like fuel for the return trip, how to extract oxygen, how to find water, among the many things necessary for survival on Mars. (*Much of this in action was shsown in the film The Martian.)*

Of course his first novel has to be about a journey to Mars, and how to survive there when things do not go as planned or expected.

First Landing is the most positive novel — though tense and dramatic — about a first expedition to Mars that has been written over the last 20 years.

True to his belief of going to Mars within a decade, he set the events in his novel 10 years ahead of the time it was written, and has his first Mars expedition arriving on Mars in 2011.

Zubrin's story begins with a nail-biting sequence where the five astronauts are unable to decouple the tether which joined the living quarters of the ship from the drive segment. Once the ship had left Earth orbit and was in transit to Mars the segments were spun around a common centre to create artificial gravity equal to that on Mars so when they land they will be accustomed to Martian gravity. If they can't uncouple the two segments the ship will tumble into the atmosphere uncontrollably and burn up killing all of them. This nail-biting sequence involves one of the crew going outside to manually uncouple the tether, but in the process she comes unstuck and is drifting in space eventually to burn up as she descends into the tenuous Martian atmosphere. Grazing the edges of the atmosphere they manage to rescue her but are forced to make an immediate landing which doesn't go too well. They crash-land the ship, but fortunately they are not too far from where a previously unmanned ship had been landed with the supplies they need for their base.

Zubrin has dramatized, with interesting characters that are not all compatible with each other, what could go wrong and how they could resolve the problems in order to survive.

But he is not just setting up scenarios and explaining how the problems presented can be solved, he is telling a story that is a result of the interaction between the five people involved, and how each is affected by each problem that occurs. Too many things go wrong and each person begins to believe that one of them could be trying to sabotage the mission. Suspicions create unbearable tension, and the reader is almost breathless wanting to know what could possibly happen next.

Meanwhile back on Earth politics intervenes with any attempts to mount a rescue party with public sentiment against them coming home fearing they will bring unknown Martian bacteria back which could devastate the population of Earth. A fanatical group not wanting the astronauts to come home has infiltrated NASA and some of them are able to sabotage the automatic maintenance of the habitats and of the previous robotic fuel producing plant sent to Mars before the astronauts arrived. The outgoing president uses a fake attempt to set up a rescue mission to enhance his political career since he is up for re-election, while back on Mars the stranded astronauts do their best to survive with whatever they can do while attempting to 'live off the land'.

The main focus throughout the story is on the five people stranded on Mars and how they overcome severe problems both personal and environmental to survive. Everything they do is plausible and can obviously be done. For actual scientific detail the reader should look at ***The Case for Mars***.

First Landing is an exciting thriller with a hopeful ending. It shows that Zubrin is a fine novelist by any criteria, and one would hope that he will produce more novels of this calibre in the future.

Robert Zubrin has another Mars book which is a quasi-fictional story called ***How To Live On Mars***, *A Trusty Guidebook to Surviving and Thriving on the Red Planet*, (published in 2008).

This is an illustrated technical book for non-technical readers that assumes well established colonies on Mars will be welcoming tourists as well as new immigrants to the Red Planet and explains everything they need to know about living on Mars, from how to get about, how to select a habitat, choosing a spacesuit, how to fly and anything else newcomers may want to know to make their stay memorable. It's basically a fictitious travel guide, as well as being a fun book that at times is quite irreverent, but it is full of wonderful ideas and some cutting edge science, all explained in such a way that anyone can understand.

It would be hard to find anyone anywhere in the world who is as enthusiastic about going to Mars as Robert Zubrin, which is why this delightful book exudes excitement and should be read by all young people interested in Mars or the possibility of going there sometime in the near future.

The Forge of Mars by Bruce Balfour (2002) is an exciting adventure that takes place on Mars and on Earth.

There is conflict between Americans and European scientists at a NASA colony and a Russian military force which has a semi-secret base on the other side of the planet.

A NASA scientist discovers artificial tunnels under the surface that contain alien machinery. When one of the scientists touches something on a machine he is instantly vaporised. NASA sends a team of archaeologists to examine the ruins and the lead archaeologist, Dr Kate McCloud, manages to activate the ancient machinery. A gateway to another world opens as she learns to communicate with the controlling machinery, an artificial intelligence. It tells her the other gate must be closed or Mars and Earth will be destroyed. The world it opens on is about to be destroyed by its sun going nova. If the gate remains open the destructive force of the nova will be transmitted to Mars and the solar system with disastrous consequences.

At the Russian military base the other open gateway leads to a world with an incredibly acidic atmosphere. Anything sent through is destroyed.

One person tried going through and he never returned. Any robot sent in comes back dissolved and falling apart. They have been unable to change it or alter its settings or even figure out how it works. After hearing of the American success they want the American archaeologist to try to communicate with their open gateway. The Russians want to use it somehow as a weapon, a way to make Russia great again.

On Earth in a secret base the Russians have another such alien device which they discovered at Tunguska. It is not a gateway but is some kind of ship. It was damaged when it crashed at Tunguska almost a century ago. They have been studying it since then but have made no headway, when suddenly it activates and appears alive after someone touches something. They don't know what happened but suspect it has to do with the other open gateway at the Russian base on Mars. The general in charge of the secret Earth base goes to Mars to take control of the military base there.

The American archaeologist Kate happens to be the lover of Tau Wolfsinger who has developed an AI capable of using and directing nano technology or nano-robots to build artificial environments. He was about to propose to her when she told him she was going to Mars to examine the alien ruins.

People are scared of Wolfsinger's technology but when one of the NASA scientists is killed by the alien machine at their base they decide to send Wolfsinger to Mars in the hope that while building additional living quarters with his nano-robots he may also be able to communicate with the alien machinery via his AI which controls the nano technology. Wolfsinger is more than happy to go because he will see Kate again.

On Mars the Russians decide to take over the NASA base and attack it with their military force. They coerce Kate to accompany them to their base and their gateway. But in the melee that occurs when they take the American base Wolfsinger with his portable AI is accidentally thrown into the gate and he disappears.

He finds himself on an alien world where giant robots battle endless wars amongst themselves as a way of evolving better and more deadly machines. They are all super intelligent. He wants to go back but he needs help from these machines. They implant an anode into his brain so he can communicate with them and they use him to teach some of their younger fighting machines unusual tactics which guarantees success. In return they agree to help him by sending a group of war machines with him to Mars for training purposes. The machines bring back a super bomb to use to destroy the rogue gateway. They also activate a self detonating device on the scout ship lost years before in an unknown region of space. Whoever activated the ship accidentally in Russia caused it to send out a distress call. The scout ship which should not have been in that part of space was damaged which is why it crashed, so a message is sent for it to self destruct. Collateral damage is the obliteration of the secret base where it was hidden.

Coming through the gateway back to Mars Wolfsinger and his robot war machines kill the Russians occupying his newly constructed base, after which they attack the Russian base and set the bomb in place to destroy the gate and its partially insane AI. While this is happening he rescues Kate and the other scientists captured by the Russians. They just manage to evacuate before the alien bomb destroys the base and the gateway.

Although the first half, set mostly on Earth, is a bit slow moving, it is necessary to give credibility to Wolfsinger and his AI as well as to his relationship with Kate.

The second half of the story takes place on Mars (as well as another alien planet) and this is non-stop action and mystery right to the end. The details regarding Mars and how it is on the surface seem accurate and don't disrupt the flow of the story but enhance it in a most enjoyable way. The robot war machine intelligences also seem credible in the way they act and think. If anything, they were probably not alien enough. But overall, I enjoyed this story.

Two views of Mars from Brian Aldiss

White Mars by Brian Aldiss in collaboration with Roger Penrose (1999) is not a novel but a polemic disguised as a novel. Its full title is: ***White Mars, or, The Mind Set Free. A 21st Century Utopia.***

Mars has been set aside as a place for scientific study and not a place to be colonised and terraformed for the benefit of humans, in much the same way as the decision was made to keep Antarctica pristine. Aldiss is in fact the president of *APIUM: the Association for the Protection and Integrity of an Unspoilt Mars.* He doesn't want to see Mars turned into a colony, or as an inferior version of Earth. This society wants Mars to be considered in the same way Antarctica was considered, as a place for scientific study, and not a place to be exploited or colonised and turned into another inferior version of Earth.

The first chapter tells of the decision by the UN to make Mars a *White Mars*, although a group of colonists already lives on the planet doing scientific studies, especially an experiment to investigate sub atomic particles away from the disturbances of Earth and the Moon.

After chapter 1, the whole book forms a flashback to the events leading up to this decision. It consists of two memoirs, one by the leader of the group of about 5000 people abandoned on Mars by the collapse of the organization that sent them there, and the other by his adopted daughter, who sees a different perspective of what is happening. These two memoir streams alternate as the story progresses.

Not really a novel at all, ***White Mars*** allows Aldiss and Penrose to describe the establishment of a Utopia and the type of scientific studies people should undertake there. Their narrative is slow-moving and inevitably boring, since all the characters do is talk and argue over what they should do and what their objectives should be. They never come alive as people. They are clearly only mouthpieces for Aldiss and Penrose to project their ideas of a *White Mars*, a Mars set aside for scientific study. There is a lot of discussion about the Higgs-Boson particle, which had not been discovered when the book was written. The novel has some exciting sections: some brief sexual encounters, and the discovery that Olympus Mons is a living thing akin to a giant barnacle eating its way across the surface of Mars and heading slowly towards the colonists. There is no real explanation of this phenomenon, and no depiction of what might happen once it reaches the colony.

In the final chapter set 20 years later, the UN sends a ship to Mars to rescue the remnants of the colony.

I was disappointed with these 233 pages of a sleep inducing utopia.

In a British SF magazine interview Brian Aldiss claimed that ***Finches of Mars*** (2013) was his final science fiction novel. This made me sad, because I like most of his work, which was endlessly innovative and certainly a lot more literary than some other popular writers. But then Brian was 88 years old when he said that. He was recently reported to be working on a major non-SF novel, but unfortunately he passed away at the age of 92 and I am not sure this last major novel was completed or anywhere near ready for publication.

Finches of Mars is a short novel about a colony on Mars and its struggle to survive. For the first ten years all children born are stillborn, malformed, or die soon after birth. No healthy baby has been born since the colony was established ten years earlier. It is suspected that this is a result of effect of the lower gravity of Mars.

As the story unfolds, communications with Earth become sporadic and supplies become unreliable. The colony on Mars was to be a new hope for mankind's future survival, but the colony may be doomed, especially if the settlers cannot solve the baby-birth problems. There seems to be no solution. The members of the colony refuse to give up hope and they are prepared to die.

Aldiss has created a problem he can't rationally solve. If the lesser gravity is the cause of the babies being born deformed and dying soon after birth, or being stillborn, the problem can't be solved. Mars's gravity can't be increased. If the constant radiation that bombards Mars is the cause, then moving under the surface could prevent it. Aldiss doesn't mention this. There is little in this book that conjures up what Mars may look like. His focus is not on Mars as a place but only as the background that causes a unique problem.

Some way into the story a newcomer to Mars in trouble out on the surface is rescued by one couple. He is ranting on about a vision he had while dying as he ran out of air; "God gives me powers," he said, "one day strange people with strange voices will land and show you strange powers you never dreamed of."

This is an obvious foreshadowing of the resolution to come so readers won't feel cheated.

Towards the end of the book with no likelihood of solving the baby problem Aldiss springs the foreshadowed surprise, one that would spoil a story if attempted by a lesser author, but Aldiss is a master and he just gets away with it. He creates a time loop. A strange ship materialises out of the air and settles down. Humanoid beings emerge to inform the settlers that they are their progeny from the future. They have come back with a solution to their problem. The time travelling descendants show the colonists how to build an oxygen generating machine to help thicken the atmosphere allowing mothers and babies to breathe freely after birth.

Mars is the key, the travellers explain, to humans going to other parts of the galaxy where they will continue to evolve, but it was necessary to come back and solve the problem of childbirth on Mars, or there will be no human progeny.

But coming back to make sure it happens only proves that they have already come back, because if they hadn't come back there would have been no future for them, and they would not have existed to be able to come back with a solution.

After producing the answer for the colonists' birth problems, the time travellers then disappear,

Aldiss is a good writer and he makes this seem plausible, but when you think about it, why would extra oxygen pressure from terraforming machines have any effect if the problems of childbirth were because of Mars' lesser gravity? That problem is still there, and won't go away because of a thicker atmosphere. If a thicker atmosphere was the solution they could have stayed indoors in the pressurized habitats (which they do anyway) and there would be no problem, and no story.

John Brunner used a similar idea back in1967 in his novel ***Born Under Mars***. Women who became pregnant stayed underground in an environment where the air was pressurized to the level of Earth's atmosphere at sea level, and stayed there until the babies were weaned, after which they would slowly be acclimatized to Mars' lesser air pressure. In 1967 Brunner, like many others, still assumed that the Martian atmosphere was breathable although of a much lesser pressure than Earth's atmosphere.

Brunner didn't have the knowledge of Mars that was available to Aldiss, but in ***The Finches of Mars,*** Aldiss doesn't exhibit any more knowledge of Mars than did Brunner almost fifty years before.

I felt cheated because it's easy to say someone from the future came back and fixed everything rather than coming up with a logical answer to the problem.

Would it not have been better if the birth problem was left with no obvious resolution in the near future? This would have made it a depressing novel, and most readers like a problem presented in a story, especially one that is the whole basis of the story, to be solved in a positive way.

Even for Aldiss, I feel this *deus ex machina* solution to an insoluble problem is a cop out.

But then if this really was his last SF novel, it is interesting for that fact alone.

Joe Haldeman's Marsbound

Marsbound (2013) is the first part of a trilogy by Joe Haldeman, but only the first volume is about Mars. It is a young adult novel, in that it follows the life of an 18 year old girl whose family decides to move to Mars for 5 years. Seen through her eyes the story is set well into the future. Mars has been settled by humans, and commerce between the Earth and the Moon and Mars is ongoing.

An adventure story in the old fashioned style, ***Marsbound*** is an alien contact story which leads us into the second volume (***Starbound***) and eventually the third volume (***Earthbound***). ***Marsbound*** has also been reprinted in 2016 with a new title ***The Mars Girl.***

We follow the family's journey from their home to the space elevator which takes them into orbit and to the waiting ship which will take them to Mars. The daughter is unhappy about the shift to Mars, but tries to make the best of it by forming new friends. This part of the story is much like the stories that enthralled us when we were young readers back in the 1950s and 60s. Our young protagonist wanders off one day to explore. She falls through a lava tube and breaks an ankle. Unable to call for help she waits to die either from the cold or when her oxygen runs out.

When she wakes up she finds she has been rescued by an alien being with four arms and four legs that seems to live underground. There are lots of them, and initially she thinks they are Martians.

They explain to her that they have been on the planet for thousands of years waiting for humans to arrive. They are actually from a star system 24 light years away, and are emissaries of an alien race that breathes liquid nitrogen and has a paranoid fear of any new species that might develop in the universe to threaten them. These emissaries are to warn the others of any new species about to develop interstellar voyaging. This novel finishes here with the eight limbed aliens helping save the children of Mars from a lung disease caused by the ubiquitous dust.

The sequels are two radically different volumes. The second, seen from multiple viewpoints, details the voyage out to the star system where the enigmatic nitrogen breathing aliens live, with the third volume returning to the first person viewpoint of our original character who is now a mature adult back on Earth where the aliens destroy the Moon and leave the shattered pieces to shroud the whole planet thus preventing any attempts humans might make to go back into space.

Robert J Sawyer's Old Mars

Red Planet Blues by Robert J Sawyer (2013) is a return to 'Old Mars' of the pulp era but updated and modernised. It has a 1940's feel to it. It is a noir murder mystery set in a lawless Mars colony called New Klondike, a Martian city set up 40 years before this story begins. The discovery of Martian fossils has started a fossil rush just like an ancient gold rush. On Earth where anything can be synthesised, Martian fossils have extraordinary value and people would kill for them. Our protagonist is the only private eye on Mars. He makes his living tracking down killers and kidnappers among the failed prospectors who try other game when they fail to find the enigmatic fossils. Full of concepts such as live humans uploading their minds to android bodies so they can live forever, and a mystery involving the murder of one of these almost immortal new beings (transfers), makes this a sheer delight to read with lots of twists and turns and loads of skulduggery. It is an expansion of his Nebula Award winning novella ***Identity Theft.***

More from Ben Bova

Mars Life by Ben Bova (2008) completes the story he began 16 years earlier in 1992 with ***Mars*** and continued in 1999 with ***Return to Mars.***

This final segment takes place some 20 years after Jamie Waterman discovered the cliff dwellings high up in the side of the Rift Valley Tithonium Chasma. By the end of the first two expeditions to Mars a permanent base has been established in the Rift valley while scientists search for the remains of life. Nothing much has been discovered other than some lichen growing in cracks in rocks at the base of the chasm where the smallest amount of moisture condenses out of the atmosphere during the freezing nights and this sustains the lichen growing in the rocks.

When the third book opens Jamie has been on Earth for just on twenty years and is the scientific head of the expedition which now numbers around 200 people on the red planet.

One of these people, is anthropologist Carter Carleton who discovers the remains of a village buried under 30 metres of detritus which has collected over the 60 million years since the meteor bombardment that destroyed Mars and its planetary ecosystem (at the same time destroying Earth's habitat and wiping out the dinosaurs). Earth's eco-system recovered, but Mars, being much smaller, lost most of its atmosphere and never recovered. It has been slowly dying ever since.

Back on Earth with greenhouse effects altering climate, religious fundamentalists are gradually taking control of the media, the universities, and even the government. They want to close down the Mars expeditions because they deny the possibility that there could have been intelligent Martians even 60 million years ago. They claim the village discovered and the fossils are all faked to make the government continue funding for the Mars explorations. The government hardly funds it anyway. Most of the money comes from private sources, but under the new fundamentalism spreading across the country; even private organizations are not willing to fund Mars exploration any more.

As a solution, limited tourism is suggested. Wealthy people would pay millions for the chance of a trip to Mars, now accomplished by super-fast fusion propelled rockets.

Jamie Waterman returns to Mars with his wife Vijay, a biologist, to maintain a Navajo presence on the planet. When he was leader of the second expedition twenty years earlier he refused to consider the idea of tourism as fund-raiser. He is even more against any kind of tourism now, adamant that it would ruin Mars forever.

The solution suggested by his business partner, and friend on Earth, Dex Trumball, who had been on Mars 20 years earlier with Jamie, (Return to Mars) is to bring everyone back so he can fund a private expedition to claim Mars once the Navajo presence is no longer there.

Jamie refuses to leave and solicits limited help from Selene, the now independent Moon colony, so he can stay with a small number of people to preserve Mars as it is forever.

He is finally convinced that this will not work, Mars will be abandoned, so a compromise is finally reached where in the long run everyone benefits while Jamie gets to stay on his beloved Mars.

Though not as vast as Kim Stanley Robinson's massive Mars trilogy, Ben Bova's Mars trilogy is certainly equal to it, and is engrossing. It is a more accessible story because it covers in total only about 25 years, and most of the characters we met at the beginning stay to the end. Bova's character development is good enough to make you care about them and about what they are trying to achieve, while at the same time he paints an accurate picture of what Mars is actually like and the difficulties involved in living there. His speculations about the way the world is being affected by climate change and the reactions of religious fundamentalists can be seen in the news headlines at this very moment.

All in all, a brilliant series that is well worth taking the time to read.

Will deep space travel be funded by private enterprise for profit, or by government agencies?

The prolific Ben Bova returns again with a story called ***Mars Inc: The Billionaires Club*** (2013).

A Billionaire businessman Art Thrasher who has been enthralled with Mars all his life sees that the cost is such that no government agency will ever be able to afford to send an expedition there. Art decides to convince twenty of his billionaire compatriots to form a club and contribute one billion dollars each a year until launch capabilities and a space ship can be developed.

The story is about the battles and petty jealousies of the members of this billionair's club as they try to outdo each other to gain the most profit from the venture they are financing. It finishes with the successful launching of a privately funded mission to Mars.

Written in a straightforward manner, Mars Inc. is full of wry comments on the way big business controlled by dominant males works.

It is quite funny and an enjoyable read. For all his hardness and business acumen, Art Thrasher comes across as a lovable character, a boy who never grew up and who never gave up on his dream to go to Mars, even if he cannot go himself.

In ***Rescue Mode*** (2014) Ben Bova is partnered with Les Johnson, a popular scientist TV presenter and physicist who works for the Advanced Concepts Office of NASA. This story is dated to the year 2035, but this time the dates that head each chapter are relevant, believable, and crucial in the building of tension for the reader.

2035 is the year of the first manned expedition to Mars. (and the actual year in which NASA plans its first manned expedition to Mars orbit.)

A ship carrying four men and four women of various nationalities is NASA's and the US's first Mission to Mars. This meets with a lot of opposition in Congress with various senators lobbying to cut funding for future missions, but the President is determined to go ahead.

When a meteoroid smashes through the ship over half way to Mars, causing considerable damage, it is too late to cancel the mission. The astronauts must continue on to Mars before they can return. This accident in space convinces many senators that it is too dangerous to send humans into space beyond the Moon. A current strong American presence on the Moon can't be cancelled, but future Mars missions can.

The astronauts on the Mars ship manage to fix broken struts that hold the two halves of the ship together, but they have lost so much water there will not be enough, even with severe rationing, for all of them to survive the year long return trip from Mars.

On Mars there is a habitat with supplies for a month's stay, which is what had been intended. NASA, when it sent the unmanned habitat ahead of the manned mission, placed enough supplies for 4 months on the site. Four months for eight people, means eight months for four people, so when they arrival on Mars, the astronauts hatch a plan that may give at least half (if not all) of them a chance. They decide to take most of the water from the habitat and transfer it to the return ship in orbit, which would give four of them enough water to make it back to Earth alive. On the surface, the other four will have enough for a month, during which they hope to obtain water for themselves from the Martian permafrost.

By deliberately stranding half their number on Mars, the astronauts hope to force NASA and the politicians to reinstate the rescue mission or the second manned mission to Mars. Since everything the astronauts do is watched live on TV they gain massive public sympathy, which in turn forces the politicians, who are accused of wanting to murder the stranded astronauts, to change their mind and re-instate the next series of missions to Mars.

The stranded astronauts find the ice they were looking for, but also discover that, when melted it contains amoeboid life. They have discovered life on Mars, which was the main reason for the mission in the first place.

This idea of forcing the continuation of the manned space missions has been used before, most notably in ***The Martian Race*** by Gregory Benford (1999), and no doubt will be used again.

Rescue Mode is not an outstanding book, but it is entertaining, well written, with believable characters and good science, and is a worthy addition to any collection of novels about Mars.

A Radically different view from Ian McDonald

Desolation Road, (1988) and **Ares Express** (2010) by Ian Mc Donald are two books I never saw when they were published. It could have been because the name ***Desolation Road***, (his first novel), didn't sound like the title of a book with a story set on Mars. I could have overlooked it thinking it was a non SF work. It was published in 1988 to great acclaim from many reviewers as well as authors like Philip Jose Farmer and Cory Doctorow. Asimov's Magazine reviewer called it '*one of the most interesting and accomplished science fiction novels of this latter day era*'. His second Mars book ***Ares Express*** was published in 2010, 22 years later.

Sometimes there are books I find difficult to read and there could be a number of reasons for this, but primarily it depends on how I feel when I start to read it. ***Desolation Road*** was one such book. It seemed interesting as I read the first chapter, the first 9 pages...

A man staggers across the desert lost, struggling to survive. He finds a small oasis where he discovers some alien technology that communicates with him and which he adapts to enable him to live in a nearby cave. He names his settlement Desolation Road. It just so happens, that not far from his initial settlement is one of the many train lines that traverse the planet.

In this book Mars has been colonised long enough to have been terraformed to have a breathable atmosphere, yet it is still basically a barren desert like world. It is crisscrossed with railroad lines joining various communities that are serviced by gigantic atomic steam powered locomotives pulling huge trains. It is almost like an updated cyberpunk version of something Ray Bradbury could have imagined, combined with a touch of magic realism found with writers such as Gabriel Garcia Marquez and Jorge Louis Borges.

Each chapter is a separate, sometimes incomplete story about someone, a misfit or a person searching for something different, who discover often accidentally, the place that is evolving into the township of Desolation Road.

The picture I get is that Mars is a very strange and fantastic place filled with the weirdest people imaginable, especially those who find their way to Desolation Road.

After about twenty chapters, a third of the way through the book and just over 100 pages, I began to lose interest because the overall story seemed to be going nowhere other than showing how a small community gradually develops into a larger one over time. Each chapter seems to be a disconnected event introducing new characters, though it is part of a whole story arc. I would have expected some interaction between the various often quite straange characters but as far as I got that wasn't happening.

It is beautifully written, but I couldn't get involved with the multiplicity of characters. Perhaps the story has too much of a fantasy feeling rather than being related to the reality of Mars as we are beginning to understand it.

I have no doubt many people will absolutely love this book, but I was unable to finish it. Perhaps I will try again one day…

Because of my experience with ***Desolation Road***, I have yet to consider the sequel which was written twenty two years later.

Ares Express does seem to be more of a complete novel rather than an episodic one, but I keep putting it aside for later, which means I may never get to it. At my age there is limited time for me to read books, and with so many being published, I prefer to read those that capture my interest within the first twenty pages or less rather than force myself to keep reading on the off-chance something interesting may happen further on in the story.

I mention these two books because they are set on a very different Mars than the one we are accustomed to reading about. They also traverse all three of my categories, being fantastical, somewhat scientifically plausible, and transformative all at the same time.

Rock spires in the 'Spirit of St Louis' crater.

Chapter Thirteen

The beginnings of a new Space Race

Celebrating the 20th anniversary of the Apollo 11 Moon landing President Bush said in a speech on the steps of the Air and Space Museum in Washington DC that NASA would go '*back to the Moon, back to the future, and this time back to stay... and then a journey into tomorrow, a journey to another planet, a manned mission to Mars.*' No doubt he tried to emulate Kennedy who told America that they would put a man on the Moon within a decade, and they did, but stopped after the so called 'Space Race' had been won. The Moon was abandoned and any chance of establishing a foothold in Space was also abandoned for the foreseeable future. It was such a waste but then that's politics. Once Americans had demonstrated their technological superiority it was time to move on to more down to earth mundane matters.

President Bush's statement was a bold, probably 'off the cuff' statement that at first seemed easy to implement, but in reality the whole idea was fraught with difficulties. President Bush's grand plan never made it through congress as both sides rejected the huge sums of money that would be needed and attempts to get humans in Space on a permanent basis failed. The only plan that got the go ahead was the ISS but this was because Europe and Japan and Russia were all part of the International Space Station even though America supplied the most money, the expertise and the use of the shuttle fleet.

Then the space shuttles were abandoned, being considered obsolete, especially after two disasters had shattered confidence. The US was terrified another disaster might occur with the aging shuttles, and budget constraints meant no alternative system was allowed to be developed as a replacement for the shuttle. Once the shuttles were abandoned the US had no means of getting into space let alone going to Mars. They turned to the Russians who still used old almost obsolete technology to get people and supplies up to the International Space Station.

The chance of going to Mars was being pushed further and further into the future.

Even going back to the Moon doesn't seem likely if we rely on Government financing.

However, private enterprise has come to the rescue with the development of rockets capable of delivering payloads into orbit and opening the possibility of near space tourism with short duration flights to the edge of space. Some private companies are even thinking of taking paying passengers on a round trip to the Moon and back in the very near future.

How much longer can it be before private enterprise takes us to Mars and beyond?

Most likely sooner than we imagine.

Mars One and other Grand plans

Ray Bradbury was spot on when he said in one of his Martian Chronicles stories that *the sky was filled with slender spaceships, like a cloud of silver locusts, taking thousands of people who wanted to go to Mars looking for a new and perhaps better life.*

He wrote this story in the mid-1940s when the memory of the massive European diaspora brought thousands upon thousands of people from the 'old world' to the new in a desperate search for a better life. Knowing people never really change, he imagined a future where thousands upon thousands would want to go to another planet in search of a better life, and he said and implied all of this in a few lines in one short story.

Now in the second decade of the 21st century there are, as always, thousands upon thousands who are also desperate to find a new life somewhere else, and these aren't always refugees from war torn countries.

There is a competition to find people willing to go to Mars on a one way trip to set up a colony (*Mars One expedition*), to start a new life on another planet with no possibility of returning. Should there be any surprise that there are more than 200,000 who want to go?

This number has already been whittled down to less than a hundred. Eventually only four of them will make that first trip to Mars. Their job will be to establish and build a self-sufficient base for themselves and for the next group of four to follow, and so until a decade later there is expected to be at least 20 people living on Mars.

Their preparations and eventual journey will be watched on TV by the whole world and it will no doubt be the greatest 'reality show' ever, and with a bit of luck will be entirely financed through advertising or private subscriptions.

Before they get to go however, another privately financed group intend to send a married astronaut couple on a flyby mission to Mars and back with the craft passing as close as 160 kilometres above the surface.

But NASA as well as ESA and other government organizations have re-entered the fray which is the race to get to Mars. NASA is developing a massive new rocket that will lift their Mars expedition ship into orbit and boost it on the journey to Mars. They plan on orbiting, on setting up a possible base on Phobos, and eventually landing on the surface before returning to Earth.

Unfortunately none of this is likely to take place before the end of the 2030s.

The *Mars One Consortium* plans to send 4 people initially to set up a base to be followed thereafter by several groups of four until that have a large base with twenty or more people there. None of them are expecting to come back, and will have to survive on their own with whatever resources they can obtain from the planet itself.

Exactly how they are testing those who volunteered and what they are looking for in the people they eventually select has been delineated in detail in a book called ***Mars One: Humanity's next great adventure***, (2016) by N Kraft, J Kass and R Kass.

This would especially interest writers thinking about a Mars story since all the physical skills, psychological, engineering, medical health and fitness, social and cultural interaction, age, adaptability to the unexpected, and much else is discussed, along with interviews from the participants about why they are willing to go to Mars knowing they will never return to Earth. It also includes a timetable of when various stages will occur and as of this writing they have finally settled on around 100 volunteers after elimination more than 2000. The stages of their training together in teams of 4 will soon begin once the 100 have been whittled down to 40 and then to 30, finally finishing with 24, in 6 teams of 4. Crew training was supposed to commence in 2017. The first manned expedition is expected to launch in 2026, less than ten years from now.

Once the above has occurred it is unlikely we will see stories about going to Mars, the focus will shift to what may happen, or could happen as a result of attempts to colonize the planet.

Unfortunately of late there has been very little news regarding the progress of the *Mars One Consortium* which leads me to suspect it may have fallen by the wayside. But there is still hope something may eventuate.

NASA is preparing to send astronauts, perhaps a married couple, on a round trip to Mars where they will orbit the planet but not land.

This will be followed perhaps a decade later with a proper expedition setting up a base from which to study the planet. This idea has been brought forward with instructions from the President to get someone on Mars sooner rather than later. New plans are being drawn up; new rockets are being developed, especially in conjunction with private companies like ***SpaceX, Blue Origin***, and ***Boeing***, all of which have serious plans to build rockets to take people to Mars in the very near future.

The European Space Agency and the Russians are also testing rockets and launch systems as well as cosmonauts, studying the effects of long term survival without contact outside of their enclosed space ship environment, in preparation for their trip to Mars in the next twenty years.

And then there are the Chinese who remain very quiet about their plans but they are certainly considering an expedition to Mars, and they will probably beat the Americans and the Russians who are both constrained by limited budgets and backward looking politicians.

The Chinese recently announced they are building a Mars Village at Haixi prefecture in Qinghai province. The region is part of the Tibet plateau which exhibits sharp ridges and mounds of rock similar to parts of the Martian surface. The village will include training facilities for Marsnauts as well as be an education centre which could contribute to tourism in the area. They are also building a Rover which they hope to deploy to Mars around 2020 if all goes well. While this is happening their plans for constructing a large space habitat to rival the ISS which will be decommissioned in another ten years or so are well on the way.

More than likely though, it will be private enterprise rather than governments who get us back into space, planetary exploration and colonization.

SpaceX and Elon Musk are already servicing the ISS on a regular basis with his rockets launched from NASA's own launch pads in Florida. Perhaps this grandest plan of all is that ***SpaceX*** wants to send hundreds of thousands of people, perhaps even a million, to Mars in the next 20 to 40 years.

His company is building huge rockets that can be re-used many times to launch space ships into orbit. Each ship will hold 100 or more passengers or colonists. He wants these ships to also be re-usable in that they will ferry people to Mars every two years when Mars is at its closest to Earth, then return to Earth orbit to be re-used for another load of passengers.

He is very determined and most likely will get people to Mars before anyone else. Recently he announced he has brought forward the expected time of his first landing on Mars to ten years from now, perhaps sooner. He is expecting to have his first Mars rocket ship completed and ready to go within five years. That is early in the 2020s. I suspect he really will be the first to send people to Mars, no matter who else is competing in this new space race.

On the other hand ***Blue Origin*** founded by Amazon's boss Jeff Bezoz is planning to go to the Moon first as well as to build a huge space station to replace the aging ISS which will be decommissioned in the near future, recently reconfirmed by President Trump who wants to bring the date forward. He then plans to send people to Mars.

SpaceX also wants to take tourists on round trips to the Moon within the next couple of years.

Soon we will see a new space race to get to the Moon first, followed shortly by another race to see who can get to Mars first. Perhaps the two will happen simultaneously. For space enthusiasts the future is looking bright.

Andy Weir's The Martian shows how it could be done

In 2014 many readers worldwide as well as many SF adventure fans hailed the publication of ***The Martian***, by Andy Weir.

Since then it has appeared as an equally successful film starring Mat Damon.

Andy Weir originally published ***The Martian*** as an eBook serial, chapter by chapter in 2011. It became so popular that Crown Publishers bought the rights in 2014 to publish it as a hardcover book. It became a best seller and was immediately optioned by Ridley Scott for a film. Since then numerous paperback editions have been published.

Andy Weir is not scientist who works for NASA but the accuracy of the details in this first novel would make you think he does. He is a lifelong space nerd, a computer programmer who loves stuff like relativistic physics, orbital mechanics, and the history of spaceflight. All this can be seen in this remarkable novel.

Just five days after the arrival of this expedition to Mars, a massive dust storm threatens to destroy the first explorer's return vehicle by blowing it over making it unable to take off. The commander orders the six-member team to abandon the mission and head for the return vehicle. As they try to board it, one member of the team is blown away by the wind and his space suit is pierced by a flying piece of aerial. When they realise one of the team is missing, some of them try to search for him, but there is no radio contact, and no telemetry to indicate he is still alive. The dust is so thick they can barely see anything. As the storm worsens threatening to blow over their return vehicle, the commander orders them to abandon the search. They blast off, back to the waiting mother ship which will take them home. With the mission abandoned, they begin the return journey with each of the team grieving for their lost companion, the first man to die on Mars.

Only he isn't dead, merely unconscious. His space suit has not leaked air and lost pressure because the blood escaping the wound the aerial made froze around the hole where the aerial pierced the suit, sealing it.

Waking up after the storm passes and realising the others have gone he makes his way to the habitat which is still standing and still pressurised. Inside, he cleans his wound and dresses it, and takes stock of what he has. There are supplies for a six person team to last three months. This will last him a lot longer than three months, but not nearly long enough until the next expedition arrives (four years away). Besides, the next expedition won't be landing anywhere near his location. The habitat has already been landed with its robot installation and return vehicle and is sitting there waiting for the astronauts to come; but it is half way around the planet 3200 kilometres away. The main character can last 9 months on his own, but unless he can supplement his supplies by growing food. But all he has are 12 potatoes. All the other food is freeze dried.

He cannot make contact Earth because the radio masts were destroyed during the storm. Nobody knows he is alive.

The rest of the book shows how he turns his habitat into a greenhouse to grow potatoes, the methods he uses to extract water, oxygen and other necessities from the Martian atmosphere and the regolith, how he discovers an old Mars rover and cannibalizes the primitive radio to finally make contact with NASA headquarters, using Morse code and written messages which orbiting satellite high resolution cameras can read. NASA decides not to tell his five companions, half way back to Earth, that he is alive. The politics involved in this decision make up a considerable section of the book.

The stranded astronaut's only option is to make it to the other expedition site, where he can wait while using the supplies already there — but even these rations will give out before the next team arrives.

Eventually NASA tells the five returning team members that their lost expedition member is still alive on Mars. Against all advice they decide on a wild rescue mission that would enable them to return to Mars just in time (after his food runs out) to rescue him. This doesn't involve turning around and going back (not at all possible), but by using Earth as a slingshot to send them back on a higher, faster trajectory back to Mars. The book tells us much about orbital mechanics and the feasibility of slingshot moves, something NASA has been doing with all the robot missions to the major planets in the outer solar system, but Weir makes it fascinating. The Martian becomes a thriller you can't put down.

The finale takes place in space, and now filmed, rivals the great opening scene in the recent film Gravity. The returning team members are travelling so fast they will not be able to go into orbit around Mars, but will have to do the same thing they did in Earth orbit; use the planet as a slingshot to shoot them around on to the return course for Earth.

The stranded astronaut has only one shot at being rescued. He must strip the return vehicle down to its minimum weight so it will reach a high enough orbit to match the velocity of the returning team's ship, and then transfer across before the retuning ship gets too far ahead in its slingshot around Mars. This grand finale is nail-bitingly tense.

The Martian is a stand-out amongst good books about Mars. It certainly was the most exciting one I have read so far.

I had barely finished reading the book when the film was released.

The film must hold up scientifically to be convincing. With Ridley Scott as director, it does exactly that. NASA was consulted regarding the design of the space suits used in space and on the surface of Mars, the base, the surface vehicles, and the ships likely to carry the astronauts down to the planet and back up to the mothership in orbit. NASA also allowed filming of major scenes at the mission control centre in Huston. No doubt it supplied photo mosaics of surface features, beamed back from the rovers on the surface and the satellites in orbit around the planet, so the most authentic depiction of Mars to date is obtained.

Since there is only one character on screen for most of the film, the choice of Mat Damon to play the role of Mark Watney, the stranded astronaut, is brilliant. He is so convincing you empathise with him as he deals with the problems of the harsh Martian environment: no breathable atmosphere, dust storms, and Antarctic temperatures with a bit above freezing to 100 below zero during the night.

Ridley Scott doesn't depart from reality. The equipment looks real, the base looks completely functional, the rovers he uses to traverse the surface actually work, and his predicament is truly believable. Being a botanist, he devises a means of growing potatoes from frozen stock in the supplies of the base camp, while fertilizing the growing medium (Martian regolith) with his own excrement. His potato crop supplements the supplies meant for an expedition of six over three months which for him alone could last for a year. But he still does not have enough to last the four years until the next expedition arrives.

He devises a means of communicating with Mission Control by cannibalising an old rover sent to Mars years before. Once it is known that he is alive, mission control must decide whether to tell the returning astronauts that their team mate is not dead. The film cross-cuts between NASA mission control, Mark Watney on the surface as he struggles to survive, and the crew of the returning space ship. This cross-cutting makes what could have been a very long film seem much shorter than it actually is. The main focus however is on Mark Watney. He carries the film with his seriousness of purpose, his determination to survive, and his self-deprecating humour as he narrates a video log.

An explosive decompression of his habitat almost kills him, and scares the shit out of anyone watching the film. It also destroys his potato crop by snap freezing it. He has no choice now but to devise a means of reaching the base that has already been established for the next expedition even though he won't have enough food to last until it arrives.

Once the members of the returning crew find out that he is alive, they contrive to slingshot around Earth to send them back to Mars so they can rescue him before his food runs out. Mission Control doesn't want them to do it but they take their own action: feeling guilty for having left him on Mars, they will do whatever they can to bring him back alive.

In the book by Andy Weir this final rescue and the preparations he must make are explicitly detailed, especially the scenes in space as the returning ship slingshots around Mars. He must get into orbit and match their speed so he can be picked up or he will end up lost in space and die when his oxygen runs out.

This final part of the film was truncated, almost as if the director thought that the film was running over time and needed to be shortened. The rescue happens very quickly and suddenly the film is done. Perhaps in a future release, a director's cut will add more to the final rescue scenes, the stripping down of the return capsule, and the rendezvous in space in orbit above Mars.

On the other hand, at the beginning of the film where the fierce storm forces the abandonment of the mission, considerable detail is shown, whereas in the book, it is over in a couple of paragraphs, and that includes how he operates on himself to remove the piece of aerial and stitches his wound.

Nevertheless, it is to date, the best and most believable film about what it would be like on the surface of Mars.

Acidalia Planitia: the Ares 3 landing site on Mars associated with the best selling book ***The Martian*** *and the film of the same name.*

In the second decade of the new millennium a new category of stories about Mars has emerged that concern a well-established colony forced to survive on its own after something disastrous has happened on Earth.

This is a sub-category of the survival in a harsh environment theme and many stories set on Mars have used this successfully, two recent examples being Geoffrey A Landis' ***Mars Crossing*** (2000) and Andy Weir's ***The Martian*** (2014). But the modern scenario is about a colony established for some time (if not for years) surviving, rather than an individual or several individuals from an initial expedition having to cope with something gone wrong.

One scenario has communication permanently cut so the colonists do not know what has happened on Earth, only that they are on their own and must survive, or the disaster could be economic, with governments no longer interested in spending vast sums of money to keep the colony going.

Another scenario is a world war, atomic, biological or traditional, started by major nations grappling for more power and control, or a war started as a result of terrorist attacks on major nations forcing them into a response with such destruction and devastation worldwide that no further expeditions to Mars, or even into orbit would be possible. Perhaps no one even survives on Earth, or at the least, very few survive.

These new stories postulate a well-established base with more than just a few people, or a very large base several generations on having to survive on Mars with no possibility of outside help.

Brian Aldiss' ***Finches of Mars*** (2013) would fall into this category, although very little emphasis was made of the deteriorating conditions on Earth. Perhaps even Lewis Shiner's ***Frontera*** (1984) could be classified as the first example of this more recent category. There always was and always will be crossovers between categories and sub-categories. The best thing is not to be too concerned but simply enjoy the story regardless of category or sub-category.

Everyone accepts the idea that there will be a Mars colony in the near future, and stories of how to get there, how to set up a base and cope with surviving until they can return, have been done many times over the latter part of the twentieth century; which is not to say stories of that kind won't be produced in the future. We haven't got to Mars yet, and until we do, there is always room for speculation about how it will be done and what possible consequences could come from that.

But the thinking now among many newer novelists is more about what an established colony would do.

What would the people of that colony do if they knew there was no way back, that they were stuck on Mars and had to make the best of it?

Chapter Fourteen

A New Age for stories about Mars

The fact that serious attempts are being made to go to Mars by many organizations, governmental, public, and private, in countries and nations around the world, has inspired a new generation of stories about Mars, many of which are written by amateurs who self-publish them.

Up to this point, all the books mentioned have been published by known publishing houses and were written mostly by SF writers whose names were familiar to me over many years of reading in this genre.

With the advent of self-publishing (relatively inexpensive compared to vanity publishing) literally millions of people now have the opportunity to write and publish their stories as eBooks as well as POD or print on demand books, usually paperbacks. No need to be rejected by major publishing houses, one can now write and publish anything at any time, either individually or through one of the many smaller companies which specialise in setting up self-published books for world distribution.

As a result, stories of all kinds have bombarded potential readers with so many choices they don't know where to start. Similarly, with the prospect of people actually going to Mars in the near future, stories about Mars, or set on Mars, or about going to live on Mars, have proliferated until there are so many it is hardly possible to read them all.

As a consequence I chose some by the synopsis if it seemed interesting, or by what appears to be an evocative cover. If the cover looked cheap and tacky I would assume the content would probably be much the same. None of the author's names were familiar to me so I had no idea of what to expect until the books arrived in the post or could be downloaded to my computer.

The stories vary from average and mediocre to quite outstanding ones that appear to have been professionally edited and printed. Some are only available as eBooks, disappointing for those who prefer a printed book, but on the other hand if the print quality is poorly produced it is better to read it as an eBook which is cheaper to download than buying a printed copy that doesn't measure up to professional standards in appearance.

And this is the biggest problem with most of the self-published books. Ignoring the fact that some do have attractive covers, and many of us choose a book, especially if buying over the internet, by its cover, on opening the book the poor quality of design and layout, old fashioned large fonts, huge paragraph indents (tab stops), or extra spacing between every paragraph because there are no indents creates the appearance of amateur production.

I'm all in favour of authors having the opportunity to publish their stories, and congratulate everyone who manages to finish writing a novel; never an easy task, but what I do feel is that those who publish these stories, the printers and distributors, need to lift their game so the resultant book at least has the appearance of a book published by a reputable publisher. I think they take advantage of the authors. They take their money for setup costs and printing costs, but what they produce is often a poor example of a book, overweight because of heavy thick paper, and large fonts with wide line spacing to make a short work appear longer and more substantial; in general a book that is not attractive to hold and read.

My only other concern here would be that the authors are sometimes in a hurry to see their work in print and usually don't take time to proof read the work for words a spellchecker will not find incorrect because they are homonyms, *words that sound the same, are spelt differently and have different meanings to that which was intended.* A careful rereading before sending the manuscript off to be setup would result in a better finished product.

'Re-inventing the wheel...'

Because Mars is now popular and many people want to write a Martian story, a major concern is that quite a few of these new self published authors haven't read any earlier books about Mars or even any current non-fiction books regarding Mars. They seem to be repeating the same old plot lines used years ago, or worse still their ideas of Mars are derived from memories of poorly made movies that do not adhere to scientific reality.

Inevitably the stories they produce are not outstanding.

One can only hope that with time and more experience in writing, and with the reading of other stories with a Martian setting their ideas will improve and the quality of their stories will be better.

Who can resist a title like *Mars Needs Books?* (2011)

This one is by Gary Lovisi, a Mystery Writers of America award nominee and a winner of the Western Writers of America's Spur award. He is also the editor of ***Hardboiled*** and of ***Paperback Parade*** magazines. ***Mars Needs Books*** is a hardboiled, mystery/spy thriller set on Mars about 150 years in the future.

The Department of Control, DOC, controls the Earth, all its peoples and everything they do. They have secret agents, like Ryan, who infiltrate workplaces or subversive organizations to eliminate recalcitrants, or to have them shipped to Mars where they will work in the mines. Almost everyone is brainwashed and compliant. Those who are eliminated are wiped from the digital records so they cease to exist with no records to prove they were there in the first place. The truth is whatever DOC says it is, and records are manipulated to reflect what truth DOC wants people to know.

However DOC suspects something is not right about Mars. They send their best agent, Ryan, to find out what is going on. DOC also sets up a plan to make those on Mars cause a rebellion which they will publicly squash to boost their power over the general populace on Earth. They do this by sending paperback, hardboiled fiction from the 1940s and 1950s hoping that by reading these old real books, a feeling of independence will result with the miners rebelling against Earth and the Department of Control. This plan backfires.

To live on Mars requires independence rather than subservience, and instead of rebelling, the population on Mars resists the brain washing TV broadcasts, and with the instigation of Ryan become collectors of old hardboiled paperback fiction. Ryan has been changed by the long voyage out to Mars and even subsequently on Mars itself. His programming has been too effective and he becomes the instigator of the resistance.

Shipments of paperbacks come from Ryan's brother on a monthly basis and everyone buys, sells, and trades these books. These old books can't be altered or doctored by the DOC without being noticed. They exhibit independence of thought, contempt for authority, and in general a strong feeling of independence; exactly as the miners see themselves. With Ryan's instigation they send reports back to Earth which are fake, which show DOC that the Mars citizens are compliant and do what they are told. This is not what DOC expected.

The middle part of the book slows down a bit as there is (too) much discussion over old paperbacks and how the miners regard the authors and storylines, appreciation of original cover art, and others aspects collectors of these books desire. But it picks up when after 20 years a group of women arrive on the planet. There were no women before, and the miners are ecstatic. Among these women, in disguise, is the head of DOC, Arabella Rashid. She has come to find out what went wrong with her plan to subjugate the Martian miners.

She immediately hooks up with her agent Ryan, and is astonished at what she finds. Nothing is as she expected. She falls in love with Ryan, and in doing this she starts to remember her past life as well as his. They were once married or at least their originals were, and this explains their intense attraction to each other. They are clones and have been alive for far longer than they thought. Together they conspire to destroy the Department of Control, but to do this they need to fake a rebellion, and take the leader of said rebellion back to Earth for interrogation to make it look real.

Ryan stays on Mars while Arrabella returns to Earth with a person who is dying anyway, but who is willing to pretend to be the rebellious leader, to be interrogated and die for the cause of keeping Mars free.

The story finishes with Arrabella returning to Mars while back on Earth resistance to DOC begins in remote areas, hinting that eventually DOC will be eliminated and Earth will once again be free.

This is a much better book than expected and the author certainly knows a lot about old last century 'noir' mysteries.

Mars Station Alpha (2011) by Stephen Penner.

The story opens with a second expedition arriving and coming in to land on the surface of Mars, on a runway beside a base established by a previous expedition, Mars Station Alpha. This is obviously a ground based station or the ship wouldn't be landing on a runway. The author makes a glaring mistake by referring to it as a space station… twice in the first two pages, yet clearly they are landing on the surface of Mars. A space station is in space, not on the surface of the planet. In space the ship would dock with the station, not land on a runway beside it.

Another mistake the author makes, which almost put me off wanting to continue reading, is the length of the Martian day. He mentions it as being 23 hours, and that the crew of the second expedition accustomed themselves to the shorter day on the way out, so they wouldn't feel strange once they had landed. He mentions the length of the day three times in the first couple of chapters, probably so readers would know they were on Mars.

The length of the Martian day (called a Sol) is 24 hours, 37 minutes and 23 seconds, measured by its rotation in relation to the stars, not 23 hours. In relation to the movement of the sun rising and setting the Martian day is 39 minutes and 35 seconds longer than Earth's 24 hour solar day. Earth's sidereal day is 23 hours, 56 minutes, 4.1 seconds. This makes the Martian Sol equivalent to 1.027 Earth days. It takes 687 days to complete one orbit of the Sun. It was known as long ago as 1686 when **Bernard le Bouvier de Fontanelle** *mentioned in his book* ***Conversations on the Plurality of Worlds****, that Mars had a day about half an hour longer than Earth's day and that its year was about two months shorter than two Earth years. It was only measured with more accuracy in the 20th century.*

They crew land, taxi to the station and as they connect to the air lock of the station there is an explosion outside the airlock and one of the crew has his faceplate smashed. Instead of suffering the effects of explosive decompression (*Mars atmosphere is approximately 1000 times less than the pressure of Earth's at sea level)* his space suit floods with poisonous carbon dioxide and he begins to suffocate. But the rest of the team get him into the ground station and he survives.

These three mistakes made me doubt that the story would be worth reading, making it obvious that the author has snot researched anything about Mars and is not familiar with SF, other than perhaps what could be seen in cheap B grade movies. SF movies are different from SF literature. They mostly rely on action, sometimes horror, with few of them having any scientific basis.

The events of this story take place inside the Mars Station Alpha with little activity outside so hardly anything of Mars is depicted. Radio communications don't function and an outside inspection reveals there are no satellite dishes or aerials, so messages can't be sent to Earth. During this inspection one of the team is injured in a fall and the leg of his suit is gashed. (Again no decompression). They get him inside quickly but immediately he suffers a virulent bacterial infection which they barely bring under control with antibiotics. Another team member starts having visions and believes there are malevolent spirits trying to sabotage them. By now the story begins to seem like a ghost story. They don't know what happened to the previous expedition members. This group was originally sent as a relief team, but now they need to find out what happened to the others.

Communications in their lander have also been sabotaged. Power cuts off intermittently. Another team member dies so there are only four left. Flashes of an unseen shape are noticed on video playback so the idea of ghosts is reinforced. The team start bickering with each other. Some want to return home while the captain insists on discovering what happened to the previous team who set up the station; all this in the first '23' hours.

During the landing one of them saw something odd. Two of them make an excursion to see what it was. They discover monolithic carved rocks set up in a circle like Stonehenge, weathered, and apparently millions of years old. Shortly after a massive sandstorm they discover that the Mars Station Alpha had been built on top of an apparent ancient burial ground, containing more of the same monolithic rocks arranged in a circle only these seem a lot newer. Immediately they believe that is the source of the ghosts.

Suddenly, at the very end, there is a twist, and the captain realizes there are no ghosts, there is a survivor from the original group manipulating events. It turns out he was the leader of the earlier expedition. He has been hiding in a secret room within the station. *How big is this station?* He killed the others and buried them outside and wants to kill the members of the second expedition. He also created the monoliths to fool the second team. Why? His motives are never explained. He is killed in a short scuffle so we don't find after all.

The characters don't come alive as individuals. There is no defining image of what Mars is like, apart from some token mentions; the incorrect 23 hour day, a sandstorm, and an atmosphere of mostly carbon dioxide.

Stuff like this can be done in a cheap film, and by the time you question it the film is over.

In a film there would be enough visuals in the background outside and inside the Alpha Station that the audience absorbs subconsciously to indicate the story is taking place on Mars while the action unfolds. But this is a novel, not a film. There needs to be character development and sufficient background information inserted into the story to convince the reader that it is taking place on Mars… and the reader also needs to know why things happened, and a promise that the resolution will make sense, or else there is no interest in continuing to read. Relying on relentless action over a short period, with events overwhelming the team, to develop drama is not enough.

The book does have a nice cover though.

Red Hope (2014) by John Dreese.

This one harks back to stories about going to Mars.

Subtitled *Book 1* it begins intriguingly with the Mars Rover sending back several photos of a fossilized five fingered hand sticking part way out of the rock and holding a small rectangular artefact with an engraved symbol on it. Before the rover can be commanded to take more images its battery power fails. The rocks containing the fossil are estimated to be 3 million or more years old. In the background of one of the photos there appears to be a stone building.

The president orders an immediate expedition to go to Mars to find that fossil and examine the nearby stone building.

This opening immediately captures the reader, but for the next 10 chapters the book bogs down with press conferences, astronaut selection and training, none of which moves the story forward. There is some character delineation so we can identify who is who in the crew of four selected to go.

It isn't until chapter 13 (page 129) that the journey to Mars commences.

Chapter 15 (page 133) starts with the line *When done correctly; space travel can be boring...*which sums up the previous 100 plus pages.

Finally at the end of Chapter 15 they come down for a landing and things go wrong. They are forced to use their aero-braking parachute which they were not supposed to use until they returned to Earth, but they had no choice; it was use it or crash.

This brief moment of excitement could have been given more prominence with the previous 10 or 11 chapters edited down to 2. It would have made it tighter and more dramatic. But then it would have been half the size.

Finally on the surface they examine the fossil and find it is only 200,000 years old which the author suggests ties in with the appearance of Homo sapiens on Earth. Suddenly the astronauts believe that Homo sapiens came from Mars and settled on Earth.

There is no explanation or suggestion of how these human ancestors arrived on Mars or where they came from if that fossil only dates back 200,000 years.

How could it be fossilised if there was no running water on Mars to lay down sedimentary rock? Mars 200,000 years ago was as desolate and dry and empty as it is today and had been like that for perhaps two billion years. A fossil is formed by being covered with layers of sedimentary deposits, put down under water until the pressure converts the sand and mud into soft stone such as sandstone, which at the same time preserves the bony structure of the thing being fossilized.

The idea of humans coming from Mars is a common theme in movies and allows scriptwriters to put in such things as the "face" on Mars, pyramids and other structures.

There is conflict between the astronauts who are comprised of Americans and Russians. Two of them are trapped inside the enigmatic stone building, where they discover a small anti-gravity device. Fiddling with this device inadvertently creates a marsquake, causing a huge boulder to roll across the entrance of the building. They can't physically move this boulder. Being close to using up all the oxygen in their suits, they use one of the oxygen tanks to blow away the boulder blocking the entrance, but that means only one of them will have enough oxygen left to get back to the lander. The other will die.

The expedition is a disaster. Only two manage to take off for the return to Earth, taking with them the anti-gravity device. There is another disaster on the returning ship and again one doesn't survive.

The last scene is the ship approaching Earth with one survivor staring at the planet as the ship goes into orbit. The other dead astronaut is being towed along behind on a tether. We don't know which one survived and which one didn't. The story stops at this point.

Obviously Book 2 ***Blue Hope*** will continue the story when the lone survivor lands on Earth, and it actually begins by reiterating the scene where one atsronaut dies as the two escape from the hut where they were trapped by a huge boulder. This also makes it clear who survived and how, which was not clear in volume one.

I didn't get much of an impression of Mars with ***Red Hope***, even though the characters had to wear pressure suits because of Mars' low atmospheric pressure. The characters don't come alive, being mouthpieces or talking heads. The story seemed to be more about conflict between American and Russian ideology rather than about Mars. If it had been set in the Sahara, or perhaps the Gobi desert, the finding of the fossil would have made more sense. But that would mean substantially changing the story. I think that would have made it a better story. I feel this one is derivative, with ideas long since abandoned by many authors, but unfortunately not by scriptwriters of B grade SF movies.

Even though I have downloaded the second volume, after reading the first ***Red Hope***, it it unlikely that I will read much beyond the opening pages of the second volume. I really don't care who made the anti-gravity device or who originally died and became fossilized.

Red Rising (2014) by Pierce Brown.

This is a story for young adults, and in keeping with the themes young adults like to read, it is a dystopian novel much in the vein of ***The Hunger Games*** or ***Maze Runner.***

Darrow is 16 years old, (not Martian years, but Earth years or else he wouldn't be a teenager) and is a member of the Red mining community on Mars. He lives underground; his people have for centuries and basically they are slave labour although they have been conditioned to think otherwise. They believe that the work they do extracting precious minerals is essential for terraforming the surface to make Mars habitable.

His reality takes a hit when his wife dies and he becomes disillusioned with life underground. He joins forces with a small rebel group who take him to the surface to see the reality. They have been living a lie.

Mars has been terraformed for centuries and there is a thriving population controlled by almost superhuman Golds. The Reds, the miners who live underground, have no idea of how well those above ground live. The Golds also control commerce between the planets many of which are colonized, and they oversee a brutal life on Mars where the children who come of age are forced into competitive games in which only the toughest survive to join the ranks of the ruling elite.

Darrow, with the help of a small group of rebels is disguised and joins the other teenage members of the ruling families to participate in the series of savage war games and competitions which eliminate the weak so only the toughest and strongest survive to become members of the Gold elite.

This book is superbly written, and if the reader is a young adult, he or she would be captivated and will certainly want to read the next four books in the series.

From my personal point of view after reading the first half which I found engaging, I couldn't go on with the second half which became an endless series of fights and battles between the various groups of teenagers as the weak are eliminated and killed. If I was 50 years younger I would absolutely love this story and would desperately look for the follow up volumes.

When I first started reading this there were two more books in the series. There are now another two which means the stories are obviously popular, and if they continue to be popular there may be even more to follow.

I suspect it won't be long before we see a series of films based on these books and I have no doubt that they will be spectacular.

Mars Base – Red 7 by David Vengley (eBook 2014)

Mars has been colonized for a couple of hundred years. The colonists mine red earth and minerals from a series of caves which they ship back to Earth where it is used to grow crops.

About to start a new mine in a large cave (Red 7) they discover a huge door slightly ajar which alters everyone's perception of Mars. The miners who enter to explore this ancient construction don't come out and a rescue team is sent in to get them but they also disappear.

The story opens with a group of marines being sent in accompanied by archaeologists and other scientists. The scientists are to examine the door and any other artefact that dates back more than 65 million years while the marines are to rescue the two previous teams. Their ship is attacked by rogue warships and is partially destroyed while some of the marines and the scientists are deep inside the cave. The cave entrance is also blocked in the battle with the two warships.

From this point on the story is full of action as the marines and the scientists are forced to find another way out. They do this by going further into the cave only to discover deep inside a hidden city with the remnants of the previous Martian population.

Back story explains that the Martian civilization became aware of a massive asteroid was about to collide with the planet.

They had five years to prepare by building 100 cities underground, linked together by tunnels in an attempt to save some of the population. They also built an ark ship to take the genetic seeds of animals and plants as well as people to search for another home. Those who stayed on the surface would not be able to survive.

When the asteroid struck, the atmosphere and the oceans were blasted into space. The magnetic field was destroyed and the planet became a barren empty world. Most of the cities underground didn't survive the impact and those that did were later destroyed by an atomic plant explosion that wiped them out. Only one city survived.

A rogue group of Russians and Chinese discovered this city by entering through an ancient lava tube in a massive caldera. They discovered in there a device they think is a weapon which they want to use to control Earth, but they can't figure out how to activate it. They have kept this secret. They dispatched two warships to attack the marines, but the marines were tougher than they expected and their two ships were destroyed.

This becomes a gung-ho action adventure from this point as we follow both the small group inside the ancient city as well as the marines who go in search of the renegades attempting to activate the ancient weapon. But there is more to it than that; with suggestions that the ark ship landed on Earth and one of the marines (Angelina, or Nina) is a direct descendant of the ancient Martians and she holds the key to activating the mysterious device which is not a weapon but a means of restoring Mars to its former glory.

With the help of the inhabitants of the city who have been waiting for millennia for this woman to save their planet they struggle to get to the location of the ancient device while the Russian renegades attempt to stop them.

There are lots of battles and near escapes not only with the renegades but with some ferocious native life as well. A war threatening on Earth between the Chinese and the American-Russian alliance is also thrown into the mix. There is a Chinese warship in Mars orbit ready to attack the Russian renegades to prevent them from using the 'weapon' but this comes abruptly to an end and the ship is withdrawn as the Chinese on Earth capitulate to the Alliance.

And right at the end in the middle of a battle to gain access to the control room where the control for the device is located, the author throws in an alien from another star system who wants to stop them activating the restoration device because it is a life form that doesn't need water and wants to keep Mars a dry cold desolate planet. It fails its attempt and leaves while Nina activates the device that begins the restoration of Mars.

This bit at the end about a mysterious alien spoilt what was a reasonable action story.

Why an alien life form from a system 1340 light years away would want anything to do with Mars doesn't make sense unless it is there to provide an entrance into another story as a kind of sequel.

Basically this is an action fantasy that would appeal to young male readers in much the same way an action movie does.

There is so much non-stop action that consideration of the story's plausibility doesn't happen. There is also not much of an impression of Mars since most of the action takes place beneath the surface where there is a breathable atmosphere.

War Dogs by Greg Bear (2014) (Orbit)

First book of a trilogy: Thirteen years before the start of the story enigmatic visitors from another star system arrived and handed out knowledge that allowed rapid scientific but especially military weapons development. But there is a catch. These aliens called Gurus claim they have been hounded from star system to star system by another much worse alien foe. These other aliens have followed the Gurus to our solar system and have established a base on Mars. The Gurus want humans to help them fight against these other aliens. Waves of Marines (both US and Russian marines) called Skyrines have been sent to Mars to establish a beachhead against the vicious aliens.

There are settlers on Mars from South Africa, Voortrekkers or Voors, and Muskies, people who came to Mars because of Elon Musk's vision to settle the planet. Both groups, having been abandoned by Earth Governments, want little to do with humans from Earth. They live underground and are antagonistic towards each other. The descendants of the original settlers are now into their third generation and subsequently their language, customs and even physical appearance has begun to differ from Earth humans.

The story is told from the viewpoint of Master Sergeant Venn who is part of a small force dropped to the surface, but the alien antagonists, Antags, attacked their orbiting ships resulting in a botched drop. Venn's platoon of Skyrines is on its own without any resources and limited time to survive on the surface. They will run out of oxygen unless they can find their lost supplies. They manage to find an abandoned Russian camp where there is an oxy-tent in which they can survive the night. Searching for the rest of their platoon they find their commanding officers in an oxy-tent that is also running out of air.

Somehow they triggered an alarm and just as they are about to expire a female Martian driving a large buggy finds them. She takes them to an abandoned base. She is a Muskie and is on the run from a group of Voors who want to kill her because she violated a marriage code. Her father used to work for the Voors and he told her about this mine and underground base which had been abandoned because it had been flooded. Inside the base they discover some weird very old and very alien stuff.

The base was part of an ancient water filled icy moon that crashed into Mars, seeding the planet with life that survived for a while before Mars once again dried up. But there is something deep down in the remnants of this icy moon, something very alien. The Voors want their old mine back. The Antags and the Gurus also want to destroy this icy remnant for reasons of their own. A huge battle ensues for possession of this mine base and very few of the Skyrines survive. Master Sergeant Venn found something in the mine, a platinum disc covered with numbers and strange symbols. He keeps it hidden but it is something others want, and they will kill him for it if they know he has it. He and several others who spent time fighting inside the ancient moon fragment encounter flaky dust like rwsidues which remind them of green tea. Some of them are infected with this 'tea' which initially causes hallucinations and dreams of intelligent bug-like creatures.

The story which is only the first part of a trilogy finishes with a few survivors being returned to Earth and with Venn on the run from authorities who believe he is infected with the green tea from the mine. They want to question him. Before they capture him he manages to send his platinum disc to one of his comrades who also managed to get back to Earth and is hiding somewhere in Canada. This person is also infected in the same way as Venn. Venn is quickly captured and placed in quarantine, and the story ends here with him waiting to be interrogated.

Mars described by Bear in this story is a very harsh place, but not without beauty. Bear is convincing in the way he depicts the physical aspects of Mars and the difficulties people have in surviving there. And his suggestion that fragments of an icy moon that once had life inside it somehow broke out of orbit and fell into the inner solar system, breaking up and impacting Mars and Earth which is how life began on on Earth and possibly Mars, is in itself intriguing.

The second volume ***Killing Titan*** (2015) begins with Venn having stranger and weirder memories as well as remembering things from alien bug like creatures that became extinct billions of years ago. They were the first life forms in the solar system while Earth was still a ball of molten rock.

The authorities and the Gurus want to find what he knows about the bugs and the very early solar system and interrogate him to the point of almost torturing him. Some of the doctors though don't agree with what the Gurus are doing and believe they are lying about their reasons for wanting humans to help them with their interstellar war. They contrive to break Venn out of the hospital where he is quaratined and manage to smuggle him onto a ship going back to Mars. They believe he can communicate with whatever is still residual in the old mines that were actually part of the icy moon that impacted with Mars and earth billions of years earlier. All but the last third of this volume takes place again on Mars where the Antags are still fighting the Guru manipulated Earth forces. As Venn's dreams become more coherent he realizes he is in contact with the remnants of an ancient billions-of-years-old computerized data base, which can supply him with unbelievable information if he can form the right questions.

Venn finds the remnants of his skyrine platoon and they discover those they thought dead, turned into black glass by whatever was in the moon remnants, are not really dead but are being absorbed into the memory banks of the very alien computer that remembers everything going back to the beginnings of life in the solar system which started on Titan and other icy moons orbiting Saturn.

The gurus have sent a large number of special forces to destroy all the remnants of the icy moon's fragments on Mars, and Venn and his small group just manage to escape in time. The alien moon fragments turn into inpenetrable black glass when an attempt is made to destroy them. The same reason some skyrines were turned into black glass when they earlier tried to destroy the larger moon fragment.

Venn and his group escape Mars following the Antags who are also leaving, heading to Titan. Venn's skyrines are followed by Guru controlled Earth forces who want them dead because they know more than they should. On Titan they find enormous Antag forces beneath the ice in hidden seas. Venn manages to communicate with the leader of the Antags, a female, mentally via the ancient computer and when the Guru led Earth forces arrive to destroy them on Titan they surrender to the Antags who they have discovered are also being misled about the war and why they are fighting humans in the solar system. They were told the same story the Humans were told, only in reverse, with the humans out to utterly destroy the Gurus (or Keepers as they are called by the Antags) along with their Antag allies. Both sides have been deliberately pitted against each other, by their respective Gurus or Keepers, for entertainment of the galactic masses. Their war is a massive reality show. Surrendering to the Antags was the only way they would survive since the massive Earth forces arriving were set to wipe out everything on Titan, especially the data base which could reveal the truth about the War that has been going on intermittently for billions of years.

This volume ends here, but the story continues exactly from this point in the third volume, ***Take Back the Sky*** (2016). These two later volumes are really one story split into two parts whereas the first volume was more a stand alone story, though open ended.

The third volume ***Take Back the Sky*** takes place on board a gigantic living ship that is invisible to Earth forces' radar detection, where the humans and their reluctant Antag allies discover their war is only a drama, an entertainment designed to be broadcast across the galaxy. On board the

Guru ship the humans are first kept in cages but later released by the Antags who need Venn and one of the Russian women who are mentally able to communicate with the computers as well as with the Gurus and the Antags. The ship is returning to the Antag homeworld after which it will return to Mars and Earth to set up a new conflict with other aliens since the audience for the Human Antag war has become bored.

The humans suffer a lot on the journey out of the solar system; they were meant to fight each other to the death while in the cage as they discovered other cages full of decomposing bodies, but the Antags released them because several of them were infected by the martian tea and could mentally communicate with the ancient data bases. One of them, a Russian skyrine takes partial control of the ship because the ship thinks she is a Guru. The Antags want her to help get the ship to take them back to their homeworld. Once the Antags have left to go down to what's left of their homeworld, she contrives to get the ship to take her fellow skyrines back to Earth. As it is returning the whole ship is re-configuring itself and producing new ships and weapons in preparation for a new conflict it will promote. When Venn and his fellow skyrines arrive downsystem, some decide to stay on Mars while Venn and Ishida (who had been seriously injured in a previous Antag Human conflict and whose body had in part been reconstructed robotically) return to Earth where they discover the war has been over for thirty years and military forces are mostly disbanded. The ship is to pick up the remaining Gurus on Earth and take them to a new location where a new entertainment is planned to commence.

The ship is going to swing around the sun before heading back out to the far reaches of the solar system but the Russian remaining on board convinces the ship to dive into the sun where it will be destroyed. There will be no more fake wars generated for entertainemnt. By the time the Guru's who left Earth on this ship realise that it is diving into the sun it is too late.

The final scene has the woman on board the ship sends to Venn an image of herself standing and watching the sun get larger and larger as the ship approaches until it finally burns out as the ship is destroyed.

After three years Venn and Ishida, who has had the robotic parts of her body rejuvenated, decide to return to Mars because Earth had changed so much there really isn't anything for them there.

The great thing about Geg Bear is that he makes the reader feel concerned about his characters, and no matter how spectacular the events occuring in the story are, it is the people they affect that the reader cares about. You have to keep reading to find out what happens to them.

The Lady Astronaut of Mars, by Mary Robinette Kowal (2014 - eBook)

A poignant story of a woman who must decide whether to leave her terminally ill husband in order to make one final trip into Space, or to stay and look after him until the end causing her to miss out on a voyage to another star.

NASA has developed a system of folding space so the journey to another star system only takes weeks instead of years. The catch is; someone must first go to the destination physically in order to set up the receiving station that enables the transportation of a ship through folded space.

On Mars they choose her because she is famous, having been the first lady astronaut who helped colonise Mars, and as a result can help maintain interest and finance for the project.

There are also other reasons why they want her; because the trip to the star system with the newly discovered earth-like planet will take three years, and she is old and it won't matter if she is affected by radiation exposure during the three year voyage because she won't be returning, and finally because she is also a pilot who dreams of going back into space again after so many years on Mars.

She desperately wants to see the stars in all their glory again.

But she doesn't want to leave her dying husband. She is his full time carer. He only has a few months to live, even less before his illness affects him adversely. If she stays they will send a younger pilot on the mission because it has to depart on a specific date.

Her husband urges her to take the job, and she refuses.

What if the mission is cancelled and no one goes? You will regret it for the rest of your life once I'm gone. Besides, I don't want you to see me when I really get bad. You should go, he insists. When the director of the proposed mission gets her husband to write special software for the mission she finally accepts the idea of going.

Her desire to be in space overwhelms her desire to stay and look after her husband. She finally relents and accepts knowing that a little part of him, in the software incorporated into the ship, will be with her throughout the duration of the long voyage.

This is a beautiful, very emotional story that will bring tears to the eyes of anyone who knows what it is like to be a carer for a dying or very ill partner.

Snowfall on Mars by Branden Frankel (2015) is something completely different,

The blurb on the back cover says *Red Planet. White Winter. Black Heart.*

This is the best of the new dystopian views of Mars that has appeared in the last couple of years. A deep character study of people struggling to survive in circumstances no one could possibly have foreseen.

Most Mars stories that involve terraforming the planet tend to be positive, looking forward to a better future where new Martian colonists can live in a more earth like environment and any problems that occur are solved usually for the better.

This story postulates the opposite. The terraforming has failed, and with disastrous results. Was it sabotaged or did it simply not work as expected over the longer term?

The colonists have to contend with constant acid rain and snowfalls interspersed with raging dust storms, rather than an improved atmosphere and this has been going on for decades.

As the story opens it is twenty years after life on Earth has been annihilated. The only humans left in the solar system are in the failing colonies on Mars where after abandoning the smaller colonies, those left are living in the original and the largest domed city called New Huston. It has seen better days and is now falling into disrepair, with only 500 colonists surviving where once there had been more than five thousand.

David Adler as a child migrated to Mars with his parents in search of a better life. Not long after that War ravaged the Earth resulting in a nuclear holocaust which destroyed all life. For the five thousand colonists on Mars there was no going back they had to make the best of their new home. But chaos descended on the planet with various factions rioting and fighting each other. Many colonists committed suicide because life on Mars was hard, and now there was no escape, no going back to Earth. Mars was all they had. But the hope of making it a better place failed as the terraforming which began okay, has increasingly changed the planet for the worse.

A few older colonists still work: someone has to supply the food and other necessities. Many have sunk into apathy and space-out on drugs to escape their awful reality. Gangs of kids who know nothing other than this run-down falling apart environment roam the partially deserted domed city, inflicting violence on themselves and anyone they come across. A religious death cult has evolved which believes they are all dead anyway. They practice torture among themselves in the hope it will help them move to the next plane of existence.

All this is backstory as we open with David Adler, now an engineer and one of those who actually work to maintain the life support systems within the colony, is asked by his former girlfriend to help solve the brutal murder of her new boyfriend, whose job it was to maintain the atmosphere within the colony.

This story is a post-apocalyptic dystopian setting with a murder mystery. This kind of setting has been around in some form for as long as science fiction has been written, but I don't recall ever seeing it used on Mars before; at least not like this. Perhaps Lewis Shiner came close with Frontera in 1984 with his particular dystopian setting both on Earth and somewhat on Mars, but this book goes well beyond that.

Post-apocalyptic dystopian fiction is popular amongst young adult readers and setting this on Mars makes it stand out from most of the recent dystopian stories (usually set in a grim futuristic Earth). It is also quite different from most other self-published Mars offerings.

As David delves deeper into what happened to the murdered engineer he discovers a plot to blow up the colony instigated by the death cult leader who believe that the non-believers need encouragement to move on to the next realm. He and his ex-girlfriend attempt to stop the death cult while at the same time solve the murder. He discovers that the worsening condition of the terraforming is the result of sabotage instigated by the leader of the death cult who once was one of the engineers who built the terraforming systems. David discovers finally that the murder was committed by one of two electronics experts who believe they have received a signal from Earth and want to go there. Before David can get to them they steal a shuttle and take off for Earth, leaving themselves no way to come back. And the reader knows there will be nothing there when they get to Earth; a fitting end.

This is a gritty, noir mystery-thriller that is hard to classify. That it takes place on a Mars no one else has imagined in this way is a bonus. The writing is better than what one would expect and the characters are fully formed and believable with all their faults and good points. It also finishes on a positive given the severe conditions that exist.

This is a book every Mars enthusiast, as well as readers of SF and mystery stories, will relish.

If it is self-published as I suspect, it's hard to tell. It has the appearance of being professionally edited, and is printed on the same paper stock top publishers use. It looks and feels very good indeed.

Here is another offering where because of a nuclear holocaust on Earth the colonists on Mars have to survive on their own.

Mars Endevour (2016) an eBook by Peter Cawdron, retitled and republished (also in paperback) as ***Retrograde*** but essentially the same story. It also has a new cover.

This story opens with the members of a newly established colony made up of Chinese, Russian American and European scientists suddenly learning that a nuclear war has devastated Earth. The colonists learn that the Eastern blocks and Western blocks blame each other for starting the war, with each claiming that all they did was retaliate.

The colony members from various countries and continents have been happily working together up until that moment. Each group has their own module connected to a central module which is a common area for meetings and recreation among other activities. Suddenly the Chinese are suspicious of the Americans. The Americans want nothing more to do with the Russians. The Europeans consisting of people from several European countries including Japan try to talk sense to the other groups without much success. They all close off their modules from each other reflecting the same paranoia and mistrust that has spread around the home planet.

But on Mars each group needs the others. They have to relearn how to trust each other or no one will survive.

One American woman, Liz, (the story is told from her viewpoint) has fallen in love with one of the Chinese scientists and it is these two who help bring suspicion down, who desperately work towards getting everyone to trust each other again, and this is in spite of one group stealing medications from the general storage area, and incidents which appear to be sabotage that each blames the other for.

Liz is convinced that some of her own team have been lying to her regarding a supply ship carrying essentials that the whole colony needs. This ship was reported by their computer system as having failed to enter the atmosphere for aero-braking and had bypassed the planet. But Liz suspects it came down exactly as it was meant to and someone is hiding this from the rest of them. She takes a rover to search for the missing supply vessel and discovers that the rover has been sabotaged and she is running out of air. She has to be rescued, and while this is happening her lover is killed. The way in which she is rescued is a truly spectacular.

Most of this story is full on action which makes it hard not to keep reading. You just have to know what is going to happen next.

At this point when the reader is suspicious of the Russian, the American, and the Chinese groups thinking that each is trying to sabotage the other for their own benefit, the author turns everything on its head.

Liz along with one of her people realizes that the computers that run the whole base are the problem. They are the only things that control everything and can falsify information. Something in a radio burst that initially seemed to be some kind of interference came to them from Earth just before the atomic war started, and this infected their computers. They thought at first it was just static and ignored it, but now they suspect it was something else, something more malevolent. Collectively on Earth computer systems have developed self-awareness or artificial intelligence and this new AI wants to rid itself of humans since it sees them as a threat to its existence. It sent a copy of itself to Mars after starting the atomic war on Earth, and this copy has automatically downloaded and installed itself into the computer systems running the colony.

The struggle of the humans to survive on Mars suddenly takes on a whole new perspective. How can they fight against logic and coldness of this AI? How can they even plan to defeat it when it monitors everything they say and do and controls their complete environment?

Suddenly the story has much greater depth. It has gone from being about surviving on their own on Mars; hard enough in itself, but it has added surviving at the same time against an AI that wants to eliminate them altogether.

I won't give away how they manage to fight back once they have realised their situation so as not to spoil the plot for the reader, but I will say that this is as much a psychological thriller dealing with suspicion and paranoia in a closed environment with no safe way to escape as it is about having to cope with the advent of Artificial Intelligence and the adverse consequences that could occur. In the hands of a lesser writer this combination could degenerate into ridiculous melodrama, but Peter Cawdron is a superb writer and he pulls this off with great skill leaving the reader breathless and exhausted.

The details of the Martian environment, how the habitat works, and what the colonists need to do for survival are utterly convincing.

It would make a great movie but unfortunately most scriptwriters would anthropomorphise the AI into an exaggeration of some monstrous evil being and spoil what could be a realistic thriller set on Mars turning it into some awful monster versus humans' story. So I hope they don't make a film of this one.

Colony One Mars, Colony Two Mars (2016) **Colony Three Mars** (2017) Gerard M Kilby

The first two short books are one story divided into two parts, originally published as eBooks on the Amazon website. They later became available as self-published paperbacks with inconsistent editing and un-matching lay-outs and the use of a large font size to make a slight story appear longer. One volume has justified text while the other one is only justified left side. The extra heavy paper used by the printer makes both books appear amateurish which can be off-putting. I was tempted to not bother with them, but after having paid for them plus postage to Australia I decided to read them. I'm glad I did.

The story in ***Colony One*** is gripping right from the first few pages, apart from a small glitch, and compels you to read to the end.

Background: all contact has been lost with the first Human settlement on Mars because of a six month long planetary sandstorm. Later observations from space show extensive damage to the colony site and no signs of any activity, so all 54 colonists are presumed to be dead.

The story opens 3 years after the apparent destruction of Colony One when a 6 person team arrives to find out what happened to it.

On arrival at the site of what is left of Colony One the team finds it is still partially functioning and that someone is still alive but hiding from them. They begin to explore the working remnants as well as the outside areas that were damaged when suddenly one of them starts acting violently. Very soon almost all of them are affected by a disease that drives them to self-destruction while trying to kill each other as violently as possible.

It was at this point I thought the author ha used that old familiar trope of some ancient virus on Mars turning people into ravening zombies. Damn!

I was about to stop reading, and would have deleted it if it had been an eBook, but because the writing was engaging I decided read a bit more.

As it turns out, a small group of scientists who were part of Colony One, which was established by a private enterprise rather than a Government agency (COM or *Colony One Mars Consortium*), had been experiment-ing with genetic research into age prolongation among other things and they had modified the Leprosy virus which attacks the nerve cells, only something went wrong and it got out of control infecting almost the whole colony driving them crazy and making them kill each other. A few escaped unharmed and they set up a smaller colony unknown to those on Earth on the other side of the crater from Colony One, where they could continue their experiments without being exposed to the disease they inadvertently unleashed. This is Colony Two.

In no time the 6 person expedition is reduced to two women, one a biologist, who appears to be unaffected, and the other, the second in command whose secret mission was to recover the results of the original experiments with mutated leprosy virus and return them to Earth. As she attempts to do this the biologist blows up the return ship module while the second in command is refuelling it to prevent her from returning to Earth with the virus which would be devastating to everyone on the planet.

This leaves her stranded permanently on Mars.

Colony Two Mars begins at this point, where the biologist Dr Jan Malbec has let herself go and doesn't care how she looks. She only has a small intelligent robot accompanying her which belonged to the person who had been hiding when her group arrived and who was killed near the end of that volume. She has given up trying to find a cure for the dangerous virus knowing that even if she wasn't infected the Earth people wouldn't let her return anyway in case she was a carrier. They want to know how to kill it first. Besides she doesn't have a return vehicle, she blew it up.

Suddenly the little robot (Gizmo is its name) rushes in to inform her that there is someone in the airlock who is coming into the station. At the airlock she finds a young man in a patched up space suit who barely says anything before he dies. She has no idea who he is and on testing his DNA she finds he was one of the original colonists, but according to the colony records he died years ago and his body should be frozen along with all the other dead colonists in a shed they call the mausoleum. Sure enough he is there, and now there are two of him only the new one is much younger.

Guessing he must be from Colony Two she and Gizmo repair the only rover they have in the habitat and head off across the huge crater to the far side where Colony Two is situated in tunnels and caverns inside the massive walls of the crater. Eschewing the main entrance she sneaks in through an isolated entrance further up the crater side, only to be captured by the inhabitants once she comes through the airlock. They had seen her coming and were waiting for her.

The underground colony is massive, much bigger that anyone would have imagined and it is filled with clones of the original Colony One people… many clones of each person, clones that are not ageing so some of the research has been successful.

This is where it starts to fall apart and we have the Mad scientist scenario where he generates clones he can use for further experiments as well a slave labour the keep his underground facility functioning. This was for me so derivative of old B grade movies where a megalomaniacal scientist is trying to control the whole world, or in this case an unknown colony on Mars. It becomes rather silly but the author writes well enough to keep it moving at a breakneck speed so the reader won't easily notice. A small group wants to escape control of the scientist. The scientist wants to use Dr Jan Malbec somehow to get himself and his superior clones back to Earth since she is the only one who knows the access codes to operate the return vehicle, still in orbit around Mars.

The clones all look to her as a figurehead and begin a revolt against the scientist who created them. She aligns herself with the clones and helps them to fight against control by the head scientists and his special in-bred superior clones used as bodyguards during which she finds out a cure has been found for the virus that drives them nuts as well as the secret to prevent ageing. Once the scientist has been defeated with a suitably grisly end, she now has the position of being the leader of the remaining colony. Earth is informed of what has happened.

She has no intention of returning to Earth and the story ends here.

Colony Three Mars begins after the conclusion of events depicted in the previous book. Two years have passed and the arrival of a Chinese group is imminent. Dr Malbec is trying to decide whether she should destroy the only remaining sample of the deadly virus so there is no way they can take it back to Earth when events begin to unfold. The colonists decide to meet the Chinese with a show of force using their rovers and a flying transport device. The colonists are armed and they warn the Chinese not to bring weapons into Colony One. The Chinese are adamant about Dr Malbec giving them a sample of the virus and she insists it no longer exists. It has been eradicated.

Before they can take it further a second expedition from Earth Arrives. These are the people from COM *Colony One Mars Consortium* who claim ownership of both colonies and when the Colony Two people try to prevent them from bringing weapons inside they use new electronic weapons to disable the colonists who resist. They ask the Chinese to leave and when they don't they attack to Colony One base and take it over. They are prepared to dissect the colonists to find the answers to how the virus has affected them genetically to prevent ageing. Dr Malbec who escaped into the tunnels and a secret laboratory when the Chinese imprisoned all the colonists in Base One inside the bio-farm area now decides she will release the virus into the air system. She knows the colonists are immune but the newcomers won't be.

As they start to become infected chaos ensues and the imprisoned colonists manage to escape while the Chinese and the COM intruders go berserk and try to kill each other as violently as possible. In the ensuing mayhem the colonists regain control of both Colony One as well as Colony Two, but one Chinese person escaped and took off as well as the commander of the Com group. The infection is carried back to Earth where millions very quickly are infected.

Dr Malbec informs the Earth Government that she has a cure but will only tell them what it is if they can guarantee the freedom of Mars to become an independent nation separate from Earth.

In the meantime a third group, an asteroid mining company has sent an expedition to Mars carrying all the basic equipment the colonists need replaced as well as much needed spare parts. This group wants to set up a base on Mars from which they can use to explore the asteroid belt for mining opportunities and wants Mars to process the ore as well as help manufacture the equipment they need for the mining. It looks as if Mars will have a future once they are independent from Earth.

Up to this point the story is all action and quite engrossing. Suddenly the pace slows and by comparison seems drawn out. Dr Malbec goes to Earth to negotiate on behalf of Mars and after this is concluded finally reaffirms she no longer wants to live on Earth, Mars is now her home.

Overall, the three volumes which are not very long make one complete story. Apart from some clichés which are obviously derivative, the story is for the most part fast moving and well written. The main character is believable as is her delightful robot companion. Some of the other characters are stereotyped but they fit into the story. It reminded me of the old fashioned type of story prevalent in the 1950s and 1960s that I grew up reading and enjoying.

Overall, I did enjoy these books. (The covers were also designed by the author and are quite attractive.)

Colony Four Mars - Jezero City (2017) an eBook by Gerard M Kilby

This is the fourth book in the series.

It begins ten years after the final events in the third book. Since it gained independence from Earth as a condition of Dr Jan Malbec giving Earth authorities the cure for the devastating genetically modified leprosy disease brought back from Mars, there has been underlying resentment from Earth towards Mars. As Mars prepares to celebrate its tenth anniversary a suspicious explosion of a rover delivering materials to an outpost causes concern to Dr Malbec. She believes the courier was murdered and that the rover had been sabotaged. No one accepts that, accusing her of being paranoid.

She enlists the help of a recent arrival amongst the colonists; an ex-police detective from New York called Mia, who doesn't want to act as a policewoman because of a terrible event in her past. Mia only decides to help so she can trace something that was stolen from her by a recent lover. This lover works for the governing UN body that once controlled Mars.

This story is fast paced and full of action. Mia discovers the suit the courier, an original Martian clone, had been sabotaged which means he was murdered. The rover was also sabotaged because normally they do not blow up. Her ex-boyfriend is involved somehow which makes her more determined to find out what happened. With the help of Gizmo, Dr Malbec's intelligent robot companion, she gets into the area controlled by the UN group to search for the rover's 'black box' which holds the clues as to what happened.

Meanwhile colonists and miners from all over Mars (the colony has expanded exponentially over the 10 years since independence) are heading to Jezero City as the original Colony One base is now called, to participate in celebrations to mark the anniversary of Martian independence.

Part of the celebrations involves the detonation of an atomic bomb to melt the carbon dioxide ice at the North Pole, releasing it into the atmosphere to begin terraforming the planet. This explosion is to be controlled from the UN controlled space station that orbits Mars.

At every turn attempts are made to prevent Mia and Gismo from discovering what has happened but she is resilient and relentless in her pursuit of the truth. They discover a weapon has been placed inside the Jezero City dome that will destroy the whole Martian population, timed to coincide with the atomic explosion at the North Pole. The explosion will be detonated by a signal from the Space station. As the countdown begins, the city's airlocks have been over-ridden and controlled by signals from the space station, which has locked all the doors trapping the population inside. Mia and Gismo are the only ones outside and they are forced to take a shuttle to the space station where she can disable the antennae sending the signals. These signals will also detonate the atomic bomb as well as the weapon inside Jezero City which turns out to be a biological weapon. It appears that Earth and the UN wants to take back control of Mars by killing the population. (Payback for the millions that died on Earth from the mutated disease from Mars… Dr Jan Malbec is blamed for their deaths by having held Earth to Ransom — the cure in return for Martian independence.)

All sorts of things go wrong as Mia and Gismo gain access to the space station but in the end they manage to prevent the destruction of Jezero City and the death of all the colonists.

This section of the story is spectacular and exciting, leaving the reader breathless. After the colony and Jezero City has been saved there is a summing up which explains several things one of which is the importance to Mia of what was stolen from her. She is promoted to become head of the newly formed police force and the story concludes satisfactorily.

It is also clear that the author has improved in the way he presents a story and promises to be someone to look out for in the future.

Killing Time on Mars (2017) an eBook by Alec Taylor

This intriguing story has the feel of a noir murder mystery combined with an explorative adventure, and is well worth reading.

A new space drive which also can be used as a weapon more powerful than earlier atomic weapons depends on using helium isotypes which can only be found on the surface of Mars.

A consortium of nations has established a mining colony on Mars to extract the helium isotypes from the regolith which are a result of radiation from the sun and only exist on Mars because it has very little atmosphere. The colony is thriving even though it is run as if it was a prison camp.

When an important person, in charge of the greenhouses, is murdered in one of her greenhouses a detective is sent to Mars by the consortium to find out what happened.

The story is divided (unnecessarily) into three acts. *Act one* being the discovery of the murder and the arrival of the detective. He doesn't fit in and isn't made welcome by those who have been there since the beginning. He is put to work with those in security, and it seems they want the murder solved quickly, since it disrupts the extraction of helium which is their primary purpose. There are very few clues and no one seems helpful.

When another worker steals a rover and heads off towards a chasm they go out after him but can't prevent him from driving over the edge to commit suicide. He was a former lover of the murdered woman in the greenhouse. Security calls the case closed since they can now blame the ex-lover for the murder, but the detective knows, feels, something is not right. He enlists the help of a computer expert to go back through digital records of events to see if they can pinpoint who was actually in the greenhouse at the time of the murder, but it is inconclusive because some records have been erased.

Act two has the colony getting back to normal and the detective plus a couple of people that he has made friends with go on an extended excursion to an old archaeological site in a deep chasm. This part of the story is pure adventure exploration. We learn about Mars and the history it shows us in the sedimentary layers deep into the chasm.

There is also another story here of a scientist who searched for ancient Martian life but who apparently had an accident and was shipped back to Earth. After that he disappeared and no one ever heard of him again or of what he may have found. The group holidaying decide they will search for fossils in the area the scientist had previously been working but a recent avalanche has completely covered the site. However they come to the conclusion that the scientists may have found something significant and the consortium covered it up because they don't want their mining operations interrupted by other scientific expeditions. There is an accident and one of them has a suit punctured necessitating a quick evacuation and a return back to the main colony. But before leaving the isolated base they discover a fossil. Mars once had life, and this is what the consortium doesn't want anyone to know.

Back on Earth there is escalating tension between the countries that are members of the consortium with each accusing the others of turning their space drives into weapons, and this tension is reflected in the additional security and monitoring of people in the mining colony. Some of them are agitating that they should be allowed to decide things for themselves rather than being told what to do by people back on Earth. In fact the murdered woman was agitating exactly for that, which is possibly what got her killed.

So we come to *act three* which reverts back to the noir feel of the first act with the detective almost killed to stop him from investigating. He survives and again with the help of his friend and the computers, they manage to dig up video files seen from the kitchen dining area of the tunnel that leads to the greenhouses. These are only partial views in the background of the dining area but they show two people went into the greenhouse at the time of the murder. One of those is most likely the killer, and it wasn't the ex-lover.

The detective has been removed from security and sent to work in a remote metal working sector, but he has discovered who the true murderer is and that perhaps there are two of them. A showdown occurs when these persons are confronted and which involves quite a few people. The two murderers escape to the launch pad where they steal the shuttle and blast off for rendezvous with the orbiting space ship that will take them back to Earth.

Meanwhile there is a ship with presumably a police or military force on board in transit from Earth to the colony.

Also back in the security centre of the colony where there is constant monitoring of the colony as well as a real time view of Earth the screen monitoring Earth suddenly flares with brilliant explosions as tensions there finally erupt into an all-out war. It appears every major city on every continent has been destroyed in what appears to be massive atomic explosions.

The Mars colony is now on its own. The two escaped murderers will find nothing when they get back to Earth.

The story ends here. The murder has been solved.

The independence of Mars and its colony has been asserted, which is reasonably satisfactory.

However it is clear that another story will follow, which is probably why there was so much back story in Act two.

What will happen to the colony now that they are entirely on their own with no possibility of help from Earth? What will happen when the ship in transit arrives and who is on board? Will the two escaped murderers turn around and come back since going on the Earth would be pointless?

Answering these questions will make a very interesting sequel which is promised for some time in the near future.

The Piranha Solution *a techno thriller* (2017) eBook by John Triptych.

This first book in the Ace of Space series has been set mostly on Mars.

The author postulates a solar system undergoing human expansion with the establishment of colonies in suitable locations, such as the Moon and Mars, some of which are government sponsored while others are private enterprise.

On Mars the original colonies established by the Russians and the Americans have been abandoned and evacuated. Only the Chinese colony still struggles to survive. Meanwhile an independent colony (licenced by NASA) has been established by a large private corporation. They hope to pay their way by developing space tourism to Mars. As the story opens a computer virus transmitted from Mars has corrupted communications not only on Mars but from Mars to Earth as well.

The private group have sent a team to investigate the old abandoned

American base, but they have disappeared. A rescue mission also vanished after losing contact.

The chief of the corporation on Earth decides to send his top problem solving investigator to Mars to find out what is happening. Their main object though is not the missing teams but the source of the corrupting virus which appears to have initially come from the old American Base. He takes with him a small team of special force combatants. NASA also sends an investigator.

The story actually opens with something very strange tearing apart the rover of the investigating team, killing its occupants. This draws the reader immediately into the story. There is quite a bit of technical detail regarding space flight, use of space suits, effects of freefall as well as about Mars which is interesting and well integrated into the story so it does set the mood for what follows.

Once the team lands on Mars it is non-stop action as the Ace of Space, the top problem solver Stilicho Jones (Stil) and his team set out to find the source of the corrupting computer code as well as to search for some missing people once thought to be dead. Not all of the team make it, several experiencing gruesome deaths, but Stil and his NASA associate do.

The latter part of the story reminded me of E C Tubb's 1953 book ***I Fight for Mars***, with its giant robotic antlike creatures (Lobants) controlled by an alien brain determined to eliminate humans from the planet. Here we have vicious spider-like robots also remotely controlled by a mad human who is no longer human because he has transformed himself into some kind of hybrid human computer monstrosity determined to eliminate all other humans from the planet.

It pays not to examine this too closely as it borders on science fantasy but to read it and go with the flow of the action in the story which is 'Blockbuster Cinematic' and would look spectacular on a big movie screen.

I enjoyed this story as it harked back to the kind of stories I read in my younger years. In fact I suspect it is aimed at younger readers rather than older more seasoned ones who may not be interested in reading eBooks or stories loaded with almost superhuman action.

For all its action and excitement it does however give a good impression of how hard it is to live on Mars and the kinds of problems settlers would need to solve in order to stay there.

Fable Hill (2017) by Christopher Uremovich is self-published through Amazon.

It begins with action off the coast of Venezuela that suggests a war between the Chinese and the USA is imminent during which Colonel Frank Nash is shot down and seriously injured. It then follows his recovery after losing both his legs and his eventual hire by the Japanese Nagoya company as a pilot for the space ship being readied for a trip to Mars. There is also a suggestion that the Chinese are also on their way to Mars as well.

I feel that too much space is given here regarding Frank's recovery, and the training in Antarctica that could have been included as back story on the flight to Mars. The story should have begun at or near chapter 8 with them taking off for orbital rendezvous with their ship while the Chinese are attacking the launch site with missiles launched from submarines. This part of the story is full of tension and excitement as the launching ship is chased up into orbit by missiles and is almost destroyed.

It slows down as the bonding of the crew takes place over the long journey out to Mars and then on Mars it takes awhile for the pace to pick up again as we go through exploration teams searching for minerals and setting up a pipeline to bring water from a nearby glaciated region. During this period contact is lost with Earth and the reader immediately suspects a major conflict between the Chinese and the Americans has taken place, though initially the characters are not aware of it. While the others are exploring Alexei, a Russian member of the crew is secretly working on a project which he won't allow anyone to see.

He is working on developing a faster than light (FTL) drive using magnetically contained anti-matter and does not allow any other crew member access to what he is doing. Tension is generated through clashes between various members of the crew as they have different explorative agendas and inevitably accidents occur and one of them is killed, which reinforces the harshness of the Martian environment. Meanwhile Frank has taken a liking to Mia and together they take a lander to go in search of the cause of unusual methane gas emanations. The methane turns out to not be caused by life but comes from oil deposits and dense coal formed by Abiogenic processes, something not proven on Earth because all our fossil fuel deposits come from biological decay of plant material even though a non biological process could theoretically produce some deposits.

Frank and Mia discover a hidden base which was established by American and Russian astronauts back in 1973. It was called Fable Hill. The astronauts at this hidden base discovered oil on Mars. There are no signs of what happened to the astronauts and no records on Earth about anything connected with Fable Hill, and since this takes place in 2043 we can presume they died long ago or else they returned to Earth long before the present expeditions were conceived.

There is not much mention of who set up the extensive base the present astronauts are using but we assume Nagoya had done it in preparation for future expeditions.

Things come to head as Alexei prepares to test his ideas of FTL drive. He generates a massive explosion using the anti-matter. It creates a black hole one kilometre up in the sky and he flies one of the landers through it and disappears. Once he has gone through the hole disappears. Mia is blinded by the explosion that opened the black hole but Frank manages to avoid looking at it which saves his eyesight. The base is destroyed including whoever was inside so Frank and Mia have no other option but to fly their lander 4000 kilometres to the Chinese base where they hope they will be helped to return to their mother ship in orbit around Mars.

Arriving at the Chinese base they are taken prisoner and it is then they find out that a war between China and American and Japan has taken place with the Chinese being the victors. America and Japan had been destroyed while only a part of China had been devastated. The Chinese astronauts assumed the Americans had come to surrender.

Frank refuses to surrender but as a prisoner he is made to work for his and everyone's survival. After a few weeks he tries to escape, to take the Chinese lander up into orbit to rendezvous with the Nagoya mother ship, but the Chinese corner him and are about to shoot him when they are in turn shot by a team of Marines arriving to take over the Chinese base.

The marines are part of a refugee group that managed to escape from Earth before total destruction of America and Japan. They arrived in time to send a reconnaissance group to seize the Chinese base and save Colonel Frank Nash from being executed.

The refugees are about to land and set up a self sustaining colony on Mars. Frank and Mia survive and Frank has a copy of the data that created the black hole so readers can imagine at some point in the future humans will venture through such a black hole on a journey to another star.

Perhaps we will find out what happened to Alexei in another story...

Although a little slow or even confusing at times it is in general an enjoyable story.

Traditional publishing still a force to be reckoned with...

Not all recent Mars stories are self-published. Top SF publishers like Tor Books still publish Mars stories if they are good, and by respected authors. ***Martians Abroad*** by prize-winning bestselling young-adult author Carrie Vaughn (with over 20 novels and numerous short stories published) is a fine example of a story imbued with a sense of excitement and wonder. Known for her modern urban fantasies, she returns to the youthful days of the books she read as a child with this young adult novel. At the age of 8 her father gave her a copy of Robert Heinlein's ***Red Planet*** to read, and she was hooked on SF (and everything those two letters imply) from that time on.

Martians Abroad (2016) by Carrie Vaughn (Tor Books)

Martians Abroad harks back to the Golden Age of SF and the sense of wonder that fired the imaginations of so many young people in the 1940s and 50s. Perhaps it pays homage to Heinlein's ***Podkayne of Mars,*** in so far as the two main characters are Martian born teenagers, a sister (Polly) and brother (Charles, clever enough to be a genius), who travel to Earth to attend an elite private school.

In ***Podkayne*** the teenager is Poddy and the brother, a genius, is Clarke. They are travelling with their uncle as emissaries to Earth from Mars, but make a side stop on Venus where most of the story takes place. As it was published originally in 1967, Poddy survives Venus and heads off to Earth, but that isn't how Heinlein wanted it. He was forced to write an upbeat happier ending. His estate have republished this story with the ending Heinlein originally wrote which has Poddy not surviving her adventures on Venus, and the story is concluded with her brother giving the reader an extract from Poddy's final diary entry.

Even considering the time Heinlein wrote ***Podkayne of Mars***, with its thinking about old civilisations on a dying Mars colonised by brash humans, and wild extremely tropical conditions on Venus, the story is not convincing when compared to ***Martians Abroad***.

My feeling is that Heinlein didn't capture the essence of a young female character.

This is not the case with ***Martians Abroad***.

The story is Polly's, but Charles is always there in the background. Sent to Earth —by their mother, a leading figure of the Mars Colony — to attend an elite private school because of the connections she would make interacting with the children of leading Earth Dynastic families, Polly doesn't want to go. All she wants is to be a spaceship pilot. Her mother has other planes. Polly is resentful, especially when she and her brother have to cope with the much heavier Earth gravity. Being outsiders or offworlders they, along with several other students from the Moon and various off-earth settlements, are bullied by the stronger Earth born students, and made to feel inadequate. They tend to stick together for most school activities.

There is enough Mars background to paint a convincing picture of what Mars is actually like as we understand it from all the knowledge gained by orbiting satellites and on ground rovers. Mars has a long established colony where many children have been born to make it viable and functioning. Although not the main feature of the story it determines how the characters think and act. Their subconscious thinking has been moulded by living on Mars and this is what saves them when something adverse unexpectedly happens.

When an accident occurs on a hiking expedition which almost kills one of the students, it is Polly who immediately comes to the rescue. Polly is used to reacting without thinking to danger, a quality needed in order to survive on Mars which could kill you instantly if a mistake is made. Saving the other girl from falling down a cliff gains her respect from other Earth born students. *It's what everyone does on Mars;* she tells them, *they look out for each other*. Polly thinks nothing of it.

As the story progresses, Polly gets into all kinds of mischief, like stealing a motorbike to go for a ride outside of the school grounds, which is forbidden, to wandering off from the group while on an excursion to New York Museums. She goes to Central Park to see a real horse, something she has never seen on Mars. When she sees one of the students being kidnapped she begins to suspect that all is not as it seems, that various events that appeared accidental were not, and she suspects they are instigated to see how she would react. Messages of encouragement from her Mother on Mars lead her to believe that her mother is behind the manipulation of events.

It all comes to a head when her school group makes a study trip to the Moon. She keeps expecting something to happen during the trip between

Earth orbit and the Moon colony, but all is well. However as her group is travelling in a smaller shuttle vehicle across the Moon's surface the pilots appear to collapse. They have been drugged. Now she knows. Someone is definitely manipulating events. Being the only one of the student group theoretically capable of piloting the shuttle she has no choice but to take the controls. She radios for help to land the shuttle at its destination, but an unfortunate accident occurs as Base Control is attempting to talk her through a landing. The shuttle starts to lose atmosphere and a crack in the hull causes an engine to explode. With her brother she organises an immediate evacuation into an escape pod but she can't release it unless she manually does it from the pilot's cockpit. That means she can't be in the escape pod with the others. She makes sure they escape while she still has some control of the shuttle.

As it starts crashing back to the moon's surface she runs out of oxygen.

By this time the tension is so high the reader's heart is pounding, hoping Polly will survive this horrible accident.

Unlike Poddy in Heinlein's story who doesn't survive, Polly does.

She is rescued almost immediately and finds herself recuperating in hospital. She confronts her mother via video link and accuses her of setting up the incidents, which her mother doesn't deny. She also tells her mother that she will not return to Mars and that she is going to gain a place in space ship piloting studies. Having saved the other students in her group with her quick response (engendered by living on Mars) she is guaranteed a spot in the pilot training programme she so much desires. Charles however will return to Mars when the school year is over.

This story has been called a retro-SF adventure and has rightly been given high praise by the likes of award winning SF authors Jack McDevitt, Gregory Benford, Greg Bear, Vernor Vinge, and Alan Steele among others.

And rightly so! It is a riveting story that embodies the sense of wonder found in those golden age stories, and that captures perfectly the young female character's feeling of angst and her desires for her own future. It is a book that should and probably will become a best seller in the young adult market where so much innovative fiction is being discovered.

Over the last decade the idea of going to Mars has definitely penetrated public awareness, not because NASA is always showing new images taken on Mars as well as talking about when they would send someone there — along with people like Elon Musk and Space X consortium having big plans to settle on Mars, nor with Mars One announcing it has finally selected its candidates to train for their mission to Mars in the mid-2020s — but because mainstream writers are now writing novels about going to Mars. *Previously it was only Science Fiction authors who wrote about going to Mars, or setting stories there.*

When mainstream writers like Meg Howrey write a novel about a voyage to Mars the idea of going must already have penetrated worldwide public consciousness. It is not marketed as an SF novel but is simply a novel, like any other novel one can find where books are sold.

The Wanderers (2017) by Meg Howrey (Scribner) opens with the initial astronaut selection and basic training before the three astronauts begin a simulated voyage to Mars. They believe that once they have successfully completed the simulated voyage they will then be sent to Mars for real.

Howrey has based the idea for her novel on the recent Russian simulation, *Mars 500*, in which six Cosmonauts (Russian, European and Chinese) spent 520 days confined in a mock space ship to test whether sending a crew to Mars and determining whether they could survive being confined in a small space together for the length of time needed to get there and back is viable.

In her scenario a smaller international crew, one American, Helen Kane, one Russian, Sergei Kuznetsov, and one Japanese Yoshsi Tanaka, will spend the two years it takes, to go to Mars, to stay there for 30 days and then return, confined in a tiny capsule of a space ship.

The training experiment will take place somewhere in Utah.

The novel is not about the training or going to Mars and there is not a lot of the technical details one would expect in a more traditional SF novel; it is about the relationships the three astronauts have with each other, and with their family members who can only communicate with them via radio and delayed video, exactly as if they were on a real journey to Mars. Equally with mission control; their communication is exactly as it would be for a real voyage.

As the astronauts begin their simulated journey they are quite aware at the start that it is a simulation, no matter how real it feels or looks via the view-screens in the vehicle. There are no windows to look out of, and all information received is digital. They watch Earth shrink to a tiny dot and eventually Mars begins to fill their view-screens as they approach. They presumably land on Mars and make some excursions and carry out some experiments, exactly as they would on a real mission. The simulation is absolutely perfect. They must wear space suits and the equipment they use, they have been told, has been specially lightened to simulate how it would feel on Mars. They have to vacuum the fine dust from their suits when they re-enter the airlock. The three of them are stunned at how real the simulated Mars appears to be.

But on one excursion when Sergei stays behind to monitor their actions (one of them always remains on board while two carry out the jobs to be done) there is a glitch with the simulation. Helen is caught in a ferocious whirlwind, enveloped in dust and feels as if she is being electrocuted. Sergei on board the ship sees a momentary black screen before it reveals a changed landscape that looks like Mars, but not the simulated Mars they have so far experienced.

It's only a brief glimpse but it starts him wondering whether they have actually been sent to Mars but were not told, that Mission Control back on Earth wants them to think it is only a simulation. They are told that a second crew is being trained for the job as a back-up crew which makes them worry that when they complete their mission they might not get picked to do it for real.

They manage to get some privacy to discuss Sergei's paranoid idea by all cramming into the toilet which is only designed to be used by one. Everywhere else within the ship they are constantly monitored by mission control.

The idea of them doing it for real rather than being simulated is reinforced when Helen's daughter goes to mission control where she supposes she could see the structure housing the simulated spaceship only to discover it isn't there where it was supposed to be.

On the space ship the three of them experience leaving Mars, the return to Earth, the braking manoeuvres, the glimpses of Earth below them, clouds and blue skies as they enter the atmosphere. Each of them is looking forward to coming home, and also to the future when they will do the voyage to Mars for Real.

The story finishes with both the reader and the astronauts wondering whether the whole voyage was a simulation in preparation for the real trip or whether they actually did do the trip for real and it wasn't a simulation. But this isn't the main focus of the novel, it is about Helen's interaction with her daughter and with her fellow astronauts, as well as their relationships, Sergei with his two young sons, and Yoshi with his wife who builds robots to look after the sick and infirm, who is herself as much a robot as those she creates.

The voyage to Mars is the catalyst which allows the author to examine human emotions and interactions in an unusual circumstance.

This is a fascinating novel and is well worth the time taken to read it and ponder about how those left behind can cope with the length of the voyage and the absence of their loved ones as well as how the astronauts themselves deal with the same problems.

As we approach a date when people will really go to Mars, more mainstream novelists will be using the long voyage as a stimulus for examining the effects of isolation and of how it will be to live on Mars, and then it will no longer be science fiction but just stories about a new reality.

One Way S J Morden (2018) (Gollancz)

NASA awards a contract to a private company Panopticon's Xenosystems Operations to build a base on Mars and to maintain it until NASA astronauts and scientists arrive.

Panopticon also runs privately owned prisons, and selects a group of murderers and other dangerous criminals who are serving life sentences to go to Mars and build the first base. They won't be free but will remain serving their life sentences, but being on Mars there is nowhere for them to escape to and so they do have much more freedom and autonomy than they would have as prisoners on Earth. By selecting seven life-serving prisoners they can save a lot of money and make a profit. Basically they are slave labour. Six months are spent training and conditioning each prisoner for specific duties, such as construction, electrical work, plumbing, driving vehicles, computer maintenance, medical services and so on. Each person needs to double up so anyone injured or incapacitated can be replaced by their second. The eighth person is their supervisor, Brack, whose only task is to keep an eye on the co-opted prisoners to make sure they do the work assigned to them. Once the base is built they are tasked to maintain it indefinitely. They won't be going home but are free to live their lives on Mars as long as they maintain the base in operational order.

Other authors have used Mars as a dumping ground for unwanted criminals: D G Compton springs to mind with ***Farewell, Earth's Bliss*** where Mars is considered useless and prisoners are sent from the Moon and left on Mars to survive or not. No one cares. Heinlein had Mars originally colonized by establishing a penal colony in ***Podkayne of Mars***, but this is only a brief mention as part of the background details. There was no further mention of that in any of his other Mars stories. Cyril Judd had Mars with criminals and other incorrigibles living in an almost lawless community with police as corrupt as those they look after as did Lester del Rey with ***Police your planet***.

But ***One Way*** is different in that it has serious criminals being used to build a permanent base for future astronauts to use.

Frank Kitterage, who murdered his son's drug dealer, is the viewpoint character and although he is a murderer he is a not a bad person. Brack asks Frank to keep an eye on the others and report back to him and in exchange, he is told, when Brack returns to Earth he will be able to go as well.

Right from the start there are problems. The capsules containing the necessary equipment for constructing the base are scattered over a wide area from 15 to 80 miles away from where the ship landed. They must be retrieved and the only way to get to the nearest capsule which contains the rovers they need is by walking. They have to assemble it, or both of them, and return them to the ship. With the rovers they can then retrieve the equipment from the other scattered capsules and start construction of the base. It takes them longer than anticipated to get there and they use up more than half of their spacesuit air supply. They have very little air left when they finish assembling the first rover and decide to return to base. They will come back the next day for the other one. Driving recklessly fast they manage to get back to the ship but Frank's partner Macy runs out of air before they can enter the airlock and dies in her space suit. Later Frank suspects the CO2 scrubber in her suit may have been sabotaged.

Brack says he will take care of the body and pushes the others to get on with retrieving the equipment from the capsules and setting up the base at the designated spot. There is a lot of tension as the base is constructed and someone else dies, again apparently by accident. The prisoners bond together for survival and each has to take on extra duties to replace the persons who died. Other accidents occur and they blame the harshness of Mars.

Frank begins to suspect they are not accidents and sets out to prove it. The remaining prisoners become suspicious of each other, and of the fact that Brack never stays with them on the base but remains in the ship. They turn on each other as two more die in accidents inside the base. They blame Frank since he discovers the bodies, but Frank thinks he is being set up, and he suspects Brack is the murderer. The remaining three are suspicious of each other and it is revealed here that Brack told each of them the same thing he told Frank. He is positive that none of them will go home because as each one completes the tasks they are responsible for they have an apparent accident. Frank suspects because they are no longer needed Brack gets rid of them but makes it look accidental so he can report their deaths as such to Xenosystems Operations.

The final confrontation between the two remaining prisoners and Brack in the Mars habitat is as dramatic as it is nail-biting.

This story would make a superb movie. Although suspenseful it describes beautifully the difficulties of surviving on Mars as we understand it today, and examines the reactions of people, who could never be more isolated, in ways that make them very human. Only Brack appears a little exaggerated, but then he's the foil against which the others react.

Before Mars (2018) by Emma Newman (Gollancz)

This story does reference some background material from her two previous novels ***Planetfall*** and ***After Atlas***, but it isn't necessary to have read those books first.

Before Mars is a brilliant evocation of a time when Democracy has failed and most countries are managed by giant business corporations. One of these corporations in effect owns Mars and has a small colony established there. A Geologist, Anna Kubrin is sent there to conduct geological surveys officially but unofficially she is there to paint pictures of Mars. She is an artist whose work is famous for its three-dimensionality and the corporation head believes her paintings made on Mars would be worth a fortune to him once they are shipped back.

After months of travel in which she was immersed in memories and training sequences using virtual reality Anna arrives somewhat disorientated. Shown to her room in the base she discovers a note painted by herself warning her not to trust the resident psychiatrist. She doesn't remember painting that note. She also discovers less canvasses than what she thought she had brought with her. Other things don't seem quite right. She feels a weird attraction for one of the colony members, the doctor, as if she has known him for a long time, but she has only just met him. She also doesn't get answers to the messages she sends home but the responses seem natural apart from ignoring things she asks about.

When she ventures out to research areas for her proposed paintings she discovers a footprint where no one is supposed to have been. She questions her own sanity knowing that her father, with whom she refuses to talk, went insane and tried to murder her mother, and is isolated in an asylum. She is almost paranoid about the Artificial Intelligence that operates everything in the colony believing it is hiding information from her. She is sure of it when she sees a communications mast from some distance away over the sand dunes, but which mysteriously disappears when the AI replays back her digital images for verification.

She also receives a strange subliminal message which bypasses the usual communications route via the AI requesting that she undertake certain actions and report back using the same methods. She knows something is wrong but can't pinpoint it. Tricking the AI so she can go outside by herself because it claims there is a massive sandstorm and won't allow anyone out of the habitat, she discovers there never was a sandstorm; the AI was lying in an attempt to prevent her from going to where she saw the mast.

She finds another base recently abandoned and when she convinces the doctor and the media consultant to go there together, they break in to discover an almost identical base to the one they live in, which must have been constructed at the same time, and that the AI also runs this base. But more than that she discovers four paintings (which explain the missing canvasses she was sure she had brought with her) that she had done but has no memory of doing them. They are however exactly like the sketches she had been doing in preparation for the paintings.

Another problem occurs when communications with Earth are abruptly cut off and the problem is not the AI but the relays in earth orbit not sending anything. The colony is isolated. They then discover Earth had been destroyed by an atomic corporate war and there were very few survivors. Only a small religious group that built a star ship duplicating the original one from years before had survived because they had already left Earth. Her sister was on board that ship.

They finally confront the colony psychiatrist who admits that she had chemically wiped all their recent memories to cover up what had been going on at the other base. It was she who took the paintings to the other base to hide them from Anna. But apparently not all memories are encoded in the brain the same way and some random ones remained which is why Anna kept feeling things were not quite right. The others are upset that they too had their memories wiped.

What had happened at the other base was they built a small star ship to follow the much larger one sent off to another star system years before. The plans for the ship had been sent to Anna subliminally and she uploads them to the AI. They can survive on Mars for several years until they finally run out of material needed to make food. Their only hope of long term survival is to duplicate the star ship and follow the others who have already left.

This is a beautifully written story and is a 'must read' for anyone interested in stories set on Mars as well as stories that delve into a woman's relationship with her husband, her daughter, her family, and the people she meets on Mars. It reads more like a mainstream novel rather than SF, but these days there is little distinction between genres since Mars is almost mainstream itself with so many proposals about how to get there as well as the media coverage of the fantastic imagery sent back from the planet by the orbiting satellites and the rovers on the surface.

Dead Red by Matthew Buza (2018)

Subtitled ***A Sci-Fi Horror Novel***

That should have put me off, but I liked the title and the cover was intriguing.

This is a derivative work that pays homage to films like ***Last Days on Mars,*** and other zombie films and stories. It begins well enough with two expeditions, one already on Mars and setting up a base, with a second group on the way. When the second group lands at a different location a third group is also sent from Earth. The idea is to have three bases set up in different locations so different aspects of Mars can be studied. The second group has barely landed when disaster strikes.

A large meteoroid tracked for months by NASA was supposed to pass between the orbit of Phobos and the surface of Mars, a very close flyby, but instead it impacts Phobos, witnessed by two geologists working on the surface (*and beautifully described*), explodes tearing off bits of Phobos which begin crashing down out of orbit to impact on the surface. There is so much debris from the collision falling that no one is safe on the surface. The falling debris churns up the surface and an enormous dust storm is produced cutting visibility to almost zero. The two who saw the collision struggle to get back to their base but their rover is hit by a large chunk of rock pounding down out of the sky. It tears the rover almost in half including one of the occupants, while the other is seriously injured with a piece of metal from the rover slicing through and severing one of his legs at the knee. The blood freezes which seals the suit and he manages to drive the damaged rover back to the base.

Up to this moment the story is well written and interesting enough with sufficient character development to be worth reading.

As if this disaster wasn't horrible enough to warrant subtitling this *A Sci-Fi Horror Story*, the author introduces rabid parasitic bacteria that immediately invade the blood stream of the dead astronaut almost consuming him within minutes. Back at the base the four others of the first team are worried that falling debris from the collision might puncture the habitat as it falls down along the orbital path of Phobos. When they see the damaged rover they immediately rush to help bring in the injured driver and the dead companion. In the sick bay the doctor tries to repair some of the damage to the injured geologist but leaves him sedated. He wakes up and with teeth chattering goes over to the dead geologist and starts tearing into him with his teeth, ripping the body apart.

There is no suggestion of where the horrible bacteria came from, out of the disturbed sand of Mars, or from the pieces of the meteoroid or from the debris of Phobos. I would presume from the meteoroid since the author would know, with Mars bathed in constant radiation from the Sun the surface is sterile.

Why would alien bacteria turn humans into ravening zombies? Why in fact would alien bacteria have any effect at all? The DNA would be sufficiently different as to be incompatible in my view, so there should be little or no effect.

The one legged geologist immediately kills another team member who rushes in to help and the rest of the team flee to the airlocks where they keep their pressure suits. As they do this the zombie tears the walls apart and the whole habitat deflates. The remaining team members manage to don their pressure suits and escape to the remaining undamaged rover. They quickly disappear into the dusst storm as they head for Base two.

The story then switches to the second team at Base Two where Jade, the wife of one of the first team members, Sean, is concerned about him. She and one associate commandeer a rover and head towards the Base One. They have to drive very slowly because the sandstorm kicked up by constantly falling debris from the orbital collision has left craters around which they must negotiate that weren't there before. During her transit to Base One Sean and the other couple who managed to escape pass them on the way to Base Two. At Base One Jade and her friend go inside to be confronted by two zombies who viciously attack them and Jade is forced to decapitate one of them while her friend isn't so lucky and is infected. She tries to stop Jade from leaving but Jade runs over her with the rover crushing her head and rendering her more or less dead permanently.

The rover runs out of power when it gets close to the second base and

Jade is forced to go the rest of the way on foot. She almost runs out of oxygen but is rescued at the door by her husband Sean.

And so the story goes: the second base is soon infected and the only two survivors are Sean and Jade who manage to escape in the rover and head for Base Three where the ship in transit from Earth is going to land. Unfortunately at the end Sean is also infected and there is no way then that they will ever leave Mars. We are left with Jade keeping Sean trapped inside an enclosed space while she searches for a cure.

There is enough horror action to satisfy people who love 'zombie' stories but I'm afraid I lost interest since I find this type of meaningless action 'horror' to be rather silly.

It could have been a remarkably good story if it showed how people could survive such a rare disaster as an asteroid colliding with Phobos with the resulting debris impacting Mars and the astronaut's bases. To survive until the third expedition arrived would have been a really interesting story. But to turn it into a zombie story spoilt it, and in my view, it lost credibility no matter how well it was written.

Phobos

Coming full circle...
Lost Mars — a Fitting Bookend

A newly published collection of superb Martian stories containing some forgotten early stories that take us back to a time when science fiction didn't exist as we know it, along with some almost forgotten stories from the Golden Age of science fiction, makes a fitting bookend to this volume.

Lost Mars: the Golden Age of the Red Planet edited by Mike Ashley (2018) brings back some superb very early stories mixed in with a scattering of other pieces from the various decades in which Mars stories were prominent.

We have ***The Crystal Egg,*** by H G Wells, published in 1897 just before his magnificent ***The War of The Worlds*** which depicts the Martians as curious, almost ethereal beings that use Crystal Eggs as a means of communication and a way to see far places. That there was one in a shop of oddities in London suggests that the Martians had already made plans regarding Earth and this was the means by which they could observe us, although all they saw was a few faces up close and the interior of a couple of rooms where the Crystal Egg was kept. It mysteriously disappears at the end of the story... and of course we know what the Martians did next...

Letters from Mars by W S Lach-Szyrma was first published in two parts as ***Letters from the Planets*** (1887) is an extension of the story of Aleriel who travelled from Venus to visit all the planets including Mars reporting his observations to fellow travellers on Venus, in a book ***Voyage to Other Worlds,*** (1883). The book was so popular it led to the further stories published in 1887, eight years before HG Wells started writing his first novel ***The Time Machine*** (1895), and ten years before his epic ***The War of The Worlds.***

The Great Sacrifice by George C Wallis (1903) is the third very welcome early Mars story in this collection, and paints a positive view of Martians, although we never see them.

The Forgotten Man of Space by P Schuyler Miller (1933) *(see page 74)* is another rare positive picture of Martians which in general were never portrayed as benign beings.

A Martian Odyssey by Stanley G Weinbaum (1934): What can I say about this classic piece? Sooner or later everyone will have to read this mind opening story.

Then there is ***YLLA*** one of Ray Bradbury's ***Martian Chronicles*** stories (1950) one of the most beautiful and poetic of his Martian series, ***Measureless to Man*** by Marion Zimmer Bradley (1962), one of her earlier stories set on Mars where human explorers encounter the minds of ancient Martians which usually sends them insane until one Martian born Human is able to understand them.

Without Bugles, by E C Tubb (1952), claimed by Mike Ashley to be the first in his Martian sequence (which may have been written first and thus started the sequence of stories originally published in *New Worlds Science Fiction*) but is actually the fourth in the completed novel ***Alien Dust.*** (1955). The colonists have been on Mars for 5 years and are still struggling to survive when a politician and a reporter arrive. The politician wants to know what they have done to justify the billions spent to maintain the colony and if it doesn't show a profit they will close it down, while the reporter wants to write a story of the heroic attempts to colonize Mars. The politician doesn't care that once you have been on Mars for several years there is no going back to Earth because they will die. The reporter is instrumental in keeping the colony alive. This is a grim story with a positive outcome and is an integral part of the sequence that became ***Alien Dust.*** *(see page 121)*

Crucifixus Etiam by Walter Miller Jr (1953) *(see page 107)* is an ideal extension to ***Without Bugles***, as it depicts an equally grim view of Mars as it could be, but looks towards a far future view of a possible better place as the planet is slowly terraformed.

Finally ***The Time Tombs*** by J G Ballard (1963) is a story that suggests it could be on Mars with tomb raiders stealing technological artefacts from ancient Tombs uncovered after sandstorms blow away some of the fine sand covering them. There is no direct mention of Mars but the idea of tombs containing ancient technology is an old idea often used in early Mars stories, but which has now been given more relevance by the discovery of what many believe to be a face carved into the top of a mesa. Of course it could be on Earth after some dire Ballardian catastrophe, who knows? It does make a good story though and a fitting end to a worthy collection, made extremely interesting by the inclusion of such early almost forgotten stories.

Brief notes on some academic studies.

Imagining Mars, a literary history (2011) by Robert Crossley
Dying Planet, Mars in science and the imagination (2005) by Robert Markley.

Robert Crossley is emeritus professor of English at the University of Massachusetts- Boston, and Robert Markley is Professor of English at the University of Illinois, Urbana-Champaign.

Both books are academic studies, as one would expect. Both books have copious pages of references cited as well as extensive indices and it is clear that these two professors have done a lot more reading of older texts than I have been able to, or even knew existed. But their object is an academic study, and as with most of the studies of this kind, the authors often draw conclusions based on present day cultural mores, ascribing motives behind the writing or reasons for the writing of the books, which I believe at the time they were written the authors never had. It seems in hindsight much more can be seen and deduced than would have been possible at the time the stories were written, especially in regard to those written 100 or more years ago.

Because we can look back in time to the books mentioned throughout the two volumes, we can see correlations between their author's projections for the future that they imagined, and compare them with what has actually happened since those books were written at the end of the 19th century or earlier. We can also see the biases both academics reveal as they find whatever it is in the books they mention which allows them to draw the conclusions they prefer.

Both authors have looked back as far as the 17th century to examine how authors writing about Mars have reflected the desires and controversies of their societies. They have unearthed obscure stories, and enlightened the way science was beginning to develop, especially in relation to observing and studying Mars during its various oppositions. Both have clearly shown how Mars has featured in the minds of ordinary people during those recent centuries, and how our general perception of the planet has also changed over time from the 17th to the 21st century.

I think one of the biggest problems with these two books, but especially with ***Dying Planet*** which is much harder to read than ***Imagining Mars,*** is the professors forget how dark and foreboding life was in the 1800s and early 1900s and that the books mentioned in the studies were written primarily to entertain the general public who wanted to escape from their hard dreary lives. They wanted to believe that the future must be better. They didn't want to read about how ugly the world was, or how difficult it was to live; they knew that because it was their life. They wanted to escape this ugly reality, to spend time in a beautiful and imaginary future.

The authors of scientific romances and fantasies gave them what they wanted. They often wrote about utopian societies where everyone was equal and life was pleasant, where people didn't have to work themselves to death in order to barely survive, but had much leisure time to enjoy themselves, and so on. Utopian fiction in which a 'perfect' society was compared against the society in which the reader lived, was the most popular form of storytelling. The stories were not propaganda for revolutions. They didn't deliberately espouse the perfection of socialism against capitalism; they were entertainments, not political manifestos, although underlying them may have been the cultural aspirations of the societies in which the authors lived.

The world was experiencing many kinds of social upheaval, with the threat of massive wars impending. Who wouldn't want to read about a perfect future where none of this occurred?

Utopian fantasies were the answer especially if some of them had some science in them. Science would provide the answers to the future. These utopian fictions were immensely popular, until they died a sudden death with the advent of H G Wells' ***War of The Worlds***. After that the stories about Mars changed radically and in the public's mind monsters from Mars came to symbolise any alien who or which was not of Earth. Men from Mars, monsters from Mars, aliens from other star systems, it was all synonymous.

Dying Planet is almost two books in one. It alternates (in long chapters) between a detailed history and evolution of science and scientific scandals involving Mars, and the examination in detail of stories, long and short about Mars, that reflect the times in which they were written and the knowledge of what was known about Mars then. Much is made of the controversies between Percival Lowell and his '*canalists*' who believed canals existed and had been built to save a dying world, and those disbelievers such as Alfred George Wallace who had different conclusions from the same data. He thought the lines were natural fissures due to planetary shrinkage because of the extreme cold.

Some of the early scientific thinking is interesting but Markley goes into far too much detail which I feel is overwhelming and makes the book hard to read for the non-scientifically minded person. The later chapters deal with the various Mars missions from the Russian Mars Probes that failed, from Mariner 3, 4 through to the rovers and other satellites inserted into Mars orbit and this in itself is interesting because there have been far more attempts to send things to Mars than to any other part of the soslar system.

A little science is good because it illuminates how people thought and what they believed in past times and how this could affect the way they wrote stories. But there is simply too much detail for me in these chapters. I always prefer to be entertained rather than educated, (I would have bought a text book otherwise...) The alternate chapters regardidng stories about Mars I found far more interesting. The last chapter before the list of notes and the index discusses Kim Stanley Robinson's Martian trilogy in great detail, one of the book's highlights.

Imagining Mars also covers the scientific history about various discoveries regarding Mars but not in exclusive chapters devoted only to the science; it is more dove-tailed into the history of the books and stories about Mars so it is less daunting to read. I read this book almost in one sitting, whereas I found ***Dying Planet*** far too difficult to do that. I had to spend a lot of time digesting the science chapters which made it hard going.

Nevertheless, both books should be essential reference works on the shelves of anyone who is interested in stories about Mars.

Along with those should be the beautifully illustrated volume by Thomas Kent Miller called ***Mars in the Movies***, (2016) which as the title suggests is about exactly that. It delineates all the plot lines of the films made about Mars or in which Mars features prominently.

It has comments from reviewers who loved the films compared with those from reviewers who hated the films. It also contains the author's own feelings about each film which he suggests should really be watched in chronological order of production, so the viewer can clearly see how ideas and science regarding Mars and the special effects needed to depict Mars has evolved over the last century that films have been made. From a technological point of view each film has improved on what has been done before. It is copiously illustrated with publicity shots as well as screen shots from the films. It also covers all the TV shows and telefilms that feature Mars, so it is a real gem for lovers of films about Mars and for those who love SF films in general.

Visions of Mars Essays on the Red Planet in Fiction and Science

Edited by Howard V Hendrix, George Slusser and Eric S Rabkin (2011).

This book contains academic essays, each one with lists of references cited for readers who want to do their own research, (or at least to prove how much work the author did in researching material for the article). I am not a fan of academic writers and so some of these essays were a bit of a slog to get through, but ultimately interesting.

One surprising thing about this book (for me) was the amount of Science Fiction that was written in Russia, France, and Europe generally in the early years of SF development. Very little of this work was translated into English so virtually none of it influenced SF as it was being developed in the USA and to a lesser extent other English speaking countries. On the other hand authors like H G Wells and later Early American authors were regularly translated into French, Russian, and other languages. There is no doubt English works translated had some effect on the early development of European SF and in particular stories about Mars, but I wonder, if some of the Russian and French works had been translated into English close to the time they were written, what way would the SF familiar to us via the American pulps have developed and how much different would it be today?

The book is divided into three sections: ***One: Approaching Mars, Two: The uses of Mars,*** and ***three: Science and fictional Mars.***

The majority of the articles fall into section two which covers Mars in Russian literature of the early Twentieth Century, Wells and the Strugatskys, Brackett and Burroughs, Bradbury's ***Martian Chronicles***, Heinlein and the ***Red Planet***, Philip K Dick's Mars, Kim Stanley Robinson's Mars. It also includes an article by Kim Stanley Robinson, *Martian Musings and the Miraculous Conjunction.*

The most interesting section from my personal viewpoint is at the conclusion of the book where there are transcripts of two panel discussions at a convention that took place in 2008; the first between Ray Bradbury and Frederick Pohl regarding their books on Mars, efforts to turn them into movies (that have been ongoing for many years with countless script drafts, but still no sign of the movies) and whether they would write another story set on Mars today.

And the second, a broader discussion about what is known about Mars today and how various authors have changed their views of Mars over recent years and what they think we should be doing about Mars in the way of exploring, scientific studies, colonizing, and the possibility of finding life and so on. The authors on the panel were David Hartwell, Geoffrey Landis, Larry Niven, and moderator Mary Turzillo, with questions from the audience including people like Jim Benford and Greg Benford among others adding immensely to the discussion.

Postscript
Continuing dreams…

Mars has always fascinated human observers from long before the ancient Greeks named the spots of light that moved across the sky Wanderers or Planets. But one in particular stood out, the blood red coloured one, the one the Greeks called Ares and the Romans Mars.

As inhospitable as it seems, Mars is still the closest likely planet that we could learn to live on. It once had running water, and a thicker atmosphere. It has a day only slightly longer than ours. It has seasons. The temperature range is not so extreme that we could not exist there. With the help of technology, just as we can live and work in Antarctica, we can do the same on Mars. It won't be easy, but has that ever stopped people who are determined?

The greatest dream of modern times is that humans will become an interplanetary species, and what better place to begin this epic expansion is there than Mars?

It's not a dream, it's a necessity. A major disaster could wipe out all life on Earth, or at the very least all major life forms, but if humans could expand into the solar system and later beyond, then any disaster to Earth that effects humankind is mitigated and we will continue elsewhere.

To establish a colony, to take those first faltering steps on our neighbouring planet is only the beginning. Now that a lake of salty water about fifteen kilometres long and one and a half kilometres below the surface has been discovered by ground penetrating radar from an orbiting satellite, (announced on the 26th of July 2018 by Italian scientists who studied the results of 29 passes over three years) those steps are guaranteed to happen sooner rather than later. Not only that, the discovery of this lake suggests there may be others in similar locations around the planet, and that it is almost certain some kind of extremophile life forms may be living in those lakes. It will certainly inspire those who are attempting to travel to Mars to bring their plans forward.

Dreams of Mars will continue on into the future as they have done in the past. But now that the reality of humans being able to go to Mars, to step on the planet's surface, to establish a base, to begin to live there, is almost upon us, will those old dreams Die?

Not likely.

Going to Mars will fire the imagination like nothing else.

New stories will be told, and establishing a human presence on Mars will give endless inspiration to writers dreaming of Mars.

Once again: it isn't possible for me to find and read every story about Mars, especially the earliest ones from more than one hundred years ago. Other more recnt publications I would be unaware of, while some I have managed to obtain I found difficult or impossible to read for various reasons.

New stories continue to appear which I have yet to see, so if I waited to read them this volume would never be finished.

I apologise for not mentioning some that readers of this text may have read, and for not including some of the more recnt publications.

J L.

Robina, Australia 2018

Books and stories mentioned: in chronological order:

1889 — Melbourne and Mars – My life on two Planets – John (Joseph) Fraser
1898 — The War of the Worlds – H G Wells
1898 — Edison's Conquest of Mars – Garrett P Serviss
1935 — Planet Plane aka Stowaway to Mars - John Wyndham
1936 — Sleepers of Mars - John Wyndham
1948 — The Martian Chronicles - Ray Bradbury
1945?— You Can't Escape from Mars – E K Jarvis
1945?— Secret of The Martians – Paul W Fairman
1949 — Red Planet – Robert A Heinlein
1949 — Queen of the Martian Catacombs – Leigh Brackett
1951 — Black Amazon of Mars – Leigh Brackett
1951 — The Sands of Mars - Arthur C Clarke
1951 — Outpost Mars/Mars Child – Cyril Judd
1952 — The Martian Way – Isaac Asimov
1952 — Atom War on Mars - E C Tubb
1953 — The Sword of Rhiannon – Leigh Brackett
1953 — Crucifus Etiam – Walter M Miller Jr
1953 — I Fight for Mars – E C Tubb
1954 — Journey to Mars – E C Tubb
1955 — Alíen Dust – E C Tubb
1956 — Police Your Planet – Eric van Lhin (Lester del Rey)
1957 — Omnilingual – H Beam Piper
1961 — The Nemesis from Terra – Leigh Brackett
1962 — The Red Planet – Russ Winterbotham.
1962 — Podkayne of Mars – Robert A Heinlein
1962 — Marooned on Mars – Lester Del Rey
1963 — A Rose for Ecclesiastes – Roger Zelazny
1964 — The Secret of Sinharat – Leigh Brackett
1964 — Martian Time Slip – Philip K Dick
1965 — The Martian Sphinx – John Brunner
1966 — Farewell Earth's Bliss – D G Compton
1966 — The Three Stigmata of Palmer Eldritch – Philip K Dick
1967 — The Coming of The Terrans – Leigh Brackett
1967 — Born Under Mars – John Brunner
1973 — The Earth is Near – Ludek Pesek
1976 — Man Plus – Frederick Pohl
1977 — The Martian Inca – Ian Watson
1977 — In the hall of the Martian Kings – John Varley
1978 — The Far Call – Gordon Dickson
1983 — Menace Under Marswood – Sterling E Lanier
1984 — Frontera – Lewis Shiner

1984 — Icehenge – Kim Stanley Robinson
1984 — The Greening of Mars – James Lovelock, Michael Allaby
1986 — Martian Spring – Michael Lindsay Williams
1988 — The Day The Martians Came – Frederick Pohl
1988 — Desolation Road – Ian McDonald
1989 — Crescent in the Sky – Donald Moffit
1990 — Voyage to the Red Planet – Terry Bisson
1991 — Red Genesis – S C Sykes
1991 — Martian Rainbow – Robert L Forward
1992 — Labyrinth of Night – Allen Steele
1992 — A Season of Passage – Christopher Pike
1992 — Beachhead – Jack Williamson
1992 — Mars – Ben Bova
1992 — Red Mars – Kim Stanley Robinson
1993 — Green Mars – Kim Stanley Robinson
1993 — Red Dust – Paul McAuley
1993 — Moving Mars – Greg Bear
1994 — Climbing Mount Olympus – Kevin J Anderson
1994 — Mars Plus – Frederick Pohl and Thomas T Thomas
1995 — Red Planet Run – Dana Stabenow
1996 — Voyage – Stephen Baxter
1996 — Blue Mars – Kim Stanley Robinson
1996 — Voyage – Stephen Baxter
1997 — Mars Underground – William Hartman
1998 — Return to Mars – Ben Bova
1998 — Semper Mars – Ian Douglas
1999 — The Martians – Kim Stanley Robinson
1999 — Rainbow Mars – Larry Niven
1999 — The Martian Race – Gregory Benford
2000 — Mars Crossing – Jeffrey A Landis
2001 — The Secret of Life – Paul McAuley
2001 — First Landing – Robert Zubrin
2002 — The Forge of Mars – Robert Balfour
2005 — The Sunborn – Gregory Benford
2008 — White Mars – Brian Aldiss
2008 — Mars Life – Ben Bova
2010 — Ares Express – Ian McDonald
2013 — Marsbound – Joe Haldeman
2013 — Finches of Mars – Brian Aldiss
2013 — Red Planet Blues – Robert J Sawyer
2013 — Mars Inc – Ben Bova
2014 — The Martian – Andy Weir
2014 — Red Rising – Pierce Brown
2014 — Rescue Mode – Ben Bova and Les Johnson
2014 — War Dogs – Greg Bear
2016 — Martians Abroad – Carrie Vaughn

2017 — The Wanderers - Meg Howrey
2017 — War of the Worlds – Retaliation – Mark Gardner and John J Rust
2018 — One Way – S J Morden
2018 — Before Mars – Emma Newman

Other books ancillary to the above:
1966 — The Saliva Tree – Brian Aldiss
1970 — The Space Machine – Christopher Priest
1979 — The Second Invasion from Mars –Strugatski brothers
1990 — The Martian War – Kevin J Anderson
1996 —War of the Worlds- Global Dispatches – ed: by Kevin J Andreson
2005 — Fourth Planet from the Sun – edited by Gordon Van Gelder
2011 — Life on Mars – edited by Jonathan Strahan
2013 — Old Mars – ed: George R R Martin and Gardner Dozois
2018 — Lost Mars – The Golden Age of the Red Planet – ed: Mike Ashley

Self-published stories: eBooks, POD books
2011 — Mars Needs Books – Gary Lovisi
2011 — Mars Station Alpha – Stephen Penner
2014 —The Lady Astronaut of Mars – Mary Robinette Kowal
2014 — Red Hope – John Dreese
2014 — Mars Base Red 7 – David Vengley
2015 — Snowfall on Mars – Brandon Frankell
2016 — Mars Endeavour – Peter Cawdron
2016 — Colony One Mars – Gerald M Kilby
2016 — Colony Two Mars – Gerald M Kilby
2017 — Colony Three Mars – Gerald M Kilby
2017 — Colony Four Mars – Jezero City – Gerald M Kilby
2017 — Killing Time on Mars – Alec Taylor
2017 — The Piranha Solution – John Triptych
2017 — Fable Hill – Christopher Uremovich
2018 — Dead Red – Matthew Buza

Non Fiction
1990 — Mission to Mars – Michael Collins
1994 — The Snows of Olympus – Arthur C Clarke
2001 — The Quest for Mars – Laurence Bergreen
2004 — The Real Mars – Michael Hanlon
2008 — Landscapes of Mars – Gregory L Vogt
2011 — The Case for Mars – Robert Zubrin (originally in 1996)
2011 — Exploring Mars – Scott Hubbard
2012 — Destination Mars – Rod Pyle
2013 — Mission to Mars – Buzz Aldrin
2016 — Mars One –N Kraft J Kass R Kass
2016 — Mars – Our Future on the Red Planet – Leonard David
2017— Destination Mars – Andrew May

Studies on Mars in fiction and in science
2005 — Dying Planet, Mars in science and the imagination - Robert Markley
2010 — Imagining Mars – a literary history – Robert Crossley
2011 — Visions of Mars Essays on the Red Planet ed: Hendrix, Slusser, Rabkin
2016 — Mars in the Movies – Thomas Kent Miller
2017 — 4th Rock from the Sun - Nicky Jenner

List of photos "Courtesy NASA/JPL-Caltech."
Page
6 –Meridianum Planum east of site where opportunity rover landed
20-21 - Gale Crater
75 - Prominent mineral veins at the 'Garden City' site on Mount Sharp
90 – Victoria Crater
118 – Streamlined crater, Lethe Vallis, part of outflow channel caused by catastrophic flood where water flowed around crater leaving a tear shaped island behind.
142 – A mesa in Noctis Labrynthus (0.4 Km) surrounded by sand dunes in fractured region at the western end of Valles Marineris.
163 – Valles Marineris extends for 4000 kilometres (2,500 miles), is 600 kilometres wide at it broadest points, and in places 10 kilometres deep.
164 – Cratered surface
166 – Early images from Mariner 4
169 -179 detailed craters211 – 'The Face' on Mars seen by Viking 1 orbiter.
230 – Polar deposits
253 – Close up of rocky sandy surface
254 – The most complex rover yet sent to Mars 'Curiosity' pauses at Namib Dune
282 – Rock spire in 'Spirit of Saint Louis' crater
291 – Acidalia Planitia
235 – Phobos
249 – Curiosity Rover

There are also an increasing number of science magazines worldwide that feature articles about Mars, going to Mars, how it can be done, how we can live there, and what the future of going to Mars holds for humankind, not to mention updates from NASA and other sources regularly appearing on YouTube that are worth a look at.

www.ingramcontent.com/pod-product-compliance
Lightning Source LLC
Chambersburg PA
CBHW022000160426
43197CB00007B/207